P9-AGD-936

Pregnancy to Parenthood

Pregnancy to Parenthood

Your Personal Step-by-Step Journey
Through the Childbirth Experience

Linda Goldberg

Ginny Brinkley

Janice Kukar

Avery Publishing Group

Garden City Park, New York

The health, medical, and nutrition information in this book is based on the training, personal experiences, and research of the authors. Because each person and situation are unique, the authors and publisher urge the reader to check with a qualified health professional before using any procedure whose appropriateness may be of concern.

The publisher does not advocate the use of any particular diet or health program, but believes the information presented in this book should be available to the public.

Because there is always some risk involved, the authors and publisher are not responsible for any adverse effects or consequences resulting from the use of any of the suggestions or procedures described in this book. This book is as timely and accurate as its publisher and authors can make it; nevertheless, they disclaim all liability and cannot be held responsible for any problems that may arise from its use. Please do not use the book if you are unwilling to assume the risk. Feel free to consult with a physician or other qualified health professional. It is a sign of wisdom, not cowardice, to seek a second or third opinion.

Cover designers: William Gonzalez and Rudy Shur
Cover photo: © Tony Stone Images; Rosanne Olson, photographer
Text photographer: Susan Torregrosa
Illustrator: Melissa Brenner
Cartoonist: Penny Banks
In-house editor: Elaine Will Sparber
Typesetter: Elaine V. McCaw
Printer: Paragon Press, Honesdale, PA

Avery Publishing Group
120 Old Broadway
Garden City Park, NY 11040
800–548–5757

Library of Congress Cataloging-in-Publication Data

Goldberg, Linda.
    Pregnancy to parenthood : your personal step-by-step journey
  through the childbirth experience / Linda Goldberg, Ginny Brinkley,
Janice Kukar.
      p.   cm.
  Includes bibliographical references and index.
  ISBN 0-89529-635-7
   1. Pregnancy. 2. Childbirth. 3. Infants (Newborn)—Care.
I. Brinkley, Ginny. II. Kukar, Janice. III. Title.
RG525.G5138 1998
618.2'4—DC21   97-46507
                                       CIP
                                       Rev.

Copyright © 1998 by Linda Goldberg, Ginny Brinkley, and Janice Kukar

All rights reserved. No part of this publication may be reproduced, stored in a retrieval system, or transmitted in any form or by any means (electronic, mechanical, photocopying, recording, or otherwise) without the prior written permission of the copyright owner.

Printed in the United States of America

10 9 8 7 6 5 4 3 2 1

Contents

Acknowledgments, xi

Preface, xiii

1. The Optimum Birth Experience, 1
2. Pregnancy, 13
3. Nutrition, 45
4. Exercise, 65
5. Tools for Labor, 81
6. Labor and Birth, 113
7. Medications and Anesthesia, 147
8. Variations and Interventions, 161
9. Cesarean Birth, 183
10. The Newborn, 201
11. Infant Feeding, 241
12. The New Parent, 273

    Appendix A: Labor Record, 305
    Appendix B: Recommended Reading List, 307

Notes, 311
Glossary, 317
Bibliography, 325
About the Authors, 329
Index, 331

To our families—our husbands, for their constant support and encouragement; our offspring, who provided the inspiration for this work and who continue to bring us pride and gratification as they travel their unique journeys into adulthood; and our grandchildren, present and future, whose births will serve to keep us current and provide the inspiration for future editions!

Permission Credits

"The Pregnant Patient's Bill of Rights" on pages 9 through 10 is used courtesy of Doris Haire and the International Childbirth Education Association.

"The Pregnant Patient's Responsibilities" on page 11 is used courtesy of Doris Haire and the International Childbirth Education Association.

The illustrations of the woman's body at the end of the first trimester on page 24, at the end of the second trimester on page 25, and at the end of the third trimester on page 26 are from *Pregnancy in Anatomical Illustrations*. They are used courtesy of Carnation Nutritional Products, a division of the Nestlé Food Company.

"The No-Risk Pregnancy Diet" on page 49 is reprinted from *The Pregnancy After 30 Workbook* © 1978 by Gail Sforza Brewer. Permission granted by Rodale Press, Inc., Emmaus, PA 18049.

The "Protein, Calcium, and Iron Counts of Selected Foods" table on pages 54 through 58 is adapted from "Composition of Foods—Raw, Processed, Prepared." It is used with the permission of the U.S. Department of Agriculture, Washington, DC.

The pudendal block illustration on page 150 is from "Regional Anesthesia in Obstetrics," Clinical Education Aid No. 17. It is used courtesy of Ross Laboratories, Columbus, Ohio.

The illustrations on pages 161, 162, and 163 depicting different categories of presentation and the illustration on page 186 depicting a prolapsed cord are from "Obstetrical Presentation and Position," Clinical Education Aid No. 18 © 1985 by Ross Products Division, Abbott Laboratories. They are used with permission of Ross Products Division, Abbott Laboratories, Columbus, OH 43216.

The skin incision illustrations on page 193 and uterine incision illustrations on page 194 are adapted from an illustration copyrighted © 1980 by Childbirth Graphics Ltd. Used with permission.

The "Methods of Contraception Used in the United States" table on pages 294 through 301 is adapted from "Family Planning Methods of Contraception." It is used courtesy of DHEW Publication No. (HSA) 80-5646, Department of Health and Human Services, Public Health Service, Health Services Administration.

Acknowledgments

Just as an optimum birth experience combines the judicious use of modern technology with the support of caring individuals, the delivery of *Pregnancy to Parenthood* was accomplished thanks to a combination of factors. Modern technology provided us with computers, modems, copy machines, and fax machines, which certainly made our labor easier. But of more importance was the support we received from a number of individuals who took the time to give us their input and assistance.

We want to thank the following for sharing their professional expertise: Sandy Arpen, RN, ICCE; Wade Barnes, MD; David Blue, DMD; Brenda Bradshaw-Csonka, LMT; Samantha Brinkley, LMT; Camie Carson, CNM; Liz Flight, IBCLC; Don Floyd, CRNA; Fred Hoover, MD; Debby Kearney, IBCLC; Miles Landis, MD; Roberta Mattix, CNM; Suzanne Paszkowski, CNM; Sandy Williamson, CNM; and Beth Wrigley, CNM. Also, thanks to Dana Delaney, for her suggestion, and to Carolyn Hewitt, for her assistance with the photos.

Special thanks go to Melissa Brenner and Rebecca Hardy, for their original artwork, and to Penny Banks, whose unique cartoon drawings provide a light touch and help make this a one-of-a-kind publication.

We are grateful to Susan Torregrosa and Terry Cuffel, whose photographic artistry can be seen throughout the book.

The following people deserve special recognition, for graciously agreeing to appear in our photos. We especially appreciate those families who shared their birth pictures or allowed us to photograph their birth and share in their joy. These people are: Helen, Peter, and Andrew Alberse; Debbie and Logan Baker; Traci, Jon, and Samantha Balao; Tracy, Zach, Jett, and Skylar Baumann; Brenda Bradshaw-Csonka; Rockett Brinkley; Zachary and Nathan Burns; Camie Carson; Natalie, Kevin, and Elizabeth Casey; Kelli Conley; Jill and Levi Corns; Rita and Kolohe Del Carmen; Jeannie, Lynn, and Jared Denbrook; Sariah, Darren, and Kirra Ellsmore; Nancy Fishalow; Colleen and Tyler Goehrig; Bill, Jeff, Becky, and Jon Goldberg; and Maryanne and Brett Hewitt.

Also, Nancy and Allison Hillis; Ashlen Johnson; Paula Jones-Marek; Leslie and David Jordan; Diana Konz; Heather and Matt Kubis; Mari Beth and Cade Langston; Roberta Mattix; Casey and Jesse Mizzone; Lisa and Sam

Nasrallah; Chiaki and Wendy Nishikawa; Josephine and John Oetjen; Suzanne Paszkowski; Clare Rogers; Karen and Nathaniel Scheer; Brette Petway Sears; Pamela and Thomas Shipley; Kendra Shortle; Julianne Stowell; Nicole, Vincent, and Tiana Tristram; Kimberly and Kayla Vincent; and Veronica and Derrick Watts.

Preface

Imagine what it would feel like to take piloting lessons and then never be allowed to actually fly an airplane. That is how many fathers-to-be felt in the early days of prepared childbirth. A couple would take Lamaze classes, but the husband would not be allowed in the delivery room for his baby's birth. In the 1970s and 1980s, the parents and older siblings of today's expectant couples fought long and hard for the right to experience husband-attended labors and deliveries, as well as for many other birthing options that were not readily available at that time.

Over the years, the efforts of these early advocates have paid off. The couples' perseverance prompted studies that showed that there actually *are* measurable benefits to having a support person during labor—that the presence of a support person can result in a shorter labor and fewer complications. Studies have even shown that continuous labor support may decrease the chances of a cesarean delivery.[1] Other birthing options have also been proven to be of benefit to the woman and baby. For example, walking during labor, rather than being confined to a bed, has been shown to speed up labor and to decrease the need for pain medication. Breastfeeding immediately after birth and on demand thereafter is now known to be extremely beneficial to the newborn. These, and many other options that were denied in the past, are presently available to most expectant couples.

Today, it is a rare hospital that does not encourage at least one support person during labor and delivery. Laboring women are often allowed to move around as they desire and to choose the position of greatest comfort. Immediate breastfeeding and bonding are encouraged, and siblings are often permitted to be included in the birthing and bonding experiences. Family involvement has become the standard in most birthing units. In addition, many out-of-hospital birth centers have opened throughout the country, allowing the greatest freedom for couples desiring to plan their own births.

Because so many options are now available, it is even more important for expectant couples to educate themselves before making decisions. The options today include the use of such technological advances as ultrasound, which is employed during labor to monitor the baby, and medications such as the epidural, which many women choose in an effort to avoid pain. Only by becoming familiar with the benefits and risks of all the available options can a couple make wise decisions. Education is the purpose of this book. Expectant couples are no longer in the position of having to push for what they want. Now their responsibility is even greater—they must learn all they can about the many choices available so that when their special day arrives, they can choose the options that are best for them. The birth of her baby is one of the most significant events in a woman's life—one of the few that she will remember in great detail even decades later. Well-thought-out decisions can help ensure an optimum birth experience and positive memories.

This book is designed to accompany couples from the early months of pregnancy through the early months of parenthood. It provides the most current information available to help you have a healthy, enjoyable pregnancy and an awake and aware childbirth experience. It also offers information on baby care and parenting. In addition, throughout the book you will find helpful hints directed to the labor partner or father-to-be. Utilizing these will increase your mate's participation in the pregnancy, labor, and birth processes, and will enhance his role in parenting.

WHAT IS FAMILY-CENTERED MATERNITY CARE?

The term *family-centered maternity care* (FCMC) implies family togetherness during the time of labor and delivery. The needs and feelings of the mother, father, and baby are of the utmost importance, second only to the safety of the mother and baby. FCMC includes such concepts as father participation in labor, delivery, and cesarean birth; bonding time; rooming-in; sibling involvement; and presence of other family members and/or friends during labor and delivery. All of these concepts are discussed in this book.

PREPARED CHILDBIRTH

Childbirth preparation comes in several forms. Some couples choose to attend the shortest class offered by their hospital, wishing simply to learn the hospital procedures or to find out how soon they can get an epidural. Other couples prefer to attend a class that teaches a prescribed format such as the Lamaze (pronounced *le MAHZ*) method or the Bradley method. This choice requires learning and practicing specific techniques for use during labor. Yet, these methods offer more than just breathing techniques. Couples are also encouraged to try other pain-reducing measures that may increase their comfort during labor. Still others prepare for birth by gaining a thorough understanding of the birth process and having the confidence that a woman who is in tune with her body will instinctively know how to labor and give birth.

Prepared childbirth, as discussed in this book, presents a variety of options, allowing you to select the tools you desire to individualize your birth. The basis for the breathing techniques is the Lamaze method, named for the French doctor, Fernand Lamaze, who discovered that laboring women could benefit from the conditioning techniques originated by the Russian scientist Ivan Pavlov. Prepared childbirth, however, is more than just relaxing and breathing. It is an attitude whereby a couple accepts responsibility for their childbirth experience. This method requires you to become familiar with many techniques and procedures. You can then utilize those that provide the most benefit and comfort during your particular labor. This is why there is no success or failure. Since each childbirth is unique and unpredictable, you are prepared to deal with any situation that may arise. The ultimate experience is achieved when you make informed decisions concerning the management of your labor and delivery. This can be accomplished only through education and preparation. It also requires the knowledgeable seeking-out of those birthing facilities and caregivers that will most enhance the type of birth you desire.

As in many scientific and medical fields, the techniques of prepared childbirth are constantly changing. The Lamaze of today is quite different from that of Dr. Lamaze's day, over 40 years ago. Aware childbirth educators are constantly updating and revising their teaching methods in order to incorporate the relaxation and breathing techniques and other pain-relief strategies that have been found most beneficial. The techniques presented in this book are the most current available today.

WHAT THIS BOOK WILL DO FOR YOU

The purpose of this book is twofold. First, the book provides the tools to be utilized by you, the expectant couple, throughout pregnancy and birth. Some of these tools must be studied and practiced many times for maximum benefit. Second, the book conveys an attitude, one of awareness and responsibility. It is through this attitude that couples can make educated decisions.

HOW TO USE THIS BOOK

This book is intended to be used in conjunction with early pregnancy, childbirth preparation, breastfeeding, and new mothers' classes. The chapter on cesarean birth also makes it an appropriate manual for cesarean preparation classes. When used individually, rather than in a class setting, the book should first be quickly read from cover to cover. Then, the various sections should be studied in more detail according to the current stage of pregnancy—for example, the nutrition chapter should be read during the early months of pregnancy, the relaxation and breathing chapter during the later months. The newborn, infant feeding, and parenting chapters can provide a handy reference guide after your baby is born.

When reading through the book, please note that for the sake of clarity, the pronoun *she* is used in reference to the woman, midwife, or nurse. The pronoun *he* is used when referring to the labor partner, baby, or doctor.

Whether this is your first birth or your first "prepared" birth, the information in this book will enable you to make your journey from pregnancy to parenthood a truly rewarding and memorable experience.

Chapter One

The Optimum Birth Experience

or *Decisions, Decisions*

Pregnancy is a time of heightened awareness. You become aware of changes in your body, in your way of thinking, and in your priorities. You must also become aware of the choices available to you that can help determine how you feel about your birth experience, your baby, and yourself as a parent. You have the right as a consumer to know about the different options from which you can choose. You have the responsibility to learn as much as possible—through classes, your doctor or midwife, and independent reading—to enable yourself to make informed, considered choices from among those options.

CHOOSING YOUR CAREGIVER

Your caregiver is the person you select to provide your prenatal care and to deliver your baby. It is the doctor or midwife that you hire to be your health-care provider.

The choice of this important person may have a significant effect on the type of birth experience you have. You should consider how to find the best caregiver as soon as your pregnancy is confirmed. Early in pregnancy, you have sufficient time for interviewing and exploring the options. However, even in late pregnancy, women have successfully changed caregivers. If possible, include your support person (husband, other family member, or friend who plans to be with you during labor and birth) in interviews with potential caregivers.

According to Dr. Silvia Feldman in her book *Choices in Childbirth,* the choice of a caregiver "should be determined by three things: his or her expertise, philosophy, and personality."[1] When the pregnancy and childbirth are expected to be normal, Dr. Feldman recommends that women interview several caregivers using an organized list of specific needs and wishes. Almost all possible birth options are now available in most areas, so it should not be difficult to locate a caregiver who is willing to go along with any reasonable requests. The important factor is communication. It is up to you to communicate your desires and to ask the doctor or midwife to explain any policies that may be unclear. An open exchange of views establishes a good rapport and a feeling of mutual trust and security.

Choose a caregiver with whom you feel comfortable and can agree on a birth plan.

Hints for the Mother-to-Be

❑ Make a list of the things that you wish to discuss with your caregiver.

❑ Start asking questions early in your pregnancy.

❑ Ask a few questions at each obstetric visit, rather than a long list of questions at one visit.

❑ Take your partner with you to the visits at which you want to discuss important issues. Your caregiver may be more willing to discuss these issues with both of you present.

Hints for the Father-to-Be

❑ Join your mate for interviews of prospective caregivers.

❑ Discuss the options with your mate prior to her office visits.

❑ Tour the local hospitals and birth centers.

❑ Ask labor and delivery nurses for recommendations of supportive doctors and midwives.

❑ Help your mate make her birth plan. Discuss the plan with her caregiver and have it signed. Make sure that it is placed on her chart when she enters the hospital or birth center in labor.

Choose your options wisely.

A conscientious, up-to-date doctor or midwife will take the time to discuss feelings and will promote careful attention to good nutrition. Such a doctor or midwife will encourage you to educate yourself by reading all you can about pregnancy and childbirth, and by attending classes. You may want to ask the doctors you interview about their cesarean rates, as well as the cesarean rates of the hospitals where they deliver. Find out, too, the reasons they consider non-negotiable for performing a cesarean. You may also want to verify the credentials of all the doctors and midwives you consider selecting. For example, a *board certified physician* has passed an exam administered by his professional society. A *certified nurse-midwife* has completed training in midwifery in addition to being a registered nurse. A few states recognize *licensed midwives,* who have completed training according to the requirements of their states. On the other hand, *lay midwives* may or may not be registered in their states, so their standards and quality of care will vary.

Many women in the United States prefer to have an obstetrician as their caregiver because of his training in handling the problems that may arise. Family and general practice physicians also deliver babies. A certified nurse-midwife's experience and training are in handling normal, uncomplicated births. This training, as well as her outlook, makes a midwife less likely to use medical intervention in the course of labor and delivery. In addition, "Midwives are willing to start in early labor and sit with a woman 14 hours," says Charles Mahan, MD, OBG, dean of the University of South Florida College of Public Health and former State Health Officer for the State of Florida. "I'm not willing to do that. Most of my colleagues aren't either. For low-risk women, they are better off with a midwife."[2] If a problem arises, however, the nurse-midwife will refer the woman to an obstetrician. Therefore, if you are considering employing a midwife, you should also interview her medical backup.

You may want to take a tour of the facility where you plan to deliver. In addition to hospitals, many areas offer out-of-hospital birth centers. Some of these freestanding birth centers are owned independently by midwives or physicians; others are financed by a hospital, but located outside the main building. Birth centers offer low-risk women the opportunity to deliver using few medical interventions. They usually cost less than the local hospitals, but still provide a high quality of care. A few areas offer the option of home birth. If you are considering a nonhospital delivery, be sure to find out about medical backup and the procedures for transfer to a hospital if complications do arise.

OPTIMUM BIRTH—THE OPTIONS INVOLVED

Table 1.1 presents a list of options in which many women have shown an interest. Not all of these options will be appropriate for you. If any of them are important to you, but your caregiver does not seem willing to accommodate your desires, encourage him to discuss his reasoning. If, following the discussion, you are still not comfortable with his responses, you have the option of seeking care elsewhere. Be sure to let your original caregiver know your reasons if you make this decision.

The options in Table 1.1 are divided into four categories—pregnancy, labor, delivery, and postpartum. They are geared to the *low-risk woman having a normal, uncomplicated labor and birth.* Read the list and check those options that are important to you. Add any other options that you may desire. This list will be your birth plan. Take it with you when choosing or consulting with your doctor or midwife. A list of cesarean options is also provided, in Table 1.2 on page 8.

After you and your caregiver have agreed on your birth plan, make several copies of it. Keep one copy with your record, give one to your labor partner, and give one to the nursing staff when you check into the hospital. You might want to have your doctor or midwife sign or initial all the copies of your birth plan to indicate his or her agreement with your desires.

Table 1.1. Options for an Optimum Birth Experience

Option	Reasoning
DURING PREGNANCY	
Optimum nutrition	The No-Risk Pregnancy Diet can reduce the danger of complications for you and your baby to the lowest possible level.[3] See Chapter 3.
Supportive caregiver willing to be flexible in your labor and delivery choices, including birth place (hospital or birth center)	Careful selection of your caregiver can eliminate the stress of trying to change the attitudes of a doctor or midwife who will not consider your individual wishes. Some low-risk women feel more at home in an out-of-hospital birth center. Others feel safer within a hospital environment. See Chapter 1.
Consumer-oriented childbirth classes	Consumer-oriented classes inform you about all the available options rather than just the routine of a particular hospital or doctor. They enable you to make educated decisions about what options you want for your childbirth experience, plus provide you with thorough training for labor and delivery.
No smoking, taking drugs, or consuming alcohol	These have been shown by experts to have adverse effects on the baby. See Chapter 3.
No routine use of ultrasound during pregnancy	Routine screening of all women is not recommended by the National Institutes of Health or the American College of Obstetricians and Gynecologists. See Chapter 2.
DURING LABOR	
Presence of a support person during the admission procedures, examinations, labor, and birth	This eliminates the stress of separation. Your partner can provide emotional support during labor and birth, as well as during any necessary procedures. His presence can enhance family bonding. See Chapter 6.
Presence of other family members or friends during labor and/or delivery	Other family members and friends can provide additional support for you and your partner. The incidence of infection does not increase as long as those present have no signs of illness (for example, runny nose or diarrhea). See Chapter 6.
Enema only if needed	An enema is unnecessary if you had a good bowel movement within 24 hours. A soapsuds enema can be very uncomfortable. However, if you have been constipated, you may desire an enema; a small disposable enema will suffice. See Chapter 6.

Option	Reasoning
DURING LABOR (continued)	
Freedom to move about and to assume a position of comfort	Walking stimulates the uterus to work more efficiently. Labors that include walking are documented to be shorter and to require less pain medication.[4] Sitting up, lying on your side, or kneeling on your hands and knees may be most comfortable for you. See Chapter 6.
Laboring in water	Laboring in a tub or shower enhances relaxation and decreases the need for pain medication. See Chapter 5.
Liquid nourishment and high-carbohydrate, low-fat snacks as desired	Foods that are high in carbohydrates and low in fat are digested quickly and supply energy that will be needed during labor. Liquids prevent dehydration. See Chapter 6.
Ice chips, sips of water or clear juice, or Popsicles	Your mouth can become very dry when you do the breathing patterns. See Chapter 6.
Personal items (for example, nightgown, music, or flowers)	Familiar articles can enhance your birth experience by encouraging relaxation and comfort. See Chapter 6.
Prep (shaving of the pubic hair) only if desired	Shaving of the pubic hair does not decrease the incidence of infection, and the regrowth of the hair is uncomfortable. See Chapter 6.
Intravenous (IV) fluids only if medically indicated	IVs restrict mobility and interfere with relaxation. Clear liquids during labor reduce the chance of dehydration. Hemorrhage is rare when the birth is unmedicated and spontaneous, and when breastfeeding is begun immediately. See Chapter 8.
Electronic fetal monitor only if medically indicated	In a low-risk woman, a trained nurse frequently listening to the fetal heart rate has been shown to be as effective in detecting fetal well-being or distress as an electronic fetal monitor.[5] Fetal monitors restrict movement and can be uncomfortable. Sometimes, women are instructed to lie on their backs, a position that can be uncomfortable and can also negatively affect labor. Intermittent use of a fetal monitor throughout labor is an alternative. See Chapter 8.
Spontaneous rupture of the membranes	The amniotic fluid contained in the membranes has a cushioning effect, equalizing the pressure on the baby, which results in less molding of his head. Artificial rupture of the membranes provides a passageway for infection and creates a time limit for delivery. See Chapter 8.
Medication administered only when requested by you and with full information regarding the possible effects on you, the baby, and the labor	All medication has the potential to affect you, your baby, and your labor. Knowledge of the benefits and risks of the medications your caregiver uses most often will enable you to make informed decisions. See Chapter 7.

Option	Reasoning
DURING LABOR (continued)	
Presence of a professional labor support person (childbirth instructor, registered nurse, trained doula, licensed massage therapist, or midwife not associated with the hospital or birth center)	A knowledgeable professional who has a strong commitment to the type of birth you desire can provide you with additional information. The presence of a doula can reduce your chances of having a cesarean by 50 percent. Also, your labor may be shorter, you may require less Pitocin and pain medication, and you may reduce your needs for an epidural and a forceps delivery. A massage therapist can perform techniques to relieve labor discomfort. See Chapter 6.
Pitocin to induce or augment labor only if medically indicated	The contractions induced by Pitocin are more difficult to handle than natural contractions for both the woman and baby. The risks of induced labor include reduction of the baby's oxygen supply and premature birth, which are not warranted just for the woman's or doctor's convenience (elective induction). The complications that may develop in a labor involving Pitocin can increase the chances for cesarean delivery.[6] See Chapter 8.
DURING DELIVERY	
Comfortable and efficient pushing and delivery position	Semireclining at a 70-degree angle, side-lying, or kneeling may be more comfortable than being flat on your back. Lying flat on your back reduces the pelvic outlet to its smallest diameter,[7] may be uncomfortable, and causes the weight of the uterus to impede blood flow. Squatting shortens the birth canal, opens the pelvic outlet to its widest diameter, and makes the contractions more efficient because the uterus is assisted by gravity.[8] See Chapter 5.
No use of stirrups	The lithotomy position, in which you lie on your back with your feet in stirrups, works against gravity and forces you to push the baby uphill. Wide stirrups, while giving the caregiver a good field of vision, cause the perineum to be stretched taut and increase the need for an episiotomy (a small incision in the vaginal outlet to enlarge the opening).[9] See Chapter 5.
Episiotomy only if needed	Allowing the baby's head to emerge slowly under uterine force alone gives the perineal tissue a better chance to stretch, which minimizes tearing. An episiotomy shortens the pushing stage. It may be necessary if fetal distress is detected and a faster delivery or the use of forceps is required. Many doctors do an episiotomy routinely, whether or not it is needed. Healing of an episiotomy may be very uncomfortable. Muscle scarring, which can negatively affect later sexual pleasure, can result. See Chapter 8.
Use of a birthing room or the same bed for labor and delivery	This avoids the stress and discomfort of being rushed to a delivery room during the expulsion stage and of then being awkwardly moved onto a delivery table. Most hospitals do provide birthing rooms for labor and delivery. See Chapter 6.

Option	Reasoning
DURING DELIVERY (continued)	
Regional anesthesia only if medical or surgical intervention becomes necessary	Anesthesia is unnecessary in an uncomplicated delivery. If an episiotomy is done, a local anesthetic may be given for the repair work after the baby is delivered. Regional anesthesia is compatible with an awake delivery; general anesthesia (gas or sodium pentothal) is not. See Chapter 7.
Leboyer delivery (gentle birth)	Gentle birth is an attitude as well as a procedure. It decreases the sensory and physical trauma to the infant as he is delivered. See Chapter 8.
Cutting the cord delayed until the pulsating stops	The delay allows the baby to continue receiving oxygen through the cord while his respiratory system begins to function. See Chapter 6.
Father cutting the umbilical cord	This increases his participation in the birth. See Chapter 6.
Collection of cord blood for banking	Collection of cord blood for donation or for storage for your own personal use may provide lifesaving benefits. See Chapter 6.
Baby placed immediately on your bare abdomen or in your arms	Immediate skin-to-skin contact is beneficial. When both mother and baby are covered with a blanket, the infant's temperature can be maintained. See Chapter 6.
Baby allowed to breastfeed as soon as possible	The baby's sucking stimulates the mother's production of the hormone oxytocin, which aids in the release of the placenta and decreases postpartum bleeding. A baby's sucking reflex is strongest during the first hours after birth. Colostrum (the first milk produced in the breasts) acts as a laxative, cleansing the baby's intestinal tract of mucus and meconium (fetal fecal matter). See Chapter 11.
Antibiotic ointment or silver nitrate drops delayed until after bonding	These can interfere with the baby's vision, which is so important during the bonding period. See Chapter 6.
Placenta allowed to detach spontaneously from the wall of the uterus	Strong traction or massaging may cause placental tissue to be retained, which can cause postpartum bleeding. See Chapter 6.
Bonding	The first hours after birth are very important in the development of maternal and paternal attachment to the newborn. See Chapter 6.
Taking snapshots or making a tape	These are wonderful ways to remember these unforgettable moments.
POSTPARTUM	
Breastfeeding	Nutritionally, your breastmilk is the perfect food for your baby. Breastfeeding is an emotionally satisfying experience for both mother and baby. It is economical. It helps the uterus return to its prepregnant state faster. See Chapter 11.

Option	Reasoning
POSTPARTUM (continued)	
No separation of mother and baby unless medically indicated	Continuous mother-baby contact enhances bonding. It also increases the opportunity for the nurse to provide baby-care instruction. The initial bath can be given in the mother's room. See Chapter 6.
No supplements (water or formula) or pacifiers if breastfeeding	Sucking on a rubber nipple may confuse your baby, since he must use a different tongue action to suck from your breast. If your baby is fed supplements between nursings, he may not breastfeed as often as necessary to stimulate milk production. See Chapter 11.
Full 24-hour rooming-in	This allows close contact between parents and baby to enhance the bonding process, depending on the mother's postpartum condition. You are able to breastfeed on demand. You can learn how to care for your baby while supervised by hospital staff. See Chapter 6.
Father staying in the room with the mother until discharge	This enhances family bonding. It enables the father to assist with the baby care. Many hospitals provide cots for fathers to spend the night.
Sibling visitation with mother and baby	This helps reassure your other children that you are fine. It encourages acceptance of the new baby by his siblings. See Chapter 6.
Circumcision only if desired	Circumcision is normally done for religious or cosmetic reasons. It should be delayed for 12 to 24 hours after birth to give the baby time to adjust to extrauterine life. It may cause bleeding or infection. See Chapter 10.
Discharge from the hospital within 24 hours after birth	This decreases the chances of a hospital-induced infection. Early discharge is safe as long as there is adequate follow-up care for the mother and baby. The decision should be made on an individual basis. It decreases the time you are separated from your other children. See Chapter 6.

CESAREAN BIRTH OPTIONS

Table 1.2 on page 8 presents a list of options for cesarean couples. With the national cesarean rate at approximately 21 percent, every couple should be prepared for both a vaginal and a cesarean birth and should explore the options for both, long before the baby's due date.

A cesarean delivery can be a very rewarding experience for couples that are prepared and participate in the birth. Even an unexpected or emergency cesarean birth can be family centered if you prepare ahead "just in case."

If you have chosen a nurse-midwife to be your caregiver, you should discuss the options in Table 1.2 with her physician backup. (See Chapter 9.)

Looking for a Midwife?

The American College of Nurse-Midwives has a toll-free number to find a certified nurse-midwife (CNM) in your area. Call 888–MIDWIFE (888–643–9433) and punch in your area code to hear a list of CNMs practicing in your area. This service is available 24 hours a day, 7 days a week.

Table 1.2. Options for an Optimum Cesarean Birth Experience

Option	Reasoning
A supportive doctor, anesthesiologist, and hospital, all willing to allow a family-centered cesarean birth	Careful selection will ensure family participation in the event of a cesarean delivery.
Participation in the birth process by your support person	Your support person can provide you with emotional security during this special experience.
Admission on the day of surgery/birth for planned cesareans	This gives you one more night at home, which can mean a better night's sleep and extra time with your husband and other children.
Labor allowed to begin before a planned cesarean is performed	Labor is nature's way of telling you that it is time to have your baby. Waiting for it to begin lessens the chance of the baby being premature.
Knowledge of the different procedures associated with cesarean birth (for example, the lab tests, prep, and urinary catheter)	Understanding what is being done allows you to be more relaxed.
Partial prep (shaving from the abdomen to the pubic bone)	This minimizes the uncomfortable feeling caused by the pubic hair growing back in.
No preoperative sedation	All medication may affect the baby. It may also affect your ability to interact with the baby at birth.[10] Instead, use relaxation techniques prior to surgery.
Use of regional anesthesia	This allows you to be awake when your baby is delivered and facilitates bonding. Except in the case of an acute emergency, adequate time is usually available for a regional anesthetic to be given.
Lowering the drape or providing mirrors during the delivery	This allows the mother and father to watch the birth of their baby.
Admitting the infant to the well newborn nursery if his condition is satisfactory	If a pediatrician or nurse evaluates the baby and approves of his condition, bonding can begin soon after birth, even in the recovery room. Rooming-in can also begin sooner. If the baby has no respiratory problems, he can be placed in the newborn nursery instead of in the neonatal intensive care unit.
Nursing the baby as soon as possible after birth (on the delivery table or in the recovery room)	This gives the baby and mother the same advantages of early nursing as does nursing following a vaginal delivery.
Bonding as soon after birth as is feasible	Holding and touching the baby can reduce parental anxiety, along with providing the benefits of early bonding.
Rooming-in on a flexible basis	This lets you care for your baby as your condition permits. It enhances bonding and breastfeeding. Help from her support person can greatly benefit the cesarean mother, as can assistance from the hospital staff.

THE PREGNANT PATIENT'S RIGHTS AND RESPONSIBILITIES

"The Pregnant Patient's Bill of Rights," below, and "The Pregnant Patient's Responsibilities," found on page 11, were prepared by the International Childbirth Education Association (ICEA) to expand awareness of the rights and responsibilities that expectant parents have.

Your obstetrician has the legal obligation to obtain your informed consent before he can perform any treatment or test. Informed consent is authorization or approval to perform a treatment or test based on a full explanation of what is involved, including the risks and hazards, the chances for recovery, the necessity of the procedure, the feasibility of alternative methods, and whether the treatment is new or unusual. Your obstetrician must explain this information to you in a way that helps you understand it thoroughly. Reasons such as, "The patient may prefer not to be told the unpleasant possibilities of the treatment"; "Full disclosure might suggest infinite dangers to a patient with an active imagination, thereby causing her to refuse treatment"; or "The patient, upon learning of the risks involved, might rationally decline treatment" are not sufficient reasons to justify failure to inform.[11]

If your obstetrician discusses medical or surgical intervention with you during your pregnancy, labor, delivery, or postpartum period, it is important that you be aware of your rights as well as your responsibilities in either accepting or refusing the suggested treatment.

THE PREGNANT PATIENT'S BILL OF RIGHTS

American parents are becoming increasingly aware that well-intentioned health professionals do not always have scientific data to support common American obstetrical practices and that many of these practices are carried out primarily because they are part of medical and hospital tradition. In the last forty years many artificial practices have been introduced which have changed childbirth from a physiological event to a very complicated medical procedure in which all kinds of drugs are used and procedures carried out, sometimes unnecessarily, and many of them potentially damaging for the baby and even for the mother. A growing body of research makes it alarmingly clear that every aspect of traditional American hospital care during labor and delivery must now be questioned as to its possible effect on the future well-being of both the obstetric patient and her unborn child.

One in every 35 children born in the United States today will eventually be diagnosed as retarded; in 75% of these cases there is no familial or genetic predisposing factor. One in every ten to seventeen children has been found to have some form of brain dysfunction or learning disability requiring special treatment. Such statistics are not confined to the lower socioeconomic group but cut across all segments of American society.

New concerns are being raised by childbearing women because no one knows what degree of oxygen depletion, head compression, or traction by forceps the unborn or newborn infant can tolerate before that child sustains permanent brain damage or dysfunction. The recent findings regarding the cancer-related drug diethylstilbestrol have alerted the public to the fact that neither the approval of a drug by the U.S. Food and Drug Administration nor the fact that a drug is prescribed by a physician serves as a guarantee that a drug or medication is safe for the mother or her unborn child. In fact, the American Academy of Pediatrics' Committee on Drugs has recently stated that there is no drug, whether prescription or over-the-counter remedy, which has been proven safe for the unborn child.

The Pregnant Patient has the right to participate in decisions involving her well-being and that of her unborn child, unless there is a clearcut medical emergency that prevents her participation. In addition to the rights set forth in the American Hospital Association's "Patient's Bill of Rights" (which has also been adopted by the New York City Department of Health), the Pregnant Patient, because she represents TWO patients rather than one, should be recognized as having the additional rights listed below.

1. *The Pregnant Patient has the right*, prior to the administration of any drug or procedure, to be informed by the health professional caring for her of any potential direct or indirect effects, risks or hazards to herself or her unborn or newborn infant which may result from the use of a drug or procedure prescribed for or administered to her during pregnancy, labor, birth or lactation.

2. *The Pregnant Patient has the right*, prior to the proposed therapy, to be informed, not only of the benefits,

risks and hazards of the proposed therapy but also of known alternative therapy, such as available childbirth education classes which could help to prepare the Pregnant Patient physically and mentally to cope with the discomfort or stress of pregnancy and the experience of childbirth, thereby reducing or eliminating her need for drugs and obstetric intervention. She should be offered such information early in her pregnancy in order that she may make a reasoned decision.

3. *The Pregnant Patient has the right*, prior to the administration of any drug, to be informed by the health professional who is prescribing or administering the drug to her that any drug which she receives during pregnancy, labor and birth, no matter how or when the drug is taken or administered, may adversely affect her unborn baby, directly or indirectly, and that there is no drug or chemical which has been proven safe for the unborn child.

4. *The Pregnant Patient has the right* if Cesarean birth is anticipated, to be informed prior to the administration of any drug, and preferably prior to her hospitalization, that minimizing her and, in turn, her baby's intake of nonessential pre-operative medicine will benefit her baby.

5. *The Pregnant Patient has the right*, prior to the administration of a drug or procedure, to be informed of the areas of uncertainty if there is NO properly controlled follow-up research which has established the safety of the drug or procedure with regard to its direct and/or indirect effects on the physiological, mental and neurological development of the child exposed, via the mother, to the drug or procedure during pregnancy, labor, birth or lactation—(this would apply to virtually all drugs and the vast majority of obstetric procedures).

6. *The Pregnant Patient has the right*, prior to the administration of any drug, to be informed of the brand name and generic name of the drug in order that she may advise the health professional of any past adverse reaction to the drug.

7. *The Pregnant Patient has the right* to determine for herself, without pressure from her attendant, whether she will accept the risks inherent in the proposed therapy or refuse a drug or procedure.

8. *The Pregnant Patient has the right* to know the name and qualifications of the individual administering a medication or procedure to her during labor or birth.

9. *The Pregnant Patient has the right* to be informed, prior to the administration of any procedure, whether that procedure is being administered to her for her or her baby's benefit (medically indicated) or as an elective procedure (for convenience, teaching purposes or research).

10. *The Pregnant Patient has the right* to be accompanied during the stress of labor and birth by someone she cares for, and to whom she looks for emotional comfort and encouragement.

11. *The Pregnant Patient has the right* after appropriate medical consultation to choose a position for labor and for birth which is least stressful to her baby and to herself.

12. *The Obstetric Patient has the right* to have her baby cared for at her bedside if her baby is normal, and to feed her baby according to her baby's needs rather than according to the hospital regimen.

13. *The Obstetric Patient has the right* to be informed in writing of the name of the person who actually delivered her baby and the professional qualifications of that person. This information should also be on the birth certificate.

14. *The Obstetric Patient has the right* to be informed if there is any known or indicated aspect of her or her baby's care or condition which may cause her or her baby later difficulty or problems.

15. *The Obstetric Patient has the right* to have her and her baby's hospital medical records complete, accurate and legible and to have their records, including Nurses' Notes, retained by the hospital until the child reaches at least the age of majority, or, alternatively, to have the records offered to her before they are destroyed.

16. *The Obstetric Patient*, both during and after her hospital stay, has the right to have access to her complete hospital medical records, including Nurses' Notes, and to receive a copy upon payment of a reasonable fee and without incurring the expense of retaining an attorney.

It is the obstetric patient and her baby, not the health professional, who must sustain any trauma or injury resulting from the use of a drug or obstetric procedure. The observation of the rights listed above will not only permit the obstetric patient to participate in the decisions involving her and her baby's health care, but will help to protect the health professional and the hospital against litigation arising from resentment or misunderstanding on the part of the mother.

Prepared by Doris Haire. Used by permission of the ICEA.

THE PREGNANT PATIENT'S RESPONSIBILITIES

In addition to understanding her rights the Pregnant Patient should also understand that she too has certain responsibilities. The Pregnant Patient's responsibilities include the following:

1. The Pregnant Patient is responsible for learning about the physical and psychological process of labor, birth and postpartum recovery. The better informed expectant parents are the better they will be able to participate in decisions concerning the planning of their care.

2. The Pregnant Patient is responsible for learning what comprises good prenatal and intranatal care and for making an effort to obtain the best care possible.

3. Expectant parents are responsible for knowing about those hospital policies and regulations which will affect their birth and postpartum experience.

4. The Pregnant Patient is responsible for arranging for a companion or support person (husband, mother, sister, friend, etc.) who will share in her plans for birth and who will accompany her during her labor and birth experience.

5. The Pregnant Patient is responsible for making her preferences known clearly to the health professionals involved in her case in a courteous and cooperative manner and for making mutually agreed-upon arrangements regarding maternity care alternatives with her physician and hospital in advance of labor.

6. Expectant parents are responsible for listening to their chosen physician or midwife with an open mind, just as they expect him or her to listen openly to them.

7. Once they have agreed to a course of health care, expectant parents are responsible, to the best of their ability, for seeing that the program is carried out in consultation with others with whom they have made the agreement.

8. The Pregnant Patient is responsible for obtaining information in advance regarding the approximate cost of her obstetric and hospital care.

9. The Pregnant Patient who intends to change her physician or hospital is responsible for notifying all concerned, well in advance of the birth if possible, and for informing both of her reasons for changing.

10. In all their interactions with medical and nursing personnel, the expectant parents should behave toward those caring for them with the same respect and consideration they themselves would like.

11. During the mother's hospital stay the mother is responsible for learning about her and her baby's continuing care after discharge from the hospital.

12. After birth, the parents should put into writing constructive comments and feelings of satisfaction and/or dissatisfaction with the care (nursing, medical and personal) they received. Good service to families in the future will be facilitated by those parents who take the time and responsibility to write letters expressing their feelings about the maternity care they received.

All the previous statements assume a normal birth and postpartum experience. Expectant parents should realize that, if complications develop in their cases, there will be an increased need to trust the expertise of the physician and hospital staff they have chosen. However, if problems occur, the childbearing woman still retains her responsibility for making informed decisions about her care or treatment and that of her baby. If she is incapable of assuming that responsibility because of her physical condition, her previously authorized companion or support person should assume responsibility for making informed decisions on her behalf.

Prepared by Members of the ICEA. Used by permission.

CONCLUSION

In this chapter, you have been given an overview of pregnancy, labor, birth, and the postpartum period, and the options that you may want to consider for each. The next eight chapters deal with these topics in greater detail. Information relevant to your first year as a new parent is presented in the final three chapters.

Chapter Two

Pregnancy

or Conception and Myth-Conceptions

Pregnancy begins with conception (fertilization) and continues until the moment of birth. It is that special time in your life when your body envelops the growth of a new being. Everything you do, everything you eat, and even your emotions may have an effect on the development of that new life. It is therefore very important for you to be aware both of the actions that you can take to most benefit the development of your baby and of the detrimental factors that you should avoid. Understanding the normal course of pregnancy will aid you in acquiring this awareness.

Each woman's pregnancy differs in some ways from every other woman's. In fact, different pregnancies in the same woman usually vary. However, some aspects of pregnancy are common to all women. Certain physical and emotional changes, resulting in similar physical and emotional needs, are seen in every pregnant woman. These common factors are discussed in this chapter.

FERTILIZATION

A baby is created by the union of an egg cell from a woman's body and a sperm cell from a man's body. This union is called fertilization and marks the beginning of pregnancy. Each egg and sperm cell contains half of the genetic material, or chromosomes, necessary to begin human life. These chromosomes contain thousands of sections called genes, which determine the various characteristics of the child. The woman and man each contribute twenty-three chromosomes to their child, making a total of forty-six. Because of the billions of possible combinations that can be produced by these forty-six chromosomes and their thousands of genes, every child is unique.

The woman's biological contribution begins in one of her two ovaries. Every month, an egg follicle ripens and swells in one of the ovaries. This ripening of the egg cell is initiated by a pituitary hormone. The walls of the follicle surrounding the ripening egg produce estrogen, which causes the lining of the uterus, or womb, to thicken. The estrogen also causes the cervical mucus to increase and to become more receptive to sperm. When the egg is mature, it bursts out of the follicle and is released near the fringed end of the fallopian tube. The release of an egg from an ovary is called ovulation.

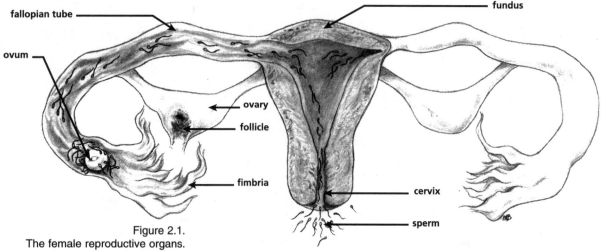

fallopian tube

ovum

fundus

ovary

follicle

fimbria

cervix

sperm

Figure 2.1.
The female reproductive organs.
Fertilization is taking place.

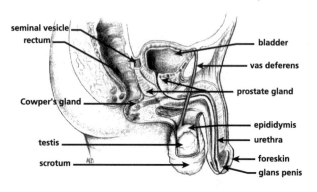

seminal vesicle
rectum

bladder

vas deferens

prostate gland

Cowper's gland

epididymis

testis

urethra

scrotum

foreskin

glans penis

Figure 2.2.
The male reproductive organs.

Ovulation usually occurs 14 days before the next menstrual period, or about midway through the cycle.

The fallopian tubes are muscular canals lined with fine hairs, called cilia, that move with a wavelike action, drawing the egg into the tube and then through it toward the uterus. (See Figure 2.1.) At the same time that the egg is traveling through the fallopian tube, the follicle, stimulated by a pituitary hormone, begins producing progesterone, another hormone, which causes the uterine lining to thicken further. The progesterone also slows down contractions in the uterus, which facilitates implantation of the fertilized egg.

The biological contribution that the man makes to the baby begins with the production of sperm cells in his testes, which are two organs that hang outside his body in a sac of skin called the scrotum. (See Figure 2.2.) Sperm cells, or spermatozoa, are produced in the seminiferous tubules within the testes and are propelled into the epididymis for storage until ejaculation. As the spermatozoa pass from the epididymis through the vas deferens to the urethra, secretions are added from the seminal vesicles, the prostate, and the Cowper's glands. The purpose of these secretions is to provide a nourishing and fluid material that helps the spermatozoa move through the vagina, where they are deposited during intercourse.

The penis becomes erect during sexual excitement as blood pours into its layers of spongy material and the veins leaving the penis begin to constrict. With further excitement, the muscles around the seminal vesicles, the vas deferens, and the prostate gland contract, driving the semen into the urethra. The muscles in the penis then contract and push the semen through the opening of the urethra. About 250 million to 500 million sperm are ejaculated, although less than 500 will reach the egg.

For fertilization to occur, sperm must reach the egg within 24 hours of ovulation. Sperm remain viable for up to 72 hours. It takes sperm from 30

"May the best sperm win!"

minutes to 2 hours to swim from the upper vagina, where they are usually deposited, to the outer third of the fallopian tube, where fertilization takes place. Sperm may reach an egg even if they are deposited externally, on the vulva. Only one sperm, out of the hundreds that may complete the journey, actually fertilizes the egg. As soon as this one sperm breaks through the egg wall, an enzyme is released that toughens the membrane of the egg and prevents penetration by any other sperm.

IMPLANTATION

The fertilized egg cell, now called an ovum, divides into two cells, then into four, and so on. By the fourth day, it is a cluster of sixteen cells called a morula. By the time it travels through the fallopian tube and reaches the uterus, a journey that takes 3 to 4 days, it is a hollow ball resembling a tiny blackberry and is known as a blastocyst.

About 8 days after fertilization, the blastocyst implants itself in the uterus, usually on the upper back wall. Projections on the outside of the blastocyst help it to attach to the thick inner lining of the uterine muscle. The blastocyst can then tap into the woman's blood supply for nourishment.

FETAL DEVELOPMENT

The terms used to date a pregnancy can be confusing. Once the pregnancy is confirmed, your caregiver will estimate your due date by counting from the first day of your last menstrual period. Since fertilization took place approximately 2 weeks after your period, you are considered as having been 2 weeks pregnant at the time of fertilization. Throughout your pregnancy, your progress will be measured in weeks of gestation (pregnancy) and the baby will be given a gestational age as measured from the first day of your last menstrual period. For example, when you are 12 weeks pregnant, the fetus is actually only 10 weeks old but is referred to as a 12-week-old fetus or as being at 12 weeks gestational age.

Pregnancy is also divided into three trimesters, each consisting of 3 calendar months. In addition, lunar months are used to describe events occurring during the pregnancy. A lunar month equals 28 days, and a pregnancy lasts 10 lunar months.

Most of the development of the fetal organs takes place during the first trimester. At the beginning of this phase, the ovum is a single cell. By the end

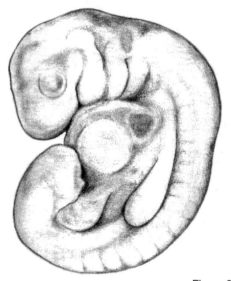

Figure 2.3.
The embryo at 4 weeks after fertilization.
Its actual size is 3/16 inch.

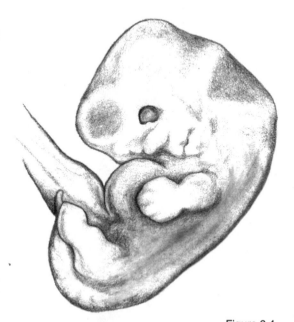

Figure 2.4.
The embryo at 5 weeks after fertilization.
Its actual size is 1/2 inch.

of the twelfth week, or third lunar month, the fetus is recognizable as a human and the placenta is fully functioning, exchanging nutrients and waste products. The second trimester is a time of continued development. Most of the fetal growth and maturation of the organs takes place during the third trimester.

First Week

During the first week following fertilization, the single cell—or ovum, as the developing being is called for the first 2 weeks—divides again and again, forming a hollow ball of three cell layers. Projections, called villi, appear on the outside of the ovum and help the ovum to burrow into the uterus, usually on the upper back wall.

Second Week

By the end of the second week following fertilization, the hollow space in the ovum has acquired two parts—an amniotic sac, which is filled with fluid, and a yolk sac, which will produce small blood vessels and cells. The yolk sac will degenerate as the developing being begins producing its own blood cells. The amniotic sac serves three functions—protecting the developing being from shocks, keeping the temperature constant, and serving as a barrier against infection from the outside. It is composed of two membranes that will eventually fuse together. The amnion, or inner layer, produces the amniotic fluid, and the chorion forms the outer layer.

Third Week

The developing being is called an embryo from the third to the eighth week after fertilization. By the end of the third week, the embryo is only 1/8 inch long. It has buds that will grow into lungs, a tube that will become a heart, and the beginning of a central nervous system. All of these are growing from the three layers of cells. Most pregnancy tests are positive at this time.

Fourth Week

By the end of the fourth week after fertilization, or 6 weeks gestational age, the embryo is 3/16 inch long. The nervous system and brain are beginning to grow, and the face is forming, with a mouth, a lower jaw, and dark circles where the eyes will be. The heart is beating and is pumping blood around the developing blood vessels. Little buds that will become the arms and legs have appeared. (See Figure 2.3.)

Fifth Week

By the end of the fifth week after fertilization, or 7 weeks gestational age, the embryo is 1/2 inch long. The brain, spinal cord, and nervous system are more developed. The head has increased in size, and the nostrils, lips, and tongue are visible. The limb buds have grown into arms and legs. (See Figure 2.4.)

Sixth Week

By the end of the sixth week after fertilization, or 8 weeks gestational age, the embryo is 7/8 inch long. The head is quite large in comparison to the trunk. External ears form elevations on either side of the head. A skeleton made of cartilage, not real bone, has appeared; and a tail is apparent at the end of the spinal cord. Fingers and toes have formed. (See Figure 2.5.)

Seventh Week

The embryo is almost an inch in length by the end of the seventh week after fertilization, or 9 weeks gestational age. The brain can be seen through the fine skin on the top of the head. The eyes are visible through the closed lids. The body may begin to move as small muscle fibers grow. Bone has begun to replace the cartilage, and the tail has almost disappeared. The embryo is now uniquely human, with most of the internal organs present.

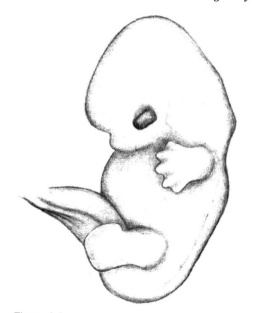

Figure 2.5.
The embryo at 6 weeks after fertilization. Its actual size is 7/8 inch.

Eighth Week

From the eighth week after fertilization, or 10 weeks gestational age, until birth, the developing baby is called a fetus. By the end of the eighth week, the fetus is approximately 1 1/2 inches long and weighs about 2 grams (1/15 ounce). The jaws and other facial features are more clearly developed, and teeth are forming. The arms begin to bend at the elbow and are long enough for the baby to touch his face. If the baby is a boy, his penis is apparent. If the baby is a girl, her clitoris has developed.

Ninth Week

By the end of the ninth week after fertilization, or 11 weeks gestational age, the fetus looks more human. It measures almost 2 inches in length and weighs 4 grams (1/6 ounce). Most of the major structures have formed. Development now consists of the growth and maturing of present structures. The scrotum has appeared, as have fingernails, toenails, and hair follicles. (See Figure 2.6.)

Third Lunar Month

By the end of the third lunar month, or 12 weeks gestational age, the fetus is over 2 1/2 inches in length and weighs 7 grams (1/3 ounce). The face is well developed, with the eyelids present, though fused. The baby can move the muscles of his face to squint, purse his lips, and open his mouth. The arms, hands, fingers, legs, feet, and toes are fully developed. The external

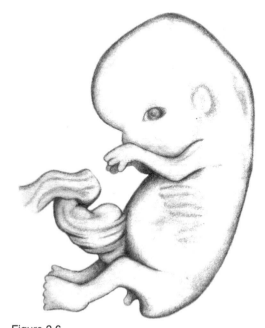

Figure 2.6.
The fetus at 9 weeks after fertilization. Its actual size is almost 2 inches.

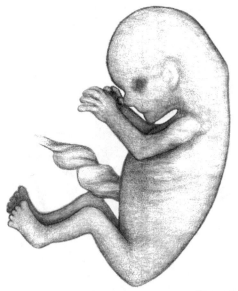

Figure 2.7.
The fetus at 3 lunar months.
Its actual size is over 2 1/2 inches.

genitalia show definite signs of male or female sex. The baby can make a fist and kick with his feet, although the woman cannot feel it yet. The uterus can be felt just above the woman's pubic bone. The fetal heartbeat can be heard with a doptone, the device used by caregivers to listen to babies. (See Figure 2.7.)

Fourth Lunar Month

By the end of the fourth lunar month, or 16 weeks gestational age, the fetus is almost 5 inches long and weighs 100 grams (3 ounces). The essential body systems are now present; most of the remaining changes will be in size. To facilitate this growth, the placenta is also growing rapidly. The baby's skin is getting thicker and less transparent, and is forming several layers. Eyebrows and eyelashes are evident. The baby may suck his thumb, and he may swallow amniotic fluid and then pass it out as urine. Meconium, the baby's first bowel movement, is beginning to collect in his intestinal tract. Some women feel the first faint fluttering movements between their pubic bone and navel. These movements are often initially confused with gas, but the feeling is "quickening," the earliest felt movements of a fetus. Usually, quickening is first perceived between the sixteenth and eighteenth weeks. (See Figure 2.8.)

Fifth Lunar Month

By the end of the fifth lunar month, or 20 weeks gestational age, the fetus is about 8 inches long and weighs 240 grams (1/2 pound). Some fat has been deposited under his skin, but he is still quite thin. His skin is less transparent. Hair has appeared on his head, and downy hair called lanugo is covering his body. This is the midpoint of pregnancy.

Sixth Lunar Month

By the end of the sixth lunar month, or 24 weeks gestational age, the fetus is almost 11 inches long and weighs 500 grams (1 pound 2 ounces). Vernix caseosa, a cheeselike coating that protects the baby's skin from its watery environment, has developed. The eyes are open, and the fetus can hear. Fingerprints and footprints have formed. Between 40 and 60 percent of the babies born at this time survive.

Seventh Lunar Month

By the end of the seventh lunar month, or 28 weeks gestational age, the baby is close to 13 inches long and weighs about 900 grams (2 pounds). The eyes can perceive light, and the baby can hear, smell, taste, and respond to touch. The baby has definite awake and sleep periods. If the baby is a boy, his testicles have descended into his scrotum. Over 90 percent of the babies born at this point survive.

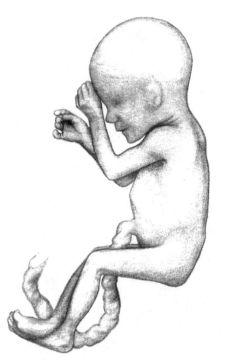

Figure 2.8.
The fetus at 4 lunar months.
Its actual size is almost 5 inches.

Eighth Lunar Month

By the end of the eighth lunar month, or 32 weeks gestational age, the average baby is 15 inches long and weighs 1,500 grams (3 pounds 5 ounces) or more. The skin is still red but is less wrinkled, and the fingernails are long. If born now, the baby's chance of survival is better than 95 percent.

Ninth Lunar Month

By the end of the ninth lunar month, or 36 weeks gestational age, the baby is almost 17 inches long and weighs between 2,160 grams (4 pounds 12 ounces) and 2,500 grams (5 pounds 9 ounces). During the last 2 months of gestation, the baby gains about an ounce of weight a day. This weight gain is important because it provides the baby with a layer of fat under his skin that will help keep his body temperature constant outside the uterus. The skin has become smoother, and the redness has faded to pink. Most of the lanugo has dropped off, remaining only on the arms and shoulders. The lungs are maturing and are producing lecithin, which is necessary for respiration.

Tenth Lunar Month

By the end of the tenth lunar month, or 40 weeks gestational age, the baby's brain has greatly increased in number of cells. This growth will continue for the first 5 to 6 months after birth. By now, 96 percent of all babies are positioned head down. During the final 2 to 4 weeks of gestation, the head or other presenting part settles down into the top of the woman's pelvis. During this last lunar month, the baby gains about 1/2 pound per week and, by the fortieth week, is an average of 20 inches in length and 7 to 7 1/2 pounds in weight. The baby is ready to be born! (See Figure 2.9.)

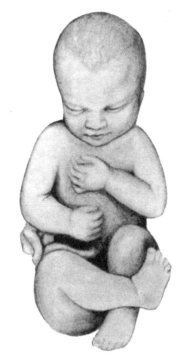

Figure 2.9.
The fetus at 10 lunar months

FETAL EMOTIONS

We now know that even while all of this physical development is taking place, the unborn child is becoming an aware, reacting human being. At as early as 8 weeks, he can express his likes and dislikes with well-placed kicks and jerks. At 28 to 32 weeks, his emerging sense of awareness transforms his physical responses into feelings. The woman's emotional state can and does have an effect on the way he perceives his world—as warm and friendly, or cold and hostile. This is not to say that fleeting anxiety or doubt about your health will negatively affect your unborn child. However, it does mean that chronic anxiety or stress, especially of a personal nature, or deep ambivalence about motherhood may affect your baby's personality.

Studies have shown that the unborn child hears well from the twenty-fourth week on. A recent discovery is that the noise

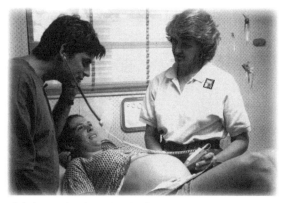

A father-to-be listens to the fetal heartbeat with the help of a certified nurse-midwife and a doptone.

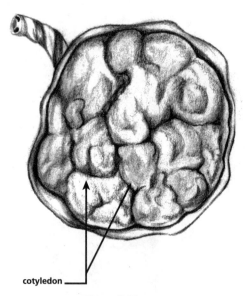

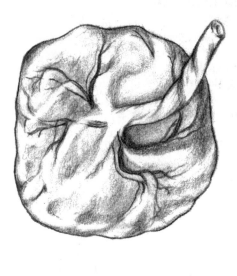

cotyledon

Figure 2.10.
The maternal side of the placenta.
This is the side that is attached to the wall of the uterus.

Figure 2.11.
The fetal side of the placenta.
The amniotic sac originates on this side.

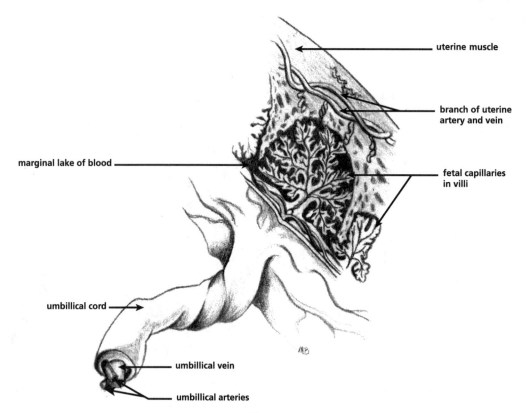

uterine muscle

branch of uterine
artery and vein

marginal lake of blood

fetal capillaries
in villi

umbillical cord

umbillical vein

umbillical arteries

Figure 2.12.
A cross section of a placenta, showing the blood supply and circulation.

level inside the uterus is much higher than was previously thought. The woman's constant heartbeat and intestinal rumblings are magnified by the amniotic fluid, providing a continuous, loud, and rhythmical background for the baby. The kinds of sounds a baby hears definitely affect him emotionally. Soft, soothing sounds and music calm him; loud sounds and music such as hard rock can make him kick violently. Some women have found that if they play soft music when resting during the last months of pregnancy, the baby, after he is born, associates this music with rest time. For a further discussion of fetal emotions, see *The Secret Life of the Unborn Child* by Thomas Verny with John Kelly.

The exciting aspect of this knowledge about fetal emotions is that you can begin shaping a positive relationship with your child before he is born. Talk soothingly to your baby and send him loving thoughts. This is also a good way to get your partner involved in the pregnancy. Encourage your partner to gently massage your abdomen and to talk to his baby as well. Try to spend a portion of each day in a relaxed, anxiety-free state of mind. Both you and your unborn child will benefit.

THE PLACENTA

By the time the developing being is 2 weeks old, the placenta, or afterbirth, has begun to develop. The villi, embedded in the lining of the uterus, are forming primitive blood vessels, which tap into the woman's blood supply. The function of the placenta is to supply the growing being with the oxygen and nutrients it needs from the woman's blood system and to pass to the woman the waste products it does not need.

The fetal blood is always separate from the maternal blood. Substances are passed back and forth through a semipermeable membrane. At one time, the placenta was thought to act as a barrier to materials that might hurt the fetus. However, it is now known that almost everything that enters the woman's body—including viruses, drugs, nicotine, and alcohol—is passed to the fetus.

The placenta continues to grow until about 2 months before delivery, when it reaches its maximum size. At that time, it is about the size and shape of a dinner plate, approximately 8 to 9 inches in diameter, but thicker and heavier, weighing 1 to 2 pounds at birth. The side that is attached to the uterine wall is dark red and has sections like circular puzzle pieces in it. (See Figure 2.10.) Scarlike areas of tissue may be apparent. These are areas of calcification, and they denote places that have degenerated. Women who smoke during pregnancy have more of these than do women who do not smoke. The side of the placenta that is next to the fetus is white and smooth, being covered by a membrane, the amniotic sac. (See Figure 2.11.)

Nutrients coming from the woman pass to the blood vessels in the placenta. From the placenta, they move through the umbilical cord into the blood circulating within the fetus.

Inside the umbilical cord are three blood vessels—one large vein and two smaller arteries. (See Figure 2.12.) Nutrients travel from the placenta to the fetus through the vein. Waste products return to the placenta through the arteries to be passed into the woman's system. A jellylike substance called Wharton's jelly surrounds the blood vessels and helps to protect them.

The umbilical cord begins to develop during the second week after conception and usually grows to about 18 inches in length, although it is possible

A Myth Disproved

At one time, the placenta was considered to be a "barrier," blocking harmful substances from reaching the fetus. It is now known, however, that almost everything that enters the woman's body passes to the fetus.

*Hints for
the Father-to-Be*

❏ Bring your mate a snack
before she gets out of
bed if she is bothered with
morning sickness.

❏ It is normal to feel uncertain
or ambivalent about the
pregnancy at first. Give
yourself time to adjust.

❏ Accompany your mate
on her prenatal visits.

❏ Take photos each month to
make a pregnancy scrapbook.
Record important national
events or pregnancy-
related items.

❏ Remind your mate how
beautiful her changing body
has become.

for it to grow to anywhere from 12 inches to 40 inches. After the birth of the baby, the cord is clamped and cut. A stump remains, but dries up and falls off in 7 to 10 days.

LENGTH OF PREGNANCY

The average length of pregnancy is 280 days. This is about 9 calendar months or 10 lunar months. A lunar month is the time it takes to go from full moon to full moon—28 days.

Your doctor calculated your estimated due date by adding 7 days to the first day of your last normal menstrual period and then counting back 3 months. For example, if the first day of your last menstrual period was February 15, he added 7 days, which brought the date to February 22, then subtracted 3 months, for an expected due date of November 22. This is about 280 days after February 15. The baby would be only about 266 days old on November 22, but the date of the last menstrual period is used because the actual date of conception is usually unknown and could be as early as day 5 or 6 of the menstrual cycle. Only about 4 percent of women carry their babies for exactly 280 days, but 66 percent deliver within 10 days before or after their due dates. The due date is only an estimate, based on an average of all pregnancies. Your baby may take more or less time to develop, the same way that some babies take more or less time to get their first tooth.

PHYSICAL AND EMOTIONAL CHANGES IN THE WOMAN

Pregnancy is generally divided into three trimesters, or three periods of 3 months each, for purposes of discussion. This is done because most women experience the same general changes during each trimester.

During pregnancy, two kinds of development go on at once—the physical changes in the mother-to-be and the physical changes in the fetus. Along with the physical changes the woman experiences, some emotional changes take place. You and your partner can use these changes as opportunities to grow, to expand your awareness of yourselves and of each other, to deepen your sense of responsibility, and to become aware of what millions of other parents-to-be have experienced.

First Trimester

The first trimester of pregnancy is the first 3 calendar months, or through the fourteenth week of gestation. You will experience many physical and emotional changes during this time, although most of the physical changes will be more noticeable to you than to anyone else.

Physical Changes

The major physical changes that women experience during the first trimester include the following:

❏ *Uterus.* For many women, a missed menstrual period is the first sign of pregnancy. Other women continue to have very light periods for the first 2 to 3 months. This lack of a regular period is due to the high levels of estrogen and progesterone that the body produces to maintain the uterine lining that nourishes the developing embryo. Many women spot slightly on the day the ovum attaches itself to the uterine wall. This is not menstrual bleeding; rather, it is called implantation bleeding.

By the time the fetus is 12 weeks old, the placenta, or afterbirth, has formed. The uterus has grown to the size of a grapefruit, with its top reaching to just above the pubic bone. The cervix has already begun softening.

❑ *Vagina.* The vagina has begun thickening and softening because of the increase in maternal hormones. It has also turned blue to violet in color as a result of the increased blood supply to the area. Vaginal secretions have become more noticeable and will increase in amount as the pregnancy progresses.

❑ *Breasts.* A tingling or prickling sensation is often felt in the breasts during the early weeks of pregnancy. This is because the blood supply is increasing and the milk-secreting glands are growing. After a few weeks or months, the tingling or prickling will disappear, but the breasts will usually continue to enlarge until the third trimester.

Around the eighth week, veins may become visible under the skin, and small round elevated areas appear on the areola, the dark area surrounding the nipple. These elevated areas are the Montgomery glands, which secrete oil to help keep the nipples soft and pliable in preparation for breastfeeding.

❑ *Urination.* Many women experience an increased need to urinate during the first trimester because the enlarging uterus is pressing on the bladder. This need usually eases during the second trimester, as the uterus rises out of the pelvis. Even though it means more trips to the bathroom, you should drink plenty of fluids to maintain good kidney function and to provide the water necessary to metabolize the protein you eat.

❑ *Digestion.* About half of all pregnant women feel nauseated and may vomit during early pregnancy, and sometimes also in later pregnancy. This condition is called morning sickness, although it can occur at any time during the day. Morning sickness is attributed to an increase in hormone levels, a lack of vitamin B_6, and/or low blood sugar. Eating foods high in the B vitamins and consuming small high-protein meals throughout the day usually help this condition. (For a further discussion of morning sickness, see "First Trimester" on page 51.)

In addition to nausea, some women also have trouble with indigestion and heartburn. The hormones relaxin and progesterone relax the smooth muscles in the body, including the sphincter at the top of the stomach, which keeps food in the stomach. Progesterone is also responsible for relaxing the intestines somewhat, thereby slowing digestion and making constipation more likely. Eating a diet high in fiber (fresh fruits and vegetables, and whole grains), drinking plenty of fluids, and exercising regularly help to minimize constipation. For some additional heartburn preventatives and remedies to try, see "Heartburn Fighters" on page 27.

❑ *Skin.* The hormones of pregnancy can affect your skin either positively or negatively. Many women experience the glow of pregnancy, and their skin radiates. Others are not so fortunate and develop acne. Continue to eat a good diet and drink plenty of water. Wash your face two or three times a day with a gentle cleanser and apply moisturizer to dry areas. Avoid the temptation to pick at or squeeze the blemishes. This will only increase the likelihood of infection and scarring. Choose makeup that does not clog the pores or try to limit the time you wear it. Wash the applicators or purchase new blush brushes or powder "puffs." If the acne is severe, you may need to see a dermatologist. Make sure that he knows you are pregnant. Two common medications used for acne, Accutane and Retin A, should not be used during pregnancy.

❏ *Fatigue.* Pregnancy brings changes to every system in the body, and these changes require a great deal of physical and emotional energy. Proper rest is extremely important for an expectant mother. You should not feel guilty about resting during the day or about going to bed early. You need rest for your body to adjust to pregnancy.

See Figure 2.13 for an illustration of the woman's body at the end of the first trimester.

Emotional Changes

Many expectant mothers spend the first trimester accepting the fact that they are pregnant and coming to terms with the implications. This is true for other family members as well. You may find yourself drawing inward and focusing on the changes in your body and on your fears and dreams. You may feel increasingly vulnerable to danger and may also fear miscarriage.

Even when the pregnancy is wanted, expectant parents usually have many questions: Can we afford a child? How will our lifestyle change? Will we have jealousy problems with our other children? The woman may wonder: Will I quit work? Both parents-to-be may feel a sense of panic at the additional responsibilities. Ambivalent feelings toward the pregnancy are very common in the early months. These feelings are not bad or wrong. By acknowledging and talking about them, you and your partner may find yourselves better able to cope with them and to accept the pregnancy. Facing your doubts and fears about pregnancy aids in emotional growth.

Many couples enjoy more sexual activity during this time of adjustment, while other couples may desire less sex. (For a discussion of sexual intimacy during the first trimester, see "Sexual Relations During Pregnancy" on page 28.) You and your partner should talk to each other openly about your feelings to prevent pent-up fears from damaging your relationship.

By the end of this first trimester, you may find that you have begun to sort out and examine your feelings toward your own parents. Think about how you will be different from or similar to them. Among the other feelings you may experience during the first trimester are excitement, increased creativity, and increased sensuality. You may feel "special" during this time.

Mood swings sometimes become more extreme during pregnancy. You may find yourself laughing or crying over insignificant things. This problem is related to the increasing levels of hormones. Researchers believe that these hormones do not cause the moods, but probably increase the intensity of the feelings.[1] Some evidence has shown that expectant mothers feel more anxiety if the baby is a boy, but the reason for this is unknown.

Women experiencing a second or later pregnancy often find that they are less preoccupied with the pregnancy than they were with their first. The major adjustment to parenthood seems to come with a first pregnancy. With later pregnancies, women have less time available and feel less of a need to ponder the meaning of each physical change.

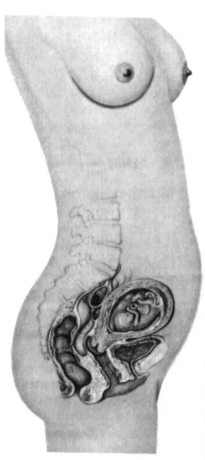

Figure 2.13.
The woman's body
at the end of the first trimester.

Second Trimester

The second trimester of pregnancy is the middle 3 months, or from the fifteenth through the twenty-eighth week of gestation. This trimester is often the most enjoyable of the three. Your initial period of adjustment has passed, and fatigue and nausea are usually less of a problem. It is during this time that your pregnancy becomes obvious to other people, and you may frequently be the center of attention. Your body, though larger, is not cumbersome, and you should find it fairly easy to move around.

Physical Changes

The major physical changes that women experience during the second trimester include the following:

❏ *Uterus.* The uterus begins to expand out of the pelvis and into the abdominal cavity by the fourteenth week. By the twentieth week, which is midway through the second trimester, the uterus is usually at the level of the navel.

A woman pregnant for the first time usually begins to feel the movements of the fetus at about 16 to 18 weeks. Women who have already borne at least one child often feel these movements earlier. When the movements are first perceived, the fetus is about 7 inches long and weighs less than 1 pound. The woman may also feel mild uterine contractions, called Braxton-Hicks contractions.

❏ *Vagina.* The tissues of the vagina continue to soften and become more elastic, preparing for the baby's passage at birth.

❏ *Pelvis.* Hormones cause the cartilage to soften and widen to provide additional mobility and relaxation in the pelvic joints. This allows a large baby to pass through more easily.

❏ *Breasts.* Colostrum, a clear yellow fluid that precedes mature breast-milk, is often present by 16 weeks.

❏ *Circulation.* By the end of the second trimester, the blood volume has increased by 40 to 60 percent and the heart has begun pumping more blood per beat. Edema (swelling) is common because of the increased blood volume, the pressure from the enlarging uterus, and the increase in estrogen. The fluid will tend to pool in your feet and hands when you stand for long periods. Resting on your side will improve your circulation and will help to relieve the edema. Increasing your protein intake will also help to decrease the swelling. If the swelling is sudden and involves the face, you should notify your doctor, since this may be a sign of pregnancy-induced hypertension. (For a discussion of this condition, see "Pregnancy-Induced Hypertension" on page 35.)

❏ *Linea nigra.* The linea nigra is a dark line that extends from the navel to the pubic hairline. It is common and is attributed to the hormonal activity of pregnancy. It fades after delivery, although it may continue to be visible.

❏ *Stretch marks.* Many women develop at least some stretch marks, or striae gravidarum, during pregnancy. Stretch marks appear when the connective tissue of the skin is stretched to the point of rupture. They are red or pink lines and may appear on the abdomen, thighs, or breasts. After delivery, they fade to white. Many women find that massaging oil or lotion into the vulnerable areas prevents stretch marks, although heredity seems to be a more important factor.

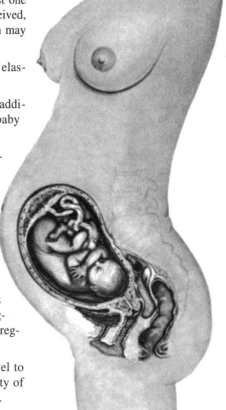

Figure 2.14.
The woman's body
at the end of the second trimester.

❑ *Mask of pregnancy.* Some women develop the mask of pregnancy, which consists of dark blotches on the face. This pigmentation is believed to result from increased levels of melanocyte stimulating hormone (MSH). Production of MSH drops after pregnancy, with the mask of pregnancy usually disappearing. Deficiency of folic acid, a B vitamin, may also be a cause. Your prenatal vitamins should include folic acid to meet your increased requirement.

See Figure 2.14 on page 25 for an illustration of the woman's body at the end of the second trimester.

Emotional Changes

Most women find the second trimester to be a more positive experience than the first, as they are now beginning to feel the movements of the life within them. Most husbands by now have accepted the existence of the pregnancy and are as excited as the woman about the movements of the baby. During this trimester, men frequently also become more aware of their wife's growing dependence on them. As the pregnancy progresses, the woman may feel more vulnerable and may need her mate's attention more. She may want him to become more involved with the pregnancy and the baby. In addition, she may become overly concerned for her husband's safety. Meanwhile, the husband may share the woman's interest in the pregnancy, or he may feel an increased creative interest in his work or hobby. He may gain weight or show other symptoms of pregnancy. These are all ways in which expectant mothers and fathers deal with the stresses and changes that are occurring. It is important for both partners to be aware of and to talk about their feelings, especially when friction arises between them.

A woman's dreams may become very real during this trimester and are sometimes disturbing. Dreams are a way of bringing fears to consciousness, where they can be dealt with more easily. Dreaming about misfortune to the baby or to herself, or about giving birth to animals is common. If a woman refuses to acknowledge her fears, she may suffer increasing anxiety.

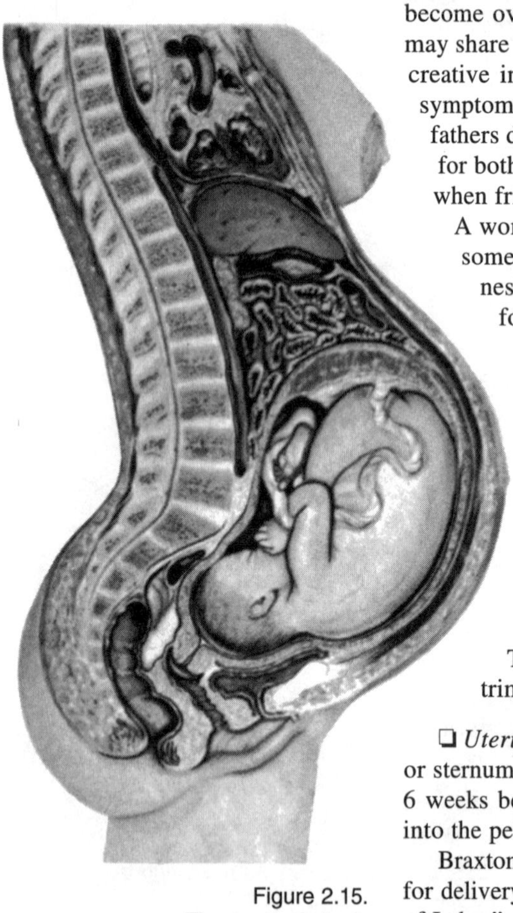

Third Trimester

The third trimester of pregnancy is the last 3 months, or from the twenty-ninth through the fortieth week of gestation. It is a time of preparing for the birth, physically, mentally, and emotionally.

Physical Changes

The major physical changes that women experience during the third trimester include the following:

❑ *Uterus.* Toward the end of pregnancy, the uterus reaches the breastbone, or sternum, and measures about 11 by 14 inches. Lightening occurs from 1 to 6 weeks before delivery. This means that the baby's head settles downward into the pelvis and may engage in the pelvic inlet.

Braxton-Hicks contractions become stronger and more apparent as the time for delivery approaches. (For a discussion of false labor, see "Warm-Up Signs of Labor" on page 120.) The cervix becomes softer during the last few weeks and may begin to thin out and open up a little in preparation for labor. The

Figure 2.15.
The woman's body
at the end of the third trimester.

woman may feel a sharp pain in the groin if she moves suddenly. This pain is caused by a spasm in or stretching of the round ligaments. These ligaments are a main support of the uterus and extend into the groin area on both sides.

❏ *Vagina.* As the pregnancy nears its end, more mucus is passed vaginally in preparation for the baby's passage. The vaginal swelling also increases at this time and may result in discomfort during sexual intercourse. (For a discussion of sexual intimacy during the third trimester, see "Sexual Relations During Pregnancy" on page 28.)

❏ *Digestion.* The growing uterus puts pressure on the stomach and intestines, pushing them up and back. Heartburn, a burning sensation felt in the chest, may occur. This is caused by the escape of gastric contents into the esophagus as a result of the relaxation of the sphincter at the top of the stomach. Problems with constipation may continue.

❏ *Breathing.* Shortness of breath is common because the uterus is pushing up on the diaphragm. This improves after lightening. Many women also experience nasal congestion and may even have nosebleeds.

❏ *Vision.* Some women experience a change in vision, possibly requiring new glasses or preventing them from wearing their contacts. Report any change in vision to your caregiver, since it may be the result of gestational diabetes, pregnancy-induced hypertension, or another serious problem.

❏ *Circulation.* Varicose veins may develop in the legs, vulva, or rectum (hemorrhoids). Varicose veins are caused by the increased pelvic pressure exerted by the uterus and growing fetus, as well as by the decrease in blood returned from the lower body and limbs. They usually diminish after delivery.

❏ *Urination.* The need to urinate usually increases, especially after lightening occurs. This is caused by the pressure of the baby on the bladder.

❏ *Fatigue.* Carrying around the extra weight causes fatigue to return during the last trimester.

See Figure 2.15 for an illustration of the woman's body at the end of the third trimester.

Emotional Changes

During the third trimester, most women focus more and more on the baby, and on labor and delivery. Both parents-to-be find that the search for the perfect name has become an important pastime. They also spend time preparing an area in the house for the baby. Almost all women by now have accepted that they are pregnant and are able to differentiate their babies as real people, separate from themselves.

Time during the third trimester seems endless. Many women count on their due date to bring the end of their discomfort and may be very discouraged if they go a week or more beyond.

Because of their large size, some women experience a drop in self-esteem during this trimester. They need the people around them, especially their husbands, to reassure them that they are still attractive.

You can use your preoccupation with labor and delivery to your advantage at this time. Gather as much information about the birth experience as possible. Read books, take classes, and talk to new mothers. However, avoid peo-

Heartburn Fighters

Many women have found the following to be helpful against heartburn:

❏ Eat frequent small meals.

❏ Avoid spicy or fried foods.

❏ Eat a small amount of yogurt before meals.

❏ Drink milk or eat ice cream.

❏ Chew gum.

❏ Never overfill your stomach with foods or liquids.

❏ Take an antacid as recommended by your caregiver.

❏ Try papaya enzyme with meals.

❏ Do not lie down after eating.

❏ Sleep with your head elevated.

❏ Avoid bending at the waist.

Your caregiver may have other heartburn fighters to add to this list.

Hints for the Father-to-Be

❏ Place your head close to your mate's abdomen and talk or sing to your baby.

❏ Continue the romance.

❏ Your desire for sexual relations with your mate may increase or decrease after you learn of the pregnancy. This is normal.

❏ Sexual relations will not harm the fetus in a normal pregnancy.

❏ Try alternate positions for lovemaking if your mate has trouble with your regular positions.

ple who repeatedly attempt to discourage you from taking prepared childbirth classes or who dwell on negative birth experiences. You need to keep a confident, relaxed attitude toward the upcoming event. Do not avoid your fears, but at the same time, do not allow negative thinking to dominate you. Your chances for a positive birth experience are to a great extent determined by your attitude. Fear and anxiety create negative experiences.

SEXUAL RELATIONS DURING PREGNANCY

During pregnancy, you undergo many changes, both physical and emotional. How you react to these changes, how openly you can talk with your partner, and whether your caregiver makes you feel comfortable discussing lovemaking all play a role in your attitude as a couple toward sex during pregnancy.

Your husband may find you more desirable now because your body is carrying his child. Or, he may worry about the effects sexual intercourse might have on the growing baby in terms of miscarriage or harm. Unless you have a history of miscarriage or other problems, this concern is unnecessary. Check with your caregiver to be reassured about a healthy pregnancy.

At the beginning of your pregnancy, you and your husband should decide together to remain physically close, even if you go through times of lessened sexual activity. Touching, snuggling, caressing, or massaging, not necessarily leading to sex, can keep both of you feeling open, warm, and loving toward one another. Accepting both positive and negative feelings is a necessary part of dealing with and coming to terms with the pregnancy. Open communication with one another and, of course, with your caregiver will help ensure that your pregnancy gets off to a good start.

Early pregnancy classes are a good place to talk about sexuality and your changing body in relation to lovemaking. Prepared childbirth classes offer another good opportunity, although much of your pregnancy will be behind you by the time you take them. An informative book on the subject is *Making Love During Pregnancy* by Elisabeth Bing and Libby Colman.

The *first trimester* of pregnancy can be an exciting time, with both you and your partner feeling very good about yourselves and your pregnant body. You may feel beautiful, exhilarated at the thought of a new life growing within you, and very close to your mate. You might also find yourself easily fatigued, nauseated, anxious, and very emotional. Your husband may be proud and excited about the new life he has helped to create. At the same time, he may feel anxious or rejected because you are now concentrating your love and attention on your developing child.

The first 3 months are certainly a time of adjustment for both you and your husband. Wide mood swings are normal for both of you. You will also experience changes in your body and in your relationship. While you continue to love each other as much as or even more than before the pregnancy, your physical expression of that love is often altered—sometimes to a surprising degree! Please be assured that this is not unique to you. Whatever your feelings, desires, needs, or concerns, they have been experienced by countless other couples. Be aware that there is a wide range of emotions, needs, and concerns. Some women experience increased sexual desires during the first trimester; others, especially if feeling nauseated or fatigued, have a decreased desire. Even if you are nauseated, you will appreciate the touching and caressing from a good back rub by your husband. Both of you will enjoy a warm hug and kiss.

During the *second trimester,* your growing uterus is beginning to bulge your abdomen, though usually not to the extent that it is in the way or makes sex uncomfortable. Some women experience a decline in sexual enjoyment as the pregnancy advances, while others feel increased pleasure. Again, if you are open with each other and responsive to each others' sexual needs, you can eliminate many of the problems.

Some of your initial physical complaints of pregnancy have probably disappeared by the third or fourth month. Usually, the nausea and fatigue have passed, and you feel more relaxed now that the chance of miscarriage has diminished.

As you move into the *third trimester,* however, you may find even simple movements—such as getting in and out of bed, bending forward, and even standing, walking, or sitting—to be very awkward and difficult. This physical clumsiness may keep you from enjoying sexual intercourse. On the other hand, increased pelvic congestion may arouse sexual desires, which are relieved by orgasm. Your partner may also feel some restraints in enjoyment. He may be uncomfortable feeling the baby moving while he is making love to you. He may also initiate sex less frequently as he assumes a more protective role. Do not misinterpret this as rejection.

As your waistline expands and your body enlarges, you may start to view yourself differently and may find it difficult to feel sexy. This feeling may be reinforced by other people's attempts at humor when they comment on your changing shape. Just remember, you are pregnant, not fat, and this growth is essential for a healthy baby. You can be assured that your former figure will return after the birth.

You may have already tried a variety of positions to increase your comfort during intercourse. If your pregnancy has advanced to the point where it is almost "in the way," you may find that having your partner on top but slightly to the side avoids the discomfort caused by his weight pressing on your abdomen. This position also gives you more mobility and lessens penetration of the penis. You might find that your being on top is more comfortable, as you can better control the degree of penetration. Some couples, however, find that this position results in deeper penetration and causes more discomfort.

You might be comfortable and satisfied with side-lying positions. Or, your mate can enter from behind, with you either kneeling or standing, using the bed for support, or lying on your side. In these positions, you can control the degree of penetration and can relieve the abdominal pressure. You can also lie close to the edge of the bed and have your partner support your legs with his arms or shoulders. Needless to say, experimenting to find the position that affords the most comfort and satisfaction is important, as is a sense of humor!

Many couples find alternatives to sexual intercourse at this point in the pregnancy. Remember that massaging, touching, and caressing provide close physical contact, which is just as important as intercourse for both of you. Some couples find that genital manipulation and mutual masturbation provide good sexual gratification. Even self-masturbation can be relieving. Some couples enjoy oral sex. However, a word of caution is necessary concerning cunnilingus (oral stimulation of the female genitals). Air should *not* be forced into the vagina at any time during pregnancy, as a rare phenomenon called air embolism can result. Because of the increased vascularity during pregnancy, air that passes into the uterus can enter the woman's bloodstream and cause serious problems and even death. If you enjoy oral sex, it is fine to continue the practice as long as you are aware of this one restriction.

When to Avoid Sex During Pregnancy

You should avoid sex during pregnancy:

❏ If you are at risk for preterm labor.

❏ If you have a placenta previa (low-lying placenta).

❏ If you have an incompetent cervix.

❏ If you experience vaginal bleeding.

❏ If your membranes have ruptured or you are leaking fluid.

❏ If you have an active herpes lesion.

❏ If you experience pain with intercourse.

❏ If you have a vaginal infection or an undiagnosed vaginal discharge.

Your caregiver will advise you in this area.

Unless you are spotting or have a history of miscarriages, you should consider pregnancy to be a sign of physical health. You should continue your life as normally as possible, keeping in mind that intercourse will not harm your baby and can be continued throughout pregnancy. If you leak fluid from your vagina, experience pain in your pelvic region, or bleed vaginally, contact your caregiver immediately. Orgasms do cause the uterus to contract. However, the uterus contracts the same way with Braxton-Hicks contractions, which are perfectly natural during pregnancy. But, if your caregiver advises against orgasm, you need to realize that this means orgasm via masturbation as well. You may also need to adjust two other practices if you are at risk for preterm labor. First, avoid touching your nipples, as this releases oxytocin, a hormone that causes uterine contractions. Second, since semen contains prostaglandins, which can also stimulate contractions, your partner may need to wear a condom, if you are permitted to continue lovemaking. In addition, your caregiver should let you know if you have a medical problem that requires you to alter your position or frequency of intercourse or to stop it altogether. Otherwise, most professionals believe that couples can continue to enjoy intercourse until labor begins or the water breaks. Therefore, experiment and enjoy!

PRENATAL CARE

You should begin receiving prenatal care the moment you suspect you are pregnant. All of your baby's vital organs will have already begun forming by this time. The person you choose as your caregiver will be the one providing your prenatal care. (For a discussion of selecting a doctor or midwife, see "Choosing Your Caregiver" on page 1.) He or she will chart your progress during your pregnancy and will watch for any signs that indicate a potential problem.

When you visit your caregiver's office for your first prenatal examination, you will have a complete medical history taken and a physical examination done. If applicable, you will be told to stop smoking, to stop the use of alcohol and drugs, and to improve your nutritional habits. You may be advised on the benefits of exercise and counseled about sex, hygiene, and any other relevant topics. Expect this first exam to take about an hour, and feel free to bring up any areas of concern that do not come up in the normal course of the exam.

The physical examination you receive will include:

❏ A breast examination.

❏ A pelvic, or vaginal, examination to:
  • confirm the pregnancy.
  • take a pap smear.
  • take a smear for gonorrhea and chlamydia.
  • take a vaginal culture.
  • estimate the size and shape of your pelvis.

A pelvic exam usually will not be done again until the last month of pregnancy.

❏ Blood tests for:
  • blood type and Rh factor.
  • complete blood count.
  • rubella titer to determine if you are immune to German measles.
  • syphilis and hepatitis B.

Some clinics and offices also provide other blood chemistry checks for a more complete analysis of the woman's health. Additional blood tests that may be offered after counseling include those for human immunodeficiency virus (HIV), toxoplasmosis, and alpha-fetoprotein. (For a discussion of alpha-feto-protein, see "Alpha-Fetoprotein Screening" on page 38.) If your racial or genetic background dictates, you may be tested for sickle cell anemia, Tay-Sachs disease, or thalassemia.

❏ Urine tests for:
   • a complete urinalysis.
   • a culture to check for infection, if indicated.

After the first examination, you will probably be given checkups on a monthly basis. Starting in the seventh calendar month, the checkups will become biweekly. In the ninth calendar month, they will become weekly. All these checkups will probably include:

❏ Checking your weight.

❏ Checking your blood pressure.

❏ Checking your urine for:
   • protein, high levels of which may indicate pregnancy-induced hypertension. (For a discussion of this condition, see "Pregnancy-Induced Hypertension" on page 35.)
   • sugar, high levels of which may indicate diabetes. (For a discussion of this condition, see "Gestational Diabetes" on page 34.)
   • infection.

❏ Checking your abdomen for:
   • growth of the uterus to estimate the progress of the pregnancy.
   • size and position of the fetus.

A mother-to-be takes an active part in her prenatal care by checking her own weight during her regular monthly office visit.

Some caregivers encourage women to participate in their prenatal care by checking their own weight and urine during their office visits.

Other screening tests that may be performed, beginning at 28 weeks, are:

❏ Blood tests, including:
   • 1-hour glucose tolerance test (GTT). About 1 hour after drinking a liquid high in sugar, blood is drawn for a glucose level to check for development of gestational diabetes. This test may be performed earlier, at around 16 weeks, if there is a family history of diabetes, previous large babies, or a history of gestational diabetes. If the test result is high, a 3-hour glucose tolerance test is given to confirm the diagnosis.
   • antibody screening. In Rh-negative women, blood is drawn to check for antibodies, and within the next week, a shot of RhoGAM, an Rh-immune globulin, is given intramuscularly. (For a complete discussion of this, see "Rh Incompatability" on page 32.)

❏ Culture of the vaginal and rectal area to check for the presence of group B streptococcal infection. In some practices, this test is not done until 36 weeks and may also be done when the woman is admitted in labor. (For a discussion of this condition, see "Group B Strep" on page 33.)

❏ Vaginal exam to check the status of the cervix and the position of the baby. This may be done weekly, starting at 36 weeks.

Your caregiver will probably discuss with you the symptoms he will want

Rh Incompatability

Blood type is identified by two major components—a letter (A, B, AB, or O) and the Rh factor. If your blood contains the Rh factor, you are Rh positive; if it lacks this factor, you are Rh negative. Therefore, if your blood type is AB and you are Rh-negative, you are said to have AB-negative blood.

If an Rh-negative person receives Rh-positive blood, she will become sensitized and her body will produce antibodies to attack the foreign red blood cells. This is significant in pregnancy for an Rh-negative woman because if her mate is Rh positive, the child can be Rh positive. During amniocentesis or the delivery of the placenta, it is possible for the baby's blood to come in contact with the mother's blood. If this happens, the mother's body will produce antibodies against the Rh-positive cells. These antibodies will attack the Rh-positive blood cells and cause them to die. This disease is called hemolytic disease of the newborn. Since the sen-

sitization does not occur until after the birth, the first baby is not affected, unless the woman was previously sensitized and not treated. If a woman is not treated and becomes pregnant again with an Rh-positive baby, the antibodies will cross the placenta and kill the fetus's red blood cells.

To prevent hemolytic disease of the newborn, RhoGAM, an Rh-immune globulin, is administered after the birth of an Rh-positive infant, as well as after a miscarriage, an abortion, or amniocentesis. It is also given at 28 weeks of pregnancy. RhoGAM acts by suppressing the specific immune response of Rh-negative individuals to Rh-positive red blood cells. Since the woman does not produce antibodies, subsequent pregnancies will not be affected, and the woman can give birth to healthy newborns in the future. Hemolytic disease of the newborn is rare since the development of RhoGAM.

you to report. These symptoms, or warning signs, may or may not indicate a serious complication. For a list of symptoms, see "Warning Signs" on page 34. If you experience any of the warning signs, notify your caregiver immediately. Do not worry about bothering him. It is his job to answer your questions about your physical well-being.

A warning sign should be taken as an indication of possible illness, infection, or threatened miscarriage. However, it is just as important that you remain calm as it is that you recognize the sign and act on it, since nothing may be wrong. Just speaking with your caregiver can be reassuring. Genital sores, vaginal discharge, and other genital discomforts are warnings of venereal or sexually transmitted diseases. Your baby will be at risk if you contract a venereal disease while pregnant. Not only gonorrhea and syphilis are serious, but the herpesvirus and chlamydia can also cause serious problems if the baby becomes infected. Inform your caregiver of any current or previous problems or venereal diseases so that he can test you and treat you if necessary during your pregnancy. In addition, recent studies indicate that pregnant women who have been exposed to HIV, the virus that causes acquired immune deficiency syndrome (AIDS), are at risk for passing the virus on to their unborn children. It is important that you be tested for HIV early in your pregnancy because early treatment may decrease the risk of transmission to the fetus.

Another condition that you should be aware of is toxoplasmosis, a disease that is contracted by eating raw or rare meat or by coming in contact with an infected cat, particularly the feces of such a cat. Toxoplasmosis can cause brain damage, malformation, blindness, or death in an unborn child. Therefore, while you are pregnant, you should avoid changing a cat's litter box and eating meat that is not well cooked.

A food item that could cause serious problems for pregnant women is soft cheese. Any soft cheese—including feta, mozzarella, goat, brie, Camembert,

Group B Strep

Group B streptococcal (GBS) infection is found in the genital area of up to 30 percent of healthy women. Most infected pregnant women show no signs of illness, but are at increased risk for kidney infections, premature rupture of the membranes, preterm labor, and stillbirth. The biggest danger is to infants who become infected during birth. While not all infants become ill, those rare infants who do contract the infection can suffer serious complications. The factors that increase the risk of complications are prematurity, fever during labor, high levels of bacteria, and prolonged rupture of the membranes prior to delivery.

According to the Centers for Disease Control (CDC), a culture of the vaginal and rectal area to check for group B strep should be performed on all pregnant women at 35 to 37 weeks of pregnancy.[2] Some facilities also perform a culture upon admission in labor. Women who tested positive during pregnancy with either the genital culture or urine culture, who previously had an infant with GBS, or who deliver before 37 weeks gestation should be treated during labor with antibiotics. Women who did not have a culture done or whose culture result is not known should be given antibiotics if they are less than 37 weeks pregnant, have had ruptured membranes for longer than 18 hours, or have a temperature of over 100.4°F (Fahrenheit). Treatment with antibiotics during labor has been shown to be highly effective in preventing complications in newborns if the antibiotics are administered 4 or more hours prior to delivery.[3] If the infant is delivered less than 4 hours following the administration of antibiotics or shows signs of infection, a partial or full septic workup may be required. This may include blood tests, a spinal tap, chest X-rays, and/or intravenous administration of antibiotics. The CDC also recommends that all infants of treated mothers be observed for 48 hours after delivery.

blue-veined, and Mexican—could contain a bacteria called listeria that causes miscarriages and stillbirths. This lethal bacteria may also be found in raw and undercooked meat, poultry, and seafood, as well as on raw vegetables. Two other foods in which listeria has been found are hummus dip and taboule salad. Listeria can be killed only by heating to the boiling point. Cold or freezing temperatures do not destroy it.

The symptoms of listeria infection include fever, chills, and other flu-like complaints, plus headache, nausea, and vomiting. They can occur 2 to 30 days after ingestion.

Although information on this bacteria is not widely available, listeria is very dangerous, so products that could be contaminated with it should be carefully avoided during pregnancy. Dr. Boris Petrikovsky, chief of maternal-fetal medicine at North Shore University Hospital on Long Island stated that listeria is "the No. 1 food-borne infection that kills fetuses."[4]

The following guidelines can help reduce your chances of ingesting this harmful bacteria:

❑ Avoid all soft cheeses.

❑ Use only pasteurized dairy products.

❑ Eat only thoroughly cooked meat, poultry, and seafood.

❑ Reheat any ready-to-eat grocery store or deli items.

❑ Thoroughly wash raw vegetables.

❑ Wash hands, countertops, and all utensils after handling uncooked foods.

Listeria is not harmful to healthy adults, but it is very dangerous to the elderly and to people with weakened immune systems, as well as to pregnant women and their fetuses.

The precautions used to avoid listeria infection will also help prevent food

Warning Signs

The following symptoms may be warning signs of complications during pregnancy:

❏ Vaginal bleeding. It is never normal to bleed during pregnancy.

❏ Sharp abdominal pain or severe cramping.

❏ Loss of fluid from the vagina.

❏ Any signs of labor before the thirty-seventh week of pregnancy.

❏ Persistent nausea or vomiting.

❏ Frequent dizzy spells or fainting.

❏ Visual disturbances such as dimness, blurring, flashes of light, or dots in front of the eyes.

❏ Sudden and excessive swelling of the face, hands, or feet.

❏ Severe and persistent headache.

❏ Pain or burning upon urination.

❏ Marked decrease in the frequency of urination.

❏ Persistent dull or sharp pains, anywhere.

❏ Fever higher than 100°F orally, or chills and fever.

❏ Vaginal discharge that is irritating.

❏ Noticeable decrease in fetal movement.

❏ Any other problem that you feel is unusual.

If you experience any of the above symptoms, contact your caregiver as soon as possible.

poisoning from E. coli and salmonella bacteria. Always cook meat, especially hamburger, until there is no pink and the thermometer registers 170°F. Poultry should be cooked to an internal temperature of 185°F.

Several other situations have been cited as possibly being hazardous during early pregnancy. For example, one investigation showed that the employees in a semiconductor plant who worked in the room where computer chips were etched with acids and gases had a miscarriage rate of 39 percent, which is nearly twice the national average.[5]

Some concern also exists about a possible correlation between exposure to electromagnetic radiation and miscarriage. Sources of this radiation include computer monitors and video display terminals, electric blankets, waterbed heaters, electric cable ceiling heat, and power lines and substations. There is no conclusive evidence to support this concern.

Other possible risks are to women who handle the chemicals used in dry cleaning and in hair dyes and permanents. In addition, the use of hot tubs and saunas by pregnant women has been associated with birth defects and fetal death. Further studies are needed to determine whether any danger actually exists in these cases. Until then, you may want to avoid these situations.

HIGHER-RISK PREGNANCY

Some pregnant women are considered to be at "higher risk" than most women. They include women who have diabetes, heart disease, or high blood pressure, or who develop these conditions during pregnancy or labor. They also include women who are carrying their fifth or later child; who are carrying more than one baby; who are under 17 or over 35; who are over 30 and carrying their first child; or who develop signs of preterm labor. The degree of risk varies with each of these conditions and should be thoroughly explained to you by your doctor.

If you are in a higher-risk category, the management of your pregnancy and labor may need to be varied from that of a low-risk woman. Consequently, not all of the options discussed in this book may be available to you.

Some of the more common conditions that place women in the higher-risk category are discussed below.

Gestational Diabetes

Diabetes is a condition characterized by a high level of sugar, or glucose, in the blood. Diabetes that occurs only in pregnancy is known as gestational diabetes. During pregnancy, hormones cause the woman's insulin to be less effective at metabolizing glucose. The resulting high blood sugar can lead to complications in both the woman and baby. The condition disappears after pregnancy for the vast majority of women, although a third of afflicted women become gestational diabetics with subsequent pregnancies. In later life, they are also more likely to develop non-insulin-dependent diabetes. Most women who are well controlled during pregnancy have good pregnancies and healthy babies.

The risk factors for developing gestational diabetes are family history, previous large babies, or previous gestational diabetes. The condition is more common in women who are obese or over the age of 25. Most practices screen all women at 28 weeks for the condition with the glucose tolerance test. (For a discussion of glucose tolerance testing, see "Prenatal Care" on page 30.) Once a positive diagnosis is confirmed, the pregnant woman is placed on a diabetic diet. Home monitoring of blood sugar is performed several times a day. If diet alone does not control the blood sugar, insulin may have to be given.

The babies of untreated diabetic women may be very large, making delivery more difficult. Other complications include respiratory difficulties, jaundice, a low level of calcium in the blood, and stillbirth. If the diabetes is not controlled, hypoglycemia (low blood sugar) may occur after birth. While in utero, a baby produces high levels of insulin to absorb the woman's high blood sugar. At birth, the woman's supply of sugar drops, and the baby's high level of insulin may cause his own blood sugar level to drop very low. Nursing soon after birth helps to prevent hypoglycemia.

Women who have diabetes are more likely to develop pregnancy-induced hypertension. To prevent stillbirths, their doctors may induce labor before or on the due date. If the induction is not successful, a cesarean section is performed. Infection and postpartum hemorrhage are also more common in diabetic women.

Pregnancy-Induced Hypertension

Hypertension (high blood pressure) that occurs during pregnancy is called pregnancy-induced hypertension (PIH). Most women who develop PIH did not have hypertension before pregnancy and will not have it after. PIH was formerly known as toxemia. While the cause of PIH is unknown, some studies suggest that the blame lies with an imbalance of the substances that regulate the constriction and dilation of the blood vessels. The risk factors include heredity, a diet low in protein or calcium, a history of preeclampsia prior to 32 weeks gestation, chronic high blood pressure, kidney disease, lupus, diabetes, multiple pregnancy, age (under 20 or over 35), and being overweight. A new theory states that PIH may be an immune response to a new sex partner, since 85 percent of cases occur in first-time pregnancies. Several studies have shown that a good diet can reduce the risk of developing PIH. A diet containing 75 to 100 grams of protein and 1,500 to 2,000 milligrams of calcium is recommended.

PIH affects both the woman and the fetus. High blood pressure constricts the blood flow to the uterus. This can result in the baby receiving less oxygen and nutrients, which will affect his growth. In addition, the placenta may separate from the wall of the uterus before delivery and result in bleeding and shock. If untreated, PIH can become preeclampsia, which is characterized by high blood pressure, protein in the urine, sudden weight gain, and swelling of the face and hands. It may be necessary to induce labor if the blood pressure is not controlled. This may lead to a premature infant. Rarely, preeclampsia progresses to eclampsia, which is marked by convulsions, coma, or even death of the woman or baby.

Treatment of PIH consists of bed rest for mild conditions. Occasionally, a woman must be hospitalized. If the blood pressure is not controlled, delivery by induction of labor or cesarean section may be necessary to save the lives of the woman and baby. The medication magnesium sulfate is administered intravenously to prevent convulsions. The risk of seizures diminishes 48 hours after delivery of the baby.

New PIH Findings

Researchers have new findings indicating that pregnancy-induced hypertension results from a cellular defect that occurs early in gestation and affects the implantation of the placenta. They are hopeful that this information will lead to the development of a test for the condition.[6]

Multiple Pregnancy

If you are pregnant with more than one baby—with twins, triplets, or more—your pregnancy is called a multiple pregnancy. Fraternal twins are more common than identical twins and are the result of two sperm fertilizing two eggs. Fraternal twins may or may not be the same sex and are no more alike in appearance than any other siblings. Identical twins occur less frequently and are the result of one sperm fertilizing one egg, which then separates. Since identical twins carry the same genetic material, they are always the same sex, always look alike, and always have the same blood type. They may be mirror images of each other.

During pregnancy, an increased demand is placed on the body of a woman carrying more than one baby as well as additional placentas or one larger placenta. The discomforts of pregnancy are accentuated, since there is an increased demand on the circulatory system and the uterus is larger in size. The chances of PIH and preterm labor are greater. For these reasons, many physicians place these women on bed rest at around 28 weeks gestation.

Women experiencing a multiple pregnancy have higher protein and caloric requirements. (For a discussion of diet during pregnancy, including multiple pregnancy, see "Nutritional Needs During Pregnancy" on page 46.) Additional protein is necessary to provide for adequate growth of the babies and to ensure good muscle tone of the overdistended uterus. Women who eat well during pregnancy decrease their chances for complications and increase their chances for delivering at term.

Preterm Labor

Signs of Preterm Labor

The following symptoms may be indications of preterm labor:

❏ More than four uterine contractions in 1 hour.

❏ Menstrual-like cramps, constant or intermittent.

❏ Abdominal cramps, with or without diarrhea.

❏ Backache, constant or intermittent.

❏ Pelvic pressure or the feeling that the baby is pushing down.

❏ Sudden increase in vaginal discharge, either watery, bloody, or mucuslike.

If you note any of the above symptoms, contact your caregiver immediately.

If a baby is born before the thirty-seventh week of pregnancy—more than 3 weeks early—the birth is called preterm and the baby premature. Preterm birth represents the greatest health risk to newborns. Preterm babies have an increased risk of neonatal problems. Their lungs and other organs may not be ready to function yet. Respiratory distress is the greatest concern, and the babies often have difficulty maintaining their body temperature. In addition, their sucking may be weak, and they are more susceptible to infection.

Women who are more likely to go into preterm labor include those who had a previous miscarriage or preterm birth; who have an overdistended uterus from a multiple pregnancy or from an excess of amniotic fluid; who smoke, take drugs, or are malnourished; who are under the age of 18 or over 35; who are experiencing a high degree of emotional distress; who have jobs that involve standing for long periods or enduring other stressful working conditions; and who have a vaginal or urinary tract infection or an infection of the membranes of the amniotic sac.

Preterm labor can often be stopped if it is caught in time. The treatment for preterm labor includes bed rest; antibiotics, if indicated, for infection; and possibly medications to relax the uterus and stop the contractions. While some studies question the efficacy of bed rest, it is the current treatment of choice.

The U.S. Food and Drug Administration (FDA) recently approved a blood test that can predict whether a pregnant woman is about to experience a preterm birth. The test detects a substance called fetal fibronectin in the woman's blood. Fetal fibronectin is an adhesive protein that serves as a "natural glue" on the placenta. The substance changes into a lubricant just before labor begins. It should not be present in the woman's blood after the twentieth week of pregnancy unless there is a problem, such as preterm labor or an infection. Its presence indicates a 30- to 50-percent risk of delivering within the next 2 weeks.[7]

In cases of impending preterm birth between 24 and 34 weeks gestation, a treatment is available that accelerates fetal lung maturity. Synthetic steroids have been shown to reduce the incidence of respiratory distress syndrome and brain hemorrhage in newborns by 50 percent and to reduce death rates by 40 percent. According to a recommendation of the National Institutes of Health (NIH), this medication should be used when delivery prior to 34 weeks gestation is likely, unless the medication will have an adverse effect on the woman or delivery is imminent.[8]

If you experience any signs of labor more than 3 weeks before your due date, contact your caregiver right away.

TESTS USED IN PREGNANCY

Various tests and procedures are used in certain cases of pregnancy complications. Like all medical procedures, they offer advantages, but also carry risks. Therefore, they should be utilized only when medically indicated, not on a routine basis for your or your doctor's convenience or to satisfy your curiosity.

When deciding whether to undergo a test, ask your caregiver if the results will in any way alter his care of you. If his answer is yes, ask him how. If his answer is no, ask him if the test is therefore necessary. Make sure you understand all the risks and benefits involved before agreeing to, or rejecting, a procedure. Continue to ask questions and to request explanations until you feel comfortable. Understanding the benefits can help to relax you and may free you from concern about the procedure. Or, it can help you decide to ask for an alternative.

Among the more common tests used in pregnancy are amniocentesis, chorionic villus sampling, alpha-fetoprotein screening, ultrasound, X-ray pelvimetry, the estriol excretion study, fetal movement evaluation, the nonstress test, and the oxytocin challenge test.

Amniocentesis

Amniocentesis is a test to detect abnormalities in the baby. It may also be done to assess fetal lung maturity if induction of labor or cesarean delivery is indicated. The test is performed by administering a local anesthetic, then withdrawing a sample of amniotic fluid using a long needle inserted through the abdominal and uterine walls. It should be done in conjunction with ultrasound, which will show the location of the fetus, the placenta, and the umbilical cord.

The amniotic fluid is sent to a lab for culturing and testing. Certain tests—such as those for Tay-Sachs disease, Hunter's syndrome, neural tube defects, and fetal lung maturity—can be performed immediately. These tests measure chemicals produced by the baby that are present in the amniotic fluid. To determine fetal lung maturity, the amniotic fluid is examined for the specific phospholipids that are present when a baby's lungs are mature.

Most tests require that the fetal cells be isolated and given sufficient time to multiply, usually 2 to 4 weeks. Then a complete chromosomal analysis is

A Hint for the Mother-to-Be

❏ Some tests involve risks. Make sure that you understand the potential benefits and risks of any procedure before you agree to have it.

done to detect the presence of Down syndrome or other genetic abnormalities. The sex of the baby is also established.

When amniocentesis is used for detecting abnormalities, it is generally performed between 16 and 18 weeks gestation. Before 14 weeks, there usually is insufficient amniotic fluid. Some caregivers are performing amniocentesis between 11 and 13 weeks. But one study found that when amniocentesis is performed before 86 days, an increase in foot deformities (turned-in and club feet) was observed.[9] When testing for gestational maturity, the procedure is done in the last trimester.

Amniocentesis is a very valuable procedure, but according to many experts, it can be misused. The risks include some chance of blood exchange between the woman and baby, creating a greater Rh incompatibility while testing for the condition; infection of the amniotic fluid; peritonitis; blood clots; placental hemorrhage; injury to the baby; and even premature labor.[10] Amniocentesis should definitely not be done just to satisfy curiosity about the baby's sex. And, unless you plan to terminate your pregnancy if an abnormality is found, or unless your doctor plans to alter your care, it is questionable whether you should have this test done just for the genetic information.

Chorionic Villus Sampling

Chorionic villus sampling (CVS) is a test that can detect genetic abnormalities earlier than amniocentesis can. It is usually done between the ninth and eleventh weeks of pregnancy. However, it is not available in all locations.

A chorionic villus is one of the fingerlike projections covering the developing embryo. It contains cells that have the same genetic composition as the embryo. In CVS, a sample of chorionic tissue about the size of a grain of cooked rice is removed. In one method, a suction catheter is inserted into the uterus through the cervix under the visual guidance of ultrasound. In another method, a needle is inserted into the uterus through the abdominal wall. Both methods take about a half-hour to complete.

The advantages of CVS are that it can be performed early in pregnancy and that results can be obtained more quickly than with amniocentesis. Up to 3 or 4 weeks may pass before amniocentesis results are known. The possible risks of CVS include infection, Rh sensitization, bleeding by the woman or baby, miscarriage, birth defects, and perforation of the fetal membrane.[11] In addition, studies in England have indicated that fetal limb deformities may result from CVS, especially when it is done early in the pregnancy (before 66 days).[12] Several American studies have failed to confirm this finding, however.

Alpha-Fetoprotein Screening

Alpha-fetoprotein (AFP) screening is a blood test done on the woman between the fifteenth and eighteenth weeks of pregnancy to screen for fetal abnormalities. AFP is a protein produced by the baby. A high level of AFP in the woman's blood indicates a possible open neural tube defect, such as spina bifida or anencephaly. A high level may also be caused by a multiple pregnancy or a miscalculation of gestational age. A low level may indicate Down syndrome. Also measuring two other substances—human chorionic gonadotropin and unconjugated estriol—increases the accuracy of detecting Down syndrome, identifying about 70 percent of Down syndrome cases.[13]

AFP testing has a history of false positive readings, however, and further testing should be done if the results are abnormal. The additional tests could include another AFP blood test, ultrasound for accurate determination of gestational age, or amniocentesis for a more accurate diagnosis.

Ultrasound

Ultrasound was developed during World War I when high-frequency sound waves were used to detect enemy submarines. A form of ultrasound used in pregnancy testing is the sonogram, which uses intermittent sound waves. The sound waves are directed into the woman's abdomen, with an outline of the baby, placenta, and other structures involved in the pregnancy transmitted to a video screen. A sonogram is often used to determine fetal position, to estimate the maturity of the baby, or to confirm a multiple pregnancy. In addition, the location of the placenta can be pinpointed when placenta previa (low implanted placenta) is suspected. Ultrasound is also used to visualize the baby and placenta when amniocentesis or CVS is being performed. Since X-rays are now considered dangerous to developing babies, ultrasound is used instead.

Many doctors use ultrasound routinely to determine the due date. When the test is performed between the fourteenth and twentieth weeks, it is accurate to within 1 week before or after the estimated date. Later in pregnancy, and especially after the thirty-second week, it is not as accurate at determining due date because of variations in fetal growth. In a higher-risk pregnancy, an accurate due date is important for making sure that the infant is delivered at the best time. Routine ultrasound is usually done between the sixteenth and nineteenth weeks of pregnancy.

Ultrasound can also be directed in a continuous wave to check the baby's heart rate. This is done during routine examinations using a doptone. Most often, it is done during labor using an electronic fetal monitor. (For a discussion of this use, see "Electronic Fetal Monitor" on page 168.)

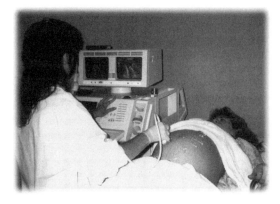

A technician moves a transducer over a woman's bare abdomen to check the condition of the developing fetus. The gel on the woman's abdomen helps improve the quality of the sound waves.

Ultrasound often provides expectant parents with the first "photograph" of their child.

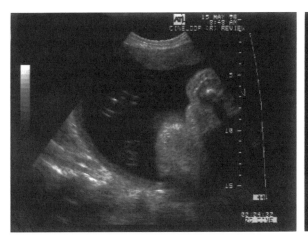
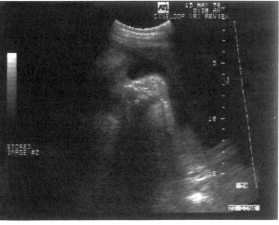

Ultrasound can also be used to measure the biophysical profile of a fetus. This type of profile includes fetal movements, muscle tone, amount of amniotic fluid, and fetal breathing movements. The test is usually done in higher-risk pregnancies to assure fetal well-being and to determine the best time for delivery.

Diagnostically, ultrasound is preferred over X-rays. However, many doctors now use ultrasound routinely during labor, as well as recommending one or more sonograms during pregnancy. The same as other procedures, ultrasound should not be used indiscriminately, and you have the legal right to refuse it. A 6-year study by the National Institute of Child Health and Human Development, a division of NIH, concluded that no benefit is derived from the routine use of ultrasound in low-risk pregnancies. This study, the largest ever conducted, found that perinatal outcome was not improved by routine screening when compared with the selective use of ultrasonography based on the caregiver's judgment. The investigators estimated that $1 billion a year could be saved if sonograms are limited to higher-risk pregnancies and other cases in which it is medically indicated.[14]

If your caregiver requests a sonogram and you do not have insurance to cover the cost, ask if the procedure is medically necessary and what information your caregiver hopes to receive. Also, ask if the information will change your care. In addition, if you are going to have a sonogram, you may want to ask about the credentials of the person performing and interpreting the test. Does that person have training or certification in ultrasonography? The FDA has guidelines regarding the intensity of the machines and the amount of time a fetus should be exposed.

Because so much information can be gained about the fetus through diagnostic ultrasound, and because studies have not shown any long-term effects on babies, many doctors feel strongly that the benefits of ultrasound outweigh the risks. Others, however, oppose its use without a medical indication, since routine screening of all women is still not recommended by the NIH or the American College of Obstetricians and Gynecologists.[15]

X-Ray Pelvimetry

X-ray pelvimetry measures the size of the woman's pelvis to determine if the passageway is adequate. It is seldom used except at the end of pregnancy when a breech presentation is suspected and the doctor needs to determine whether a vaginal delivery is possible. X-rays are avoided because they carry the risk of being carcinogenic (cancer producing).

Estriol Excretion Study

Estriol is an estrogen-type hormone made by the placenta and excreted in the woman's blood and urine. The estriol excretion study measures the estriol level and helps to determine the functioning of the placenta, as well as the baby's well-being. The test can be conducted using urine collected over a 24-hour period or a single sample of blood.

A drop in the estriol level indicates that the placenta's functioning is declining. Several consecutive studies may need to be done to assess the degree of placental functioning.

The estriol excretion study is used, along with other tests, to determine the best time for delivery in cases of diabetes or other difficulties.

Fetal Movement Evaluation

Around the eighth month of your pregnancy, your caregiver may suggest that you keep track of your baby's movements. You can do this best by setting aside a certain time each day and recording how long it takes your baby to move ten different times. A healthy baby moves about the same amount each day. Report any decrease in movement to your caregiver immediately. Fetal movement evaluation is a noninvasive test that can provide valuable information about your baby's health and well-being.

Nonstress Test

A nonstress test can be a very reliable noninvasive test for fetal well-being. It is done by measuring the fetal heart rate in response to fetal activity as observed on a fetal monitor.

In a nonstress test, the woman is placed on an electonic fetal monitor and a baseline heart rate is noted. The woman is given a control to push when she feels the baby move. The control places a mark on the readout. Sometimes, a small transducer is used to make a buzzing sound over the baby's head. When this is done, the test is called a vibroacoustic stimulation test (VST).

An increase in the fetal heart rate indicates fetal well-being. If the result is negative, additional testing, such as an oxytocin challenge test, is usually performed.

Nonstress test results can be affected by low blood sugar, so you should make sure to eat before taking the test. The results can also be affected by sleepiness of the fetus.

Oxytocin Challenge Test

The oxytocin challenge test (OCT) is done in the hospital to help determine how well the baby will undergo the stress of labor. The OCT is also known as a stress test.

Oxytocin is a medication that causes uterine contractions. While reclining at a 45-degree angle, the woman is given oxytocin intravenously until she has contractions 3 to 4 minutes apart for a full half-hour. At the same time, the baby's heart rate is electronically monitored to check the effect of the contractions on him. If the results are positive—that is, the fetal heart rate appears abnormal during the stress of the contractions—the doctor may recommend a cesarean birth, since the baby may not be able to tolerate the stress of labor. If the results are negative—that is, the heart rate remains normal during the contractions—the baby will most likely do well during labor.

When taking the OCT, avoid lying flat on your back. This can cause your blood pressure to drop, decreasing oxygen to the baby and possibly causing the appearance of fetal distress on the monitor.

WORKING DURING PREGNANCY

More than 1 million working women become pregnant each year. For most of these women, continuing to work until right before their due dates is not a problem. As long as you and your fetus are healthy and your job presents no greater risks than those encountered in everyday life, working should not give you any added concerns.

Certain conditions, however, do require that you take precautions. If your

Hints for the Father-to-Be

❑ Be understanding of your mate's mood swings.

❑ Sometimes, fathers-to-be gain weight and show other symptoms of pregnancy.

❑ Massage oil or lotion into your mate's abdomen to help reduce the number and severity of stretch marks.

❑ Attend your mate's ultrasound examinations and take along a blank videotape for the technician to make a copy of the procedure for you.

❑ Encourage your mate to take naps.

job includes a lot of lifting, standing, or walking, for example, your caregiver may suggest that you cut back on your hours. If you are exposed to potentially toxic materials (including X-rays, lead, and chemotherapy medications) on the job, you will want to ask to be reassigned to another area. If reassignment is not possible, your caregiver may advise you to quit your job. If you work with any substances that you feel may be harmful, be sure to talk to your caregiver about them.

Additionally, some medical conditions may prevent you from working. Such problems as diabetes, kidney disease, heart disease, back pain, and high blood pressure may require you to restrict your activities. If you previously had a miscarriage or preterm birth, or if you are experiencing a multiple pregnancy, your caregiver may advise you to stop or cut back on your work.

Everyone encounters some stress in life. If your job involves an unusually high amount, however, it could possibly lead to problems in your pregnancy. You will need to modify your work environment to provide less stress, or learn some stress-relieving techniques to help you deal with the situation.

In rare cases, a condition related to your pregnancy may qualify you as disabled. Even such symptoms as nausea, dizziness, and swollen ankles may cause a temporary disability. More serious complications such as infection, bleeding, premature labor, premature rupture of the membranes, heart disease, diabetes, or high blood pressure may cause disability. Other disabilities are related to exposure to high levels of toxic substances that could harm the fetus. If your caregiver determines that your pregnancy is disabling, he can sign a statement verifying your disability. Your employer will be required to give you the same preferences and benefits that are provided to any other disabled employee. If your employer does not routinely provide disability benefits, you may be eligible for benefits from the state.

There may be times during your pregnancy when you find it difficult to cope with your job. If you have morning sickness or are extremely tired or sleepy, making it through another day at work will be a challenge. Make maximum use of your breaks to rest and elevate your feet. Keep nutritious snacks handy to provide energy and relieve nausea. If you sit all day, remember to maintain good posture. Get up and walk around often to improve your circulation and reduce swelling. Above all, listen to your body's signals. You may find it best to cut back on your hours or just take a day or two of vacation. With common sense on your part and cooperation from your employer, you should be able to make it over the rough spots.

CAR SAFETY DURING PREGNANCY

Most pregnant women wonder if it is advisable to wear a seat belt while riding in a car. The answer is a definite *yes*. If you protect yourself from injury, you also protect your baby. In auto accidents, most fetal injuries and deaths result from the woman being injured or killed.

Many women are concerned that the seat belt could squeeze the baby and cause a miscarriage. However, there is no evidence that wearing a seat belt results in fetal injury, no matter how serious the collision. Your baby is well cushioned inside your body, surrounded by amniotic fluid and your body organs. A properly worn seat belt is his best protection.

You should wear a lap-shoulder belt whenever you ride in a car. Place the lap portion of the belt underneath your abdominal bulge, as low on your hips

Place the belt under your abdomen and the shoulder strap between your breasts.

as possible. Never put it above your abdomen. Position the shoulder portion of the belt between your breasts. Do not slip the belt off your shoulder. Adjust both parts as snugly as possible.

Always fastening a seat belt around yourself and always using a car seat for your baby after his birth are important ways to protect both of you.

TRAVEL DURING PREGNANCY

If you are like most women, traveling during pregnancy is no problem, as long as you follow a few guidelines. These guidelines are:

❏ Check with your caregiver to make sure there are no special healthcare concerns that would prevent you from traveling.

❏ Try to plan any trips for your second trimester, when comfort is the greatest.

❏ While traveling, walk around often to improve circulation and reduce swelling.

❏ Wear comfortable shoes and clothing.

❏ Take along light snacks and juice to prevent hunger and decrease nausea.

❏ Do not take motion sickness pills or any other medications before checking with your caregiver.

❏ Take time to eat regular, nutritious meals.

❏ Eat plenty of high fiber foods to ease constipation.

❏ Get your usual amount of sleep, and rest often, elevating your feet.

❏ If you are traveling far from home, take a copy of your medical record and get the name of a doctor or facility where you could go for treatment if necessary.

❏ If traveling by car, do not ride for more than 6 hours a day. Stop every 1 to 2 hours to walk around. Always wear a seat belt.

❏ If traveling by air, sit in an aisle seat for the greatest comfort. Wear layers of clothing so that you can adjust as the cabin temperature changes. Drink plenty of fluids.

❏ If traveling overseas, drink only bottled beverages, do not use ice in your drinks, and do not eat raw, unpeeled fruits or vegetables. Also, avoid raw or undercooked meat, and make sure that any milk you drink has been pasteurized.

The best guideline you can follow is to keep your plans flexible and to change them according to your body's signals. If you use common sense, traveling during pregnancy can be a pleasure, not an inconvenience.

CONCLUSION

This chapter has presented many aspects of pregnancy to give you an idea of what you may experience during the next few months. Keep in mind, too, that pregnancy is a normal, natural condition, one of wellness, not illness. With a few exceptions, you should be able to continue the same daily activities and experience the same good health and lifestyle that you enjoyed prior to becoming pregnant.

Nutrition
or Food for Thought

Because Americans are among the wealthiest people in the world, they are often thought to be the most well nourished. Unfortunately, this belief is not true. The average American diet includes a good deal of fat, sugar, and highly processed food. This "junk food" provides only empty calories—that is, it has a high caloric content with no corresponding nutritional value.

A diet comprised of junk food is not healthy for anyone, but for a developing fetus, it is disastrous! Your baby's entire body—including his liver, his heart, his bones, and his brain—is formed completely from the nutrients you provide him. Your baby is not a parasite drawing from your body's reserves. Only the nutrients that you consume are available for his formation and growth. For him to develop to his full potential, both physically and mentally, you must eat properly throughout your pregnancy. Even his intelligence quotient (IQ) in later life can be affected by your diet, since his tiny brain cells need adequate protein from which to develop. Remember this as you plan your meals every day.

If you are already nutrition conscious and eating a healthy diet, your main concern will simply be to increase your protein intake. However, if you are a "junk food junkie," now is the time to change. By eliminating empty calories from your diet as well as increasing your consumption of protein, you can be confident that you are providing your baby with the optimum building blocks. And as a bonus, you will feel better, too!

Fortunately, many women begin to pay closer attention to their diets during pregnancy. Some are motivated by a desire to do everything possible to ensure a healthy child. Some are prompted by problems with constipation, heartburn, morning sickness, or fatigue. An expanding abdomen and weight gain are factors that negatively concern still other women, who fear never losing the added pounds. It is important for you to realize that gaining weight is necessary during pregnancy and that you will lose the added weight afterwards.

A poor diet can cause a multitude of problems for the woman including anemia, infection, placental malfunction, difficult labor, cesarean delivery, poor postpartum healing, and failure at breastfeeding. The effects of a poor diet on the baby run from prematurity and low birth weight to brain damage and stillbirth.[1]

This chapter discusses exactly why mothers-to-be need certain food substances. It also explains how to plan a diet to best get them.

NUTRITIONAL NEEDS DURING PREGNANCY

When a woman is pregnant, she is growing not only a baby, but also a placenta. This placenta, like the baby, needs to be adequately nourished, to ensure proper implantation and development for efficient functioning. The placenta carries out many essential life functions for the baby. Along with the umbilical cord, amniotic sac, and uterus, the placenta is a life support system for this tiny person.

The placenta, in providing nourishment for the baby, works very much like a fuel pump. If the fuel is of poor quality or the wrong octane for the particular engine, the pump will work ineffectively or may even stop completely. Also, if the pressure or the volume of the fuel coming through the pump is affected, the pump's efficiency will be altered. If you think of the nutrients in the bloodstream as fuel, you can see that a poor diet results in a poor quality of nutrients moving through the "placenta-pump." If the volume of fluid in the bloodstream is inadequate, then the pressure of the blood coming through the "placenta-pump" will be low and the nutrients will not be able to get through in sufficient quantity to adequately nourish the fetus.

The body's blood volume needs to increase by more than 50 percent during the last half of pregnancy to enable the placenta to be an efficient pump.[2] This increase requires an adequate intake of sodium (salt), along with a sufficient intake of fluids. Many women experience an increased desire for salt during pregnancy. This is the body's way of ensuring the supply that is needed to help increase its blood volume. Thus, restricting salt may hinder the body's performance of this vital function and can result in intrauterine growth retardation.[3]

Sufficient fluid intake is also needed for the production of amniotic fluid. By the last weeks of pregnancy, the amniotic sac contains about 1 quart of amniotic fluid to cushion and protect the baby. This fluid is replaced every 3 hours. In addition, tissue fluid increases by an estimated 2 to 3 quarts during pregnancy. You need to drink at least 2 quarts of liquid a day to maintain these levels and to ensure a healthy pregnancy. The best fluids to drink are water, milk, and fruit juices. Stay away from alcohol and drinks that contain caffeine. (For a discussion of the use of alcohol and caffeine by pregnant women, see "Nonfood Items and Drugs During Pregnancy" on page 59.)

Many women and doctors are overly concerned about edema (swelling) during pregnancy. Some degree of swelling is normal. The enlarging uterus pressing on the veins of the legs causes dependent edema in women who stand or sit for long periods. In addition, estrogen, which is manufactured by the placenta during pregnancy, causes the tissues to retain extra fluid. Before you were pregnant, you may have noticed water retention just before your menstrual period. Women who took birth control pills may also have experienced it. This was caused by the increased estrogen in the body.

In years past, doctors often treated this normal swelling with diuretics (water pills), as well as with a diet restricted in salt. Fortunately, they no longer follow these practices because of the potential side effects. In addition, almost all obstetrical authors now warn that diuretics can actually increase the symptoms and may even cause more serious side effects, including a rise in

the blood pH (the relative acidity or alkalinity of substances), reduced placental exchange of nutrients and waste products, decreased tolerance of carbohydrates, generalized edema, severe loss of calcium through the urine, and sodium depletion.[4] If the swelling is a result of hypovolemia (low blood volume), diuretics may drive salt and water from the circulation and lower the blood volume even further. This could actually cause or accentuate the PIH that the diuretic was supposed to prevent. Sometimes, however, diuretics are indicated in pregnancy, such as when the woman has abnormal swelling due to heart disease or kidney disease.

Rather than resort to diuretics or salt restriction, the normal pregnant woman should make certain that her protein consumption is ample (75 to 100 grams) and that her salt intake is adequate. Salt is contained naturally in many foods. During pregnancy, "salt to taste" is a good rule to follow.

Your liver also helps to maintain an increased blood volume during pregnancy. It does this by providing albumin, a protein that keeps water in circulation. An inadequate intake of protein prevents the liver from producing enough albumin to hold water in the bloodstream. The water therefore leaks out into the woman's tissues, creating abnormal puffiness.

The liver also filters the pregnancy-induced hormones, manufactured by the body in amounts equal to what is supplied by 100 birth control pills taken daily, and rids the body of toxins normally produced in the lower bowel. Altogether, the liver performs approximately 500 functions. Since the liver is under increasing stress as the baby grows, you need to increase your intake of calories, protein, vitamins, and sodium during the last half of your pregnancy to counteract this stress.

The baby's brain grows the most during the last 2 months, and an adequate intake of protein is essential at this time for building brain cells. So even if your diet has been unstructured up to your seventh month, a change now can still greatly benefit your baby. Conversely, if your diet has been adequate up to your seventh month, but you now begin restricting calories in an effort to control your weight gain, your baby may suffer.

Weight gain is often the focus of too much concern during pregnancy. Gaining weight is expected and necessary for the well-being of the mother-to-be and baby. The amount of weight gain varies from woman to woman, as does the pattern of weight gain. Total weight gain is determined by prepregnant weight, eating habits, daily activities, and metabolism. Since every woman is unique, there is no specific weight gain that is correct for all pregnant women. However, if a woman was underweight before becoming pregnant, she will need to gain more weight than what is expected in the average woman.

Even for overweight women, dieting during pregnancy is risky for both mother-to-be and child. Changing the woman's diet to eliminate high-calorie junk foods and to include only nutritionally beneficial foods will provide the baby with adequate nourishment. A diet that provides less than 2,300 calories will not provide the nutrients necessary for the baby to grow or for the woman to gain an adequate amount of weight.

During the last weeks of pregnancy, the baby lays down stores of vital minerals and insulating body fat essential for his survival. He builds his stores of iron because his diet for the first 6 months of extrauterine life will be low in it. Even the iron supplement in infant formula is poorly absorbed by babies. Therefore, during the last months of pregnancy, you must eat foods that will provide you and your baby with a sufficient supply of iron. After birth, breast-

Hints for the Mother-to-Be

❑ *Do not* restrict your salt intake unless your doctor can give you documented proof that it is necessary in your particular case.

❑ *Do not* take a diuretic for normal swelling.

❑ *Do not* restrict your calories to "hold down" your weight gain.

❑ *Do not* go for even 24 hours without good food.

feeding will help. Breastmilk contains just a small amount of iron, but this iron is efficiently absorbed and utilized by the baby, which allows the infant's iron supply to last longer.

If you are experiencing a multiple pregnancy, your increased nutritional needs are greater than those of a woman carrying a single baby. Each day, you need to consume an additional 20 to 25 grams of protein per baby and take in at least 300 more calories per baby. Physiologic swelling is even more exaggerated, as you may have additional placentas or one larger placenta producing a greater quantity of estrogen. The larger and heavier uterus restricts the blood flow from the veins of your legs more than normal, increasing dependent edema. The weight gain in a woman carrying twins can be as much as 40 to 50 pounds if she is eating correctly. Women who eat a healthy diet and do not restrict their salt intake often give birth to babies who are of normal weight (not less than 5 1/2 pounds) and who arrive at term, not prematurely, as is usually expected.

Gail Sforza Brewer presented the No-Risk Pregnancy Diet in her book *The Pregnancy After 30 Workbook.* The diet includes daily and weekly food patterns designed to supply the woman and baby with adequate building materials and reserves. The plan is still recognized as an excellent guide for providing maximum nutrition during pregnancy. For a description of the diet plan, see "The No-Risk Pregnancy Diet."

NUTRITION BASICS

Proteins are the building blocks of all cells. They are composed of amino acids and are necessary for the growth and repair of tissues, for building blood and amniotic fluid, and for forming antibodies in both the woman and baby. There are two kinds of proteins—complete and incomplete. A complete protein supplies all eight of the essential amino acids. Protein from animal sources is usually complete. Vegetable protein is usually incomplete. If you are a vegetarian, you will need to learn all about protein composition to plan a diet that is balanced and provides all eight of the essential amino acids. Including both animal and vegetable sources of protein is the best way to get all of them. Some good sources of protein are meat, fish, poultry, eggs, milk, cheese, dried beans and peas, peanut butter, nuts, and whole-grain breads and cereals.

Carbohydrates also come in two forms. Sugars, the simpler form, are found in fruit and milk. Starches, the more complex form, are found in vegetables and cereals. Carbohydrates are especially important during pregnancy because they supply the woman with energy, allowing protein to be spared for the important work of building tissues. Many snacks—such as potato chips, cookies, and candy—are largely carbohydrates that supply empty calories and little else. Vegetables and fruit supply not only energy, but vitamins and minerals that benefit both the woman and the developing baby. Some carbohydrates also provide fiber, which helps minimize the problem of constipation. Good sources of carbohydrates are fresh fruits and vegetables, and whole-grain breads and cereals.

A small amount of fat is essential for the body to be able to process vitamins A, D, E, and K, which are fat soluble. Nutritionists believe that vegetable fat is more beneficial than animal fat in the human body. Good sources of fat include cooking oil, butter, margarine, nuts, peanut butter, and cheese.

The No-Risk Pregnancy Diet

When you are pregnant, you need more of good-quality foods than when you are not pregnant. To meet your own needs and those of your developing baby, you must have, *every day,* at least:

1. One quart (four glasses) of milk—any kind: whole milk, low-fat, skim, powdered skim, or buttermilk. If you do not like milk, you can substitute one cup of yogurt for each cup of milk
2. Two eggs
3. Two servings of fish, shellfish, chicken or turkey, lean beef, veal, lamb, pork, liver, or kidney

Alternative combinations include:

Rice with: beans, cheese, sesame seeds, milk

Cornmeal with: beans, cheese, tofu, milk

Beans with: rice, bulgur, cornmeal, wheat noodles, sesame seeds, milk

Peanuts with: sunflower seeds, milk

Whole wheat bread or noodles with: beans, cheese, peanut butter, tofu, milk

For each serving of meat, you can substitute these quantities of cheese*:

Brick	– 4 oz.	Longhorn	– 3 oz.
Camembert	– 6 oz.	Muenster	– 4 oz.
Cheddar	– 3 oz.	Monterey jack	– 4 oz.
Cottage	– 6 oz.	Swiss	– 3 oz.

4. Two servings of fresh, green leafy vegetables: mustard, beet, collard, dandelion or turnip greens, spinach, lettuce, cabbage, broccoli, kale, Swiss chard
5. Five servings of whole-grain breads, rolls, cereals or pancakes: Wheatena, bran flakes, granola, shredded wheat, wheat germ, oatmeal, buckwheat or whole wheat pancakes, corn bread, corn tortillas, corn or bran or whole wheat muffins, waffles, brown rice
6. Two choices from: a whole potato (any style), large green pepper, orange, grapefruit, lemon, lime, papaya, tomato (one piece of fruit or one large glass of juice)
7. Three pats of margarine, vitamin A–enriched, or butter, or oil

Also include in your diet:

8. A yellow- or orange-colored vegetable or fruit five times a week
9. Liver once a week, if you like it†
10. Table salt: *salt your food to taste*
11. Water: drink to thirst

It is not healthy for you and your unborn baby to go even 24 hours without good food!

Note: Vitamin supplements are in routine use in prenatal care; they do not take the place of a sound, balanced diet of nutritional foods.

From *The Pregnancy After 30 Workbook* (Emmaus, PA: Rodale Press, Inc., 1978). Used with permission.

* Soft cheese may be contaminated with listeria. For a discussion of this, see page 32.

† Although liver is a good source of protein and iron, some experts advise against eating it during pregnancy. One function of the liver is to detoxify the blood. There is a concern that liver may contain toxins or pesticides that may be harmful to the fetus. Therefore, it might be safer to fulfill your protein and iron requirements by consuming sufficient amounts of dairy products, eggs, and other meats.

Calcium builds bones and teeth, aids in blood clotting, regulates the body's use of other minerals, and functions in muscle tone and relaxation. An imbalance of calcium and phosphorus can lead to leg cramps. Just one bottle of a soft drink may contain enough other minerals to have a negative effect on the availability of calcium to the body's cells.[5] Eliminate soft drinks from your diet and eat good sources of calcium. Decreased amounts of calcium in the diet are associated with decreased strength in infant bones. In addition, a daily intake of 1,500 to 2,000 milligrams of calcium may decrease the risk of developing

PIH.[6] Good sources of calcium are dairy products, broccoli, dark green leafy vegetables, and some seafood.

Iron is essential for the formation of hemoglobin, the element that carries oxygen to the tissues and cells. Because of the increase in total blood volume during pregnancy, the ratio of hemoglobin to blood volume goes down in the last trimester. This is normal, although it is sometimes confused with true anemia. During pregnancy, iron intake must be increased to build up the baby's supply while preventing anemia in the woman. If necessary, an iron supplement may be recommended to be taken along with the prenatal vitamins. Iron supplements, however, can cause constipation and nausea. Talk with your caregiver about finding an iron supplement that will agree with your digestive system. Good sources of dietary iron are red meat, egg yolk, shellfish, dried fruit, and enriched whole-grain breads and cereals.

The best way to obtain vitamins is through a diet that includes both the water-soluble B complex and C vitamins as well as the fat-soluble A, D, E, and K vitamins. Vitamin supplements are essentially just that—supplements. They will not compensate for an inadequate diet and should not be thought of as the best way to obtain vitamins. They contain only those vitamins for which nutritional recommendations have been established. There are many trace vitamins in a well-balanced diet for which recommendations have not been set or requirements are not even known.

A vitamin for which a supplement is strongly recommended is folic acid, a B vitamin. Studies indicate that daily consumption of 400 micrograms (but not more than 1,000 micrograms) of folic acid, beginning before pregnancy and continuing through the first trimester, can prevent up to 70 percent of neural tube defects in babies. There is also evidence that folic acid may prevent cleft lip and palate,[7] and certain heart and limb defects.[8] Good dietary sources of folic acid include orange juice, green leafy vegetables, beans, peas, liver, and some fortified cereals. The FDA enacted a regulation, beginning in 1998, to require manufacturers to fortify grain products—including breads, flours, cornmeal, pasta, and rice—with folic acid to ensure that women receive this important vitamin.

Not all vitamins are safe. Extra doses of vitamin A, even two or three multivitamins a day, may cause birth defects if taken in early pregnancy. A study published in the *New England Journal of Medicine* in 1995 cautions that more than 10,000 international units of vitamin A each day may be dangerous to the fetus. The problems involve malformation of the face, head, heart, or nervous system.[9] Most prenatal vitamins contain 4,000 units. Some multivitamins, especially those sold in health food stores, contain higher levels, and vitamin A capsules may have as much as 25,000 units. It is also recommended that women be careful combining supplements with large servings of liver, which is high in vitamin A, and with vitamin-enriched cereals, which may contain 5,000 units of vitamin A per bowl.

A Hint for the Mother-to-Be

❏ Make sure that your diet includes 400 micrograms of folic acid daily.

NUTRITIONAL CHANGES DURING PREGNANCY

As your pregnancy progresses, the nutritional demands that are made on your body increase. A look at these increasing needs by trimester can provide further insight.

First Trimester

During the early weeks of pregnancy, you may not be aware of the baby within your body. Therefore, you should consume an adequate diet even before you become pregnant. Once you realize that you are pregnant, you may experience morning sickness, which tends to minimize thoughts of food. But even this early in pregnancy, you need to make sure that you eat a good diet. This should not be difficult, since your nutritional requirements at this point are still essentially the same as those for a nonpregnant woman, with the exception of your additional folic acid requirement.

Lack of certain nutrients in the diet, primarily vitamin B_6, is thought to contribute to morning sickness. Morning sickness may also occur because of low blood sugar after not eating all night. Some women experience nausea throughout the day, however, especially if they go for long periods without food. Many women find that natural remedies can bring relief from morning sickness. However, if natural remedies do not help you, and nausea and vomiting become a severe problem, your doctor can prescribe medication. Gratefully, morning sickness usually disappears by the fourth month.

Second Trimester

During the second trimester, nutritional needs increase, and you should begin consuming additional calories, vitamins, and minerals by following the No-Risk Pregnancy Diet. The baby puts on very little weight during the second trimester. However, the maternal tissues greatly increase. The woman begins to lay down a store of fat for her body to utilize during lactation. Her uterus and breasts enlarge, the volume of amniotic fluid increases, the placenta grows in size, and the blood volume expands. Therefore, increased protein and fluid intakes are essential.

Third Trimester

During the last trimester, the baby gains weight rapidly. His brain grows the fastest during the last 2 months, and his liver stores up iron. Continue following the No-Risk Pregnancy Diet during this time—and beyond, if you breastfeed. You must take in sufficient calories and protein to ensure optimum development of the baby's brain and body. Dieting at this point is not beneficial for either of you, and fasting before doctor's appointments to minimize weight gain is foolish. Make certain that you eat well, and your weight gain will guarantee the health of both you and your baby.

If you experience increased swelling as your due date approaches, try adding more protein to your diet. In rare cases, swelling puts pressure on the nerves in the wrist, resulting in tingling, numbness, and pain in the hands and fingers. This is called carpal tunnel syndrome. Additional vitamin B_6 may help relieve this condition or prevent its further development. Occasionally, a hand splint is necessary to provide relief. The symptoms of carpal tunnel syndrome will gradually subside following delivery.

NUTRITIONAL HINTS

The handling and processing of food can affect its nutritional value. A knowledge of the various food preparation methods can help you derive the maximum nutrients from the meals and snacks you prepare each day.

Natural Remedies for Morning Sickness

If you suffer from morning sickness, try the following natural remedies:

❏ Eat dry crackers or toast before rising in the morning.

❏ Avoid greasy, fried, or highly spiced foods.

❏ Drink teas made from small amounts of herbs such as raspberry leaf, peppermint, or chamomile.

❏ Eat frequent high-protein snacks during the day and at bedtime.

❏ Increase your intake of the B vitamins, especially B_6, or eat foods rich in vitamin B.

❏ Wear the wristbands that are designed to prevent motion sickness using acupressure on the wrists. They can be purchased in dive shops and sporting goods stores.

Your caregiver may recommend other natural remedies.

Vegetables

Buy fresh vegetables that are in season. Steam them or cook them quickly in a small amount of water to preserve the nutrients. Cook them just until tender.

Frozen vegetables can add variety to your menus when fresh ones are not available. Cook frozen vegetables the same as fresh, using just a little water (usually 1/2 cup per regular-size box). Be careful not to overcook them.

Canned vegetables are just slightly less nutritious than fresh and frozen if they are prepared properly. Because they have already been fully cooked during the canning process, they should only be warmed. Further cooking will decrease their nutritional value.

For maximum benefit from the vegetables you prepare, save all the cooking water. This water often contains more vitamins and minerals than the vegetables themselves do. Use the water in spaghetti sauce, chili, gravies, soups, stews, casseroles, stuffings, cream sauces, pot roasts, and other recipes. Mild-tasting cooking water—from vegetables such as corn, peas, or green beans—can be used in any recipe that calls for water, even cakes and muffins. If you have no immediate use for the water, freeze it.

Wheat Germ

Wheat germ is a versatile and nutritious food that can be added to almost any dish. Its concentrations of protein, vitamin B_1 (thiamine), vitamin E, and iron can fortify cake, muffin, and pancake mixes. Add about 1/2 cup of wheat germ per regular-size box of mix. You can also use wheat germ as a topping for casseroles. You can add it to most ground beef recipes, at the rate of about 1/2 cup per pound of meat. Mix it with peanut butter for a nutritious sandwich spread, or add it to your baby's mashed banana. Use wheat germ as a cereal, served with milk, or add it to any cooked or cold cereal for extra nutrition. It can be used in almost any cookie recipe, in addition to or in place of nuts. Its nutlike flavor will enhance the taste of most foods. Let your imagination create new uses for wheat germ.

Brewer's Yeast

Brewer's yeast is a natural vitamin B complex concentrate that can be purchased in health food stores. Because its flavor is somewhat strong, you will probably want to use it first in recipes that require cooking. Cooking seems to produce a milder flavor. For example, you can add brewer's yeast to a recipe for dark-colored cookies. Use about 1 tablespoon per average batch. You can also add brewer's yeast to pancakes, cakes, and breads. For instant energy, stir 1 to 3 tablespoons into 12 ounces of vegetable or fruit juice.

The most nutritious brewer's yeast is the powdered form, but the instant flakes dissolve better and have a milder taste. Tasteless brewer's yeast is also available. In addition, brewer's yeast comes in tablets, but huge quantities must be consumed to be of value.

Honey

Honey is a natural form of sugar that is slightly more nutritious than processed sugar. It contains 1 milligram of calcium per tablespoon, but brown sugar contains more—nearly 12 milligrams per tablespoon. Honey contains 65 calories per tablespoon, as compared to 40 calories per tablespoon for granulated sugar. As with all sweets, honey should have a limited place in your diet. The best way to obtain sugar is to consume fruits, vegetables, and milk.

Do not give raw honey to a baby under 1 year of age. In addition, never dip a pacifier in honey to encourage the baby to accept it. The baby could develop infantile botulism from spores that may be present in the honey.

Peanut Butter

Peanut butter is a very rich source of protein, as are all nut butters. You can easily make peanut butter yourself in a blender, or you can buy freshly ground or natural peanut butter in your health food store or supermarket. Many commercial manufacturers use too much salt, extra (often unhealthy) fat, and unnecessary sugar, as well as other additives. Lower-fat versions of many brands are now available.

General Hints

Get in the habit of fortifying almost everything you cook. Add wheat germ, powdered milk, brewer's yeast, or anything else that is nutritious. For example, doctor up a frozen pizza with wheat germ, freshly sliced tomato, 1/2 pound freshly cooked hamburger, and extra cheese.

Cooking nutritionally is a challenge, but it can also be fun. Many nutrition books are available that contain recipes which are easy to prepare as well as nutritionally superior. You can compensate for the additional cost by not buying "valueless" foods such as soft drinks, cookies, and potato chips. In time, you will witness even greater savings because of fewer doctor and dentist bills.

If your family has well-established but poor eating habits, make dietary changes slowly. You will neither reach your nutritional goal nor have a happy family if you try to change a lifetime of eating habits in 1 week. Make only one change at a time—and do not mention it! Gradually, as the weeks change into months, you will have a family that is eating and enjoying truly nutritious foods. The highly refined and valueless foods will simply have fallen by the wayside, forgotten and not missed.

To calculate the amount of protein, calcium, and iron that you are eating each day, see Table 3.1 on page 54. Although these are not the only nutrients you need, they are very important and need to be consumed in adequate amounts. By eating sufficient quantities of these nutrients, as well as a vitamin C–rich food every day, you can be sure that you are getting all the nutrients necessary for a balanced diet. Follow the No-Risk Pregnancy Diet when planning your meals.

To use Table 3.1, write down everything you eat and drink for 24 hours. Calculate how much protein, calcium, and iron you consumed using the table and compare your totals to the daily requirements for a pregnant woman. If you are deficient in your consumption of a certain nutrient, refer back to the table to find foods that are high in that nutrient. Another good way to test yourself is to add up your day's totals after dinner. If you are low in any category, you can look through the chart to identify which foods would be best for your evening snack.

In addition to protein, calcium, and iron counts, Table 3.1 also includes the calorie count for each food listed. This is to help you determine which foods supply the most nutrition for the least number of calories.

Honey Warning

Do *not* dip a pacifier in honey to entice your infant to accept it. Honey may contain botulism spores.

Table 3.1. Protein, Calcium, and Iron Counts of Selected Foods

	Serving Size	Protein (gms)	Calcium (mgs)	Iron (mgs)	Calories
Daily requirement		75–100	1,500–2,000	36	2,600
DAIRY					
Cheese					
Natural (such as	1 (1-inch) cube	4	128	0.2	70
Cheddar or Swiss)	1 ounce	7	213	0.3	105
Pasteurized processed	1 (3/4-ounce) slice	4	120	0.2	70
Parmesan, grated	1 tablespoon	3	80	0.1	45
Cottage cheese					
Creamed	1/2 cup	15	106	0.4	120
Uncreamed	1/2 cup	19	101	0.4	98
Custard (baked)	1/2 cup	7	139	0.5	148
Egg (raw)	1 large	6	27	1.1	80
Frozen yogurt	1 cup	6	295	0.1	200
Ice cream	1 cup	6	175	0.1	300
Milk					
Whole	1 cup	9	288	0.1	160
2-percent	1 cup	9	288	0.1	145
1-percent	1 cup	9	293	0.1	110
Skim	1 cup	9	298	0.1	90
Buttermilk	1 cup	9	298	0.1	90
Yogurt (made from partially skimmed milk)	1 cup	8	295	0.1	120
DRY BEANS AND PEAS, NUTS, AND PEANUTS					
Almonds (roasted)	1/2 cup	13	166	3.4	425
Beans, canned (such as Great Northern or Navy)	1/2 cup	8	37	2.3	115
Black-eyed peas, dry (cooked)	1/2 cup	7	21	1.6	95
Cashew nuts, salted or unsalted (roasted)	1/2 cup	12	26	2.6	380
Lima beans (cooked)	1/2 cup	8	28	2.8	130
Peanut butter	1 tablespoon	4	9	0.3	95
Peanuts (roasted)	1/2 cup	19	54	1.5	420
Pork and beans, canned	1/2 cup	8	70	2.4	155

	Serving Size	Protein (gms)	Calcium (mgs)	Iron (mgs)	Calories
FRUITS					
Apple	1 medium	trace	8	0.4	70
Apple juice	8 ounces	trace	15	1.5	120
Apricots					
Fresh	3 average	1	18	0.5	55
Dried	1/2 cup	4	50	4.1	195
Banana (3 per pound)	1 banana	1	8	0.7	85
Cantaloupe	1/2 medium	1	27	0.8	60
Grapefruit	1/2 average	1	22	0.6	55
Grapes, seedless	1 cup	1	17	0.6	95
Orange, Florida variety	1 average	1	67	0.3	75
Orange juice					
Florida, fresh	1 cup	2	25	0.5	110
Frozen, reconstituted	1 cup	2	25	0.5	110
Prune juice	1 cup	1	36	10.5	200
Prunes					
Fresh	4 average	1	14	1.1	70
Cooked	1/2 cup	1	30	2.3	148
Raisins, dark	1/2 cup	2	50	2.8	230
Strawberries, fresh	1 cup	1	31	1.5	55
Watermelon	1 (4-x-8-inch) wedge	2	30	2.1	115
GRAIN PRODUCTS					
Biscuit	1 average	3	46	0.6	140
Bran flakes	1 cup	3	20	1.2	95
Bread					
Rye	1 slice	2	17	0.4	55
White	1 slice	2	19	0.6	60
Whole-wheat	1 slice	2	23	0.5	55
Corn flakes	1 cup	2	5	0.4	110
Corn muffin	1 average	3	50	0.8	150
Crackers, saltines	4 (2-x-2-inch) crackers	2	4	0.2	70
Oat cereal, flakes	1 cup	3	44	1.3	115
Oatmeal (cooked)	1 cup	5	21	1.4	130

	Serving Size	Protein (gms)	Calcium (mgs)	Iron (mgs)	Calories
GRAIN PRODUCTS (continued)					
Pancakes	1 (4-inch) pancake	2	27	0.4	60
Pasta (such as macaroni or spaghetti), enriched (cooked)	1 cup	5	11	1.3	155
Pizza, cheese	1/8 of 14-inch pie	7	107	0.7	185
Popcorn					
Plain	1 cup	1	1	0.3	25
With butter-flavored oil	1 cup	1	1	0.3	65
Rice (cooked)					
Enriched, long grain, converted	1 cup	4	20	1.6	170
Brown, whole grain	1 cup	5	4	0.8	170
Rice cereal, flakes	1 cup	2	9	0.5	115
Waffle, enriched	1 (7-inch) waffle	7	179	1.0	210
Wheat cereal					
Shredded	1 ounce	3	12	1.0	100
Flakes	1 cup	3	12	1.3	105
Wheat germ	1/2 cup	9	25	3.2	123
MEAT, POULTRY, AND FISH					
Bacon (broiled or fried crisp)	2 average slices	5	2	0.5	95
Beef, lean					
Ground (broiled)	4 ounces	23	10	2.9	185
Sirloin (broiled)	4 ounces	36	14	4.4	230
Chicken					
Breast (fried)	1/2 average	25	9	1.3	155
Drumstick (fried)	2 average	24	12	1.8	180
White meat (broiled)	3 ounces	20	8	1.4	115
Chile con carne, canned					
With beans	1 cup	19	80	4.2	335
Without beans	1 cup	26	97	3.6	510
Fish (baked)	3 ounces	22	25	0.6	135
Fish sticks, breaded (baked)	5 average	19	13	0.5	200
Ham (boiled)	1 (2-ounce) slice	11	6	1.6	135
Hot dog (8 per 1-pound package) (broiled)	2 hot dogs	12	6	1.6	310

	Serving Size	Protein (gms)	Calcium (mgs)	Iron (mgs)	Calories
MEAT, POULTRY, AND FISH (continued)					
Liver, beef (sautéed)	4 ounces	30	12	10.0	260
Pork					
Chop (broiled)	1 average	16	8	2.2	260
Ham (baked)	3 ounces	18	8	2.2	245
Sausage					
Links (pan-fried)	2 (1-ounce) links	5	2	0.6	125
Patty (pan-fried)	1 average	5	2	0.6	125
Shrimp, meat only (steamed)	3 ounces	21	98	2.6	100
Tuna, canned	3 ounces	24	7	1.6	170
VEGETABLES					
Asparagus, canned	6 average spears	2	18	1.8	20
Broccoli, fresh	1/2 cup	3	66	0.6	20
Brussels sprouts, frozen	1/2 cup	3	21	0.7	23
Cabbage (cooked)	1 cup	2	75	0.5	35
Carrot, fresh	1 average	1	18	0.4	20
Coleslaw	1 cup	1	52	0.5	120
Corn					
On the cob, fresh	1 (5-inch) ear	3	2	0.5	70
Canned	1/2 cup	3	5	0.5	85
Cucumber, fresh	6 (1/8-inch) slices	trace	8	0.2	5
Green beans, fresh	1/2 cup	1	31	0.4	15
Lettuce, fresh	1/4 average head	1	23	0.6	15
Okra, fresh	8 average pods	2	78	0.4	25
Peas, frozen	1/2 cup	5	19	1.5	58
Potatoes					
Baked	1 average	3	9	0.7	90
French fried, frozen, fried in fat	10 (2-×-1/2-×-1/2-inch) pieces	2	9	0.7	155
French fried, frozen, heated in oven	10 (2-×-1/2-×-1/2-inch) pieces	2	5	1.0	125
Spinach, fresh (cooked)	1/2 cup	3	84	2.0	20
Tomato, fresh	1 medium	2	20	0.8	35

	Serving Size	Protein (gms)	Calcium (mgs)	Iron (mgs)	Calories
MISCELLANEOUS					
Brownie, from mix	1 average	1	8	0.4	95
Cookie					
Chocolate chip	1 average	1	4	0.2	50
Vanilla or chocolate sandwich	1 average	1	2	0.1	50
Doughnut, cake type	1 average	1	13	0.4	125
Fat					
Butter	1 tablespoon	trace	3	0.0	100
Margarine	1 tablespoon	trace	3	0.0	100
Cooking oil	1 tablespoon	1	0	0.0	125
Pie					
Apple	1/7 of 9-inch pie	3	11	0.4	350
Cherry	1/7 of 9-inch pie	4	19	0.4	350
Pumpkin	1/7 of 9-inch pie	5	66	0.7	275
Soft drink					
Cola	12 ounces	0	0	0.0	145
Ginger ale	12 ounces	0	0	0.0	115
Root beer	12 ounces	0	0	0.0	150
Soup					
Beef bouillon	1 cup	5	trace	0.5	30
Chicken noodle	1 cup	4	10	0.5	65
Clam chowder	1 cup	2	36	1.0	85
Split pea	1 cup	6	32	1.5	140
Vegetable with beef broth	1 cup	3	20	0.8	80

Adapted from *Composition of Foods—Raw, Processed, Prepared* (Washington, DC: U.S. Department of Agriculture, 1963). Used with permission.

NONFOOD ITEMS AND DRUGS DURING PREGNANCY

Americans are a drug-oriented society. As adults, we routinely consume—and encourage our children to consume—many medicines without considering that even most over-the-counter substances are drugs.

Virtually all drugs and medications taken during pregnancy cross the placenta and reach the baby. The baby often gets an equal amount of the drug dosage, although the drug is taken with the woman's age and weight in mind. Fetal growth and development are so rapid that a drug can have a profound effect on the baby even though it is considered mild. Many drugs are harmful only at particular points in pregnancy or only if used in conjunction with other drugs or agents. The exact connections between some drugs and birth defects are difficult to trace, since humans are not used as experimental subjects. Therefore, you should be careful about taking or using *any* drug during pregnancy. No drug is *known* to be safe, even though it may not be considered harmful. Always weigh the potential risks against the possible benefits before taking any medication.

Often, a drug-free treatment can provide relief. For example, a headache may be caused by tension or by going for a long period without eating. Lie down with some relaxing music or apply an ice bag. Try eating, if you have not done so for a while. Some women have found headache relief by applying firm fingertip pressure to the following acupressure points—the temples, the area midway between the eyebrows, and the back of the neck, along the hairline. You may find circular massage to be more effective than direct pressure. The pressure points will be tender to the touch. This tenderness will help you locate the correct points. (For a further discussion of this method of pain relief, see "Acupressure" on page 102.)

Backaches are often caused by poor posture. Using good body mechanics and the pelvic rock may be more beneficial than taking a pill. (For a discussion of proper body mechanics as well as descriptions of several conditioning exercises including the pelvic rock, see Chapter 4.) Constipation can be avoided by consuming a high-fiber diet, drinking plenty of fluids, and getting enough exercise. Colds can be relieved by resting, drinking extra fluids, and using a vaporizer for a stuffy nose. Cold and flu medications do not cure; they just relieve symptoms. Taking them will not make you well faster and may harm your baby.

If you do develop a medical problem, such as a urinary tract infection, or have a pre-existing condition, such as diabetes or heart disease, you may need to take medication. If a problem is not treated, it could be more dangerous to the fetus than the medication. Your doctor will recommend the medication or treatment that he feels is the safest during pregnancy.

A number of nonfood items have been shown to have harmful effects on the developing fetus. These items include cigarettes, alcohol, marijuana and recreational drugs, caffeine, some food additives, and certain medications.

Cigarettes

Smoking during pregnancy is considered to be one of the leading preventable causes of low birth weight.[10] Pregnant smokers give birth to smaller babies, have greater chances of premature birth and placental malformations, and have more premature rupture of the membranes and stillbirths. Their babies also have

"Those cigarettes are killing me."

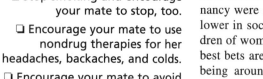

Hints for the Father-to-Be

❑ Stop smoking and encourage your mate to stop, too.

❑ Encourage your mate to use nondrug therapies for her headaches, backaches, and colds.

❑ Encourage your mate to avoid alcohol and recreational drugs.

a higher incidence of sudden infant death syndrome (SIDS)[11] and have been shown to be intellectually 3 to 5 months behind the children of nonsmokers.

In addition, some effects have been found to be lasting. Follow-up studies have shown that the 7-year-old children of women who smoked during pregnancy were shorter in stature, tended to have retarded reading abilities, rated lower in social adjustment, and had more behavioral problems than the children of women who did not smoke during pregnancy.[12] While pregnant, your best bets are to stop smoking or cut down as much as possible, and to avoid being around others who are heavy smokers. A direct relationship exists between the number of cigarettes a woman smokes per day and the degree to which her baby is affected.

Even if their mothers did not smoke during pregnancy, infants living in households where others smoke are at increased risk. They are more than twice as likely to die of SIDS than those living in smoke-free environments.[13] According to an article in *Pediatrics*, the infants of women who smoke more than twenty cigarettes a day are more likely to have recurrent ear infections. Researchers believe that "sidestream cigarette smoke causes a buildup of mucus and there is evidence that smoke can paralyze the cells that move this mucus out of the middle ear. Evidence also indicates that smoke interferes with the ability of white cells to fight infection in the middle ear."[14] These researchers also suggest that women who smoke are less likely to breastfeed, thus depriving their infants of this important immunity booster.

If you are a smoker, pregnancy is the best time to stop. The immediate and future benefits for you and your unborn baby are immeasurable.

Alcohol

Current research has proven that alcohol has a toxic effect on the developing fetus. If you drink during pregnancy, the alcohol quickly crosses the placenta and saturates the fetal blood supply in the same concentration that is present in your blood. According to a report to the U.S. Congress, prenatal alcohol exposure is a leading cause of mental retardation in the Western world.[15]

A study published in the *Journal of the National Cancer Institute* in 1996 links consumption of alcohol during the last 6 months of pregnancy with infant leukemia, a rare disease.[16] The National Cancer Institute (NCI) recommends further studies to verify this finding.

Babies born to women who are heavy drinkers have a 50-percent chance of having fetal alcohol syndrome (FAS). This syndrome includes mental retardation, slowed body growth before and after birth, learning difficulties, lower IQs, and physical abnormalities. Less severe symptoms, known collectively as fetal alcohol effect (FAE), are associated with behavioral and mental problems, poor physical coordination, short attention span, and hyperactivity.[17]

There is no known safe level of alcohol consumption for a pregnant woman. Even two drinks a day may cause a lowered birth weight in babies. Be sure to avoid any type of drinking binge during pregnancy or if you just suspect you are pregnant. One big party is not worth the risk to your baby. You would be wise to give up drinking alcoholic beverages completely while pregnant.

Marijuana, Cocaine, and Other Recreational Drugs

Marijuana affects the baby as much as it does the woman. In animal studies, temporary brain cell alterations occurred in the fetuses of rats exposed to mar-

"I wish I could tell her what those drinks do to me."

ijuana smoke.[18] Some reports have indicated that pregnant women who smoke marijuana in excess, as well as women who take lysergic acid (LSD), may cause chromosomal damage in their babies.[19]

The effects of crack cocaine are equally alarming. They include possible miscarriage, low birth weight, malformations, and stillbirth. With any drug addiction, the newborn must suffer the horrors of withdrawal. Follow-up studies on children whose mothers used cocaine during pregnancy concluded that this exposure "has a significant effect on three-year cognitive abilities as measured on the Stanford-Binet scale."[20] Do not risk ruining your child's development. Stay away from marijuana, crack, and other drugs while you are pregnant.

Caffeine

Caffeine is a stimulant present in coffee, tea, cola drinks, chocolate, and some over-the-counter medications. Recent studies have shown that heavy caffeine consumption—that is, over 300 milligrams per day—can increase a woman's chance of delivering a baby with a low birth weight.[21]

A 1993 study in the *Journal of the American Medical Association* reported that consuming the amount of caffeine in 1 1/2 to 3 cups of coffee per day

Table 3.2. Caffeine Levels in Common Sources

Source	Amount	Caffeine Content
Barqs root beer	12 ounces	23 milligrams
Caffeinated water	16.9 ounces	50–125 milligrams
Cappuccino, instant	8 ounces	25–102 milligrams
Cappuccino flavored ice cream	1 cup	8–15 milligrams
Chocolate bar	1 average	10–31 milligrams
Cocoa, prepared	1 cup	6–42 milligrams
Coffee, brewed	8 ounces	135 milligrams
Coffee, decaffeinated, brewed	5 ounces	3 milligrams
Coffee, instant, prepared	5 ounces	66 milligrams
Coffee flavored ice cream	1 cup	40–85 milligrams
Coffee flavored yogurt	8 ounces	45 milligrams
Cola	12 ounces	37–47 milligrams
Dr. Pepper	12 ounces	41 milligrams
Excedrin or Anacin	1 tablet	60 milligrams
Josta	12 ounces	58 milligrams
Mellow Yello	12 ounces	51 milligrams
Mountain Dew	12 ounces	55 milligrams
Sunkist Orange Soda	12 ounces	40 milligrams
Surge	12 ounces	51 milligrams
Tea, brewed	5 ounces	50 milligrams
Tea, iced, bottled	16 ounces	15–100 milligrams
Tea, instant, prepared	5 ounces	30 milligrams

Hints for the Father-to-Be

❏ Give your mate early morning snacks if she has morning sickness.

❏ Remind your mate that morning sickness is usually over after the first trimester.

❏ Cook nutritious meals for your mate.

❏ Encourage your mate to follow the No-Risk Pregnancy Diet.

❏ Help your mate in the kitchen if cooking smells make her nauseated.

❏ Provide healthy snacks for your mate.

nearly doubled the risk of miscarriage. In addition, drinking 3 or more cups of coffee a day during the month before becoming pregnant also increased this risk. Other studies have not always agreed. An article in the same journal 10 months earlier reported that drinking three or fewer 8-ounce cups of coffee per day did not increase the risk of miscarriage or affect fetal development.[22] Drinking 1 or 2 cups a day may not harm your baby. On the other hand, you are pregnant for only 9 months and should do everything possible to ensure a healthy child.

Caffeine is found in many common food and nonfood items. It is also present in products that you may not associate with being high in caffeine. See Table 3.2 on page 61 for a listing of the more popular ones, along with their caffeine contents.

Many delicious decaffeinated coffees and teas are now available. However, milk, water, and fruit juices should make up the bulk of your fluid intake for maximum nutrition. Coffee has no nutritional value.

Food Additives

Food additives such as saccharin, nitrates, nitrites, artificial colors, artificial flavors, preservatives, and PCB and PBB (industrial chemical wastes often found in freshwater fish) are possibly related to increased susceptibility to cancer and birth defects.[23] Saccharin presents a special risk to a male fetus if consumed by his mother. The FDA reports that studies indicate a positive correlation (a 60- to 100-percent increased risk) between saccharin ingestion during pregnancy and bladder cancer in male offspring.[24] Aspartame—which is marketed as Nutrasweet, an artificial sweetener used in soft drinks and packaged foods, and Equal, a granulated sugar substitute—has not yet been fully tested. The FDA has recommended moderation in its use during pregnancy. For optimum safety, you should eliminate all artificially sweetened substances from your diet while pregnant.

Medications

Over-the-counter and prescription medications all pass through the placenta to the baby. Therefore, you should check with your caregiver before taking any medication during pregnancy. Drugs used to treat such symptoms as pain, nervousness, sleeplessness, runny nose, heartburn, nausea, cough, or constipation can be avoided by using common sense, good nutrition, and relaxation techniques. Do not take aspirin, sedatives, antihistamines, barbiturates, diuretics, hormones, diet pills, antacids, cough medicines, or tranquilizers. Some of these are thought to be associated with jaundice, bleeding, or cleft palate in babies.[25] Pseudoephedrine, a common decongestant, has been linked to a rare abdominal defect in which the abdominal wall has a hole that allows the intestines to protrude outside the body.[26]

The drug Accutane, used to treat severe acne, is known to cause major birth defects when taken during the first 3 months of pregnancy.[27] Avoid taking this drug if there is any chance that you are pregnant.

PICA

Pregnant women are often known to have unusual cravings for everyday foods. Pica is the craving for and ingestion of bizarre items, such as laundry starch, detergent, clay, dirt, flour, baking powder, baking soda, or frost scraped from the refrigerator. Some of these cravings may indicate a severe iron deficiency, and some may be harmful. Clay from specific geographic areas, such as Georgia and Mississippi, has been found to impair the absorption of iron, although this is not the case for the clay from Texas. Argo Gloss Starch also does not impair iron absorption.

The hazard of pica is that the craved items are consumed in place of nutritious food. Pica may also cause profuse salivation, impactions in the bowel, or parasitic infection in the intestine. You should inform your caregiver if you experience pica.

CONCLUSION

Every day, you make decisions that affect your health. You choose what foods or substances you will consume and what you will avoid. These decisions are particularly important when they also affect the health and development of another person—that tiny being growing inside of you who is totally dependent on your choices. Providing him with the best possible building blocks, while avoiding toxic substances, is the most important thing you can do for him while you are pregnant. Women who are well nourished have better pregnancies, shorter labors, and healthier babies.

Chapter Four

Exercise

or Moving Through Pregnancy

Most experts agree that women who exercise during pregnancy feel better, look better, and get back into shape faster after their babies are born than women who do not exercise. Many women have an uncomfortable pregnancy. They move laboriously from chair to chair, feeling tired, constipated, and depressed. They look at the rippling fat on their legs and sigh, not realizing that with a good exercise program, it would not have to be that way.

There are two basic types of exercise—sustained and conditioning. Running, walking, and bicycling are popular kinds of sustained exercise. During sustained exercise, the heart rate increases and thus strengthens the heart and lungs (cardiopulmonary system). Also during sustained exercise, breathing becomes deeper, resulting in more oxygen getting into the bloodstream. This means that more oxygen gets to the baby as well.

Conditioning exercises, such as calisthenics and isometrics, improve muscle tone by using a muscle over and over again. Using muscles during exercise also prevents fat deposits from building up in those areas and keeps the muscles stretched. Doing a combination of both types of exercise—sustained and conditioning—provides the best overall benefit. You burn calories, tone your muscles, develop your cardiovascular system, and saturate your body with oxygen.

In this chapter, specific exercises to prepare the body for labor and delivery are presented. Proper body mechanics are also discussed, as are measures to relieve some of the minor discomforts of pregnancy.

SOME CAUTIONS

When exercising, you must make some concessions to your pregnancy. Because your circulatory and other systems have more work to do when you are pregnant, you may find that you are not able to exercise for as long at one time as you did before you were pregnant. You may also find that you require more time to rest and recover after exercise. You should never exercise to the point of breathlessness. If you are out of breath, your baby may be low on oxygen. You should always be able to talk as you exercise. If you cannot talk while exercising, slow down and catch your breath.

Overdoing an exercise session can affect the fetus. The negative effects include elevated fetal temperature, changes in the blood flow through the pla-

Best and Worst Exercises

The following exercises are the best during pregnancy:

❑ Walking
❑ Swimming
❑ Water aerobics
❑ Low-impact aerobics
❑ Stationary cycling
❑ Jogging (if it was done prior to pregnancy)
❑ Tennis (preferably doubles)
❑ Golf
❑ Bowling

The following exercises should be avoided during pregnancy:

❑ Scuba diving
❑ Water skiing
❑ Surfing
❑ Downhill skiing
❑ Cross-country skiing
❑ Horseback riding
❑ Snowmobiling
❑ Contact sports

Your caregiver may have other exercises to add to these lists.

Exercise Guidelines

If you choose to exercise during your pregnancy, make sure that you observe the following guidelines:

❑ Check with your caregiver before you begin an exercise program.

❑ Wear loose, comfortable clothing and a support bra.

❑ Always include warm-up and cool-down periods.

❑ Start slowly, gradually increasing the length and intensity of your exercise.

❑ Stop and rest when you feel out of breath.

❑ Choose activities with smooth, continuous movements rather than jerky, bouncy ones.

❑ Avoid straining.

❑ Stop if you feel pain or experience any other warning signs.

❑ After the first trimester, do not lie on your back.

❑ Do not hold your breath.

❑ Drink plenty of fluids.

❑ As you get larger, avoid exercises that require balance.

❑ Make sure that your pulse rate does not rise above 140 beats per minute.

❑ Avoid exercising in hot, humid weather.

❑ Avoid hot tubs, steam rooms, and saunas.

Your caregiver may have additional guidelines for you.

centa, reduced levels of maternal glucose, and increased uterine contractions.[1] Regular 20- to 30-minute exercise sessions several times per week are safer than one long session per week. Moderate to high levels of sustained maternal exercise have been associated with reduced birth weight.[2] Women who exercise regularly should increase their caloric intake to ensure having a baby of normal birth weight.

Stop exercising and consult your caregiver if you feel pain. You may just have performed an exercise incorrectly, or you may have overdone it a bit. Discontinue exercising if you begin bleeding or cramping. Get your caregiver's okay before beginning to exercise again. Be careful not to overstretch while doing an exercise or even while doing an everyday activity such as getting out of bed. During pregnancy, the body secretes a hormone that loosens joints and ligaments slightly in preparation for birth. This makes it easier to strain ligaments and muscles. In addition, the center of gravity changes as the baby grows and the uterus enlarges. This increases the risk of sprains, stress fractures, and falls.

Most doctors feel that women can continue the activities they enjoyed before becoming pregnant, even something as strenuous as jogging. The exercises considered to be the best during pregnancy are walking, swimming, water aerobics, low-impact aerobics, stationary cycling, jogging (if it was done prior to the pregnancy), tennis (preferably doubles), golf, and bowling. Avoid scuba diving, water skiing, surfing, downhill skiing, cross-country skiing, horseback riding, snowmobiling, and contact sports. These pose a higher risk of injury for the pregnant woman and her fetus. No matter what kind of exercise you choose to do, begin it slowly, as early in your pregnancy as possible, and gradually increase your stamina.

The American College of Obstetricians and Gynecologists supports exercise for women who have been performing it regularly and do not overdo it. In a recent study, brisk walking was the exercise preferred by pregnant women. The researchers found that the exercise group in the study experienced less maternal weight gain, but greater infant birth weight and gestational age. They also experienced shorter labors. The women in the sedentary group complained of more discomforts such as swelling, leg cramps, fatigue, and shortness of breath.[3]

Another benefit of exercising regularly throughout pregnancy is increased secretion of endorphins, natural painkillers produced in the body. These natural opiates give a feeling of well-being during and after exercise. In addition, they cross the placenta and may provide pleasant sensations to the baby. Researchers have found that women who exercise regularly have higher levels of endorphins while exercising than do women who exercise irregularly.

PROPER BODY MECHANICS

The way you use the different parts of your body to move, as well as to lift, hold, and carry things, is called body mechanics. Having proper body mechanics is important during pregnancy to help minimize discomforts as your body gets larger. The first step in achieving proper body mechanics is maintaining good posture. Good posture is essential throughout pregnancy because your center of gravity changes. You will be tempted to compensate for the change by slumping. Instead, you should maintain the same good posture you had before becoming pregnant. Standing erect lessens back discomfort, improves digestion, and enhances body image.

While standing, the way you hold your head influences the position of the rest of your body. If you let your head hang forward, your body will droop like a wilted flower. Instead, think tall! Hold your head up, with your chin tucked in and your neck straight. Lift your shoulders up and pull them back. This position will keep you from cramping your rib cage, which can make breathing difficult and possibly cause indigestion.

Pay special attention to your pelvic area, which contains the weight of the growing baby. Think of your pelvis as a bowl filled with liquid. To prevent the liquid from spilling out, tilt the "bowl" back by tightening your abdominal muscles and tucking your buttocks under. By keeping the pelvis tilted back, you can prevent excess tension in the muscles of your lower back. You can maintain proper pelvic alignment by bending your knees slightly and keeping your body weight over your feet. Place your body weight on the center of each foot, never on the inside. If you stand for long periods, put one foot on a small stool to flex the hip.

While sitting in a chair, use the back of the chair as a guide to sit up straight. Do not slump forward. Straight-back chairs are preferable over cushioned chairs during pregnancy for this reason. Place a pillow behind your neck or the small of your back to increase your comfort. Rest the entire length of your thigh on the seat of the chair. The chair seat should be high enough for you to keep your knees even with your hips.

Tailor sitting, or sitting Indian style, is an excellent position during pregnancy. It is comfortable and improves the circulation in the legs while stretching and increasing the flexibility of the inner thigh muscles. Sit this way whenever possible—for example, when you watch television, read the newspaper, fold clothes, or peel potatoes. If your legs become tired, stretch them out in front of you.

The supine position, or lying flat on your back, for extended periods of time is not recommended after the first trimester. This position puts the increasing weight of the baby and uterus on your major vessels, causing them to be compressed. This can lower your blood pressure, thereby reducing the amount of blood traveling to the placenta and the baby. If you must lie on your back (during an examination, for example), modify the position by placing a pillow in the small of your back for support and bending your knees. Refrain from doing exercises that require you to lie on your back.

Side-lying is a position that takes the weight of the baby off your back and groin, and allows the joints to be flexed loosely. A pillow placed lengthwise between your legs will make it easier for you to relax. Position another pillow under your abdomen to take the strain off your lower back. You may feel comfortable lying further over on your abdomen, in a three-quarter position. Place your lower arm behind your back and position your upper arm and leg forward, supported by pillows.

Good Posture   Poor Posture

Maintaining good posture during pregnancy lessens back discomfort, improves digestion, and enhances body image.

Poor posture can cramp the rib cage, making breathing difficult and causing indigestion.

Good posture is also important when sitting in a chair.

Tailor sitting is not only comfortable, but improves the circulation in the legs and increases the flexibility of the inner thigh muscles.

To get up from a supine position, roll onto your side and push yourself to a sitting position with your arms.

Lifting incorrectly using the back muscles can cause back strain. Instead . . .

. . . lower yourself to one knee, grasp the object, then return to a standing position by pushing yourself up with your rear foot.

To get up from a supine position, first roll onto your side and then push yourself to a sitting position with your arms. If you are in bed, swing your legs over the side of the bed. Be careful not to twist your body as you get up. This technique will help you to avoid strain to both your back and abdominal muscles.

When walking, remember all the points of correct posture described in the preceding pages. Bring your legs straight forward from the hip. Do not swing them sideways in a "waddle."

Be careful when climbing stairs. Lift your body up using your legs, rather than pulling yourself up with your arms. Lean slightly forward as you go up, placing your foot completely on each step. During your postpartum period, climb steps slowly, tightening your abdominal and pelvic floor muscles, and let your leg muscles do the work.

Many women, especially those with small children or toddlers, find that some lifting is necessary during pregnancy. Incorrect lifting can put excessive strain on the back and the pelvic floor. Therefore, it is important to learn how to lift correctly.

Avoid lifting heavy objects. Lift only what you can lift easily with one arm. To lift, get close to the object and lower yourself into a squat, bending at the knees, not at the waist. Keep your feet parallel and your back straight, and as you lift the object, straighten your legs without twisting your body. An alternate method is to place one foot in front of the other and slowly lower yourself to one knee. Lift the object by pushing yourself up with your rear foot, keeping your back straight.

A small child can climb onto a stool or chair, enabling you to lift him or her without straining your back.

CLOTHING

The kind of shoes you wear can affect your posture. During pregnancy, it is best to wear flat shoes with good support. High-heeled shoes thrust your body weight forward, putting strain on your lower back and on the ligaments of your hips and knees. You might also have difficulty maintaining your balance. Wearing high heels habitually causes the calf muscles to tighten into a knot and to actually become shorter. If you routinely wear high heels, wear progressively lower and lower heels to allow your calf muscles to stretch slowly.

You may find that support hose relieve your tired leg muscles and help prevent varicose veins. Avoid garters because they constrict circulation in the leg and cause varicose veins.

A good bra is important during pregnancy to provide support for your breasts as they increase in weight. This support will minimize upper backache as well as improve posture. If your breasts do not have support, the tissues will stretch and the breasts may sag. Select a maternity/nursing bra with wide, nonelastic straps that provides support during pregnancy and that can be used later while breastfeeding. (For tips on purchasing a maternity/nursing bra, see "How to Select a Nursing Bra" on page 118.)

Many women have found that a maternity support helps backache and provides extra support to the abdomen. It is especially helpful for women carrying more than one baby. The support lifts the uterus up and may also help to relieve pelvic and bladder pressure. It encourages the pregnant woman to maintain good posture. A maternity support is not a girdle. It can be either a one-piece body suit or an abdominal support with or without straps that go over the shoulders. It is usually made of a washable spandex-type material.

The kind of panties you wear is also important. Cotton panties are preferable over nylon because the fabric absorbs moisture. This helps prevent irritation and infection. All your maternity clothing should be made of absorbent fabric that does not trap body heat. Pregnant women often feel warmer than nonpregnant individuals do, and clothing made from nonabsorbent fabrics such as polyesters hold onto body heat. Cotton clothes are more comfortable. Maternity clothing should also be loose fitting and allow for growth.

SUSTAINED EXERCISE

If you have not been exercising, then begin with an activity such as walking. Walking is an excellent exercise for pregnant women. A brisk walk of 15 to 20 minutes each day helps develop cardiovascular strength and uses almost every muscle in the body. Even women with little extra time can usually find some time to walk.

Bicycling (ideally on a stationary bicycle for safety reasons) is another excellent sustained exercise. In addition to improving cardiovascular strength, it develops the abdominal muscles that support the baby. Swimming is unique because the buoyancy of the water helps support the baby, thus allowing you to use your leg, arm, and back muscles more freely. Swimming for 15 to 20 minutes several times a week builds muscle tone and strength.

CONDITIONING EXERCISES

Conditioning exercises are designed to improve the muscle tone of specific areas—in this case, those areas involved in childbirth—and to relieve tension and minor discomforts. Do all of the following exercises slowly and smoothly; jerky movements can overstretch tendons and ligaments, and possibly dislocate joints. In the beginning, do each exercise only two to three times per session. Increase the number of repetitions (reps) gradually until you reach the recommended amount. For maximum benefit, exercise twice a day. Make sure you continue to breathe normally as you exercise. Do not hold your breath. For ease of practice, do the exercises in the order they are given.

Rib Cage Stretch

Benefits: Relieves tension in the shoulders. Strengthens the upper back. Helps relieve indigestion.

Directions: Inhale slowly while raising both your arms over your head to the count of 5. Then exhale, slowly lowering both your arms, first straight out in front of you, then down by your sides, and then behind your back, to the count of 5.

Caution: Do not arch your back while doing this exercise.

Note: Raising your arms above your head will *not* harm the baby, as an old wives' tale suggests.

Frequency: 5 reps per exercise session. In addition, do this exercise whenever you feel tension in your upper body or have indigestion.

Rib cage stretch: Raise your arms above your head . . .

. . . then lower them behind your back.

Arm Circles

Benefits: Strengthen the upper back and upper arm muscles. Relieve tension.

Directions: Stretch your arms out to your sides with your palms up. Make small circles to the count of 10, gradually increasing the size of the circles. Then reverse the direction of the circles, starting with large circles and gradually decreasing their size to another count of 10.

Frequency: 2 reps per exercise session.

Arm circles. Shoulder rotation.

Shoulder Rotation

Benefit: Helps relieve upper backache caused by poor posture or heavy breasts.

Directions: Place your fingertips on your shoulders and make backward circles with your elbows. Then reverse the direction and make forward circles.

Frequency: 10 reps per exercise session. In addition, do this exercise whenever you have an upper backache.

Calf Stretch

Benefits: May help decrease leg cramps and improve circulation.

Directions: Stand facing a wall or your partner with one leg well forward and the foot flat on the floor (lunge position). Stretch the other leg behind you with the knee straight and the foot flat on the floor. Press your hands flat against the wall or your partner's hands. Lunge forward, bending the front leg at the knee and stretching the other calf. Stretch gradually for 15 to 20 seconds. Repeat with the other leg forward.

Frequency: 3 to 5 reps per exercise session.

Calf stretch.

Pelvic Rock

Benefits: Improves posture. Relieves back discomfort and pelvic congestion. Increases abdominal muscle tone.

Directions: This exercise can be performed in several positions. Among the more popular are the following:

Pelvic rock while kneeling: Kneel on your hands and knees . . .

. . . then press your spine up at the lower back.

Pelvic rock while standing.

1. Kneel on the floor on your hands and knees. Do not let your spine sag. Align your head with your spine, tuck in your bottom, pull up your abdominal muscles, and press your spine up at the lower back just enough to erase the spinal curve; do *not* hump your back. Hold this position for a few seconds, then return to the starting position. Repeat the exercise using a constant rhythm and a rocking motion. *Note:* This exercise in this position is beneficial during labor if you are experiencing back labor.

2. Stand erect in front of a mirror and check your posture from the side. With one hand on your pubic bone and the other at the small of your back (to help you get the motion), rotate your pelvis forward, tucking in your bottom and abdomen. Relax and repeat, using a constant rhythm and a rocking motion. (This movement is exhibited to a degree by belly dancers.)

Frequency: 10 reps per exercise session.

Tailor Press

Benefits: Stretches the ligaments and muscles on the insides of the thighs and increases their elasticity.

Directions: Sit on the floor with your legs in front of you and the soles of your feet pressed together and pulled toward your body. Using only the muscles of your legs, press your knees downward. You will feel your inner thigh muscles pull slightly.

Cautions: Do not bounce your knees. Discontinue the exercise if you feel pain around your pubic bone, which may indicate some separation at the joints. Do not do this exercise after birth until the perineum has healed.

Note: Preparing the ligaments and muscles on the insides of the thighs promotes comfort during the birth process. Practicing the exercise also helps you to relax and feel at ease in this position while giving birth.

Tailor press.

Frequency: 10 reps per exercise session.

Isometric Tailor Press

Benefits: Strengthens the inner thigh muscles. Strengthens the pectoral muscles, which support the breasts.

Directions: Sit on the floor with your legs in front of you and the soles of your feet pressed together and pulled toward your body. Cup your hands around the outsides of your knees and try to pull your knees up with your hands while pushing them down with your leg muscles. Hold for a count of 5. Now place your hands on top of your knees and try to press your knees down with your hands while pulling them up with your leg muscles. Hold for another count of 5. There should be no movement in either of these positions, just stationary counterpressure.

Isometric tailor press: Pull your knees up . . .

. . . then press your knees down.

Cautions: Do not bounce your knees. Discontinue the exercise if you feel pain around your pubic bone, which may indicate some separation at the joints. Do not do this exercise after birth until the perineum has healed.

Frequency: 5 reps per exercise session.

Tailor Stretch

Tailor stretch.

Benefits: Stretches the ligaments and muscles on the insides of the thighs and increases their elasticity. Stretches the lower back and calf muscles.

Directions: Sit on the floor with your legs stretched out in front of you and angled apart. Lean forward and either reach each hand to its corresponding ankle, right hand to right ankle and left hand to left ankle, or slide both hands down the same leg until you reach the toes, then repeat with the other leg.

Cautions: Discontinue the exercise if you feel pain around your pubic bone, which may indicate some separation at the joints. Do not do this exercise after birth until the perineum has healed.

Frequency: 10 reps per exercise session.

KEGEL EXERCISES

The Kegel (pronounced *KEE gull*) exercises are named after Dr. Arnold Kegel, the doctor who developed them. They are designed to restore or improve pelvic floor muscle tone and to increase control over those muscles. Figure 4.1 on page 74 shows the results of a well-toned pelvic floor, while Figure 4.2 on page 74 shows the consequences of a poorly toned pelvic floor.

The muscles of the pelvic floor can be pictured as a hammock that is attached to the pubic bone in the front and to the coccyx in the back. (See Figure 4.1.) This muscle group is also called the pubococcygeus, named for its position. Part of this group—the sphincters—forms a figure *8* around the urethra and vagina in the front and the anus in the back. (See Figure 4.3 on page 74.)

With exercise, you can achieve voluntary control of the pelvic floor, which will enable you to release the area consciously during birth. Relaxation of the pelvic floor will allow your baby an easier passage during expulsion and perhaps reduce the need for an episiotomy. During birth, the pelvic floor muscles are stretched, and Kegel exercises can help eliminate the problems that often result from this stretching—prolapsed (sagging) uterus, prolapsed bladder, and urinary stress incontinence (uncontrolled leaking of urine caused by sudden movements such as coughing or sneezing). If done shortly after birth, contracting the muscles of the pelvic floor shortens the muscle fibers that were stretched during birth and thus aids their restoration. After an episiotomy, doing this exercise increases the blood flow to the area, reducing swelling and aiding healing.

An added bonus of the Kegels is increased sensitivity in the vagina during sexual intercourse. Improving the pelvic floor muscle tone causes the vagina to become more snug, and the response from the nerve endings beneath the vaginal walls is improved. Your husband, too, will appreciate this extra snugness! The benefits of the Kegels therefore are not limited to the period of birth, but extend into the immediate postpartum period and can continue throughout life.

To exercise the pelvic floor muscles, your first step should be to locate the muscles. Do this by contracting the muscles around the urethra as if you were trying to hold back urine. Next, try urinating at a time when your bladder is not full, stopping and starting the flow of urine several times. Stopping the flow tightens the pelvic floor, while releasing the flow relaxes it.

Another way to check for pelvic floor tension and relaxation is to tighten your vaginal muscles around your partner's penis during sexual intercourse. Your partner can give you feedback on the effectiveness of this exercise.

Once you recognize your pelvic floor muscles, you should discontinue practicing the exercise during urination. Instead, practice after urinating, contracting the pelvic floor by lifting and tightening the muscles and holding for a count of 20 seconds. Try to maintain the contraction. If you feel the muscles relaxing, tighten them again. Do 1 rep of this exercise ten times a day. This particular Kegel exercise has been labeled the super Kegel by Penny Simkin, a well-known childbirth educator and author. It increases the awareness of and the strength of the pelvic floor muscles.

Hint: Do a super Kegel while washing your hands after urinating, since it is best to perform this exercise with an empty bladder. Or, use everyday activities such as washing the dishes and stopping at red lights as reminders to do a super Kegel. After the baby comes, doing a super Kegel with every diaper change will ensure plenty of practice.

Hints for the Father-to-Be

❏ Compliment your mate on her good posture.

❏ Do not let your mate lift heavy items.

❏ Exercise with your mate.

❏ Remind your mate to do her Kegels.

❏ Take walks with your mate.

❏ Discourage your mate from becoming overheated in hot tubs, saunas, and steam rooms.

❏ Discourage your mate from performing strenuous exercise on hot, humid days.

❏ Start performing perineal massage on your mate at 34 weeks.

❏ Offer to give your mate a massage.

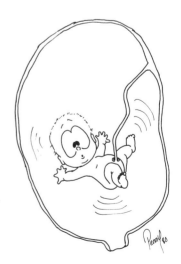

I know she needs to exercise— but on a TRAMPOLINE?!

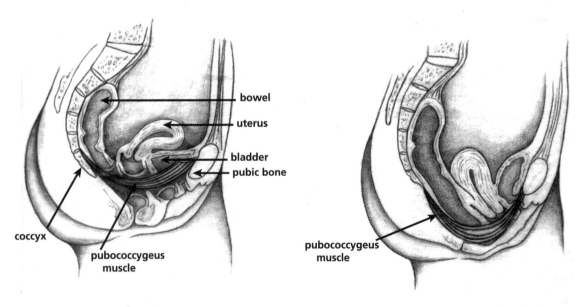

Figure 4.1. A well-toned pelvic floor.

Figure 4.2. A poorly toned pelvic floor.

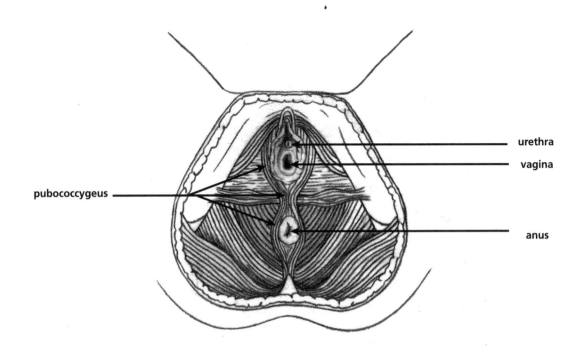

Figure 4.3. A cross section of the pelvic floor muscles.

Another Kegel exercise that will help prepare you for birth is the elevator exercise. This exercise is done by imagining the pelvic floor to be an elevator. Contract the muscles upward, from the first floor to the fifth floor, stopping at each floor and getting tighter as you go higher. Then, relax downward, releasing tension at each floor, from the fifth to the first. Continue to release the muscles completely, to a basement level, by giving them a slight push. This is the degree of relaxation you will need to achieve while pushing the baby down the birth canal. Always return to the second level to maintain a constant degree of tension in the pelvic floor. Imagine a hammock returning to its normal, higher position when you get up.

With continued practice, you should develop enough control to lift the elevator ten floors. Make sure that you do not hold your breath. This Kegel exercise helps you to achieve deeper muscle control in preparation for pushing. Practice this exercise, with your bladder empty, at least twice a day.

You should practice super Kegels for the rest of your life, not just while you are pregnant. Super Kegels will help you maintain optimum muscular condition of the pelvic floor. According to Penny Simkin, this is the most important exercise a woman of any age can do.

PERINEAL MASSAGE

Just as you prepare your muscles for delivery by toning them through exercise, you should also prepare your perineum for the stretching required to accommodate the baby's head. Perineal preparation is especially important if you want to avoid an episiotomy. Many caregivers feel that prenatal preparation of the perineum increases the chances of delivering with an intact perineum.

Prenatal preparation includes several steps. The most important is to determine your caregiver's philosophy about episiotomies. Is he willing to support you in your desire to deliver without one? Secondly, excellent nutrition will contribute to healthy tissues that stretch and heal rapidly. Some caregivers feel that taking a supplement of vitamin E will also enhance your tissues' ability to stretch. Practicing relaxation, pushing, and Kegels will help you gain additional control over the perineal area, which is so important during labor.

Perineal massage will prepare you for the sensations of stretching that you will feel during your baby's birth. It also increases the elasticity of the perineal tissues and thus reduces your need for an episiotomy. You should begin practicing perineal massage around the thirty-fourth week. You can either do the massage yourself or have your partner perform the massage for you. The person doing the massage should have clean hands and short fingernails. For lubrication, use your body's secretions or some K-Y jelly, vitamin E oil, or vegetable oil. If you have a scar from a previous episiotomy, spend additional time massaging vitamin E oil into the scar tissue. Some women find that taking a warm bath prior to the massage is helpful. You may want to use a mirror the first few times for optimum vision.

To perform the massage yourself, insert your thumbs into your vagina about 1 inch and press them toward your rectum. Stretch your perineal tissues outward toward your thighs using your thumbs. Keep the knuckles of your thumbs together to prevent overstretching. You should feel a stinging or burning sensation. Continue to hold this pressure for an additional 2 minutes, until the perineum becomes somewhat numb and the tingling is less distinct. Then gently slide the tips of the thumbs back and forth as you continue to stretch

A Hint for a Lifetime

Kegels are exercises for the rest of your life.

the tissues outward. Continue this action for another couple of minutes. If your partner does the massage, he should insert his index fingers into your vagina and keep his thumbs on the outside. The knuckles of his index fingers should remain together.

Note: Do not practice perineal massage if you have active herpes lesions or another infection. Also, avoid the urethral area to prevent a bladder infection.

EXERCISES FOR THE RELIEF OF DISCOMFORT

The following exercises are designed to provide relief for specific discomforts. Become familiar with them, so that you can use them when necessary.

Rib Cage Stretch

Benefits: Relieves tension in the upper body. Helps relieve indigestion.

Directions: See "Rib Cage Stretch" on page 69.

Neck Circles

Benefit: Relieve tension in the neck and shoulder area.

Directions: Begin with your chin resting on your chest. Slowly rotate your head around to the right, then to the back, then to the left, and finally to the front again. Rotate your head in this clockwise motion two more times, then reverse the direction and rotate your head three full times in a counterclockwise motion. Try to totally relax the muscles of your neck as you do this.

Caution: Rotate your head very slowly and carefully if you have ever had a neck injury.

Frequency: Whenever you feel tension in your neck or shoulders.

Shoulder Rotation

Benefit: Helps relieve upper backache.

Directions: See "Shoulder Rotation" on page 70.

Foot Bending and Stretching

Benefits: May help to prevent varicosities, swollen ankles, and leg cramps by improving circulation.

Directions: Sit or lie down and elevate your legs. Flex your ankles, drawing your toes toward you. Rotate your feet first in one direction, then in the opposite direction.

Caution: Do not point your toes. If you develop leg cramps, pull your toes toward your head until the cramps subside.

Frequency: Whenever you sit for long periods, do 1 rep three to four times per hour.

Calf Stretch

Benefit: Relieves leg cramps.

Directions: Sit on the floor with your legs straight out in front of you. Have your partner press down on the knee of the cramped leg with one hand and

Calf stretch.

grasp your foot, pushing your toes toward your head, with his other hand. Use steady pressure. Continue until the cramp is relieved.

Frequency: Whenever necessary.

PREGNANCY MASSAGE

Massage has been a vital part of prenatal and postpartum care in many cultures for centuries. In this country, women have only recently begun to experience the pleasures and benefits of pregnancy massage. Many of the stresses that your body undergoes as a result of pregnancy can be alleviated at the hands of a professional massage therapist who is specially trained in working with pregnant women. Some of the benefits of regular massage during pregnancy include:

❑ Relief from muscle spasms and cramps, especially in the back and neck.

❑ Increased blood circulation, which brings more blood to the tissues and to the placenta, providing greater nutrition to the tissues and enhanced waste product removal.

❑ Increased circulation of the lymphatic system, resulting in less swelling and more energy.

❑ Improved muscle tone.

❑ Increased relaxation, brought about by the sedating effect of massage on the nervous system, as well as by the release of endorphins.

❑ Reduction of stress.

❑ Development of sensory awareness.

❑ Alleviation of stress on weight-bearing joints.

❑ Emotional support and physical nurturance.

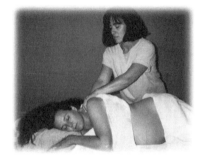

An expectant mother enjoys a massage administered by a licensed massage therapist trained in working with pregnant women.

If you are interested in experiencing this type of therapy, be sure to use a licensed massage therapist. He or she should be aware of any pregnancy restraints, such as the contraindication of deep tissue work.

You may prefer to have your partner massage you. This can be a pleasurable experience for you both, as long as he uses a gentle touch. You can sit up, straddling a chair and facing backwards, or you can lie down on the edge of a bed, in a side-lying position with pillows under your neck and abdomen, and between your legs. If you use the latter position, your partner can kneel on the floor or sit in a chair, and massage one side of your body. Then you can roll to the other edge of the bed so that he can massage your other side. Choose the position that you find most comfortable. Select a warm, quiet place, and use scented candles and soft music for a soothing and relaxing atmosphere. The use of oil or lotion will make stroking easier. It is important that you take a few minutes to rest following the massage and have assistance when getting up. Make sure you drink plenty of water to flush out the toxins that are released during the massage.

The following are suggested massage routines for your partner to try on you. Your partner can vary the techniques according to your preferences and as he feels comfortable. Be sure to let him know if any of his stroking causes pain or discomfort.

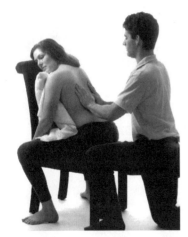

Gently move your hands up her back, across her shoulders, and then down along the sides of her back.

Make small circular movements with your thumbs.

For the Labor Partner: Back and Shoulder Massage

The following routine is excellent for relieving tension in the back and shoulder area:

1. Have the woman sit backwards on a chair, leaning over a pillow on the chair back. Stand, kneel, or sit on another chair directly behind her.

2. Pour a little oil into the palm of your hand and rub your hands together until they are warm.

3. Place your hands on the woman's lower back, with your palms on either side of her spine. Slowly and gently move your hands up her back, across her shoulders, and then down along the sides of her back. Repeat this motion several times, covering her whole back with oil and checking for tension.

4. On the woman's lower back, place your thumbs in the grooves on either side of the spine. Using moderate pressure, make small circular movements with your thumbs, slowly moving up the back. When you reach the top of the spine, place your index fingers on either side and gently bring your hands down the back. Repeat this motion three times.

5. Massage the woman's neck area by cupping one hand on the back of her neck at the base of the skull. Gently squeeze, then gradually move your hand down the neck, continuing to squeeze and release. Repeat this three times.

6. Cup your hands on the woman's shoulders close to her neck. Squeeze her shoulders, using your full hands, and work from the neck out to the ends of the shoulders. Be careful not to pinch. Repeat this three times.

7. Finish with a light full-hand massage, beginning at the top of the woman's head and slowly moving down her back to her buttocks. Repeat this three times.

Have the woman rest for a few minutes before getting up. Or, have her remain seated so that you can give her the following hand and arm massage.

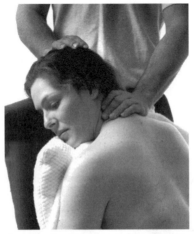

Cup your hand on her neck and gently squeeze, gradually moving down.

Squeeze her shoulders, using your full hands.

For the Labor Partner: Hand and Arm Massage

The following routine helps to relax the woman's hands and arms:

1. Have the woman sit backwards on a chair, leaning over a pillow on the chair back. Stand in front and slightly to the side of the woman.

2. Pour a little oil into the palm of your hand and rub your hands together until they are warm.

3. Gently lift one of the woman's arms at the wrist using both your hands. Apply gentle traction and use an easy jiggle motion to relax the arm.

4. Turn the woman's palm up and use your thumbs to make small circles over the entire palm.

5. Turn her hand over and, starting at the pinky fingernail, lightly compress the entire length of the finger as you move toward the base. Apply gentle traction to the finger when you reach the base. Repeat with the remaining three fingers and the thumb.

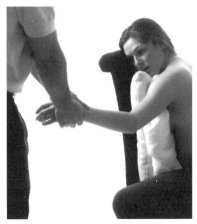

Apply gentle traction and use an easy jiggle motion to relax the arm.

Use your thumbs to make small circles over the entire palm.

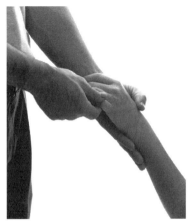

Lightly compress the entire length of each finger.

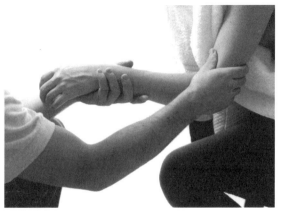

Hold the woman's wrist with one hand as you stroke the outer aspect of her arm.

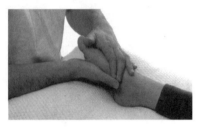

Pull down and off her foot as if you were "pulling" out her tension.

Cup your hand around her heel and gently squeeze.

Place your thumbs just below her ankle bone and gently circle.

Gently work the arch with your thumbs, using circular motions.

Lightly stroke each toe.

6. Hold the woman's wrist with one hand as you stroke the outer aspect of her arm, starting at the wrist and slowly moving up the entire length of the arm. You can use long strokes or a gentle cupping and squeezing motion. Repeat this motion three times.

7. Switch your hands and stroke the inner aspect of her same arm. Repeat this motion three times.

8. Massage the muscle at the top of her shoulder with your full palm, making circular motions.

9. Finish the massage by stroking down the entire length of the arm.

Repeat the sequence with the other hand and arm.

For the Labor Partner: Foot Massage

The following routine soothes not only the feet, but the entire body:

1. Have the woman sit in a chair; sit in another chair facing her. Rest her foot on a pillow in your lap.

2. Pour a little oil into the palm of your hand and rub your hands together until they are warm.

3. Place one hand on the bottom of the woman's foot and the other hand on top. Pull down and off her foot as if you were "pulling" out her tension. Repeat this motion three times.

4. Cup your hand around her heel. Gently squeeze the back of her foot.

5. Place your thumb just below her ankle bone and gently circle this area with firm pressure. *It is important that you do not go any higher than the ankle bone.* An acupressure point is located just above the ankle, and stimulating it could initiate labor.

6. Gently work the arch with your thumbs, using circular motions to cover the entire arch area.

7. Lightly stroke each toe, working from the big toe to the little one.

8. Finish by again putting one hand on the bottom of the woman's foot, one hand on top of her foot, and pulling down and off the foot. Repeat this motion three times.

Repeat the entire sequence with the other foot.

CONCLUSION

If you did not exercise on a regular basis prior to becoming pregnant, now is a good time to start. Exercising can increase your energy, relieve constipation and backache, stimulate the baby, and condition your muscles for birth. It will also help you feel better mentally, knowing that you are doing something positive for yourself and your baby.

Choose the type of exercise that suits you best and that you can fit into your lifestyle. Some women prefer several short sessions throughout the day, while others find it easier to stay motivated if they join a pregnancy exercise class. Toward the end of your pregnancy, you will need to taper off. Walking is the best exercise to do during the last month before giving birth.

Chapter Five

Tools for Labor

or Beyond "Hee Hee" Breathing

Childbirth training prepares you for birth on three levels—mentally, emotionally, and physically. You prepare mentally by learning all that you can about the natural process of labor and birth, and about the complications that sometimes arise. You also become aware of various comfort measures that can reduce pain perception and provide relief. Emotionally, you are encouraged to think positively about your birth experience and to openly face your anxieties and fears. Physically, you practice exercises that promote comfort during pregnancy and birth, as well as techniques that encourage relaxation, offer distraction, and help focus attention during labor.

Fernand Lamaze, a French obstetrician, first realized the importance of preparing for childbirth while observing the labors and deliveries of Russian women using the techniques of psychoprophylaxis. The word *psychoprophylaxis* means "mind prevention," and the techniques involve using the mind to reduce the awareness of pain sensations. Upon returning to France, Dr. Lamaze modified the techniques and began practicing them in his clinic. The techniques have since become synonymous with his name. Marjorie Karmel introduced the Lamaze method into the United States in the 1950s after having a baby under Dr. Lamaze's guidance in France.

The Lamaze method is based primarily on the principles of conditioned response training discovered by the Russian physiologist Ivan Pavlov during experiments with dogs. Each time Dr. Pavlov fed the dogs, he would ring a bell. When the dogs saw the food, they would naturally salivate. After a period of time, whenever the dogs heard the bell, they would salivate. In other words, they became conditioned.

Using Pavlov's theory for childbirth preparation, you will learn new, positive responses to the contractions of labor. When you feel a contraction begin, you will consciously relax and breathe in a patterned, controlled way, rather than holding your breath and tensing your muscles the way an unprepared woman does.

Your preparation will also break the fear-tension-pain cycle, first identified by Dr. Grantly Dick-Read as a major contributor to the pain of childbirth. This cycle accurately describes the labor experience of an unprepared woman, who enters labor full of fear—fear of the unknown; fear of what she was taught to expect by television, books, friends, family, and other sources; and fear of being alone. Her natural response to this fear is to tense her muscles. (Consider how you react to narrowly missing a traffic accident or watching a terrifying movie.) This muscular tension creates painful contractions, which make her more fearful of the next contraction, which is then more painful because of the increased tension. The cycle continues, increasing in intensity throughout the labor.

Adequate preparation, however, breaks the cycle. The fear is eliminated by gaining information about labor and birth, which promotes a positive attitude. The tension is relieved by using relaxation techniques, and the painful sensations of labor are reduced by using breathing techniques and other comfort measures. The fear-tension-pain cycle is therefore eliminated before it can even begin during labor. Other methods of prepared childbirth are based on the same principles, but offer variations in techniques.

In France, during the early days of Lamaze, the laboring woman was accompanied and aided by her *monitrice*, the woman who taught her the techniques. In the United States, the labor companion is usually someone emotionally close to the woman, such as her husband, boyfriend, mother, sister, or close friend, who is also trained in the techniques. In addition, some women choose to hire a professional labor support person, or *doula*. The love and support of the labor companions are other important factors in creating a confident, positive attitude toward the childbirth experience.

Chapter 4 presented physical exercises to enhance comfort during pregnancy and to prepare the body for giving birth. Chapter 6 will discuss the physical process of labor and birth, as well as normal hospital and birthing center procedures. This chapter focuses on the relaxation techniques and breathing patterns that will become your response to the contractions of your uterus during labor. A variety of other comfort measures that can be used by you or your partner during labor are also provided.

RELAXATION

A Skill for Life

Relaxation is not just a tool for labor, but also a skill for life.

Learning to relax is not just a skill for labor, but for life. This tool will benefit both you and your partner, who also learns the techniques. Many tribal cultures believe that pregnant women should be protected in a calm environment to ensure the health of the baby and a good delivery. Modern medicine is just beginning to understand the effects of stress on the body, especially during pregnancy and birth. Studies have shown that women who have more stress-producing factors in their lives during pregnancy develop a greater number of complications during pregnancy, labor, and birth.[1]

Stress and anxiety cause the release of hormones and chemicals that produce the fight-or-flight reaction. These substances cause the body to be able to react quickly to a life-threatening event. Long-term stress keeps the body at constant readiness, but it can also lead to illness.

During pregnancy, stress can cause insomnia, fatigue, headache, nausea and vomiting, high blood pressure, and preterm labor. Long-term stress in pregnancy may result in a low-birth-weight baby, as the hormones constrict the woman's blood vessels and reduce the amount of nutrients and oxygen that reach the fetus. In addition, the hormones cross the placenta and enter the baby's circulation. This may predispose the infant to increased irritability, restlessness, crying, and digestive upsets.

During labor, the stress hormones can cause fatigue, a longer and more painful labor, and an increased need for interventions. The hormones can also reduce the blood flow to the uterus and placenta, and can cause the baby to have distress. Stress increases the risk of cesarean section, for either failure to progress or fetal distress.

After the birth, stress can interfere with the woman's milk production and her ability to cope as a new parent. The body is less able to fight infection, as the stress hormones lower the white blood cells' ability to recognize germs and to produce antibodies against them. Prolonged stress leads to high blood pressure, heart attack, and stroke.

Learning how to relax your body is the single most important skill to develop as you prepare yourself for labor. Labor is hard work. The uterine muscle will contract intermittently over a period of hours to open the cervix and move the baby down the birth canal. This takes a great deal of energy. One source estimated that the same amount of energy is expended during labor as during a nonstop 12- to 18-mile hike. By relaxing all your muscles except the one that needs to contract—the uterus—you will keep more energy and oxygen available. You are less likely to become fatigued and may require less medical intervention.

When you hear the word *relaxed,* certain images come to mind—a rag doll, spaghetti, a drooping flower, a floppy hat. These are all images of extreme passiveness. A sleeping child is the picture of passive relaxation. What you will learn in the following pages is a more active, conscious form of relaxation, in which the mind is alert while the body is relaxed. Active relaxation involves the awareness and intentional release of tension. For example, slowly contract the muscles of your right arm. Now let the arm flop. That is passive relaxation. Again slowly contract the muscles of your right arm. Now slowly, with concentration, relax the different parts of your right arm. Feel the biceps, lower arm, hand, and fingers gradually relax. That is active relaxation. As you prepare for labor, you will learn to relax your body consciously. This process is technically called neuromuscular control (mind control of the muscles). You will learn a number of exercises designed to help you become skilled at relaxation.

Relaxation Basics

When preparing to practice any of the relaxation exercises described in this chapter, find or prepare a physical environment that is conducive to relaxation. Use a room that is comfortable and warm. Wear loose clothing and no shoes. Play soft music that is soothing and that you can take with you to the hospital or birth center.

Make sure that the supporting surface on which you lie is firm. If it sags, the support will be lost, and strain and muscle tension will result.

Assume a comfortable position, with all the parts of your body completely supported. Otherwise, the force of gravity will cause your unsupported body parts to do muscle work (contract). Several good positions in which to practice are:

❏ *Semireclining at a 45-degree angle.* This position makes it easy for your partner to check for muscle tension. Because of this, it is the best position in which to begin relaxation practice. To assume the position, recline at a 45-degree angle with pillows under your head, back, knees, and arms.

Hints for the Labor Partner

❏ Attend childbirth classes with your partner.

❏ Learn relaxation as a tool for your own benefit.

❏ Practice relaxation with your partner.

❏ Learn and practice breathing and pushing techniques with your partner.

❏ Help your partner practice breathing and pushing in the different labor positions.

❏ Provide your partner with sufficient pillows for support and comfort.

❏ Offer your partner a massage.

A Hint for the Mother-to-Be

❏ Relaxation will become automatic in labor if practiced frequently during pregnancy.

Sims' position.

❏ *Side-lying.* This position is the most comfortable for many women during labor while in bed. Lie on your side with pillows under your head, abdomen, and upper leg and foot.

❏ *The Sims' position.* This position is excellent for resting during pregnancy and for helping to alleviate back pain during labor. With the body positioned more forward than side-lying (three-quarters over), the weight of the uterus is taken off the back. Lie with your lower arm behind your back and pillows supporting your head, front shoulder and upper arm, front leg, and abdomen.

As you develop skill in relaxation, you can also practice your techniques while sitting up or kneeling on your hands and knees. Finally, no matter which position you use, remember to keep all your joints bent. This helps to reduce muscle tension, which can use the energy your body needs for labor.

For the Labor Partner: The Labor Partner's Role in Relaxation

A very important part of your role as a labor partner is to recognize tension in the woman. During labor, the woman may be so involved in what her body is doing that she becomes tense without even being aware of it. During practice, you should visually and physically check her for signs of tension. During labor, to avoid disturbing her, check her only visually for relaxation both during contractions and, as labor progresses, between contractions to ascertain that she is resting completely. If you observe tension, you will need to begin using one or more of the various techniques presented in this chapter to help her relax. Because each woman responds differently, it will be up to you to determine which techniques and comfort measures are the most effective for your partner. Additionally, certain measures may be more effective at different times in her labor.

To check your partner for relaxation, first check her visually. Is she frowning? Is her jaw clenched? Do her shoulders and neck look rigid? Are her toes flexed or curled? Are her fingers clenched?

Second, check her physically for relaxation by doing the following:

❏ Check her neck by gently rotating her head from side to side.

❏ Check her shoulders by placing your hands on them and gently moving them from side to side. Tense shoulders stay put, while relaxed ones move easily.

❏ Gently pick up her arm, firmly supporting it under the elbow and wrist. The upper arm, lower arm, and wrist should each move separately and feel heavy in your hands. If the arm is rigid and stiff, or if your partner lifts it for you, the arm is tense. Gently lower the arm to the supporting surface; never drop it! If you move her arm too abruptly, your partner will not trust you and will tense, rather than relax, to your touch. Repeat with the other arm.

❏ Check your partner's hips by placing your hands on the outside of each hip and moving the pelvis from side to side. Relaxed hips move easily.

❏ Lift one of her legs, supporting it under the knee and ankle, and check it the same way you checked the arm. A relaxed leg will be very heavy and its parts will move separately, the same as the arm. Gently lower the leg. The knee should flop to one side when the leg is set down on the pillow. Repeat with the other leg.

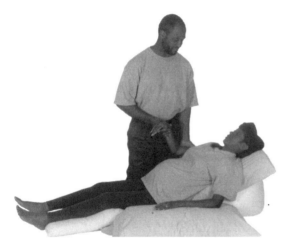

Checking the arm for relaxation.

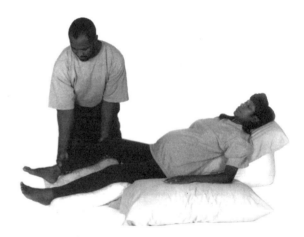

Checking the leg for relaxation.

If, in your checking, you find body parts that are not completely relaxed, try one of the following techniques:

❏ Quietly repeat, "Let your (body part) relax."

❏ Tell your partner to tense the body part as tightly as possible, then to slowly release it to the count of 10.

❏ Firmly stroke the tense body part or lightly massage it using circular motions.

Use whichever technique, or combination of techniques, works best for your partner.

Relaxation Techniques

Several steps are involved in learning to achieve total relaxation. Once you have mastered the Body Awareness/Tension Recognition Guide, you can move on to the more advanced relaxation guides. Practice with your partner, and make an audiotape that you can use if your partner is unavailable.

Body Awareness/Tension Recognition

The first step in learning relaxation involves developing a sense of body awareness and learning to recognize muscle tension. The goal of this first exercise is to make you aware of what your different body parts feel like when they are tense and when they are relaxed. You should practice this exercise with your labor partner, who can give you the verbal cues.

The verbal cues for the Body Awareness/Tension Recognition exercise, as well as the woman's actions and the labor partner's reactions, are presented in Table 5.1. When your partner gives you a verbal cue, breathe in slowly through your nose while tensing the specified body part. Feel the tightening of the muscles used to perform the action. Then breathe out slowly through your mouth and relax the body part. Feel the release as you relax the muscles. Have your partner observe the physical appearance of the tensed muscles, then check the body part both visually and physically for the degree of relaxation. For ease of checking, practice this exercise in the semireclining position.

Go through the Body Awareness/Tension Recognition Guide in order. When you have finished tensing and relaxing the final body part, take a few moments to go back over your body. If there are areas that are still tense, repeat the tensing and releasing of that muscle group. Before getting up, take several deep breaths, then slowly rise to an upright position.

Table 5.1. Body Awareness/Tension Recognition Guide

Verbal Cue	Woman's Action	Partner's Reaction
Pull up your toes.	Inhale slowly through nose and tense toes. Exhale slowly through mouth and relax toes.	Visually check tensed toes, then visually and physically check for relaxation.
Turn out your ankles.	Inhale slowly through nose and tense ankles outward. Exhale slowly through mouth and relax ankles inward.	Visually check tensed ankles, then visually and physically check for relaxation.
Bend your knees.	Inhale slowly through nose and flex knees with feet on floor. Exhale slowly through mouth and straighten legs, letting knees flop outward.	Visually check tensed knees, then visually and physically check for relaxation.
Squeeze your thighs together.	Inhale slowly through nose and press thighs inward. Exhale slowly through mouth and let thighs relax outward.	Visually check tensed thighs, then visually and physically check for relaxation.

Verbal Cue	Woman's Action	Partner's Reaction
Press your thighs toward the floor.	Inhale slowly through nose and press thighs downward. Exhale slowly through mouth and relax thighs.	Visually check tensed thighs, then visually and physically check for relaxation.
Tighten your buttocks.	Inhale slowly through nose and tense buttocks. Exhale slowly through mouth and relax buttocks.	Visually check tensed buttocks, then visually and physically check for relaxation.
Arch your back.	Inhale slowly through nose and tense upper and lower back. Exhale slowly through mouth and relax upper and lower back.	Visually check tensed back, then visually and physically check for relaxation.
Pull in your abdomen.	Inhale slowly through nose and tense abdomen. Exhale slowly through mouth and relax abdomen.	Visually check tensed abdomen, then visually and physically check for relaxation.
Expand your chest.	Inhale slowly through nose and fill lungs with air, tensing chest. Exhale slowly through mouth and relax chest.	Visually check tensed chest, then visually and physically check for relaxation.
Press your shoulder blades back.	Inhale slowly through nose and tense shoulders, pressing them back as far as possible. Exhale slowly through mouth and relax shoulders.	Visually check tensed shoulders, then visually and physically check for relaxation.
Shrug shoulders.	Inhale slowly through nose and shrug shoulders. Exhale slowly through mouth and relax shoulders.	Visually check tensed shoulders, then visually and physically check for relaxation.
Tense your hands by making fists.	Inhale slowly through nose and make tight fists. Exhale slowly through mouth and relax hands.	Visually check tensed hands, then visually and physically check for relaxation.
Extend your head backwards.	Inhale slowly through nose and tense neck muscles. Exhale slowly through mouth and relax neck muscles.	Visually check tensed neck muscles, then visually and physically check for relaxation.
Grimace.	Inhale slowly through nose and tense lips. Exhale slowly through mouth and relax lips.	Visually check tensed lips, then visually and physically check for relaxation.
Frown.	Inhale slowly through nose and tense mouth area. Exhale slowly through mouth and relax mouth area.	Visually check tensed mouth area, then visually and physically check for relaxation.
Clench your teeth.	Inhale slowly through nose and tense jaw. Exhale slowly through mouth and relax jaw.	Visually check tensed jaw, then visually and physically check for relaxation.

Verbal Cue	Woman's Action	Partner's Reaction
Wrinkle your nose.	Inhale slowly through nose and tense area above nose. Exhale slowly through mouth and relax area above nose.	Visually check tensed nose area, then visually and physically check for relaxation.
Close your eyes tightly.	Inhale slowly through nose and close eyes tightly. Exhale slowly through mouth and relax eyes.	Visually check tensed eyes, then visually and physically check for relaxation.
Lift your eyebrows.	Inhale slowly through nose and raise eyebrows as high as possible. Exhale slowly through mouth and relax eyebrows.	Visually check tensed eyebrows, then visually and physically check for relaxation.

Total Body Relaxation

The next step in refining your relaxation skills is to relax your entire body. The Total Body Relaxation exercise will help you to do this using verbal cues and mental images. As with the Body Awareness/Tension Recognition exercise, have your partner give you the cues and then observe you for relaxation. Table 5.2 presents the verbal cues, what you should do, and what your labor partner should observe. When you have completed the entire sequence, your partner can physically check your body for relaxation. Then take a moment to come back to the present, take 2 deep breaths, open your eyes, and slowly get up with your partner's assistance. After performing this exercise several times, you may be able to mentally take yourself through the routine, without the verbal cues from your partner.

Table 5.2. Total Body Relaxation Guide

Verbal Cue	Woman's Action	Partner's Reaction
Close your eyes, take several deep breaths, and begin to let the tension flow from your body. (Pause.) *Start at the top of your head and release any tightness in your scalp, moving it down the sides and back of your head.*	Relax scalp area.	Observe relaxation of face.
Lower your eyebrows.	Let eyebrows drop.	Observe relaxation of eyebrows.
Close your eyes. Feel your eyelids becoming heavy, your eyes sinking back into your head.	Relax eyes, lids, temples, forehead, and surrounding area.	Observe relaxation of eye area.
Let your jaw drop. Your lips should become slightly parted.	Relax jaw and slightly open mouth.	Observe relaxation of jaw.

Verbal Cue	Woman's Action	Partner's Reaction
Allow your head to rest against the pillow. (If her head is not supported, say: *Slightly lower your chin.*)	Relax head against support (or lower chin).	Observe relaxation of head.
Feel your shoulder blades open outward, like a dress falling off a hanger.	Relax neck, shoulders, and upper arms.	Observe relaxation of upper body.
Starting at your right shoulder, move any tightness down your upper arm, past your elbow, down your lower arm, past your wrist, through your hand, and out your fingers. (Read very slowly.)	Relax right arm from shoulder down to fingers.	Observe relaxation of right arm.
Repeating this on your left side, start at your left shoulder and move any tightness down your upper arm, past your elbow, down your lower arm, past your wrist, through your hand, and out your fingers. (Read very slowly.)	Relax left arm from shoulder down to fingers.	Observe relaxation of left arm.
Concentrate on your breathing. Slowly breathe in oxygen to your baby and slowly exhale carbon dioxide and tension. With each out-breath, sigh out a little more tension.	Exhale and relax body further. Be aware of tension release.	Observe relaxation of body.
Breathe in through your nose and out through your mouth, making each breath a little longer, until you feel very relaxed. Try to feel as if you are breathing right down your back, starting at the base of your neck and slowly moving down your upper back, past your ribs, down into your waist, and into your hips. (Read very slowly.)	Focus on breathing and relax back muscles.	Observe relaxation of back.
Starting at your right hip, move any tightness down your thigh, past your knee, down your calf, past your ankle, through your foot, and out your toes. (Read very slowly.)	Relax right leg from hip down to toes.	Observe relaxation of right leg.
Repeating this on your left side, start at your left hip and move any tightness down your thigh, past your knee, down your calf, past your ankle, through your foot, and out your toes. (Read very slowly.)	Relax left leg from hip down to toes.	Observe relaxation of left leg.
Feel every limb become heavy—your feet, lower legs, thighs, hips, hands, arms, shoulders.	Experience feeling of heaviness.	Observe relaxation of arms and legs.

Verbal Cue	Woman's Action	Partner's Reaction
The force of gravity is pulling you down into the Earth.	Experience feeling of sinking.	Observe relaxation of body.
Your knees are so heavy that they need to flop apart to the sides.	Feel legs become limp and open to sides.	Observe relaxation of legs.
Your whole body is melting and spreading across the floor.	Feel sensation of tension flowing outward.	Observe relaxation of body.
Now take a minute to go over your body. If you feel there is any area that is still holding tension, think about bringing some heat to the area, and release the area to the warmth.	Feel warmth of sun on tense area.	Observe relaxation of body, then physically check for *total* relaxation.

Touch Relaxation

Another technique that can aid dramatically in developing your skill at relaxation is touch relaxation. In touch relaxation, you respond to your partner's touch by relaxing tense muscles toward his hand. Practicing this nonverbal form of communication helps you learn to respond during labor to your partner's touching, stroking, and massaging with complete relaxation.

Touch relaxation is an effective method for learning how to relax the body.

To practice touch relaxation, contract a set of muscles upon your partner's verbal cue, then have your partner rest his hand on the contracted muscles. As soon as you feel your partner's touch, you should begin to release the contracted muscles toward his hand. See Table 5.3 for the recommended verbal cues, actions, and labor partner's reactions.

Note to the labor partner: Be sure to touch the contracted muscles with a relaxed but firm hand. Slowly mold your hand to the shape of the body part. If touching the body part does not bring about complete relaxation, stroke or massage the body part until it does relax.

Touch relaxation is one of the best techniques to use during labor.

Table 5.3. Touch Relaxation Guide

Verbal Cue	Woman's Action	Partner's Reaction
Contract your forehead.	Frown and wrinkle forehead.	Rest hand on forehead.
	Relax forehead.	Feel forehead relax.
Tense your face.	Grit teeth and clench jaw.	Place hands on sides of jaw.
	Relax jaw.	Feel jaw drop.
Tense your scalp.	Raise eyebrows.	Place hands on sides of scalp.
	Lower eyebrows.	Feel eyebrows lower.
Tense your right arm.	Clench right fist and stiffen entire right arm.	Rest hands on fist, stroke palm with thumbs, then slowly move hands up sides of arm to shoulder and press shoulder firmly.
	Relax right arm.	Feel muscles gradually relax from hand up to shoulder.
Tense your left arm.	Clench left fist and stiffen entire left arm.	Rest hands on fist, stroke palm with thumbs, then slowly move hands up sides of arm to shoulder and press shoulder firmly.
	Relax left arm.	Feel muscles gradually relax from hand up to shoulder.
Tense your abdomen.	Pull in abdomen.	Rest hand on curve of upper abdomen.
	Relax abdomen.	Feel abdomen expand outward.
Tense your shoulders.	Press shoulder blades back against supporting surface.	Rest hands on fronts of shoulders.
	Relax shoulders.	Feel shoulders move forward.
Tense your thighs together.	Press upper thighs together.	Touch outsides of thighs.
	Relax thighs.	Feel legs fall outward.
Tense your thighs downward.	Press legs and knees against floor.	Rest hands on tops of thighs.
	Relax thighs.	Feel legs rise and fall outward.
Tense your right leg.	Straighten and stiffen right leg, pointing toes upward.	Firmly touch instep of foot, stroke instep with fingers, then slowly move hands up to knee and then up to top of leg.
	Relax right leg.	Feel muscles gradually relax from foot to top of leg, with thigh falling outward.

Verbal Cue	Woman's Action	Partner's Reaction
Tense your left leg.	Straighten and stiffen left leg, pointing toes upward.	Firmly touch instep of foot, stroke instep with fingers, then slowly move hands up to knee and then up to top of leg.
	Relax left leg.	Feel muscles gradually relax from foot to top of leg, with thigh falling outward.
Tense your neck.	Raise chin in air and contract back of neck.	Rest hand on nape of neck.
	Relax neck.	Feel chin fall forward and muscles relax.
Tense your back.	Arch small of back.	Rest hands on sides of sacrum.
	Relax back.	Feel back drop toward floor.
Tense any other body part that you would like to.	Tense desired muscle group.	Touch tensed body part.
	Relax that muscle group.	Feel it relax.

Visualization

The final relaxation technique is visualization. Also known as imagery, visualization is the technique of picturing an image in your mind. It can be used as a preparation for labor and birth. You may have heard about this technique in reference to athletes preparing for competition. Prior to competing in an event, a gymnast will visualize her routine, a downhill skier will visualize the gates on the run, and an ice skater will mentally run through his upcoming performance. Prenatally, visualization can be practiced to aid relaxation and to mentally help you develop a positive attitude toward birth. During labor, it can keep you relaxed and help you focus on your body. For example, while in labor, picture your baby's head coming through your cervix, with your cervix resembling a turtleneck sweater. Other examples can be found in the following sample visualizations. Practice both visualizations in preparation for labor. During labor and delivery, choose the phrases and images that work best for you.

To practice, sit or lie in a comfortable, supported position. Play soft, soothing music in the background. (Use this same music during labor.) Your practice sessions will be most effective if your partner uses a soft, soothing tone of voice. He should speak slowly and pause frequently to allow the images to develop. In addition, he should pause for a count of 1 whenever he sees a dot; for example, ". . ." should prompt a pause of 1-2-3. The pause should be slightly longer at the end of a paragraph.

A Special Place. A Special Place is a visualization that can aid relaxation and that can be used during labor. For many women, entering the labor unit can be an unsettling experience. This is because the environment is unfamiliar. When you are in labor, use this visualization during your contractions to mentally take yourself away from the labor unit and to a familiar or secure place.

Have your labor partner recite the following to you:

> *Close your eyes . . . . take in a deep breath . . . . exhale . . . . and relax your body . . . . starting at your head . . . . and moving down to your toes . . . Take in another deep breath . . . exhale slowly . . . . and once more, slowly breathing in . . . . and out . . . . As you relax, picture in your mind a place that makes you feel very comfortable . . . . A place where you feel safe and secure . . . . A place where you are so protected that nothing can harm you or interfere with your thoughts . . . . A place where you can leave all your worries and surrender yourself to being at peace.*
>
> *This special place may be in a room in your home . . . . in the home where you spent your childhood . . . . a favorite vacation or honeymoon spot . . . . or a place you have dreamed about visiting . . . . . It may be a scene from a book . . . a movie . . . . or even a fantasy, a place that doesn't exist . . . . But, enter this place and look around . . . . Are you standing, sitting, or lying down? . . . . Is the temperature warm or cool? . . . . Is there a breeze blowing? . . . What are you wearing? . . . . Are there any familiar fragrances? . . . Are you alone? . . . . Take a few moments to familiarize yourself with your special place.*
>
> *As you gaze at your surroundings, focus on an object . . . . Stare at this object and allow it to become your focal point . . . . As you continue to stare at the object . . . concentrate . . . breathe slowly . . . and allow yourself to enter a level of deeper relaxation.* (Take a longer pause before continuing.)
>
> *Now, take several deep breaths . . . . mentally travel back to your present environment . . . . and slowly open your eyes . . . . Think about the serenity and peace you just experienced . . . and know that you can go back to this place whenever you choose.*

Practice this visualization during pregnancy. When you are in labor, you can either close your eyes and return to your special place during every contraction, or, if you keep your eyes open, you can stare at the focal point that you brought with you. For your focal point, use a picture of the object from your visualizations or, if possible, use the object itself. If you visited a place with water during your visualizations, you may find that laboring in a tub or shower enhances your relaxation.

Birth Visualization. The Birth Visualization will help you to prepare emotionally for birth as a normal, healthy event. You use your imagination to picture the process of labor and delivery. Do this visualization following a relaxation practice, such as the Special Place visualization, when you are calm and receptive to suggestion. Have your partner use a soothing tone of voice, increasing in volume and speed as the contractions accelerate and becoming softer and slower as the contractions recede.

Your partner should recite the following:

> *Concentrate on your breathing . . . . breathing deeply and peacefully . . . With each breath, allow yourself to let go more and more . . . . As you relax, picture in your mind a special place where you would like*

Hints for the Labor Partner

❑ Play soothing music while you recite a visualization.

❑ Speak slowly and pause frequently while reciting a visualization to allow the images to develop in your partner's mind.

to have your baby . . . . . . Take yourself there and become comfortable . . . . . Notice the surroundings . . . . What do you see? . . . . Are there any fragrances? . . . . . What textures do you feel? . . . . . Do you hear any sounds?

As you continue to breathe slowly and deeply, picture the uterus in your mind . . . large and pear shaped . . . round and full at the top . . . tapered and narrow at the bottom . . . a strong, muscular organ, capable of much hard work.

See the round, healthy, red placenta on the back of the uterine wall . . . . See the pulsating umbilical cord sending oxygen and food to your baby . . . . Watch your baby floating freely and peacefully in the warm, clear amniotic fluid . . . . His head is down in the pelvic cradle, just waiting for the day he will be born . . . . Hear your baby's heartbeat, strong and sure . . . . See the downy lanugo hair . . . . Look at the vernix covering his body like a protective coat . . . . Count his fingers and toes . . . Look at how long his nails have grown . . . It may be a boy . . . it may be a girl . . . but it is your baby continuing to grow and waiting to be born.

From your baby's point of view, look down at the cervix . . . See it puffy and soft, with the mucous plug sealing its opening . . . much like a cork in the neck of a bottle . . . protecting your baby from infection until it is time to be born.

Now take yourself forward in time to the day labor begins . . . . . See the cervix . . . . The mucous plug is gone, and the cervix is getting shorter and shorter as your uterus begins to contract . . . . Feel your baby's head pressing firmly against the cervix . . . helping it to stretch, and become thinner and thinner, and slowly open up.

You feel a contraction starting, much like a train approaching on a distant track . . getting closer and closer, and the contraction is getting stronger and stronger. Your baby's head is pressing harder and harder on the cervix. The cervix is stretching more and more, and the baby's head is coming down and down, and you open and open more, and the contraction begins to fade and fade, just as the train moves off into the distance . . . . Feel your body relax . . . Let all the tension go . . . Gather strength from within for the next contraction . . . Rest, and your baby also rests. (Repeat this paragraph two more times.)

As the next contraction comes, feel it growing in intensity, much like a large wave, rising higher and higher. Feel the cervix stretching and stretching as you feel the baby's head moving down, down, down into the cervix. Now feel the contraction subsiding . . . just as the wave comes to shore, as you know it always will . . . And you rest, and your baby rests. (Repeat this paragraph one more time.)

Quickly another contraction begins to build, getting stronger and stronger, and stretching the cervix further and further as the uterine muscles pull it up and back, over the baby's head. Feel your baby straining to get through as the amniotic sac bulges into your vagina, and feel relief and warmth as the water gushes out onto the bed and the contraction subsides as the baby slips back.

Now you feel another contraction. It is very hard and builds rapidly. See your vagina unfold to receive the rapidly advancing head, just as the petals on a flower open up. Feel the baby's head moving through the pelvis and under the pubic bone. Then the contraction begins to fade . . . and you rest, and your baby rests.

And still another contraction comes, massaging your baby's skin, preparing him to breathe on his own very soon, very soon. Feel the pressure of your baby's head on your perineum . . . . As your perineum stretches more and more, you feel burning and stinging, and you are panting, panting, relaxing your bottom so that your baby can ease his way out. Slowly, very slowly, here comes the head . . . and now the top shoulder . . then the bottom shoulder . . . Hear your baby breathe . . . . You are reaching down, then lifting your baby onto your chest . . . . Feel his warm wetness against your skin . . . . Watch his chest rise and fall as he begins to breathe and his color turns from blue to pink . . . . He looks intently at your face . . then begins rooting for your breast till he finds it and begins nursing . . . . Such peace and joy . . Your baby has been born!

And now, as you are enjoying the sensations of touching, seeing, hearing, and smelling your new baby, you are aware of another contraction, a milder contraction as your placenta is delivered . . . Your uterus continues to contract very firmly to prevent bleeding, just as it should.

Now bring yourself back to the present and know that your baby is growing and getting ready for that day when he will be born . . . It is still a few weeks off, but getting closer with each passing day.

Continue to breathe deeply and relax, and in a moment, you can open your eyes, feeling renewed and refreshed, knowing that your body will perform just as it should when the baby's birthday arrives.[2]

Continue to sit or lie quietly for as long as you wish. When you are ready, get up slowly. The positive feelings that you are experiencing can remain with you throughout the day.

BREATHING TECHNIQUES FOR LABOR

For some women, relaxation is sufficient for dealing with the sensations of labor. Others need additional coping strategies. This section will cover specific breathing patterns. The following section will present additional tools that can provide comfort during labor. To be properly prepared, you should learn all of these techniques. Then you can use those tools that you need during your unique labor situation, modifying them as you desire.

Breathing in a rhythmical pattern maintains a constant, balanced exchange of oxygen and carbon dioxide to ward off hyperventilation and to ensure a good oxygen supply to the working uterus, the placenta, and the baby. In addition, the focusing required to maintain slow or patterned breathing techniques may reduce your perception of pain. According to the gate control theory, pain sensations must travel up to the brain through a limited number of pathways. If the laboring woman keeps her mind busy with concentrating on a specific breathing pattern, focal point, or visualization, the gate closes, allowing fewer pain sensations to reach the brain. Thus, the perception of the contractions will be diminished. In other words, you distract yourself from perceiving the intensity of the pain. It is an experience similar to having a headache but forgetting about it while watching an exciting or engrossing movie. When the

A Hint for the Mother-to-Be

❑ Choose a focal point that reminds you of your "special place."

movie ends, the headache returns. Athletes frequently continue to play through an injury, and do not perceive the intensity of the pain until the game is over and they begin to focus on it.

Another method of utilizing the gate control mechanism is to physically stimulate specific points on the body. Examples of this include the use of heat, cold, massage, and acupressure, which will be discussed in the following section in this chapter.

Breathing Basics

Several elements are the same for all the breathing patterns presented in the following pages. They are:

❑ As each contraction begins and ends, you should take in a smooth, deep breath through your nose, then let the air out like a sigh through your mouth. This is known as a relaxing breath, and it is your cue to relax your body. This breath gives you a good boost of oxygen for the baby and for the uterus at the start of the contraction, and it is a signal to your labor partner that the contraction has begun or ended.

❑ You can focus your eyes on some object or spot in the room for the duration of the contraction. This object or spot is called your focal point. If you practice at home with a particularly pleasing object—such as a picture of a baby, a pleasant scene, a religious symbol, or the object that you visualize in your Special Place—take it with you to the birthing room. A focal point gives you something outside of yourself on which to concentrate and thus helps to lessen your awareness of the strength of your contractions.

Some women prefer to keep their eyes closed during contractions because it helps them to be in tune with their bodies. It also helps them to block out their surroundings when performing a visualization.

❑ When practicing a breathing pattern, have your partner give you the verbal cues "Contraction begins" and "Contraction ends." During labor, you will automatically transfer your practiced responses from the verbal cues to the physical sensations of the uterine contractions.

❑ Have your partner call out the passing seconds in 15-second intervals. This will help you gauge the duration of each contraction when you are in labor.

The practice steps for all the breathing patterns are:

1. Have your labor partner say, "Contraction begins."

2. Take a relaxing breath and release the tension from your body.

3. Concentrate on a focal point, if desired.

4. Begin the breathing pattern.

5. Have your partner "time the contraction" by calling out in 15-second intervals.

6. Have your partner say, "Contraction ends."

7. Take a relaxing breath and totally relax your body.

Rest for a few seconds, then repeat the steps.

Breathing Patterns

Now that you are familiar with the elements common to all the breathing techniques, you can begin to learn the individual patterns. Keep in mind that every person's breathing rate is different and that the patterns should be modified for your personal comfort. Before you begin, determine your normal resting rate of breathing by having your partner count your breaths for 1 full minute. During your practice sessions, you can either take air in through your nose and let it out through your mouth, do all nasal breathing, or do all mouth breathing. If your nose is congested, you may find mouth breathing easiest.

When you go into labor, do not use the special breathing patterns until you really need them. As long as you can walk and talk through your contractions, you will not need to do anything special except stay relaxed. As the contractions become stronger, begin slow paced breathing. Continue using this pattern for as long as possible. Many women find that slow paced breathing is the most effective in keeping them relaxed. The faster patterns require more energy and make relaxation more difficult. The longer you can comfortably wait before starting the special patterns, the more energy you will save.

Slow Paced Breathing

Slow paced breathing is the first, and possibly the only, breathing pattern that you will use in labor. It is done by breathing at approximately half your normal rate. (See Figure 5.1.) When doing slow paced breathing, breathe in a relaxed and comfortable manner.

Moaning

If it feels better for you to make noise, try humming or moaning in low tones during your contractions. Low pitched sounds will help to keep you relaxed. Many women have found that moaning is one of their best comfort tools.

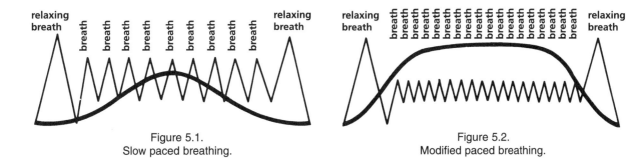

Figure 5.1.
Slow paced breathing.

Figure 5.2.
Modified paced breathing.

Modified Paced Breathing

If and when slow paced breathing no longer keeps you relaxed and comfortable, you can switch to the next breathing pattern, modified paced breathing. Modified paced breathing is more rapid than slow paced breathing, but no faster than twice your normal breathing rate. (See Figure 5.2.) Since it is a more fatiguing pattern, you should return to slow paced breathing when possible.

If you use mouth breathing, you can reduce dryness by placing your tongue behind your lower teeth. Strive for light, effortless, quiet breathing, taking in and letting out the same amount of air. At first, making a *hee* or *ha* sound when you exhale may help you to get the rhythm correctly. Later, your breathing should be quiet.

Do not go for speed. Rather, try to develop a slow, even rate. Try breathing in a 4/4 rhythm by mentally counting your breaths up to 4 and then starting

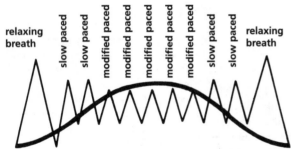

Figure 5.3.
Accelerated-decelerated
breathing (slow paced and
modified paced breathing).

again. Or, pace yourself by mentally reciting a nursery rhyme, such as "Jack and Jill went up the hill to fetch a pail of water."

When you are in labor, your breathing will accelerate naturally in response to your contractions. You might find yourself using slow paced breathing at the beginning of a contraction, gradually increasing the rate as the contraction builds, and then slowly decreasing the rate as the contraction subsides. (See Figure 5.3.) This pattern is called accelerated-decelerated breathing.

Breathing too fast is not only exhausting, but could make you hyperventilate. Hyperventilation is the result of exhaling too much carbon dioxide. You may feel dizzy, or have numbness or tingling in your fingertips, nose, or tongue. To combat this, breathe into your cupped hands or a small paper bag to rebreathe the same air and slow down your breathing rate.

Patterned Paced Breathing (Pant-Blow)

The last breathing pattern is designed to help with the long, strong, and often erratic contractions of transition. You should wait to use it until you find modified paced breathing no longer effective. It is the most tiring pattern and will prove exhausting if you use it too early.

Most women prefer mouth breathing with this pattern. As with the other breathing patterns, begin with a relaxing breath. You may need to make the relaxing breath short if the contraction peaks quickly. Otherwise, the contraction will get ahead of you and may cause you to lose control. If the contraction peaks immediately, skip the relaxing breath and start the breathing pattern at once.

The patterned paced breathing pattern is composed of 3 to 6 shallow breaths or pants followed by a short blowing-out breath through pursed lips. Do not forget to inhale before you blow out! The blow should be only a short accent; do *not* overemphasize it by breathing too slowly. When practicing, position your hand about 12 inches from your mouth and blow at it as if you were blowing out a candle. You should feel the blow lightly. During labor, repeat the pattern until the end of the contraction. Work for a light, even rhythm.

When practicing, try several of the variations. These include 3 pants and 1 blow, 4 pants and 1 blow, 5 pants and 1 blow, and 6 pants and 1 blow. (See Figure 5.4.) Decide which is the most comfortable for you and practice it for use in labor.

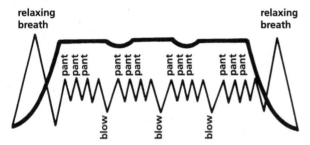

Figure 5.4.
Patterned paced breathing
(pant-blow).

You may find yourself moving in rhythm with your breathing when you practice this pattern. This uses extra energy unnecessarily. Instead, try to keep your shoulders and face relaxed and quiet.

You can also practice a more complicated form of this breathing pattern—increasing and then decreasing the number of pants before each blow. This demands even greater concentration. For example, during a contraction, do 2 pants and 1 blow, then 3 pants and 1 blow, then 4 pants and 1 blow, then 3 pants and 1 blow, and finally 2 pants and 1 blow. You can design your own combination of pants and blows.

Blowing for Premature Urge to Push

If, during a contraction, you feel a strong urge to push, blow out repeatedly and forcefully until the urge passes. It is difficult to bear down or push effectively when you are blowing out strongly. Remember to breathe in air before you blow out. When the urge to push is gone, return to the breathing pattern you had been using. (See Figure 5.5.)

POSITIONS FOR LABOR

If given the choice, most women prefer to move about and change position when they are in labor. Being mobile and upright decreases pain perception, shortens labor, and decreases the need for medication and interventions. Unfortunately, many women assume that they must remain in bed once they are admitted to the hospital, or they wait for the nurse to recommend a position change. If you are connected to an electronic fetal monitor or intravenous fluids, it becomes more difficult to move about freely. You may request intermittent monitoring or being monitored while out of bed. The use of IVs may not be necessary, or you may request a heparin lock or saline lock. (For a discussion of heparin locks and saline locks, see "Intravenous Fluids" on page 167.)

Trust your body and get into the position that makes you feel most comfortable. Try several positions during labor, and change your position frequently. Certain positions can encourage proper rotation of the baby as he moves through the pelvis.

Upright Position

Being upright during labor takes advantage of gravity and pulls the baby into the pelvis. Standing decreases the perception of pain while producing more effective contractions, which may help to shorten labor. This position also encourages the proper rotation and descent of the baby through the pelvis. If a shower is available, using it will give you the added benefit of warm water on your body. Some facilities even provide a hand-held showerhead, which allows you to direct the spray over your lower back.

The upright position includes standing next to the bed or a wall, walking between contractions, and lunging. If you stand next to the labor bed, you can lean over and use the side rail or bed for support. A fetal monitor can be applied, and your partner can easily massage your lower back in this position. If you stand next to a wall, place your fists into your lower back if you experience back pain.

If you walk between contractions, your partner can support you by holding onto your arm. When a contraction begins, face your partner, bend your knees, place your arms around his neck with your head on his shoulder, and allow him to support your weight. If your partner is taller than you, lean your head against his chest and allow your arms to drop to your sides as he places his hands around your waist for support. Some women have found that swaying their hips, as if dancing, can be soothing during a contraction. Another variation of standing is to press your back against your partner and have him place his arms around your abdomen. You can also sway in this position.

The lunge position can help to widen the pelvis, especially if the baby is in a posterior position. To get into the lunge position, stand beside the bed or a chair. Place one foot on the bed or seat of the chair, and one foot on the

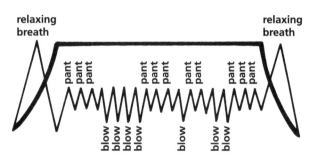

Figure 5.5.
Patterned paced breathing with blowing for a premature urge to push.

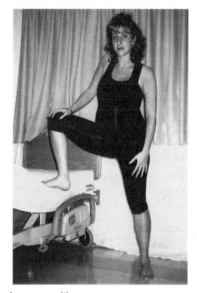

Lunge position.

floor. If you know which side of the pelvis the back of the baby's head is facing, lunge with that leg. If you do not know the position of the baby, lunge in the direction that is most comfortable. You should feel a stretch in the inner thigh. During a contraction, repeatedly lunge sideways and hold for 5 to 10 seconds, using your partner for support.

Sitting

Sitting in the labor bed or on a chair provides the benefit of gravity, although not as much as standing does. It is a comfortable position for most women and can be used with the fetal monitor. The rocking motion when sitting in a rocking chair is especially soothing. If your back is sore, you can straddle or sit on the edge of the bed or chair, and lean forward so that your partner can rub your lower back.

Side-Lying

Side-lying is a comfortable position for most women. It is beneficial in a long labor if the woman needs to rest. Place pillows under your head and abdomen, and between your legs. Side-lying does not restrict the use of the fetal monitor or other interventions. It also helps to lower blood pressure and can be used if the woman is medicated.

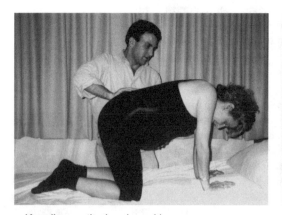

Kneeling on the hands and knees.

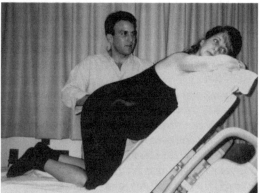

Another kneeling alternative is to raise the head of the bed and lean against the elevated section.

Kneeling with the aid of a birthing ball.

Kneeling

Kneeling on the hands and knees is the most comfortable position for back labor. It takes the weight of the baby off the spine and may encourage proper rotation. Your partner is able to apply firm counterpressure to the painful areas. You can also perform the pelvic rock in this position. If you are out of bed, you can kneel in front of a chair, with your upper body resting on the chair seat. If you are in bed, raise the head of the bed and lean your upper body on the elevated section, using pillows for support. Some women have found that a birthing ball (an extremely large, flexible ball that can be used for a variety of positions during labor and birth) is comfortable to lean against.

OTHER TOOLS FOR LABOR

Relaxation, patterned breathing, and comfortable labor positions are very important for coping with labor. Other tools that reduce pain perception during labor are massage, counterpressure, acupressure, laboring in water, and application of heat or cold. These latter techniques can be easily learned by the woman and her labor partner. Several additional techniques—such as transcutaneous electrical nerve stimulation, intradermal injections of sterile water, and acupuncture—require professional assistance. All these nondrug remedies should be attempted before using medication, since the risks to the woman and baby are lower. They may also reduce the need for other interventions.

Labor Massage

Massage can be an effective tool during labor to promote relaxation, relieve stress, conserve energy, facilitate breathing, and assist in the relief of muscle cramping and pain. While some women prefer not to be touched at all during labor, others appreciate the relief it brings, as well as the loving care and support it represents.

Effleurage is a light fingertip massage. It can be performed by you or your labor partner during contractions. To do effleurage, lightly place the fingertips of both hands on your abdomen just above your pubic bone. Slowly bring the fingertips upward, still using light pressure, to a point near the top of your abdomen. Then gently draw the fingertips outward, downward, and back to the beginning point. Continue drawing these circles on your abdomen for the duration of the contraction. If desired, draw the circles in rhythm with the breathing pattern.

Other massage techniques that your partner can try on you during labor are:

Effleurage is a light fingertip massage that can aid relaxation during contractions.

❏ Gently stroking your arms and legs using his full hand and going toward your heart.

❏ Gently massaging your face using light stroking of your jaw area to help relax your jaw during active labor.

❏ Applying pressure along the base of your skull with his fingertips in between contractions.

❏ Grasping and lightly holding together the first three toes (the big toe and the next two) on each foot during contractions. Grasping and releasing these toes rhythmically helps to relax the pelvic floor.

❏ Gently rubbing your neck and shoulders.

You may want to hire a professional massage therapist to attend your labor. Because of her knowledge and expertise, she would be able to incorporate such other techniques as reflexology and the use of pressure points.

Counterpressure

Counterpressure can also be used to provide relief during labor. Your partner can use his fist or the heel of his hand on your back to reduce the pain if you are experiencing back labor. You will need to direct him to the exact location on both sides of your lower back and let him know the amount of pressure you

Double hip squeeze.   Knee press.

desire. He can apply firm pressure during contractions. The pressure points will become lower as your labor progresses and your baby's head descends through the pelvis.

Performing the double hip squeeze can also help to relieve back pain. To accomplish this technique, you can either stand while bending over at the waist and supporting your upper body against a chair or bed, or kneel on all fours. Standing or kneeling behind you, your partner should place his hands high on your buttocks, on the meatiest areas. Using his full hands, he should then press your hips together, which opens the outlet at the pubic joint.

Another counterpressure method for relieving back pain is the knee press. For this technique, you should sit in a straight-back chair, with a small pillow or towel supporting your lower back. Your partner should kneel in front of you and place his hands on your knees. The heel of his hand should be at the lower margin of your knee, where the tibia ends. During a contraction, your partner should lean forward, pressing your upper legs toward the back of your chair.

Acupressure

The Russian theorists who originated the idea of psychoprophylaxis in childbirth included acupressure massage in their approach. They identified certain "pain prevention points" in the body and recommended applying pressure to these areas to aid in pain relief. This technique was omitted as a component of prepared childbirth when it became Westernized. Acupressure interferes with and alters the pain impulses as they travel to the brain (the gate theory), and it may also encourage the release of endorphins.

Acupressure, or pressure point massage, involves applying pressure, heat, or cold over certain acupressure points. It is a method of stimulating these points to provide pain relief in other specific areas. Pressure is applied with the fingertips or thumbs, either held stationary or moved in very small circles over the acupressure points, without the use of lubricants. When the point has been accurately located, the person being treated feels a tenderness or tingling sensation. If the area is *very* painful, it may be necessary to begin with light pressure, then to gradually increase it. Pressure should be applied for 5 to 10

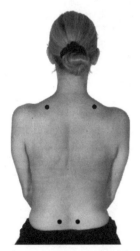

Acupressure points on the back. The shoulder points are for relieving headache or pain in the neck or upper back. The lower points are for relieving low-back discomfort.

seconds, and it may be repeated. Since acupressure points exist in pairs—one on each side of the body—remember to treat both sides.

Acupressure can be used along with patterned breathing to enhance the effects of both. Steady pressure works well with patterned breathing, as do circular and intermittent pressure.

You can either perform acupressure on yourself or have it done by your partner. Because the positive support and reinforcement of another person's touch tends to have a soothing effect and promotes relaxation, having your partner do it for you may be most effective.

The following are acupressure techniques for dealing with the discomforts of labor and postpartum, as well as of pregnancy:

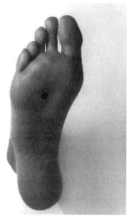

This acupressure point in the center of the foot helps to relax the lower part of the body.

❏ To relieve headache or pain in the neck or upper back, place your fingers or thumbs on the muscles at the tops of the shoulders, slightly toward the back and in a vertical line with the nipples. Apply circular pressure.

❏ For low-back discomfort, pelvic pain or pressure, or back labor, press firmly, in an inward direction, on either side of the spine just below waist level. Use circular pressure during contractions and either circular or intermittent pressure between contractions.

❏ To relieve hip or sciatic pain, alternately apply heat and cold to the upper outer quadrant of the affected buttock.

❏ To assist in relaxing the lower part of the body, massage the point in the center of the foot, just below the ball of the foot.

The following techniques are also effective for labor pain. *They should not be used before 38 weeks of pregnancy because they can cause labor to begin.* The techniques are:

Applying pressure between the thumb and forefinger may help to speed up a difficult labor.

❏ To speed up the progress of a difficult labor, apply pressure on the point at the end of the crease in between the thumb and forefinger. This relaxes the vagina and cervix.

❏ To aid a difficult labor, apply pressure to the point located approximately three finger widths above the inner ankle. Pressing around the whole area of the inner ankle will locate the point. The place that is the most tender is the correct spot. Use strong, steady pressure.

❏ For pain relief, pinch or apply pressure to the outside corners of both little toes during contractions. Press down very hard and hold for 7 to 10 seconds.

The ankle has an acupressure point that can stimulate labor.

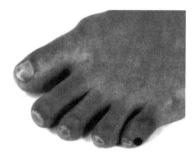

Pinching or applying pressure to the little toes can provide pain relief during contractions.

Acupressure is noninvasive, easy to learn, and effective. It is another important tool that can be added to your repertoire of pain relief techniques to be called upon and utilized as needed during labor and postpartum. For more information on acupressure and how it is used, see *The Pregnant Woman's Comfort Guide* by Sherry L. M. Jiménez.

Laboring in Water

More and more birthing facilities are providing tubs or showers for laboring women. Many women find that being in warm water aids relaxation. Submersion in a tub reduces external stimuli and provides buoyancy to eliminate pressure on the joints. Pain medication is required less often, as the body is able to produce endorphins, which reduce perception of pain. Studies have shown that women who have high blood pressure experience a lowering of their blood pressure within 10 to 15 minutes after entering a tub.[3]

Laboring in water has not been associated with any increase in complications, such as infection, even if the membranes have ruptured. The temperature of the water should not exceed 100°F, to prevent elevation of the body temperature. Since your contractions may slow if you are in early labor, wait to get into the tub until you are in active labor. A doptone can be used to monitor the baby while you are in the tub, or you may have to use the tub intermittently with electronic fetal monitoring.

If a shower is available, have the nurse place a chair in the stall so that you can rest. If the shower has a hand-held showerhead, your partner can direct the spray onto your abdomen or lower back, if desired.

Heat

The use of heat during labor can be soothing and provide pain relief. The application of heat can be accomplished through submersion in a tub or shower or by use of a hot water bottle, heat pack, or hot wet compresses. A prewarmed blanket will also provide comfort. Heat increases skin and muscle temperature, allowing relaxation. Muscle spasms are also decreased. If you are experiencing a back labor, you can labor in water or you can alternately apply hot packs and ice packs to the lower back. The application of heat increases blood flow to the area. As the perineum stretches during pushing, the application of hot compresses helps increase elasticity and decreases the burning sensations associated with the skin stretching.

Cold

The use of cold packs can provide good pain relief, as the cold temperature provides a numbing effect. Cold works particularly well for back labor. You can use an ice bag, frozen gel packs, a rubber glove filled with crushed ice, a washcloth or small towel soaked in ice water, a cold can of soda, or even a bag of frozen vegetables (a bag of peas molds nicely). Use a layer of cloth between your skin and the ice pack. If you are standing, ask the nurse to place the ice pack under the elastic strap used to secure the fetal monitor.

Transcutaneous Electrical Nerve Stimulation

Transcutaneous electrical nerve stimulation (TENS) units are most common-

"Okay, honey, I'm ready to help now!"

Homemade Heat Pack

Make your own heat pack by filling a long cotton sock with rice. Place the rice-filled sock in the microwave for 2 minutes. It will remain warm for 15 to 20 minutes. *Caution:* To avoid burns, do not overcook the heat pack or lie on top of it.

ly used to treat chronic pain, but have been found to be helpful for some women in labor. A TENS unit is a small hand-held, battery-operated device that is connected to the skin by four electrode pads. The area is stimulated and controlled by the person wearing the device. The device provides a tingling sensation that the wearer can increase during contractions and decrease between contractions. TENS units cannot be used by women who labor in water.

Intradermal Injections of Sterile Water

The intradermal injection of sterile water is a new technique in which small amounts of sterile water are injected directly under the skin to form blister-like bumps. The injections cause an intense stinging sensation, lasting for less than 30 seconds, followed by relief of back pain for 60 to 90 minutes. It is believed that the injections cause a release of endorphins. The technique requires knowledge about the specific injection sites and about intradermal injections.

Acupuncture

Acupuncture involves the insertion of fine needles into specific points on the body. Stimulation of these points is believed to release endorphins. This technique requires expertise in acupuncture administration and knowledge about the specific sites. It can be used to reduce labor pain and to increase the strength of contractions. Check with your caregiver if you would like to use this technique. You would need to hire a professional who is proficient in acupuncture to attend your labor.

PUSHING TECHNIQUES

When your cervix has completely effaced and dilated, you can actively help the uterus move the baby down the birth canal by bearing down or pushing with the contractions. Most women feel a strong desire to push, but a few do not. If you do not immediately feel an urge to push, just continue to breathe through the contractions. In addition, assume an upright position to help the baby descend into the pelvis. His head may not be deep enough to press on the sensors that trigger the bearing-down reflex. It has been found that if a woman delays bearing down, she eventually does feel the urge to push. But if the woman starts pushing without having the urge, she may never feel it. Absence of the urge to push makes the pushing stage more difficult and less satisfying. If you do not feel the urge to push as the result of an epidural, request that the medication be turned down or off, and delay pushing until you feel the urge.

Use your body's natural messages, and bear down or push only as your uterus directs. You may have a desire to bear down just mildly, or you may feel a need to push strongly. Many woman are surprised that they make noise as they bear down. Use low moans or deep guttural sounds, rather than high-pitched screams or squeals. Low tones encourage a relaxed pelvic floor. Also, during the contractions, try not to completely release the bearing-down effort between breaths. If you can continue to apply some pressure as you get the next breath, you will help to hold the position of the baby and make better progress.

A Hint for the Mother-to-Be

❑ If you would like to utilize a comfort measure such as intradermal injections of sterile water, acupuncture, massage therapy, or TENS, you may need to make arrangements before labor.

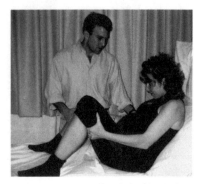

"Look for the baby."

You should also assume the position for pushing that you prefer, not necessarily the one that you practiced in childbirth class or observed in childbirth films. You may find side-lying, squatting, standing, kneeling with your upper body elevated, or kneeling on all fours to be the most comfortable for you and the one most advantageous to your baby's descent. In any pushing position, tuck your chin down onto your chest to curve your body into a *C* position. This curves the lower back and aids the descent of the baby under the pubic bone. Avoid the temptation to throw your head back, which would cause an unnatural arch in your back. Your partner can remind you to "look for the baby."

While natural or gentle pushing may not produce results as quickly as forceful breath holding does, no evidence exists that a longer second stage is harmful to a baby who is not in distress. In fact, babies may benefit from experiencing a slower, more gentle birth, instead of a forceful surge down the birth canal.[4]

Breathing Patterns for Pushing

There are two primary breathing patterns for pushing that women use to move the baby down the birth canal. The first pattern is more natural and incorporates an exhalation during the strong physical work of pushing. Exhaling during a strenuous action is a technique used by athletes to prevent injury. For many women, this first pattern is sufficient. Other women need to push more forcefully to make any progress. The second pattern, which incorporates breath holding, limits the time the breath is held. Long breath holding and forceful pushing, called the Valsalva maneuver, is not recommended, since it can cause your blood pressure to drop and thus decrease the amount of oxygen your baby receives.

Gentle Pushing

Gentle pushing is the preferred method of helping the baby down the birth canal. As the contraction begins, take relaxing breaths until you feel the urge to push. Then inhale deeply to expand your lungs, tuck your chin onto your chest, purse your lips, and exhale slowly and steadily as you bear down using your diaphragm. When you need to take another breath, lift your head, inhale slowly while continuing to maintain some pressure against the uterus, tuck your chin, and exhale through your mouth as you bear down. Repeat this pattern until the contraction ends. When the contraction is over, take several relaxing breaths and try to completely relax your body until the next contraction begins. (See Figure 5.6.)

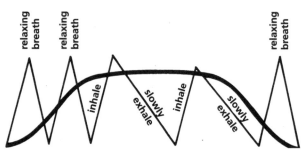

Figure 5.6. Breathing pattern for gentle pushing.

Breath Holding While Pushing

Pushing while holding your breath, also known as the modified Valsalva maneuver, is used by women who need to apply more force to help their baby in the trip down the birth canal. As the contraction begins, take relaxing breaths until you feel the urge to push. Then inhale deeply, let a little air out, tuck your chin, hold your breath, and bear down using your diaphragm. Directing the air downward, rather than holding the air in your cheeks, reduces the tension in your face and neck, and lessens your chance of breaking small blood vessels in your face and in the whites of your eyes.

While you hold your breath and push, your partner should count slowly to 6 to pace your effort. When he reaches 6, ease the breath out *slowly* to maintain abdominal pressure and to keep your diaphragm down on top of the uterus. Straighten your neck and inhale again, let a little air out, hold, tuck your chin, and push while your partner counts. Repeat the pattern as many times as needed during the contraction. When the contraction ends, gradually stop pushing as you exhale slowly. Take 1 or 2 relaxing breaths and relax completely. (See Figure 5.7.)

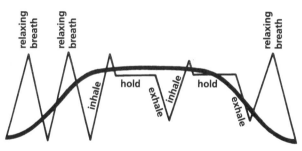

Figure 5.7. Breathing pattern for breath holding while pushing.

Pushing Positions

The positions that you use during your pushing effort will be determined largely by your comfort and your caregiver's preferences. The choices include semireclining, squatting, side-lying, kneeling, and the lithotomy position. Most nurses and doctors encourage the semireclining position, but you may not find it the most comfortable. Many hospitals now offer birthing rooms, eliminating the need to be transferred to a separate delivery room with a conventional delivery table. Birthing rooms contain birthing beds that can be adjusted to your comfort and also transformed into a delivery table, complete with stirrups. Discuss all of the possible pushing positions with your caregiver to learn what he prefers and to let him know what you would like. Then practice pushing in all of the positions, so that you can use what feels best to you when you are in labor.

Semireclined Position

Semireclining is the most common position used in the birthing room. It is a comfortable position for the woman and provides a good visual field for the caregiver. If you have back labor, this position is not recommended, as it places the weight of the baby onto your back and increases your discomfort. The head of the birthing bed can be elevated 70 degrees, and you can place your feet on the bed or in the footrests. Or, the bottom third of the birthing bed can be lowered 6 to 12 inches as a footrest.

Semireclined position.

To practice pushing in the semireclined position, have your partner sit behind you as your back support. Place pillows between his legs and your back. Lie against your partner at a 70-degree angle, being sure to sit on the small of your back, not on your rectum. Bend your knees, spread your legs, and place your feet flat on the floor or bed. Rest your hands on his knees or your inner thighs to keep your legs and perineum relaxed. If you need to hold something while pushing, grasp your inner thighs and draw them toward you. Then begin your selected breathing pattern, tuck your chin onto your chest, and *push*. When the contraction is over, lie back and relax.

Squatting Position

Squatting is physiologically the best position to use while pushing. You can support yourself in a squat by keeping your feet flat on the floor and holding onto a bed rail or your partner. Many birthing beds come equipped with a squat bar to hold onto for support. A comfortable squat can be accomplished by having your partner sit on a chair, with you squatting between his legs, your arms draped over his thighs. Squat only during the contraction, and

Squatting position.

A birthing chair.

A birthing stool.

either stand up or kneel during the rest period. During a long labor, it may be necessary for your partner to assist you out of the squat. As with other patterns, tuck your chin onto your chest as you bear down. Women delivering in birth centers are often encouraged to sit on a toilet to achieve the squat position. A birthing stool or birthing chair can also help you push in this position.

Squatting is an ideal pushing position because it allows gravity to assist the uterus, which makes the contractions more efficient, longer, and more frequent. The pelvic outlet is at its widest, the birth canal is shortened, and episiotomies are needed less frequently. Delivery time is shortened because pushing is more effective. Do not get into the position before the baby's presenting part is engaged because the descent and engagement could be hampered.[5] In case of complications, squatting may present some manual and visual inconveniences for the caregiver. It may become necessary to assume a different position.

Side-Lying Position

Also called the lateral Sims' position, side-lying is very comfortable for most women, especially those having a back labor or leg cramps. It can aid rotation of the head if the baby is not yet in a facedown position, and it can help in a breech delivery as well.

When you lie on your side, your uterus does not press on your vena cava (large blood vessel). Your chances for supine hypotension (low blood pressure) are therefore decreased. The perineum is relaxed, so episiotomies are needed less often and tears are less likely to occur. However, side-lying does not utilize the force of gravity as well as squatting does, and your view of the birth is not as good. If a difficult forceps delivery or repair of lacerations is necessary, this position is not recommended.

To get into the side-lying position, lie on your side with one or more pillows supporting your head. Try to lie on your left side because this improves blood flow to the uterus. When you are ready to push, curve your upper body into a *C* shape by tucking your chin onto your chest. Have your partner support your upper leg with his arms or hands, or place the leg on the lowest bed rail, which you can pad with pillows.

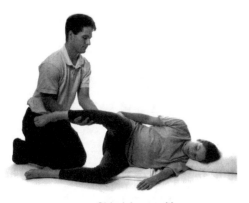

Side-lying position.

Then begin your selected breathing pattern and *push*. When the contraction is over, relax, lowering your leg onto the bed, supported by pillows.

Kneeling Position

The kneeling position is preferred by some women. Physiologically, it is a good position for pushing because it takes advantage of the force of gravity. It may be especially helpful if your baby is slow in coming down the birth canal or if you are having back labor. As you push, tuck your chin onto your chest to improve the angle of your pelvis.

To push in the kneeling position, kneel on the bed facing your partner. Put your arms around your partner's shoulders for support, begin your selected breathing pattern, tuck your chin, and *push*. When the contraction is over, relax.

Other kneeling positions include leaning forward against the raised head of the birthing bed or pillows. You may want to try placing one knee and the sole of the other foot on the bed and lunging with each contraction. If out of bed, kneel on the floor and support your upper body on pillows placed on the seat of a chair. A variation of the kneeling position is to kneel on your hands and knees. On all fours, you can do the pelvic rock exercise if you are experiencing back pain. Women whose babies are in a posterior position often find that this position eases discomfort.

Lithotomy Position

You may be encouraged to give birth in the lithotomy position, lying flat on your back with your feet up in stirrups. While this position has advantages for the doctor—such as allowing him to observe your abdomen and perineum, check the fetal heart rate, apply forceps or the vacuum extractor if necessary, and manage postpartum hemorrhage—it has definite disadvantages for you.

Pushing in the lithotomy position reduces your pelvic outlet to its smallest diameter. In addition, your contractions may become more irregular and less frequent. With your legs in stirrups, the strength of your contractions might actually lift your hips off the table, resulting in your having to push the baby uphill and against gravity. Episiotomies are done more frequently to women using this position because of the narrowed vaginal opening as well as the perineum being stretched taut. The weight of the uterus on your vena cava may lower your blood pressure and thereby decrease the amount of oxygen reaching your baby.[6] In an experiment using a device that continuously monitors fetal oxygenation, a pregnant woman was made to roll onto her back. Within 2 minutes, the fetal oxygen level was in the danger range. The woman was immediately rolled back onto her side and given oxygen, but it took 8 minutes for the fetal oxygen level to return to a safe range.[7] Finally, the lithotomy position might strain your back because your feet will be so widely separated in the stirrups.

If you do deliver in the lithotomy position, make sure that the stirrups are adjusted for your comfort and not strapped on too tight.

To simulate the lithotomy position during practice sessions, lie on the floor on your back and place your legs on the seat of a chair or sofa. When you are ready to push, have your partner raise your back to a 70-degree angle, tuck your chin onto your chest, begin your selected breathing pattern, and *push*. When the contraction is over, lie back and relax.

Lunging position.

Kneeling with the aid of a chair.

Pushing Practice

Once you feel comfortable with the breathing patterns for pushing, practice them in the various pushing positions. To push, slowly exhale or hold your breath, and bear down by doing the following:

❑ Take 2 relaxing breaths, take a deep breath to expand your lungs, and start bearing down using your diaphragm.

❑ Tuck your chin onto your chest and "look for the baby."

❑ Bulge your lower abdominal muscles down and forward.

❑ Totally relax your pelvic floor by doing basement Kegels. Your perineum should feel as if it is bulging out.

❑ Keep your diaphragm down on your uterus between breaths by inhaling slowly.

❑ Try to push three or four times during each practice contraction.

❑ Slowly lessen your pushing effort as the contraction comes to an end. This will help to maintain the baby's position in the birth canal, preventing his moving back up.

When you practice pushing, do not push forcefully, just enough to get the proper feeling. You may find it helpful to think of pushing as being like forcefully emptying your bladder. Also, visualize your baby coming down lower and lower as you push, and consciously relax your legs and bottom. A tight perineum can cause a longer, more difficult birth and almost certainly ensure having an episiotomy.

During actual labor, your first pushes will move your baby gradually down the birth canal. Your partner may even see a little of the baby's hair showing as you push. But the hair will disappear as the baby moves back up at the end of the contraction. When the top of the baby's head stays in view between contractions, it is called crowning. Your caregiver may ask you to stop pushing. Pant or blow out at this time to keep from pushing. This will allow your baby's head to gradually stretch the birth outlet and perineum, resulting in a more controlled delivery of the baby's head and hopefully reducing the need for an episiotomy.

PRACTICE FOR LABOR

You should practice your conditioning exercises, relaxation exercises, and breathing patterns every day. If possible, get in two practice sessions per day—one alone and one with your labor partner. You can do the relaxation exercises and breathing patterns the same time you do the conditioning exercises, or you can do them in separate sessions. Try to practice when you are rested and can fully concentrate on your efforts.

Rehearse in your mind the labor and birth of your baby. Start with early labor and continue through transition, pushing, and delivery. Learn your role so completely that you will automatically begin a breathing pattern and relax your body when a contraction begins.

Following is a suggested sequence for practicing your exercises and patterns. Add to it as you learn new techniques.

1. Do each conditioning exercise the recommended number of times.

2. Practice a relaxation exercise. Vary the choice of exercise.

3. Practice the slow paced breathing pattern, with the contractions lasting 60 seconds each. Do a series of three contractions, with 60-second rests in between the contractions. Practice a massage technique as a comfort measure at the same time.

4. Practice the modified paced breathing pattern, with three contractions lasting 60 to 90 seconds each. Maintain a steady, even breathing rate throughout each contraction. Then practice the accelerated-decelerated breathing pattern while your partner applies manual pressure. (See "For the Labor Partner: Helpful Hints.")

5. Practice the patterned paced breathing pattern, with the contractions lasting 90 seconds each. Do a series of three contractions, with 30-second rests in between the contractions. Have your partner call out a premature urge to push lasting 15 seconds during one or more of the contractions. Blow out forcefully and continuously until your partner signals that the urge to push has passed. Then return to the patterned paced breathing pattern to finish the contraction.

6. Practice both gentle pushing and breath holding pushing three times each. Have the contractions last 60 seconds each, with 1 to 2 minutes of rest in between the contractions. Practice with the different pushing positions, so that you will be comfortable in all of them.

Once you become familiar with all of the breathing patterns, practice your relaxation and breathing in various positions—standing, semireclining, sitting in a rocking chair, side-lying, or kneeling on your hands and knees. This will ensure maximum comfort and relaxation in all positions during labor.

To be even more prepared, simulate various kinds of labor situations as you practice. This will help you to cope better with a problem, if one should arise. Some examples of labor variations are back labor, induced or very rapid labor, loss of control, and hyperventilation.

For the Labor Partner: Helpful Hints

Several additional ways in which you can help out are the following:

❑ Simulate contractions during practice by applying manual pressure to the bony part of your partner's wrist, elbow, or knee to cause discomfort. As you call out the contraction, gradually build to a peak, then gradually ease the pressure. Increase and decrease the pressure in varying patterns, so that your partner can respond to different sensations. For example, slowly increase the pressure to a peak, then rapidly decline; peak quickly and maintain strength through most of the contraction; or peak several times during the same contraction. This technique is especially helpful for practicing accelerated-decelerated breathing. *Remember, this technique is only for practice.*

❑ Call out the passing seconds in 15-second intervals. Pacing the contraction helps your partner to keep her perspective.

❑ Observe for tension in your partner both during and between contractions. The longer the labor continues, the greater is the chance of tension slowly spreading. Use both touch and verbal cues as needed to encourage relaxation.

❑ Help your partner to maintain breathing rhythm by counting or breathing

Hints for the Labor Partner

❑ Learn about alternative methods of pain relief for labor and discuss them with your partner.

❑ Learn the acupressure points for pain relief.

❑ Recite a visualization for your partner.

❑ Encourage a daily practice session during the last month of pregnancy.

with her. Tapping on a hard surface or moving your hand in front of her face may also keep her on track.

❏ Encourage your partner to take advantage of Braxton-Hicks contractions as signals to practice relaxation and breathing patterns.

The ways in which labor partners can help out during pregnancy, labor, and delivery are innumerable. This book has suggestions in every chapter. With a little common sense, imagination, and teamwork, pregnancy and childbirth can be one of the more fulfilling times in a relationship.

"Gee, honey, can't you loosen up just a little?"

CONCLUSION

By practicing the exercises in Chapters 4 and 5 together, you and your labor partner will develop teamwork, as well as learn specific skills. The ability to work together as a team—to communicate clearly and to trust each other—is as important to the labor experience as are the skills you are learning. Teamwork takes time to develop, however, so give each other encouragement and positive feedback at first. As you become comfortable working with each other, slowly begin discussing where you need improvement.

Take time each day to practice together. The quality of your labor experience will depend greatly upon the amount of time you prepare together and the quality of those sessions.

Labor and Birth

or I Gotta Get Out of This Place

For 9 months, your body has been working to grow and nurture your baby. During the last weeks of pregnancy, changes occur that begin working toward getting your baby into the world. The baby starts to descend into the pelvis, and the mild contractions that take place only occasionally prior to the last few weeks may increase in frequency and begin the job of thinning and opening your cervix. These "warm up" contractions become more frequent and stronger, and eventually push your baby out.

Labor is the natural process at the end of pregnancy that begins with regular uterine contractions and culminates in the birth of the baby and the delivery of the placenta. Each labor is unique, differing from one woman to another, and even from one labor to the next in the same woman. Some of the factors that will affect the course of your labor are your health, nutrition, emotional make-up, size and shape of your pelvis, preparation for labor and birth through classes and reading, and practice of the conditioning exercises, relaxation exercises, and breathing techniques. The size and presentation of the baby are also important factors. Additionally, the emotional support you receive, along with any medical interventions used, may also affect the course of your labor.

"If only giving birth were as easy as getting pregnant!"

Even though each labor is different, certain aspects of all labors are similar. For ease of explanation, labor is divided into four stages. The first stage begins with the onset of labor and ends with the complete effacement and dilation of the cervix. The second stage of labor, expulsion, begins with the complete dilation of the cervix and ends with the birth of the baby. The third stage of labor is the delivery of the placenta. The fourth stage is the first hours after birth, or the recovery period.

It is most important that you go into labor trusting your body. Women have been giving birth successfully for centuries. Your body was built for carrying and nourishing your baby, and for safely delivering him into the world.

THINGS TO DO BEFORE YOUR DUE DATE

As your due date approaches, you will want to make sure that you have completed your preparations for labor and for the arrival of your baby. The following are suggested things to accomplish by your last month of pregnancy.

Confirm Your Choice of Labor Partner

Your labor partner is the person who will be with you during labor and birth to provide you with emotional support as well as to assist you with the comfort measures and techniques that you learned in childbirth class. He will also serve as your go-between with the medical staff. Many women choose their husband, their boyfriend, or the father of their baby as their labor partner. Others choose a close friend or relative. Some choose more than one person.

"But you said I could bring more than one person!"

Your labor partner should prepare for the birth by attending your childbirth classes with you, by helping you practice your relaxation and breathing techniques, and by reading books on birth. An excellent book on the childbirth experience aimed at the labor partner is *The Birth Partner* by Penny Simkin.

In addition to a labor partner, you may also want either a medical professional or a doula to support and assist you during labor. Some women hire their childbirth instructor, or a nurse or midwife not associated with the hospital in which they will deliver.

Other women hire a doula, a woman specifically trained to assist women and their partners during labor. Doulas go through a special course to become skillful in providing a reassuring, nurturing, and constant presence to help women and their partners cope during labor. Studies have shown that the presence of a doula significantly reduces the chance of complications. Women have shorter labors and require less Pitocin (a synthetic form of the hormone oxytocin used to induce or augment labor), pain medication, epidurals, and forceps deliveries. In addition, the risk of having a cesarean is reduced by 50 percent.[1] Currently, two national organizations train doulas. They are:

Doulas of North America
1100 23rd Avenue East
Seattle, Washington 98112
Telephone 206–324–5440
FAX 206–325–0472

International Childbirth Education
  Association
P.O. Box 20048
Minneapolis, Minnesota 55420
Telephone 612–854–8660
FAX 612–854–8772

If you would like a labor assistant, you can also ask your childbirth instructor about local organizations. The payment of a fee may be required.

Take a Tour of the Hospital or Birth Center

Taking a tour of the hospital or birth center where you plan to have your baby will allow you to become familiar with your labor setting before you check in. You can also discuss your desires with the staff and learn about the facility's policies. If you are planning a birth center delivery, you may want to tour the affiliated hospital in case you are transferred there during delivery.

Pre-Register

Pre-register at your hospital to shorten the admittance procedure when you arrive in labor. If you are planning to deliver at a birth center, you may want to pre-register at the hospital in case you are transferred during labor. To complete the required forms, you will need your insurance information. You should also be prepared to make a deposit. Any consent forms concerning items such as medication, epidural anesthesia, and circumcision should be read carefully at this time and modified according to your desires before being signed. You may also be asked to sign a paper indicating whether you have a living will.

Make Arrangements for Cord Blood Banking

It is now possible to collect and store the blood from your baby's umbilical cord. Cryobanks throughout the country freeze umbilical cord blood for future use. Many couples are donating this otherwise discarded blood for use in place of bone marrow transplants. There is usually no charge for this service. Some families prefer to bank the cord blood for their own possible future use. They are charged collection and yearly storage fees. These include families who have a history of leukemia or other cancers, sickle cell anemia, hemophilia, or another disease that may require a bone marrow transplant. Minority and mixed-race families are also using this option to increase the likelihood of a match, since tissue matches are much more difficult to obtain in these instances.

Umbilical cord blood contains a high level of stem cells. These immature cells produce the oxygen-carrying red blood cells, the white blood cells that make up the immune system, and the platelets that help blood to clot. There are many benefits to using cord blood instead of bone marrow. The concentration of stem cells is greater in cord blood than it is in bone marrow. Stem cells from the umbilical cord have not built up antibodies and are more compatible when donated. The collection procedure is not invasive and involves no pain to the donor, as does the traditional bone marrow transplant. The collection is usually done after the cord is cut and before the placenta is delivered.

If you are interested in cord blood banking, you must contact your nearest cryobank and make arrangements prior to your due date. If there is no cryobank in your area, call Cord Blood Registry, a company that provides the service nationwide for public donation or private storage; the toll-free number is 888–CORD BLOOD (888–267–3256). Several other banks that offer services nationwide, but only for private storage, are CorCell, Inc., telephone 888–3CORCELL (888–326–7235); CRYO-CELL International, Inc., telephone 800–STORCELL (800–786–7235); and Viacord, Inc., telephone 800–99–VIACORD (800–998–4226). Also, you must make sure that your caregiver is aware of your desires so that the collection will be performed.

Choose Your Baby's Pediatrician

Begin your search for a pediatrician during your last trimester of pregnancy. You may want to ask family members and friends who have small children for recommendations. You could also ask your obstetrician, midwife, or primary care physician. Arrange a prenatal interview. This may be in a group setting or a personal meeting. Some pediatricians charge for a private prenatal consultation. Be prepared with a list of questions you want answered.

There are some factors to consider. Are the location and office hours convenient? Many practices have several locations, and offer evening and weekend hours. If this is a solo practice, find out who covers for the physician. How many doctors are in the group and can you request a certain pediatrician? Are the pediatricians board certified? Some practices also have pediatric nurse practitioners and certified lactation consultants on staff. Who will answer your questions if you call the office? Will you speak with the doctor, a nurse, or the

Hints for the Father-to-Be

❏ Decorate the nursery.

❏ Stock up on baby supplies when you shop.

❏ Baby-proof the house.

❏ Buy an infant safety seat and install it in the car.

❏ Continue to perform perineal massage on your partner.

receptionist? How do they handle emergencies that occur after office hours? Does the office have a sick and a well waiting room? What is the average wait time? What hospitals are the doctors affiliated with? What are the costs of care? Do they accept your insurance?

It is also important to discuss the pediatrician's philosophy on breastfeeding, supplementing, introducing solids, jaundice, circumcision, and any other questions related to baby care. After the interview, you should have a good feeling about whether you are comfortable with his practice.

Prepare Your Home for the Baby

Gather all the baby equipment and furniture you need and set it up ready to use. Assemble the baby clothes, wash them, and put them away. The last months of pregnancy are a good time to reorganize your home, making it safe for a small child. Lock up all medicines and poisons. Ask friends who have small children to help you spot potential hazards. (For specific baby-proofing suggestions, see "Baby-Proofing Your House" on page 226.)

Organize Your Household

Organize your household for your absence and take measures to simplify your work when you return with the new baby. If relatives or friends will be coming to help you, be sure they understand that they will be there to help with the housework, not to take care of the baby. Organize your shopping and cleaning on a weekly or monthly basis. Buy ahead and store as many items as you have room for. Make double portions of casseroles and recipes such as spaghetti sauce, then freeze the extra portions for later use. Stock up on disposables such as paper plates and napkins.

Try to locate a 24-hour pharmacy or one that will deliver to your home. Some deliver only prescriptions. Others have a minimum purchase policy. In addition, stock up on sanitary pads—you will need plenty of them the first 2 weeks you are home. If you plan to nurse, you may want to purchase nursing pads. Men's handkerchiefs and squares of old diaper material also serve this purpose well.

Plan for the Next Couple of Months

You can save yourself a lot of trouble after the baby arrives if you go out now and buy things such as gifts and cards for upcoming birthdays, graduations, and other holidays. You may also want to purchase some special gifts for your other children, as well as several "busy things"— such as coloring books and crayons, marking pens, and perhaps a video game or favorite movie—that you can bring out on a rough day. (For more suggestions concerning siblings, see "Helping Your Other Children Adjust" on page 280.)

If someone will be helping you care for your other children after you bring home the new baby, make a schedule of meals, naps, bedtimes, school, car pools, and after-school activities. Be sure to specify anything that is an absolute no-no. Leave a list of important numbers (pediatrician, school, car pool drivers, neighbors, and friends) next to the phone.

Finally, address and stamp the envelopes for your birth announcements before you go to the hospital. Then you will only need to fill in the details, which you can do in the hospital.

Pack Your Bags

Do not forget to pack your bags for the hospital or birth center. Doing this by your thirty-fifth week is not too early. Prepacked bags will mean one thing less to worry about if your baby decides that he does not want to wait for his due date.

To be fully prepared, you should pack the following bags:

❏ *Lamaze bag.* This should be the only bag that you bring with you when you check into the hospital or birth center in labor. It should contain all the items that you and your labor partner might need during labor, such as the following:

• This book for reference.

• A copy of your birth plan, signed by your caregiver. The original should be attached to your chart.

• Playing cards, books, or games to use for amusement if you are admitted early in labor.

• A watch with a second hand to time your contractions.

• Your Labor Record (see Appendix A on page 305) or paper and a pencil to record your contractions.

• A comfortable pair of shoes for walking during labor.

• An object or picture to use as a focal point.

• Extra pillows for support and comfort.

• Tennis balls tied in a sock to lie on if you have a backache.

• A wooden roller-type foot massager to help reduce your labor pain through acupressure.

• Cornstarch, oil, or lotion to reduce friction while doing effleurage or having your back rubbed.

• A small paper bag to breathe into if you hyperventilate.

• A washcloth for cooling your face.

• Sour lollipops to help prevent your mouth from becoming dry.

• A toothbrush, toothpaste, and mouthwash to help with a dry mouth.

• Lip balm or lip gloss to soothe dry lips.

• Heavy socks to keep your feet warm.

• A hand-held fan for your partner to cool you.

• Music tapes or compact disks and a player if music is not available in the labor room.

• Snacks and beverages for your labor partner to keep his energy up without having to leave the room to get food.

• A camera, a video camera, or a tape recorder to record the birth.

• Your baby book so the staff can record the baby's footprints directly in it.

A wooden roller-type foot massager can provide pain relief during labor using the acupressure points on the bottom of the feet. Place the foot massager on the floor in front of a chair, then move your feet over the roller as you sit in the chair and rock. You may prefer alternating feet.

• A list of all the people you need to notify, as well as their phone numbers and your calling card.

❏ *Hospital bag for yourself.* This should be left in the car until you are moved into your room after the birth. It should contain all the items that you will need for your hospital stay, such as the following:

• Nightgowns. (If you plan to breastfeed, make sure that they button in the front or are special nursing gowns.)

• A robe and slippers.

• Two to three nursing bras. (For help in purchasing this important undergarment, see "How to Select a Nursing Bra.")

• Your usual cosmetics and grooming aids.

• A shower cap.

• Birth announcements.

• Your going-home clothes, preferably a loose-fitting dress or maternity clothes, since it will be some weeks before you regain your prepregnant figure.

Ouch

Do not purchase sanitary pads with hi-tech weaves in case you have stitches. The stitches could "catch."

• Sanitary pads (plain pads, not ones with a hi-tech woven barrier, which "catches" perineal stitches) and peri-care items such as a squeeze bottle, medicated cleansing pads, and anesthetic spray. (These are usually supplied by the hospital and charged to your bill. However, if you have inadequate or no insurance, you will save money by purchasing them yourself. Just remember to inform the nursing staff so that you will not be billed, then *double-check your bill when you receive it.*)

❏ *Hospital bag for the baby.* Leave this in the car until after the birth. It should contain all the items that you will need for bringing the baby home, such as the following:

• A going-home outfit.

• Diapers.

• A pair of socks or booties.

• A hat (optional).

• A sweater or warm outer covering, depending on the weather.

• A receiving blanket and, if necessary, an outside blanket.

In addition to the items listed, you may want to add items of personal significance, such as a stuffed animal to comfort you during labor or photographs

---

How to Select a Nursing Bra

You should shop for a nursing bra during your last month of pregnancy in order to ensure a proper fit. Try to find one that is comfortable. The cups should be loose on top to allow for the use of breast pads or fullness as your milk comes in. The bra should not be tight around the rib cage. It also should not have underwires. Underwires can cause constriction of the milk flow and possibly result in plugged ducts. Cotton fabric is the softest and most absorbent. Avoid lace and any fabrics that may scratch or irritate your baby's skin. Look for a cup style that is easy to latch and unlatch with one hand, since you will be holding your infant with the other.

When you find a bra you like, purchase just one initially. Try it out to check for comfort. If it is comfortable, purchase two more so you will always have a spare.

of your other children to keep on your nightstand. However, leave items of value, such as jewelry, at home. Birth center clients may receive an additional list of supplies, including foods and beverages.

Prepare an Emergency Birth Kit

If you have a history of rapid labors, live some distance from the hospital, or just want to be prepared in case your baby arrives unexpectedly, pack an emergency birth kit. The items that you might need for an emergency delivery include the following:

❑ A flashlight for better vision or at night.

❑ Clean towels, newspapers, or crib pads to absorb the amniotic fluid.

❑ Clean handkerchiefs to wipe the baby's face.

❑ Blankets, including baby blankets to dry off the infant and a larger one to keep the mother and baby warm.

❑ A new ear syringe to suction the newborn's mouth and nose.

❑ New shoelaces to tie the umbilical cord after it stops pulsating. You do not need to cut the cord.

❑ A plastic bag to hold the placenta when it is delivered. Take the placenta with you to the hospital for examination.

Keep these items wrapped tightly in a clean plastic bag. Store the bag in a convenient place and take it with you when you leave for the hospital. (For additional tips, see "Emergency Childbirth" on page 175.)

Buy and Install a Safety Seat

In addition to the Lamaze bag, hospital bags, and emergency birth kit, you should also have a safety seat ready for the ride home. The safest place to install a car seat is in the middle of the back seat, facing the rear of the car. A special mirror can be installed to give you a view of your infant. If your car has dual air bags, *never* place the safety seat on the front passenger seat. In fact, no child under the age of 13 should ride in the front seat of a car with dual air bags. The force of a discharged air bag can injure or kill a child facing forward, and can even propel an infant seat, with possible fatal results.

Read and follow the instructions that come with the safety seat. In addition, read your car's owner's manual. It may be necessary to obtain an additional seat belt or a locking clip to ensure that the safety seat is securely fastened. The car seat should not slide side-to-side or forward if tugged on. If the safety seat does not pass the tug test, call the National Highway Traffic Safety Administration's Auto Safety Hotline at 800–424–9393. It may be necessary to exchange your safety seat for another model.

If you purchase a new seat, send in the warranty card. You will be notified directly of any recalls. If you have a seat that was previously used, call the manufacturer or the Auto Safety Hotline to confirm that the safety seat has not been recalled. Never use a car seat after it has been involved in an accident, no matter how minor. Such a seat is no longer considered safe. If you cannot afford to buy a safety seat, contact your local branch of the American Red Cross or your hospital to find out about renting a car seat. All fifty states have passed laws that require infants and small children to ride in safety seats.

*"We're still 'just a couple,'
but I think something is
coming between us!"*

For a further discussion of safety seats, see "Automobile Safety" on page 231.

Arrange for Care for Your Pets

If you have pets, you may want to designate someone to take care of them while you are at the hospital or birth center. Provide your "pet sitter" with written instructions and a key, and call him or her before you leave the house in labor. Ideally, the person you choose is already familiar with your pets.

Spend Time Together

The last weeks of pregnancy are a time of waiting and expectancy. If this is your first baby, this will be the last time you will be just "a couple." Spend time together doing favorite activities, going out to eat, or enjoying quiet evenings at home. Soon your life will change forever with the addition of the new baby. If you already have other children, include them in the preparations so that they feel important.

WARM-UP SIGNS OF LABOR

Prior to the onset of labor, you will notice several signs indicating that it is approaching. Some will happen several days or even weeks in advance. Others will occur when labor is imminent.

Lightening, or "dropping," refers to the fetus's head settling into the pelvis. After lightening, your abdomen may appear lower and protrude more. (See Figures 6.1 and 6.2.) You will be able to breathe easier and to eat more at one time. In addition, you may feel relief from heartburn. However, lightening increases the pressure in the pelvis, possibly causing greater frequency of urination. You may have increased backache because of the lower position of the fetus as well as its greater size. Your center of gravity will change with the new angle of the baby, which may cause you to become more awkward when walking. In addition, finding a comfortable sleeping position may be difficult.

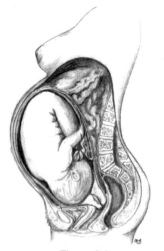

Figure 6.1.
The position of the baby
before lightening.

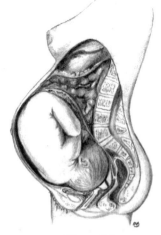

Figure 6.2.
The position of the baby
after lightening.

Try using relaxation techniques and extra pillows. If this is your first baby, lightening may happen 2 to 4 weeks before the onset of labor. With subsequent pregnancies, it may occur earlier or not until labor begins.

Your vaginal secretions will increase during the last weeks of pregnancy as your body prepares for the passage of the baby through the vagina. Effacement (thinning) and dilation (opening) of the cervix may start weeks before the onset of labor. Your mucous plug, a slightly brown, pink, or blood-tinged mucus, may be released.

Anxiety and depression are very common as the due date approaches or if it passes without labor beginning. Try to remain occupied and active.

A loss or leveling off of weight may be noticed in the last few days before labor begins. You could lose as much as 2 to 3 pounds due to excretion of excess tissue fluid. About 24 to 48 hours before delivery, some women notice a spurt of energy. You may have an urge to clean the entire house, wash floors or carpets, clean closets, or do some other chore that requires a great deal of work. *Do not give in to this "nesting" urge!* Nature gives you this extra energy to help you during labor.

Frequent bowel movements may be experienced within 48 hours of labor, cleansing the lower bowel in preparation for birth. You may notice more frequent Braxton-Hicks contractions. These contractions, named after the man who first described them, can be felt as early as the fourth month of pregnancy. These "practice" contractions prepare the uterus for labor and may cause some effacement and dilation to occur during the warm-up period. They do not ordinarily cause pain, but may be sufficiently strong and regular during the last weeks of pregnancy to be confused with true labor. When this happens, it is called false labor, or prelabor. For a comparison of prelabor and true labor contractions, see "True or False Labor."

Hints for the Labor Partner

During the warm-up phase:

❏ Spend time with your partner—for example, take her out to eat, take her out on a "date," accompany her on long walks.

❏ Continue to give your partner prenatal perineal massages.

❏ Help your partner pack her hospital and Lamaze bags. Place them in the car.

❏ Keep your car's gas tank full.

True or False Labor

Prelabor can be differentiated from true labor only by an internal examination. However, there are certain signs that can help to distinguish the two. These signs include the following:

True Labor	Prelabor
The contractions may be felt more in the back.	The contractions are felt more in the abdomen.
The contractions become stronger, last longer, and come closer together over time.	The contractions do not increase in intensity or length, even though sometimes they are strong and close together.
A bloody or pink mucous discharge is usually present.	There is no bloody mucous discharge.
The contractions continue or become more intense with a change in activity or a warm shower.	The contractions slow down or become less intense with a change in activity or a warm shower.
The contractions continue after eating.	The contractions slow or stop after eating.

True labor contractions effect changes in the cervix, causing it to thin out and open, while encouraging the baby to descend through the pelvis. Prelabor contractions do not do this.

ONSET OF LABOR

Researchers are continuing to analyze what factors are actually responsible for causing labor to begin. While the exact cause and mechanisms are not known, most evidence points to hormonal changes. Current research suggests that a complicated process that starts in the baby's brain causes labor to begin. The baby's hypothalamus, located in his brain, sends a hormone to his pituitary that causes the adrenal glands to increase their production of a chemical that the placenta turns into estrogen. This estrogen then causes the placenta to produce hormones called prostaglandins that cause contractions of the uterus. Thus, the process of chemical reactions that begins with the baby results in the uterine contractions of labor.

CONTRACTIONS AND HOW TO TIME THEM

**Table 6.1.
A sample chart of
timed contractions**

Start of Contraction	Duration of Contraction
10:00	45 seconds
10:10	45 seconds
10:15	60 seconds
10:20	55 seconds
10:25	60 seconds
10:29	60 seconds
10:33	65 seconds
10:37	60 seconds
10:40	60 seconds
10:43	65 seconds
10:47	60 seconds
10:51	60 seconds

Contractions are the periodic tightening and relaxing of the uterine muscles. They can be felt in different ways. Most commonly, a contraction is perceived as starting in the back and radiating to the front. The abdomen becomes very hard to the touch. Some women feel their contractions or discomfort just in the lower back or hip area. Many women describe contractions as exaggerated menstrual cramps or pressure in the groin or upper thighs. Others perceive contractions as severe gas pains, which they sometimes confuse with flu symptoms or intestinal disorders.

A contraction gradually builds in intensity until it reaches a peak, or strongest point. Then it gradually subsides. It is described by many women as a wave action. (See Figure 6.3.) Contractions are intermittent, with a rest period following each one. When timing contractions, time them from the beginning of one contraction to the beginning of the next. The easiest way to time contractions is to write down the time each one starts. You can also note the duration in seconds. A sample chart of timed contractions is presented in Table 6.1. Using this chart, you would tell your caregiver, "The contractions started at 10:00 and were 10 minutes apart, lasting 45 seconds. Now they are 3 to 4 minutes apart, lasting 60 to 65 seconds."

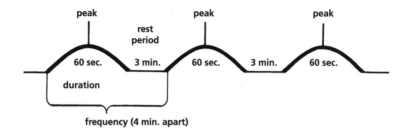

Figure 6.3.
A typical
contraction pattern.

SIGNS OF TRUE LABOR

True labor has begun when certain signs are present. If you notice any of these signs before your thirty-seventh week, contact your caregiver immediately. You could be experiencing preterm labor. The signs of true labor include the following:

❑ *Progressive contractions.* The contractions of true labor become longer, stronger, and closer together as labor advances. When they are timed, they show some regularity or pattern. Persistent contractions that have no rhythm but come less that 7 minutes apart should be reported to your caregiver.

❑ *Rupture of the membranes.* The rupture of the amniotic sac may be noticed as a gush or uncontrollable leakage of fluid from the vagina. This occurs as a first sign of labor in a small percentage of women. Most commonly, the membranes remain intact until late in labor. Amniotic fluid can usually be distinguished from urine or heavy vaginal secretions. It is colorless and odorless, and its leakage cannot be stopped by doing Kegel exercises. If you are uncertain, your caregiver can perform a test on the fluid to determine its source. If the fluid has a greenish appearance, your baby has had a bowel movement, called meconium, usually as a result of an episode of fetal distress. This will require closer monitoring during labor and extra suctioning of the baby after the delivery to prevent aspiration of this substance.

Contractions will generally start within 6 to 12 hours following the rupture of the amniotic sac. Contact your caregiver as soon as the membranes rupture because a passageway will now be open for infection. If contractions do not start on their own, your caregiver may want to induce labor with the drug Pitocin. In addition, do not douche or have intercourse after this time.

Although most doctors insist that babies be delivered 24 hours or less after the rupture of the membranes to prevent infection, some allow women to labor longer with good results. Frequent temperature checks and white blood cell counts can be used to monitor for infection. Of utmost importance is the avoidance of vaginal exams to prevent the introduction of bacteria into the vagina.

There is no such thing as a "dry birth." Approximately one-third of the amniotic fluid is replaced every hour. Also, the pressure from the baby's head acts as a cork against the cervix. You may notice intermittent leakage with the contractions as the pressure forces a small amount of fluid around the baby's head.

❑ *Loss of the mucous plug from the cervix.* Loss of the mucous plug is indicated by the presence of thick mucus, usually tinged with blood from small capillaries that were broken as the cervix began to dilate. This mucus is also called bloody show. Although the mucous plug usually is lost 24 to 48 hours before labor begins, it may be passed as much as a week in advance. Sometimes it is not noticed until labor is well established. The loss of the mucous plug without other signs is not labor.

Once labor is established, notify your caregiver. Be prepared to tell him:

❑ How far apart the contractions are, their length and their intensity, and if you are using breathing techniques.

❑ Whether the membranes have ruptured and, if they have, the color of the fluid and the time of the rupture.

❑ If a bloody show is present.

You will be instructed when to leave for the hospital or birth center.

Signs of Labor

The signs of true labor are:

❑ Progressive contractions

❑ Rupture of the membranes

❑ Loss of the mucous plug from the cervix

Call your caregiver if you are in labor.

**"Now let's see . . .
did I forget anything?"**

GOING TO THE HOSPITAL
OR BIRTH CENTER

Sometime during early or active labor, you will decide to go to your place of delivery. Whether or not this is your first baby, the distance to the hospital or birth center, your previous labor history, and your caregiver's opinion are factors to consider. Learning to recognize the signs of the various labor phases will allow you to judge your progress and thus avoid arriving too early.

When you go to the hospital or birth center, leave all your valuables at home. Take your suitcase, but leave it in the car. Do not forget your Lamaze bag. At a hospital, you generally go to the admissions office during the day and to the emergency room entrance at night. In many hospitals, you go directly to the labor and delivery unit.

When you arrive at the labor and delivery unit, your partner may be directed to a waiting room. This allows the nurse to speak privately with you. If you wish to remain together, inform the nurse. Not all facilities separate couples upon admission.

When you arrive in the birthing room, you will be asked questions about your medical history, your allergies to medications, and your present labor symptoms. You will also be asked if you plan to breastfeed or bottle feed. If a contraction starts during the questioning, stop talking and go into your breathing pattern. The nurse will wait. Finally, you will be given a vaginal exam to determine cervical dilation and effacement, and station of the presenting part.

After your labor has been verified and you have been admitted, you may be asked to undergo certain procedures depending on your caregiver, desires, and labor progress. Do not consider any of these procedures routine. Depending on your circumstances, they may or may not be necessary.

If delivering in a hospital, you will be placed on an electronic fetal monitor to determine the regularity and duration of the contractions. The nurse will also observe the baby's heart rate to assess fetal well-being in response to the contractions. (For a further discussion of this, see "Electronic Fetal Monitor" on page 168.) If delivering in a birth center, the nurse-midwife will assess your baby's heart rate by using a doptone and will observe your contractions for strength and frequency. Your blood pressure, temperature, pulse, and respiration will be taken. You will be asked to provide a urine sample, your blood will be drawn, and a vaginal culture may be done to detect the presence of group B strep.

If you are still in early labor, you may be instructed to walk around for a while to increase the strength of the contractions. Your physician may order an enema to cleanse the lower bowel. This is usually a soapsuds enema, which is made with about 1 quart of water and a soap solution. In addition to emptying the bowel, the enema also increases the strength and frequency of the contractions. This procedure will not be done if you are in advanced labor. Many doctors feel that an enema is unnecessary, especially if you have had a good bowel movement within the previous 24 hours. Occasionally, a woman may request an enema if she has been constipated or if she feels that she will not be able to effectively relax her bottom during the pushing stage for fear of soiling the bed. In this case, a small disposable will suffice.

Many facilities provide tubs or showers for laboring women. After the stress of the trip to the hospital or birth center and the admission procedures, relaxing in water can be soothing and can lower your blood pressure. The warm water provides buoyancy and reduces external stimuli, which allows you to relax both physically and mentally. Your relaxed body is better able to produce endorphins, the natural pain relievers. The more comfortable a woman is, the less likely she is to produce stress-related hormones, which can raise her blood pressure or slow the labor. There has been no increase in complications, such as infection, associated with laboring in water, even if the membranes have ruptured.

Most caregivers no longer prep laboring women (shave their pubic hair), since studies have shown that there is no increase in infection and the mother is spared the itching and discomfort associated with the regrowth of hair. If the hair is long, it may be trimmed with scissors. Some doctors do a mini prep (shave the area between the vaginal outlet and the rectum, which is where the episiotomy would be done). This is usually done prior to the actual delivery.

"Couldn't we just talk first?"

An IV may be started if indicated. To allow for increased mobility, some physicians place a saline lock or heparin lock in the vein. The procedure is the same as for starting an IV, but the bag of fluid is not connected and the line is flushed with either saline or a heparin solution to keep the vcin open. (For a discussion of this, see "Intravenous Fluids" on page 167.)

For the Labor Partner: The Labor Partner's Role as a Support Person

Many women have more than one support person for labor and birth. If you and another person are serving as labor partners, you can work together at times, while allowing each other a break occasionally. Your job is to provide comfort, support, and encouragement to the laboring woman and to remind her of her breathing and relaxation techniques and other comfort measures. If the other labor partner is a trained professional, she can supply the knowledge and technical expertise, while you provide the emotional support.

If you are separated from the mother-to-be during admission, you will be reunited with her within 30 to 45 minutes. When you are finally reunited with your partner, you may find her tense and losing control without your assistance. Immediately start encouraging her to relax and help her with her breathing techniques. Some couples do not want to be separated at all during labor so that the labor partner can assist the woman in remaining relaxed and cooperative from the start and can help her avoid the panic some women feel when they are left alone. Make your request during the admission procedure.

A few physicians still ask the labor partner to leave during exams and other procedures. Discuss this with your caregiver in advance.

For a summary of the labor partner's role during labor, birth, delivery of the placenta, and bonding and recovery, see Table 6.2 on page 142.

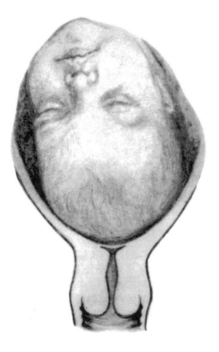

No effacement or dilation of the cervix.

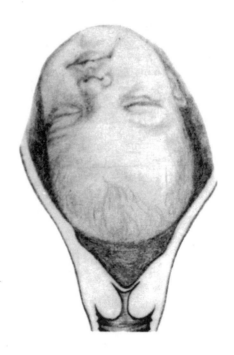

Cervix effaced 60 percent.

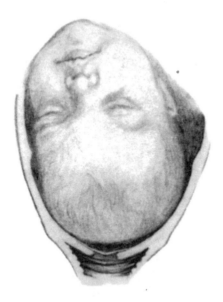

*Cervix effaced 100 percent
and dilated 2 centimeters.*

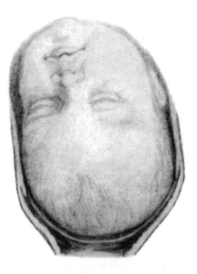

*Cervix effaced 100 percent
and dilated 10 centimeters.*

Figure 6.4. Effacement and dilation of the cervix.

FIRST STAGE OF LABOR

During the first stage of labor, the contractions of the uterine muscles cause the cervix to efface and dilate. (See Figure 6.4.) *Effacement* refers to the shortening and thinning of the cervix. It is expressed in percentages, from 0 percent (long and thick) to 100 percent (completely thinned out).

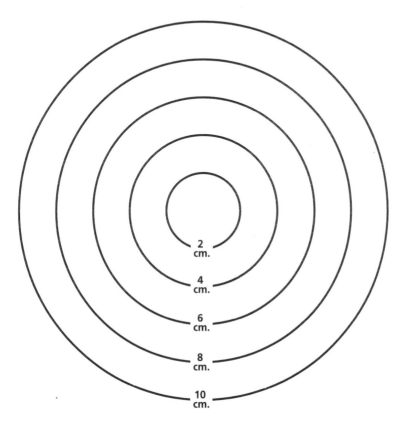

2 cm.

4 cm.

6 cm.

8 cm.

10 cm.

Figure 6.5.
Dilation chart (actual size).

Dilation refers to the opening of the cervix. It is measured in centimeters, from 0 centimeters (closed) to 10 centimeters (completely opened). (See Figure 6.5.) Dilation may also be expressed in fingers, with 5 fingers equal to 10 centimeters (approximately 4 inches). Dilation is complete when the cervix has opened wide enough for the baby's head to pass through into the vagina.

Another term used to measure labor progress is *station*. *Station* refers to the location of the baby's presenting part, usually the head, in relation to the level of ischial spines of the pelvis. (See Figure 6.6.) It indicates the degree of descent of the baby through the pelvis. The station of the baby is expressed in centimeters above (minus) or below (plus) the level of the ischial spines (zero station). The head is usually engaged when it reaches zero station.

Your caregiver or a nurse will determine your progress during labor by vaginal examination. He or she will measure the effacement and dilation of the cervix and determine the station of the baby. Though sometimes uncomfortable, these examinations will help assess your progress.

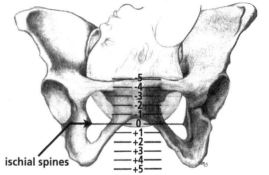

ischial spines

-5
-4
-3
-2
-1
0
+1
+2
+3
+4
+5

Figure 6.6.
The baby's head at zero station, which is even with the ischial spines.

*Hints for
the Labor Partner*

During early labor:

❑ Time your partner's
contractions.

❑ Help your partner determine
if it is true labor or prelabor.

❑ Encourage your partner to
sleep if labor begins at night.

❑ Stop and support your
partner during contractions
if you are walking with her.

❑ Remind your partner
to urinate every 1 to 2 hours.

❑ Offer your partner
snacks and liquids.

❑ Offer to give your partner
a massage or back rub.

❑ Tell your partner that
she is doing great.

The first stage of labor is divided into three phases—early, active, and transition. These phases will be discussed individually.

Early Labor

Early labor is the easiest but longest phase of labor. It usually lasts from 2 to 9 hours. Along with effacing, the cervix dilates from 0 to 4 centimeters. Contractions during this phase are from 30 to 60 seconds long. They usually start 15 to 20 minutes apart and get progressively closer until they are about 5 minutes apart. They start out mild to slightly uncomfortable, and become stronger and longer as labor progresses.

During the rest period between contractions, you should feel good, be talkative, and be able to walk around and continue your normal activities. You will probably be at home for most of this phase. Prepared women generally feel very confident during this time and handle the labor well. Some women express anxiety, realizing that once labor has begun, it will not stop.

If labor starts during the day, walk around and keep active to help stimulate the contractions. If labor begins at night, get some sleep or rest so that you can better handle the active phase. Be assured that when your contractions become strong, you will awaken!

During early labor, you can enjoy sweet liquids such as decaffeinated tea, apple juice, and sports drinks, as well as Jell-O, broth, and Popsicles. Avoid diet beverages, caffeinated beverages, milk, and citrus juices. You may also eat nutritious snacks that are high in carbohydrates and low in fat, such as crackers, fruit, toast, pasta, cereal, and waffles. These foods provide the nourishment needed for labor. In one study, women who were encouraged to eat and drink during labor required less pain relief and less Pitocin, and experienced a shortening of their labor by an average of 90 minutes.[2] Digestion slows during more active labor, and the laboring woman's desire for food diminishes.

The needs of a woman in labor are similar to those of an athlete. Prior to an event, an athlete loads up on carbohydrates in order to have the energy supplies that his or her body needs during the event. These needs are similar during labor and especially during the hard physical work of pushing. Fasting while in labor increases the production of ketones in the woman's system, since her body must use fat stores to supply the body with glucose. Frequently, IVs are started during labor to prevent dehydration, electrolyte imbalance, and ketosis. Being required to fast is often mentioned by women as a factor that increased their stress during labor. If women were encouraged to simply eat and drink, these negative side effects would be reduced. Permitting women to eat and drink as they desire provides hydration, nutrition, increased comfort, and a feeling of being in control.[3]

Eating during labor remains controversial because of the possibility of vomiting and aspirating the stomach contents into the lungs if general anesthesia is given. On the other hand, general anesthesia is seldom used, and if you vomit while you are awake and alert, you will not have a problem. Aspiration of stomach contents by a woman who fasted can be more serious than by a woman who ate. These contents are highly acidic from the hydrochloric acid that is produced in the stomach. Also, aspiration pneumonia is more common if the woman is given a general anesthetic and not intubated (having a breathing tube inserted into the windpipe) or intubated incorrectly. Current guidelines require that all laboring women be treated as if they had eaten and require the use of techniques to prevent aspiration of stomach contents.

Early labor.

For the Labor Partner: The Labor Partner's Role in Early Labor

Early labor is the time to become familiar with contractions. If you place your hand on your partner's abdomen, you can feel the uterus become very hard. Sometimes you can feel a contraction beginning even before your partner is aware of it and can help her prepare for it. Help out by timing the contractions and making sure that your partner is relaxing with them. If you notice her tensing or expressing discomfort during contractions, encourage her to relax, begin slow paced breathing, change position, or urinate. (A full bladder often causes discomfort during labor.) Suggest that she lie in a tub of warm water or take a shower.

Active labor.

Active Labor

During active labor, the cervix dilates from 4 to 8 centimeters. After 5 centimeters, labor may progress very rapidly. In fact, labor is more than half over at this point, with the contractions becoming stronger and peaking faster. The peaks also last longer now. The contractions usually last from 45 to 60 seconds and are 2 to 4 minutes apart. If the membranes rupture now, they usually do so with a gush. Many women notice an increase in the intensity of the contractions after the water breaks.

During the active phase, your mood will become serious and very birth-oriented. You may not want to be distracted and may begin to doubt your ability to cope with the contractions. You will no longer want to play cards or games, will be less talkative between contractions, and may need more help in remaining relaxed. You may want to change position or try laboring in a tub or shower.

For the Labor Partner: The Labor Partner's Role in Active Labor

Continue reassuring and encouraging your partner. It is important to keep her informed of her progress at this time. Help her to maintain control during contractions and assist her with breathing if necessary. She may want to use your eyes as her focal point. Keep your commands to your partner short, since she may not be interested in long conversations. Continue to remind her to empty her bladder every 1 to 2 hours.

Offer your partner comfort measures as needed. If her mouth is dry, help her sip juice, suck on ice chips or a Popsicle, brush her teeth, or rinse with mouthwash. For dry lips, help her apply lip balm or lip gloss. Wiping her face with a cool cloth may help her feel refreshed. If you are walking with her, you may need to stop and support her during a contraction. If she is in bed, have her change position often, about every 20 to 30 minutes, and help her adjust the bed for comfort. You can start to utilize some of the other tools for labor, such as massage, counterpressure, acupressure, or hot or cold compresses.

Hints for the Labor Partner

During active labor:

❑ Encourage your partner to take a bath or shower.

❑ Drive your partner safely to the hospital or birth center.

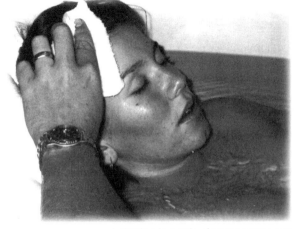

Laboring in a tub of warm water can aid relaxation during active labor.

*Hints for
the Labor Partner*

During active labor and
transition:

❑ Be positive.

❑ Encourage your partner to
change position.

❑ Do not leave your partner
for any reason.

❑ Tell your partner that
she is wonderful.

❑ Wipe your partner's face
with a cool cloth.

❑ Offer your partner sips of
liquids or ice chips.

❑ Help your partner apply lip
balm to prevent dry lips.

❑ Try acupressure.

❑ Stay calm.

❑ Maintain eye contact with
your partner if she becomes
confused or panicky.

❑ Tell your partner that
labor is almost over.

❑ Encourage your partner to
breathe evenly and slowly.

❑ Breathe with your partner
if she begins to breathe
too rapidly.

❑ Get your partner to focus on
you and to imitate your rate
of breathing.

❑ If your partner feels "tingly,"
help her to stop hyperventilating
by directing her to cup her hands
around her mouth and rebreathe
the air she exhales.

Transition

The transition from the first stage of labor to the second stage is the shortest phase, but it is also the most intense. The cervix dilates from 8 to 10 centimeters. The contractions are usually 60 to 90 seconds in duration and peak very suddenly, possibly more than once. In addition, the contractions may be as close as 1 1/2 to 2 minutes apart. Even though there is a short rest period, some women say that the contractions feel as though they are right on top of one another with no relief. Transition may last 10 minutes to 1 1/2 hours. Think positive—labor is almost over!

Certain signs will alert you and your labor partner to the fact that you are in transition. These signs, which you may or may not experience, are:

❑ Premature urge to push or bear down. You may mistakenly think that you need to have a bowel movement.

❑ Belching or hiccups.

❑ Nausea and/or vomiting.

❑ Shaking or uncontrollable trembling of your legs or body.

❑ Chills and/or extreme warmth.

❑ Loss of modesty. You may throw off your covers.

❑ Cramps in your legs and buttocks.

❑ Sensitivity to touch. You may not want to be touched.

❑ Spontaneous rupture of the membranes now if it did not yet happen. At this point, it usually happens with a gush.

❑ Dopey feeling, amnesia between contractions, or sleeping between contractions. This is probably caused by the release of endorphins.

❑ Increased bloody mucous discharge.

❑ Confusion and/or a tendency to give up. You may say, "I can't do it," or "I can't take another contraction."

❑ Feeling of getting nowhere, that labor will never end.

❑ Panic if left alone.

❑ Susceptibility to suggestion, especially if offered medication.

❑ Inability to comprehend direction and a need for your labor partner to do the breathing patterns with you.

❑ Irritability and restlessness.

❑ Feeling of being out of control. You may feel overwhelmed by the contractions.

❑ Flushed face.

Be assured that you will not experience all of these signs.

For the Labor Partner: The Labor Partner's Role in Transition

During transition, your encouragement and presence are vital. *Do not leave your partner during this time for any reason.* She may panic if left alone, even for a short period. She may more than likely accept any medication that is offered or may possibly ask for medication, even though her decision was not to use drugs. Remind her that she is in transition and any medication taken at this time may not take effect until the phase is over. However, any drugs taken now might have a strong effect on the baby. An epidural may not begin to provide relief until the pushing stage, at which time she will need to be able to feel the sensations to push effectively. Many women find that relaxing in water during transition provides sufficient pain relief to avoid the need for medication.

If your partner says that she needs to move her bowels or begins to bear down, inform the nurse so that an examination can be performed. If the cervix is not fully dilated but is stretchy, the nurse may instruct the woman to bear down with the contraction to see if the cervix will open completely. But if the cervix is unyielding and tight around the baby's head, pushing will only cause exhaustion. In this case, you will have to instruct your partner to blow out forcefully during the urge to push.

You must make sure during transition that your partner "catches" each contraction. If she sleeps or has amnesia between contractions, you must make sure that she starts her breathing pattern in time. Let her know when the contraction ends and help her to relax in between. *Remain calm.* Even if your partner yells at you, do not argue. Make your commands short and precise. If your partner becomes confused, have her sit up in bed.

If your partner says that she wants to give up, keep reminding her that this is the shortest phase and that labor is almost over. Occasionally, a woman will want to squeeze something. Be careful what you offer her! If her fingernails are long, they may dig into your skin. Give her a pillow to hold. Offer her two fingers to grasp, rather than your full hand, especially if you wear a ring.

Transition.

For the Labor Partner: What Should I Do If She Panics?

You may notice that your partner is not using a focal point, is rocking her head from side to side, or is gripping the bed sheet, your hand, or a bed rail. She may stop her breathing pattern and hold her breath, yell, or cry out. She may even thrash around in the bed. Your partner is panicking. To help her regain control, you should first stand up. This puts you in an authority position. Grasp her face or wrists with your hands and call her name. Bring your face close to hers and do the breathing pattern with her. If she is vocal, encourage low moaning, but direct high squeals to a lower octave. You may need to be firm with her during this time and take full command of the situation. Generally, when the contractions become unbearable, transition is almost over, with just a few contractions left. Be sure to tell your partner this.

Continue with the other comfort measures as needed. If your partner's back is uncomfortable, perform counterpressure or acupressure, massage the area, or apply a warm or cool cloth. If her feet are cold, put warm socks on them. If her legs are trembling, firmly massage her inner thighs or grasp her legs. Keep a cool cloth on her forehead or neck if she is nauseated. Tell her she is doing wonderfully and keep her informed of her progress. Above all else, keep a positive attitude!

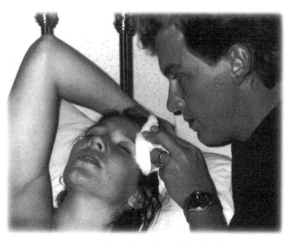

A cool cloth on the forehead can be soothing during transition.

Pushing.

SECOND STAGE OF LABOR

The second stage of labor begins when the cervix is completely dilated and effaced, and ends with the birth of the baby. The contractions are more like those experienced during active labor, lasting approximately 60 to 75 seconds. They slow in frequency and are usually 3 to 5 minutes apart. The pushing stage may last from 10 minutes to 2 hours. For a woman who has given birth before, this stage is generally short.

During the peaks of the contractions, you will feel a strong urge to push. If you do not feel the urge to push, ask to wait to begin pushing and continue to use your breathing patterns. Get into a more upright position to allow gravity to aid the descent of the baby in the pelvis. Avoid pushing until you feel the urge develop. Pushing without your body's direction is difficult and unsatisfying. If you were given an epidural, ask to have the medication reduced or turned off so that you can feel the contractions. If you are unable to move your legs or feel the contractions, it may take a while for the epidural's effects to diminish. Your pushing will be more effective if you wait until you can feel the urge to push and are able to move your legs.

You might find yourself enjoying a rest period between the first and second stages of labor. The contractions may stop for 10 to 15 minutes. Use this opportunity to rest and to prepare for the hard work of pushing.

During the pushing stage, your mood will greatly improve. You will become sociable, even talkative, and will feel more positive about your progress in labor. If you have been blowing to combat a premature urge to push, you will feel tremendous relief at being able to work actively with the contractions. Many women feel great satisfaction while pushing the baby down the birth canal, even though they are working very hard. Some women even equate the baby's emerging from the vagina with an orgasmic experience.

As the baby descends the birth canal, you may experience an increased bloody show, a burning or splitting sensation, or leg cramps. Your face may turn red or begin perspiring, and you may have a look of intense concentration. You may grunt or groan involuntarily as you actively work with the contractions. Your partner may misinterpret these normal responses as expressions of pain. Some women express discomfort or pain with pushing, which is usually associated with an unusual presentation or position of the baby, poor position of the woman, a large baby, or an unrelaxed pelvic floor. You may have a strong feeling of needing to have a bowel movement, to which you may respond by tightening the pelvic floor so that you will not soil the bed. This feeling is a normal sensation as the baby's head presses against the bowel. Do not react to this sensation by tensing. Instead, concentrate on relaxing your bottom for maximum comfort and progress. (If you relax your jaw, your pelvic floor will also relax. When you practice your Kegel exercises, you should notice that if you tense your jaw, you feel a tightening in the pelvic floor. Conversely, if you relax your jaw, your pelvic floor also relaxes.)

The intensity of pushing is reflected in the faces of both the woman and her labor partner.

You will feel a large amount of pressure or a burning sensation as the baby nears the perineum. Your caregiver may perform perineal massage to stretch

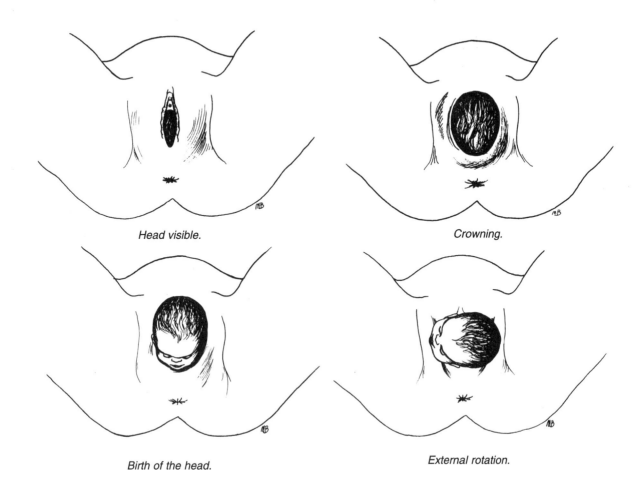

Head visible.

Crowning.

Birth of the head.

External rotation.

Figure 6.7.
Birth of the baby's head.

the tissues. During contractions, you may notice the baby's head at the vaginal outlet, along with some bulging of the perineum and separation of the vaginal lips. The head may appear wrinkled and covered with wet hair. It will recede between contractions until, finally, the top part remains visible between contractions. This is known as crowning. (See Figure 6.7.) With the next few contractions, the head will be born. It will then rotate, the face turning toward your thigh. The shoulders will be delivered, and the body will slide out with ease, often accompanied by a gush of amniotic fluid. Many couples help with the delivery of the baby. Once the shoulders are free, the woman and/or labor partner can reach down and pull the baby onto the woman's abdomen. The labor partner can then cut the umbilical cord after it has stopped pulsating.

At this point, you and your labor partner will probably be so overwhelmed by the sight, sound, and feel of your new infant that you will not notice any of the other activity going on around you.

For a discussion of the differences between laboring and delivering in a birth center and in a hospital, see "Delivery Procedures in Out-of-Hospital Birth Centers and Hospital Birthing Rooms."

Delivery Procedures in Out-of-Hospital Birth Centers and Hospital Birthing Rooms

Out-of-hospital birth centers and in-hospital birthing rooms offer a number of options to couples expecting an uncomplicated labor. Most birthing centers are run by certified nurse-midwives, with a physician as a backup in case a complication arises. They are usually located outside a hospital and accept only low-risk women as clients. In-hospital birthing rooms offer many of the same options as birthing centers do, but are located in the labor and delivery area of a hospital and utilize the hospital staff. If your caregiver is a physician, the nursing staff will monitor and care for you during labor. Your physician will arrive for the delivery. Occasionally, if your physician is in the hospital, he may visit several times during your labor. If you have chosen a nurse-midwife as your caregiver, she will often remain with you during labor to monitor your progress, as well as to perform the delivery.

Only a few hospitals still require women to labor in one room, transfer to a delivery room, move to a recovery and bonding room, and finally go to a postpartum room. The majority of hospitals have birthing rooms, also known as LDRs (labor, delivery, recovery), where a woman stays until she is transferred to a postpartum room. The newest form of birthing room is the LDRP (labor, delivery, recovery, postpartum), in which a woman remains for her entire hospital stay. This type of birthing room is the closest in concept to the birth center.

In both birth centers and birthing rooms, attractive surroundings make the room homelike, with the necessary medical equipment hidden within furniture. Restrictions on visitors are minimal or nonexistent. Siblings may even be present for the birth. A woman is free to move about the room and halls, and to labor in a comfortable recliner or rocking chair. Many facilities offer showers or tubs in which women can relax during labor.

In out-of-hospital birth centers, few interventions are used and only if medically necessary—for example, IVs, fetal monitors, and draping are not routine. Women are encouraged to eat and drink as they desire. Most birth centers have regular beds, which allow the woman to choose whatever position feels most comfortable to her. She may even deliver on a birthing chair or stool. At the moment of birth, the mother and father can reach down and lift their baby up onto the mother's bare abdomen. The infant is never separated from the parents to go to a nursery; all exams are done in the same room. Several hours after birth, when the mother is ready to get washed, she may take her baby into the tub with her for his first bath. Birth center philosophy considers not only the mother's physical needs, but also her emotional and spiritual concerns. Families play an integral part in planning the birth to provide a safe delivery in a loving, caring atmosphere. The woman and the baby usually go home within 6 hours after the birth and are followed closely by the nurse-midwife via telephone conversations and an office or home visit during the first days.

Most in-hospital birthing rooms have birthing beds that can be maneuvered into various positions. A common delivery position elevates the woman's back and places her feet in footrests or stirrups. The lithotomy position should be avoided. Many doctors are willing to try alternate positions that are more comfortable for the woman. At the time of delivery, the bottom of the bed is removed, an antiseptic solution is poured over the woman's perineum, and her legs are draped. Not all doctors require stirrups or leg drapes to be used. Others do not use abdominal drapes, recognizing the importance of the skin-to-skin contact that is obtained when the newborn is placed on the mother's bare abdomen following delivery. Many supportive doctors hand the newborn right to the mother to touch and caress as the family begins the bonding process immediately after birth. If you choose to deliver in a hospital, discuss these and all options with your caregiver to ensure an optimum birth experience.

For the Labor Partner: The Labor Partner's Role During the Second Stage of Labor

Help your partner into a comfortable pushing position. If she holds her breath while pushing, count for her. In addition, make sure that she releases a small amount of air before holding her breath. Check her jaw to make sure that it is relaxed. Place warm wet compresses or washcloths on her perineum. They will be very comforting and can help ease the burning sensation. They may also help her relax and may reduce her chance of needing an episiotomy. As the baby's head is delivered and the caregiver instructs your partner how to push and when not to push, you may need to repeat the instructions to her.

Have your camera or recording equipment ready. Make sure that the mirror is adjusted correctly and that your partner is wearing her contacts or eyeglasses if needed. Encourage her to keep her eyes open while pushing so that she can see her progress in the mirror and not miss the actual birth.

Cutting the Cord

Once the baby is born and breathing on his own, he no longer needs the umbilical cord. The caregiver will clamp the cord and then may ask the partner if he wants to cut it. Some caregivers do this immediately after birth. Others wait until the cord has stopped pulsating, which may take up to 5 minutes. Dr. Frederick Leboyer, a noted French obstetrician, advocated delay in cutting the cord. Delay benefits the infant, as he receives oxygen from two sources—his lungs and the placenta—until his lungs can adjust and take over on their own. This decreases the incidence of anoxia (lack of oxygen).

If you made arrangements to have the cord blood collected, it will be done at this time. (For a full discussion of this, see "Make Arrangements for Cord Blood Banking" on page 115.)

THIRD STAGE OF LABOR

The third stage of labor is the shortest stage, lasting from 5 to 20 minutes. After the baby is born, the uterus continues contracting, although with less intensity than during the first two stages. The placenta spontaneously separates from the wall of the uterus and is expelled. You may be asked to push with the contractions to deliver the placenta, or your caregiver may guide the placenta out using firm fundal pressure. The placenta should be allowed to separate without strong traction or pulling on the cord. Otherwise, placental tissue may be retained inside the uterus, which can result in postpartum hemorrhaging.

Once the placenta is delivered, your caregiver will examine it to determine if it is intact. If necessary, he may do an internal examination of the uterus to make sure that no placental tissue has been retained. This examination is uncomfortable, but you can reduce the discomfort by doing a breathing pattern.

FOURTH STAGE OF LABOR

During the fourth stage of labor, your caregiver will repair the episiotomy, if one was done, as well as any vaginal or perineal lacerations. If the repair work becomes uncomfortable, ask for another injection of local anesthetic.

Hints for the Labor Partner

During pushing:

❏ Assist your partner in finding a comfortable position.

❏ Tell your partner to "look for the baby" as she bears down.

❏ Apply warm washcloths to your partner's perineum.

❏ If your partner is breath holding while pushing, make sure she first lets a little air out, then pace her efforts by counting to 6.

❏ Provide a mirror so she can see her progress.

❏ Continue telling her that she is doing great.

Bonding.

If you were given medication to help contract the uterus, or if you have already started breastfeeding, you may notice uterine contractions. In addition, you may feel exhilarated and very excited about the baby. If your labor was long or difficult, you may feel relieved or exhausted. Your legs and/or your body may tremble involuntarily.

Bonding

Bonding refers to the development of the attachment that a mother and father feel for their child. This process actually begins before birth, when the parents-to-be feel their baby's movements and anticipate his arrival. The feeling is heightened at the first sight of the newborn. For centuries, mothers have felt the desire to hold and cuddle their new babies as soon as possible after birth. Studies confirm that this is best for the babies, too.

The current emphasis on bonding is the result of research first done in connection with battered, abused, and "failure to thrive" children. "Failure to thrive" babies do not grow, gain weight, or develop behaviorally at a normal rate, even though they have no sign of an organic disease. A profound number of the infants studied had been separated from their mothers at birth for a period of time. A significant correlation was found between this early separation and the subsequent development of these disastrous conditions.[4] In addition, researchers have documented that in the animal kingdom, when a mother and baby are separated, the mother abandons or rejects the baby. As a result, neonatal intensive care nurseries now encourage families to visit, touch, cuddle, and even assist in the care of their premature or sick newborns during hospitalization.

Numerous studies by Marshall Klaus and John Kennell have confirmed these original findings. Parents who spent time with their newborns immediately after birth and for an extended period while in the hospital were found to be more responsive to their babies' needs in the following weeks, months, and even years.[5] This, in turn, had a positive effect on the learning abilities and the social and emotional development of these children. The children were found to be better adjusted, have more self-esteem, and develop their own sense of identity and independence sooner.

Mother, father, and baby bonding.

Because of these findings, Drs. Klaus and Kennell suggest that a father, mother, and infant be allowed to spend at least 1 hour together in privacy soon after birth, and that the mother and baby be allowed to stay together as much as the mother desires while in the hospital. During the first 45 minutes of life, the baby is in a quiet alert state. In this state, the baby is awake and responsive to his environment. He looks intently at his mother's face and gazes into her eyes. It is now known that babies can see at birth and that they focus best on objects 8 to 10 inches away—the distance between an infant's face and his mother's face when he is being breastfed. It is suggested that a newborn's eyes not be treated with antibiotic ointment or silver nitrate drops until after this initial bonding period to avoid interference with vision.

Ideally, breastfeeding should also be initiated soon after birth. Many studies have shown that if the baby nurses within this first hour, the mother and baby will be more successful at breastfeeding.[6] In addition, the colostrum that the baby ingests during the first nursing period provides him with protection against infection and acts as a laxative, cleansing his system of mucus and meconium. The mother also benefits from early nursing. The baby's sucking releases the hormone prolactin, which enhances maternal feelings. Oxytocin, which is also released, causes the uterus to contract and reduces blood loss following birth.

Most hospitals no longer separate mothers and infants right after birth. Parents begin bonding with their newborns in the same room where the woman labored and gave birth. In complete privacy, the new parents can explore and marvel at their creation. The mother can hold her naked infant close to her bare breast, provide skin-to-skin contact, and begin the nursing relationship. By covering mother and baby with a blanket, a drop in the baby's temperature can be prevented, even without a heat lamp. Both parents can hold, talk to, and caress the baby. Do not be surprised if you find yourselves talking to your newborn in high-pitched voices. This is almost instinctive, and babies respond very positively to these sounds.

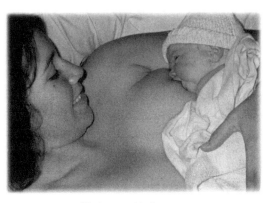

Mother and baby nurse soon after delivery.

When you hold your baby in your arms, you will notice that he is especially attracted to your eyes and facial features. He will respond by gazing, listening, imitating, possibly crying (he can be soothed), and following you with his eyes. He is so new, yet so alert!

A positive childbirth experience usually fosters the bonding process. Similarly, a negative childbirth experience may adversely affect a mother's feelings toward her child for a while and thus cause a delay in maternal attachment. Some parents simply take a little longer to develop loving emotions toward their newborns. In these cases, bonding takes place in the weeks following birth, rather than during the first few minutes. The newborn stage is not the only time in a baby's life when a strong parent-baby bond can be established. The initial bonding period can be compared to a honeymoon: If a couple become ardent, completely satisfied lovers, then so much the better. But a less-than-perfect honeymoon does not doom a marriage. Nor does a less-than-perfect birth-bonding experience doom the parent-child relationship.

Any medications used during labor and delivery may also adversely affect the bonding experience. If a mother is heavily sedated, she will not be able to interact with her baby immediately. In this case, she should bond with her baby as soon as she is able. In addition, the father can arrange to bond with the baby right after delivery.

A baby who received medication via the placenta may be sleepy and less responsive right after birth. The medication may remain in his system for as long as 30 days[7] and may affect his responses and sucking ability. Bonding is more difficult in this situation.

Active participation in the birth of their child enhances the parents' strong feelings of attachment toward the baby. In addition, when a woman and man work together to bring about the birth of their baby, they feel a closeness toward one another that is not easily forgotten. The bonding between mother and father can be tremendous. They should work to maintain this close feeling, especially during those difficult first 6 weeks after birth.

Make the most of your opportunity for bonding. Find out about your hospital's policies on bonding and about 24-hour rooming-in. Some hospitals do not separate the mother from her infant at all, moving them directly from the

Hints for the Labor Partner

After the birth:

❑ Take photos of the mother and baby.

❑ Cut the cord when it has stopped pulsating.

❑ Hold and talk to the newborn.

❑ Tell your partner that she was wonderful!

birthing room to a postpartum room. All the care and examinations are done in the mother's room. Other hospitals take the baby to the nursery after delivery for the initial bath and for routine examinations by the nurse or pediatrician. You should discuss your desires for bonding and extended contact with both your caregiver and your baby's pediatrician. Bonding is very important in family-centered maternity care, enabling parents to love and cuddle their new baby as they welcome him into their lives.

Recovery

While you are bonding with your new baby, you will be closely observed for about 1 to 2 hours. This is the time it usually takes for the vital signs—blood pressure, pulse, and respiration—to stabilize.

The nursing staff will check your uterus for firmness and for position in the abdomen. A nurse will massage your fundus, or instruct you to do so, to keep the uterus in a contracted state. The amount and consistency of the lochia will be closely watched. Lochia is the normal discharge of blood, excess tissue, and fluids from the uterus after birth. You will be asked to urinate before you are allowed to leave the birthing room because a distended bladder can force the uterus up and out of position and cause it to relax. However, you may not feel the need to urinate, since other sensations after birth can mask awareness of a full bladder. If necessary, the nurse will insert a catheter into your bladder to empty it.

A blanket will help stop your legs from trembling, an experience that is common postpartum. An ice bag will be placed on your perineum to reduce swelling and relieve discomfort. If you have afterbirth contractions caused by your uterus continuing to contract and grow smaller, use slow paced breathing. These afterbirth pains are more noticeable after second and subsequent births.

During recovery, you should try to do Kegel exercises. Contracting the pelvic floor muscles increases blood flow to the area, which reduces swelling and speeds healing of the episiotomy site. If you did not have an episiotomy, you should still do Kegels to help restore the muscle tone of your pelvic floor.

You may be hungry and thirsty after the work of labor and birth. The nursing staff should give you some well-deserved nourishment. If a meal or snack is not offered, ask for one.

Both you and your partner will experience an emotional high, feeling proud of your accomplishment. Together, you will probably relive the details of the birth over and over again.

ROOMING-IN

Rooming-in is available in most hospitals and should be initiated as soon after birth as possible. It allows the mother to keep the baby in the room with her for all or part of the day. With complete rooming-in, the baby stays with the mother day and night, while with partial rooming-in, the baby stays with the mother from morning until evening and then goes to the nursery for the night. With the latter, the mother can have the baby brought to her for nighttime feedings. With flexible rooming-in, the baby stays with the mother but can be returned to the nursery whenever the mother desires.

Even with complete rooming-in, many hospitals return the baby to the nursery for a short period each morning for a pediatric examination. During this time, the mother can shower and receive any required nursing care. In other hospitals, the pediatrician examines the baby in the mother's room.

The bond of affection formed immediately after birth can grow and deepen during the hospital stay. The close association and interaction between mother and baby continue as the mother cares for her infant. Mothers who opt for rooming-in feel more confident and competent at caring for their babies than do mothers who are separated from their babies by traditional hospital routines. Since hospital stays are approximately 24 hours after a vaginal birth, the more time you can spend with your baby under the guidance of a nurse, the more competent you will feel when you take your baby home.

Drs. Klaus and Kennell believe that while in the hospital, mothers should have complete care of their infants, with nurses available as consultants. As a result of extended contact with their babies, rooming-in mothers seem to develop maternal feelings more quickly and to resume physical activities earlier than mothers who do not room-in. Babies who interact with just one caregiver—the mother—appear to be more content. They cry less and organize their sleep-awake rhythms and feeding patterns more quickly than babies who interact with several caregivers and are fed on a rigid schedule. Rooming-in on a 24-hour basis provides the best opportunity for successful breastfeeding.

Rooming-in also gives the father a chance to hold, care for, and enjoy his baby before bringing him home. This strengthens the paternal bond and helps the father adjust to the new baby.

SIBLING VISITATION

A mother's ability to adjust to a home situation that includes other children will be greatly improved if the other children are allowed to visit her in the hospital. Visiting their mother will reduce any separation anxieties the children may be experiencing. Many hospitals allow children to visit their mother and new brother or sister. A number also allow children to be present for their sibling's birth. (For a discussion of this, see "Children at Birth" on page 140.) Early involvement by all family members enhances family bonding. *Note:* Have all visitors wash their hands well before handling the baby.

HOSPITAL STAY

The length of the hospital stay will be determined by the mother's health insurance, the health of the mother and baby, the needs of the other children at home, and monetary concerns. Some mothers choose to be discharged hours after birth, while others prefer to stay the full 2 days. In many areas of the country, discharge within 24 hours after birth is common. A federal law that went into effect in 1997 mandates insurance companies to pay for no less than a 48-hour stay for women following a vaginal delivery and for no less than 96 hours following a cesarean. Most birth centers allow mothers to go home 4 to 6 hours after delivery, but provide daily phone consultations and a follow-up visit within 3 days after birth.

The new law grew out of a great concern over the decreasing amount of time women stayed in the hospital. A primary concern was that many breastfeeding women did not recognize the signs indicating that an infant is not receiving enough milk. The National Association of Childbearing Centers,

Children at Birth

Many facilities now offer the opportunity for children to be present for the birth of their sibling. The decision to include your other child should be discussed first with your partner. During the pregnancy, as you discuss the new baby, you can also begin to offer the opportunity for your child to learn more about the changes in your body and about the actual birth. If he shows an interest in being present at the birth, you may want to prepare him in greater detail. Make sure that the information is age appropriate.

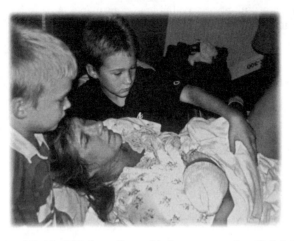

Discuss anatomy and show pictures of fetal development corresponding to your week of gestation. You should become more comfortable with your child seeing your undressed pregnant body. As you get closer to the end of pregnancy, discuss labor and birth. Show photos, slides, and films, and discuss the presence of blood and fluids. Reinforce that these are normal and expected, since most children associate blood with injuries and death. Some films also show the delivery of the placenta. Do not be surprised if the child describes the placenta as gross or disgusting. You can ask the child if he would like to help the father cut the umbilical cord. Reassure him that this procedure is not painful to the baby. Ask him to draw pictures. These offer insight into his level of understanding of the information and also provide clues about his concerns.

Prepare your child for the sights and sounds associated with hard labor and giving birth. Practice breathing and pushing, making sure to demonstrate positions and simulate moans, grunts, and groans.

Have your child attend your prenatal visits. He will become familiar with the staff and become comfortable with examinations. It will also be exciting for him to hear his sibling's heartbeat. Some offices have birthing dolls that can be used for demonstration. If you are delivering in a birth center, show your child the birthing rooms and have him assist you in your choice for the birth. If you are delivering in a hospital, take a tour of the facility and meet the staff. This will allow him to be comfortable in the hospital environment.

Choose a support person for the child that he likes and knows well. It is important that the child feel comfortable talking to or expressing his feelings to this person. Occasionally, children need to remove themselves from the birthing room because of boredom or concerns. The support person needs to understand that she must accompany the child, even if this means missing the birth. This person should also attend sibling preparation classes with the child so she knows what information the child is given.

Allow the child to make the final decision about attending the birth. Give him the freedom to be present in the room as much or as little as he chooses, and to even decide that he does not want to attend. Discuss the possibility of changes in the birth plan. These would include transfer from an out-of-hospital birth center to a hospital, interventions such as delivery with forceps or a vacuum extractor, or even a cesarean section. Occasionally, a woman goes into labor while the child is asleep or in school, or the labor progresses much faster than expected. Preparing children for the unpredictability of labor will help to prevent disappointments.

During labor, provide diversions such as books, crafts, and video games. Young children may want to bring a favorite stuffed animal or doll, or a blanket and pillow for naptime. Pack plenty of drinks and snacks. If the labor is long, make sure the child eats regular meals. Give the child several tasks to perform during labor, such as offering you drinks, wiping your face with cool washcloths, or selecting the cassette tapes or compact discs. An older child may want to be responsible for taking photographs or videotaping.

Participation in the birth of a sibling can be a rewarding experience for a child. It can start the bonding process and make him feel a special part of the birth. But, if you or your child have any reservations, alter the plans to make this a positive experience for everyone. Rather than have your child present for the actual birth, you may want to have the child arrive soon after. Celebrate the birth and make this a memorable experience for everyone.

whose members have had over 20 years of early discharge experience, has issued a statement saying that early discharge should be determined by the mother and her caregiver. Early discharge is appropriate only as part of a comprehensive program of care that includes intensive prenatal education and close postpartum and newborn follow-up. One benefit of early discharge is the avoidance of hospital-induced infections. The problems of early discharge are most likely related to lack of education and follow-up, rather than to the time of discharge.[8]

During the hospital stay, the nursing staff will provide medical care for both you and your baby. You will be taught perineal care to prevent infection and to promote healing of the vagina and perineum. If you had an episiotomy or laceration, or if you have hemorrhoids, you will be offered medicated pads, an anesthetic spray, or a warm soaking called a sitz bath. In the first 24 to 48 hours after delivery, the body begins to eliminate the fluid that was retained during pregnancy. The nursing staff may ask you to urinate into a container several times to ensure that you are emptying your bladder adequately.

Because your abdominal muscles will be relaxed, your perineum will be sore, and perhaps you will have hemorrhoids, you may have difficulty moving your bowels. If a proper diet (fresh fruits and vegetables, whole grains, and sufficient water) does not help, you can ask to have a stool softener prescribed. When cleaning yourself, make sure that you wipe from front to back to avoid fecal contamination and infection.

The nursing staff will monitor your vital signs along with observing the height and tone of your fundus, type and amount of lochia, and condition of your perineum. You can expect a daily visit from your caregiver and the baby's pediatrician.

If you are an Rh-negative mother who gave birth to an Rh-positive infant, you will be given an injection of Rh-immune globulin (RhoGAM) within 72 hours after birth. This injection will prevent your body from producing antibodies that could endanger subsequent babies during pregnancy.

Hopefully, you can utilize the first few days of your baby's life to the fullest in establishing a close family bond. Most hospitals have policies that promote mother-father-baby-sibling contact. If your hospital allows family involvement, make sure you take full advantage of it. If your hospital does not allow the options that are important to you, request them anyway. You need to make your wishes known. Perhaps the hospital will make allowances to accommodate your desires. Interaction and bonding of the family members during the first days after birth will help to promote a loving, thriving family.

CONCLUSION

The act of giving birth is something that will remain with you for the rest of your life. It can be a positive, empowering experience, providing an opportunity for you to grow as a woman. Trust your body to do the work of labor and giving birth to your baby. A woman's body was perfectly designed to perform this miraculous, natural function. Allow yourself to view birth as healthy and normal, instead of as a medical or surgical procedure. There will be hard work and pain, but the incredible feeling of accomplishment that follows will provide great satisfaction that will positively impact the rest of your life. Experience the joy of actively bringing forth your baby into this world, confident that your body knows exactly what to do.

Hints for the New Father

During the hospital stay:

❏ Room-in with the mother and baby.

❏ Bring in a cake with a *0* candle and have a birthday party.

❏ Bring your mate her favorite snacks and other foods.

❏ Learn how to change diapers.

❏ Encourage your mate to empty her bladder and do a super Kegel every 2 hours.

Trust Yourself

Trust your body to do the work of labor and bring your baby safely into the world.

Table 6.2. Labor Partner's Summary

Stage of Labor		What Is Going On?	How Is She Feeling?
Warm-Up	***Before Labor Begins***	Lightening. Increased frequency of Braxton-Hicks contractions. Early effacement and dilation. Increased vaginal discharge. Leveling off or loss of weight.	Excited; a sense of anticipation. Depressed. Difficulty sleeping; very tired. Spurt of energy.
First Stage	***Beginning of Labor***	Contractions. Loss of the mucous plug. Leaking or rupture of the membranes. Frequent bowel movements.	Excited. Apprehensive. Talkative.
	Early Labor	Contractions from 5 to 20 minutes apart, lasting from 30 to 60 seconds, becoming longer, stronger, and more frequent. Effacement and dilation from 0 to 4 centimeters.	Confident. Sociable.
	Active Labor	Contractions from 2 to 4 minutes apart, lasting from 45 to 60 seconds, with greater intensity and longer peaks. Dilation from 4 to 8 centimeters, with more effacement.	Anxious. Apprehensive; doubts her ability to handle labor. Serious mood; birth-oriented. Attention turned inward. Quiet.
	Transition	Contractions from 1 1/2 to 2 minutes apart, lasting from 60 to 90 seconds, extremely strong and erratic, possibly with more than one peak. Dilation from 8 to 10 centimeters.	Panicky; wants to give up. Irritable. Does not want to be touched. Forgetful; disoriented; amnesic. Rectal pressure; premature urge to push. Nausea; vomiting. Alternating between feeling hot and cold. Trembling legs.

What Should She Do?	How Can I Help?
Simplify the housekeeping. Pack suitcases and Lamaze bag. Conserve energy; take naps. Pre-register at the hospital; take a tour. Practice exercises, relaxation, and breathing *daily*.	Assist her with the household chores. Encourage her to rest. Provide diversion—for example, take her on walks, take her out to eat. Help her practice relaxation and breathing.
If it is nighttime, try to sleep. If it is daytime, continue normal activities. Take a walk. Take a shower; wash hair; shave legs. Eat carbohydrates; drink juice.	Time the contractions. Reassure her of her readiness for labor. Call the baby sitter. If it is nighttime, encourage her to sleep; sleep yourself.
Relax with the contractions. Begin slow paced breathing if necessary. Stay in an upright position as much as possible. Empty bladder every hour. Call caregiver. Drink sweetened liquids, eat light snacks.	Time and record the contractions. Remind her to relax; use touch relaxation. Encourage and praise her. Help her with the breathing pattern if necessary. Encourage her to walk. Remind her to urinate. Use distractions—for example, play cards or games with her, take her to a movie.
Continue relaxation and breathing. Use a focal point. Do effleurage. Relax in a tub or shower. Change position frequently. Continue to urinate hourly. Drink liquids. Adjust pillows for comfort. Go to the hospital or birth center.	When walking with her, stop and support her body during contractions. Administer massages or back rubs. Give her a cool washcloth for her face. Give her ice chips or Popsicles to suck on. Offer her cool liquids if allowed. Remind her to change position and to urinate. Keep her informed of her progress. Encourage her to relax and help her to do the breathing pattern. If her breathing seems ineffective, suggest changing the pattern. Watch for signs of transition.
Remember that this phase is intense but *short*. Take the contractions one at a time. Change breathing patterns as needed. Eliminate the relaxing breath if the contraction peaks immediately. Blow with a premature urge to push. Use slow paced breathing in between contractions.	*Do not leave her for any reason.* Remind her that the *labor is almost over*—the baby is coming. Praise her lavishly for her efforts. Communicate with the medical staff. Keep her calm; do not argue with her. Apply counterpressure to her back. Call the nurse if she feels an urge to push. Breathe with her; have her mimic you. Help her catch the contractions at the start. Help her relax between contractions. *Be positive!*

Stage of Labor		What Is Going On?	How Is She Feeling?
Second Stage	*Birth of the Baby*	Contractions from 3 to 5 minutes apart, lasting from 60 to 75 seconds, with an urge to push at the peak. Effacement and dilation complete. Baby is moving down the birth canal. Head is crowning. Delivery of the head, the shoulders, and then the rest of the body.	Strong urge to push. Relieved to be able to push. Renewed energy level. Great deal of rectal pressure. Burning, splitting sensation. Sociable again between contractions.
Third Stage	*Delivery of the Placenta*	Mild uterine contractions. Separation and expulsion of the placenta.	Exhilarated. Fatigued.
Fourth Stage	*Bonding and Recovery*	Perineal repair if necessary. Identification procedures for the baby. Intermittent uterine contractions. Checking of the mother's physical status. Possible removal of the baby to the nursery after bonding.	Emotionally high. Proud. Happy. Tired. Motherly. Hungry and thirsty.

What Should She Do?	How Can I Help?
Assume a comfortable pushing position. Use the most comfortable pushing technique. Push only when feeling the urge. Pant or blow as the head is delivered. Relax the perineum. Keep eyes open.	Help her assume a comfortable position for pushing. If she is holding her breath, count to 6 to pace her pushing. Make sure she lets a little air out before holding her breath. Remind her to relax her bottom; check her face for relaxation. Coach her to pant or blow as the head is delivered. Remind her to keep her eyes open. Be sure she can see the birth in the mirror. Take pictures as the baby is born.
Push with the contractions as instructed. Hold and soothe the new baby. Initiate breastfeeding. Use a breathing pattern if necessary.	Take pictures of the mother and baby. Hold the baby.
Examine, caress, nurse, and talk to the baby. Make eye contact with the baby. Take pictures of the father and baby. Massage the fundus of the uterus. Eat and drink.	Share in bonding with the baby. Take more pictures. Make telephone calls.

Chapter Seven

Medications and Anesthesia

or How Do You Spell Relief?

The avoidance of the use of medications during pregnancy was thoroughly covered in Chapter 2. This chapter focuses on the use of medications and anesthetics during labor, delivery, and postpartum. Also discussed are medications for special situations.

MEDICATION AND ANESTHESIA DURING CHILDBIRTH

In a normal, uncomplicated labor and delivery, the use of medication is often unnecessary. Relaxation, breathing patterns, and other comfort measures can be very effective in combating the sensations of pain. The presence of a loving support person is probably the best tranquilizer available. In addition, the support given by the hospital staff and your caregiver may affect your need for medication. If you are given positive reinforcement ("You're doing great!" "It's almost over!"), are permitted to move about freely, and receive a minimum of medical interventions, you will probably experience very little need for medication. On the other hand, if you are frequently asked if you need something for pain, if you are made to lie in one position, or if medical interventions are used, you may have an increased desire for some type of medication.

Nature has provided its own painkiller for laboring women. Labor prompts the pituitary to release endorphins, called natural painkillers. Endorphins are narcotic-like pain relievers that are said to be several times more potent than morphine. They produce a sensation of enormous pleasure after a tremendous exertion such as labor. Scientists have found that if a woman is given any kind of drug during labor, production of this natural painkiller is disturbed.[1]

"Look! All benefit and no risk!!"

Knowledge of the labor and birth process can also enhance a woman's ability to cope with labor. During labor, before you decide to take a medication, find out how far along you are. Even if it has been only a short time since you were examined, get checked one more time, just to make sure you are not progressing rapidly. If you are in transition, your labor is almost over and you may have just a few more contractions left before completing the first stage. By the time the nurse goes out, prepares the medication, and returns with it, you may have reached 10 centimeters and no longer need it. Medication taken at this time may make you sleepy, interfering with your ability to push during delivery and to bond immediately after birth, plus it may have a strong effect on the baby. If you request an epidural, it may take approximately 30 minutes to be administered and take effect, and you do not want to be numb for the pushing stage.

Before you go into labor, you should discuss with your caregiver which medications and types of anesthesia you will be offered if the need arises. You must also make sure that your labor partner is aware of your desires long before your due date arrives. Labor is stressful and is not the time to decide which medication or anesthesia is best for you. If you wait until you are in active labor or transition, you may agree to something that is really not acceptable to you.

Know your alternatives and how they will affect both your and your partner's participation in the labor and birth. When you discuss medications with your caregiver prior to labor, or when you are deciding whether to accept a medication or any prescribed treatment during labor, you should ask the following questions:

❏ How will this medication (or treatment) affect my labor, me, and my baby?

❏ What are the benefits and the risks?

❏ If I decide not to accept this medication (or treatment), what will happen?

❏ Is there an alternative form of treatment?

Even though relaxation and breathing work extremely well for many women, some find that these tools do not provide enough relief of pain or promote adequate relaxation. You may want to try some of the other techniques suggested in Chapter 5. Then, if you are still experiencing unbearable pain, medication or anesthesia is available. In a prolonged or difficult labor, some women feel they need medication to help them cope with their contractions. During a complicated delivery, in which forceps or a vacuum extractor is necessary, anesthesia may be beneficial. For a cesarean section, anesthesia is a necessity.

No one perfect medication exists for all circumstances. Since you cannot foresee what your labor will be like, except in the case of a planned cesarean, you must remain flexible in your attitude. Every medication and anesthetic has benefits and risks, and you need to be aware of them to make an informed decision. Only when the benefits outweigh the risks should you consider using a particular medication.

BENEFITS OF MEDICATIONS AND ANESTHESIA

In a difficult labor, a small amount of medication can decrease some of the pain sensations and may aid relaxation, especially between contractions. You should realize, however, that an analgesic will not take away all your pain, although it may lessen it enough to enable you to better cope.

An epidural offers the most effective pain relief for labor, hence its popularity. If a woman previously had a cesarean after a long, hard labor and is afraid to attempt a vaginal birth, an epidural may give her the reassurance to go through labor again. For a woman who is delivering a breech baby vaginally, an epidural may provide both the pelvic relaxation and the anesthesia that would be necessary if the use of forceps is suddenly required.

In a prolonged labor, Demerol, or another narcotic, may relax the cervix, helping to speed up labor. It may also provide some needed rest if the woman has been in early labor for many hours without sleep. If an intervention such as the use of forceps or a cesarean section becomes necessary, a regional anesthetic can relieve pain, while allowing you to be awake for your baby's birth. Epidural anesthesia also presents fewer risks to the woman and baby than general anesthesia does. In addition, after surgery, further pain relief can be provided by an injection of narcotics through the epidural catheter. This provides excellent pain relief for 24 hours without the disadvantages of repeated narcotic injections, intravenously (IV) or intramuscularly (IM). These disadvantages include drowsiness, intermittent pain relief, pain of an intramuscular injection, and transfer of the medication to the baby via the breastmilk.

RISKS OF MEDICATIONS AND ANESTHESIA

When weighing the risks of accepting a medication or anesthesia, you must take many factors into consideration. While the dosage of a medication is geared to the woman, two individuals are involved, one much smaller than the other. All medications affect the fetus in one way or another. The American Academy of Pediatrics' Committee on Drugs has warned that there is no medication that has yet been proven safe for the unborn child.

The fetus may be affected either directly or indirectly by medication used during labor or delivery. Both effects are highly influenced by the dose of the medication and the time it is given before birth. If enough time passes between the administration of the medication and the birth, much of the medication will be metabolized by the woman, thereby decreasing some of the side effects in the infant. But, if the baby is born while a large amount of the medication is in his system, his immature liver will have to excrete the medication on its own. Liver enzyme activity is immature in the fetus and newborn, taking 4 to 8 weeks after birth to reach adult capacity.[2] In a premature infant, the effects of a medication are even greater.

The direct effects of medication on the baby include toxicity or alteration of the central nervous system, respiratory system, or temperature regulating centers, and change in muscle tone.[3] The indirect effects are caused by a medication's influence on the woman's physiology. If the medication depresses the woman's respirations or blood pressure, the infant receives reduced amounts of oxygen.

The use of a medication or anesthetic may increase the need for additional interventions. For example, oxytocin used during labor intensifies the contractions, thereby increasing the possibility of needing pain medication. Stronger contractions may decrease the amount of oxygen the fetus receives. Conversely, some medications slow down or prolong labor, thus increasing the need for oxytocin. Certain anesthetics dull the urge to push, which can increase the need for a forceps delivery.

The decision to accept or refuse medication is not an easy one. You must learn what is available, and then, if the need arises, you can choose the medication with which you are most comfortable. If you have an allergy to a medication, make sure you tell your caregiver, who should note it on your chart.

Also, before accepting any medication, ask, "What are you giving me?" If you are very sensitive to medication, tell your caregiver and ask him to order a reduced dose. If the smaller dose is not sufficient, you can always ask for more. If the dose is too strong, however, you may not be able to handle the contractions effectively. Remember, once a medication has been given, it cannot be taken back.

REGIONAL ANALGESICS AND ANESTHETICS

A regional *analgesic* provides adequate pain relief without affecting motor abilities or level of consciousness. A regional *anesthetic* provides not only excellent pain relief, but it also results in the loss of motor sensations, depending on the dose of medication. Both are administered into the spinal area. Over the past several years, the administration of epidurals has improved to provide greater options for laboring women. Low-dose epidurals, walking epidurals, and ultra-light epidurals allow greater movement while still providing adequate pain relief. This may help to reduce some of the negative side effects of a traditional epidural.

In addition to the epidural, the most commonly used methods of regional analgesia and anesthesia include local infiltration, the pudendal block (see Figure 7.1), the spinal (see Figure 7.2), and the combined spinal/epidural. For a list of other analgesics and anesthetics commonly used during labor and delivery, see Table 7.1 on page 152.

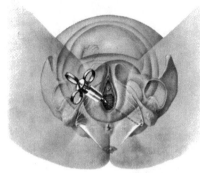

Figure 7.1.
A pudendal block numbs the vagina and perineum.

Epidural Anesthesia and Analgesia

The use of epidural anesthesia for pain relief during labor has increased dramatically over the past 20 years. In many hospitals, more than 70 percent of women use epidurals in labor. Epidurals have been called the "Cadillac of anesthesia." While they are an excellent choice of anesthesia for cesarean delivery, they have side effects that you should know about before you choose one for an uncomplicated birth. For example, it can take more than 30 minutes for an epidural to be administered and take effect. Therefore, if you are well into transition, the epidural may not kick in until you are ready to push. Also, you will have to deal with the intense contractions of transition in an uncomfortable position. During the second stage, you will find it very difficult to push without feeling the natural urge. If you do receive an epidural during labor, you could request that the dosage of medication be reduced or that it be allowed to wear off so that you will be able to push effectively.

Among the benefits of epidurals, a woman experiencing a prolonged labor or difficult back labor may find that an epidural helps her to relax or cope better. Also, if a woman was given Pitocin during labor, she may need the relief provided by an epidural because of the increased intensity of the contractions.

Epidural medication consists of two types. Local anesthetics, or "caine" drugs (such as procaine, bupivacaine, lidocaine, and ropivacaine), provide anesthesia, the complete loss of motor control and sensation. Narcotics provide analgesia, or pain relief. The single or combined use of these two drugs can be adjusted for different results. Low-dose and ultra-light epidurals administer narcotics with little or no "caine" drugs. These allow women to retain motor function while providing adequate pain relief.

If you decide to accept an epidural, you will need to undergo several procedures. An IV will be started, and you will be given 1 to 2 liters of fluid to reduce the chance of your blood pressure dropping. You will be asked to sit on the edge of the bed or to lie on your side with your back curved while an anesthesiologist or certified registered nurse anesthetist (CRNA) administers the epidural. In addition to an IV, you will be attached to a fetal monitor and an automatic blood pressure cuff, and therefore restricted to the bed. Since your mobility and your ability to feel sensations will be greatly diminished, you may need to have a urinary catheter inserted. This is to prevent a full bladder, which could impede the baby's progress through your pelvis.

Multiple studies have shown that epidurals prolong both the first and second stages of labor. Women are more likely to require Pitocin to improve contractions. Epidurals relax the pelvic floor muscles, which affects the rotation of the baby through the pelvis and increases the chance that assistance with forceps or a vacuum extractor will be necessary. It also increases the chance of needing a cesarean. Women having their first babies are two to three times more likely to have a cesarean for dystocia (an abnormal or prolonged labor) if they accept an epidural before 6 centimeters dilation. If given before 2 centimeters, an epidural causes prolonged labor.[4]

Studies have also shown that if the blood pressure drops as a result of an epidural, the amount of blood flow to the uterus and placenta is reduced, and the baby's heart rate may drop to a level that can lead to interventions and even a cesarean delivery for fetal distress.[5]

While most caregivers state that the medication does not reach the fetus, recent studies indicate that the drugs do enter the baby's circulation. This occurs as the medication diffuses from the epidural space into the woman's veins and crosses the placenta. The concentration increases with the length of the epidural. The baby's level is about one-third of the amount found in the maternal blood.[6]

Many women are extremely satisfied with their choice of epidural anesthesia. Others, especially those who experienced side effects, are not so enthusiastic. Occasionally, an epidural does not provide adequate relief or "takes" on only one side. It can also increase the risk of postpartum hemorrhage. Among the more common side effects are itching, nausea, vomiting, a drop in blood pressure, and difficulty urinating postpartum, which may require catheterization. Residual backache, sometimes lasting for months after birth, is a common complaint. It is uncertain if this is from the procedure or, more likely, the stressful position that the woman is placed in during the second stage. Because she is numb, she cannot tell if she is in a position that is actually harmful to her back.

Less frequently, a severe headache results from the epidural needle inadvertently puncturing the dura, the membrane that separates the epidural space from the spinal fluid. These spinal headaches, which can include neck aches and migraines, may start within 3 months of delivery and require a blood patch to seal the puncture and eliminate the headache. This invasive procedure may require an additional epidural injection if the epidural catheter has been removed.

When an epidural is given for longer than 5 hours, one-third of women and

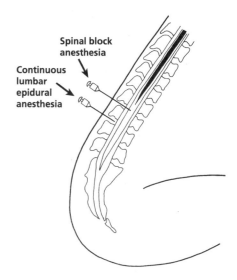

Spinal block anesthesia

Continuous lumbar epidural anesthesia

Figure 7.2.
The spinal needle is placed into the spinal fluid, and the epidural needle and catheter are positioned in the epidural space, just outside the membrane.

Table 7.1. Medications and Anesthetics Commonly Used in Childbirth

Type	How Given	When Given	Uses and Benefits
Sedatives Hypnotics For example: Seconal Nembutal Restoril	Orally	Prelabor Early labor	Help differentiate prelabor from true labor. Effects depend on dose. Sedatives allay anxiety or excitement, and induce rest, but do not relieve pain. Hypnotics may induce sleep.
Tranquilizers Antiemetics For example: Vistaril (Atarax) Compazine Phenergan Largon	Orally IM IV	Early labor Active labor or transition, alone or combined with analgesic	Relieve tension and anxiety. Promote relaxation. Prevent nausea and vomiting when used with analgesic; also potentiate effects of analgesics.
Analgesics For example: Demerol Nisentil Stadol Nubain	IM IV	Active labor	Reduce or alter pain perception. Demerol may relax cervix and hasten dilation. Stadol and Nubain contain narcotic antagonist that reduces side effects to baby.
Narcotic antagonist For example: Narcan	IM or IV to woman IM or in umbilical vein to baby	Second stage After birth	Reverses respiratory depression caused by narcotics.
Oxytocics (synthetic hormones to contract uterus) For example: Pitocin Syntocinon Oxytocin Ergotrate Methergine	IV (dosage best controlled when diluted in IV fluid) IM (postpartum only)	Prior to labor During labor Postpartum	Induce or stimulate contractions. Control postpartum bleeding.

IV = intravenously, IM = intramuscularly.

*Dependent on maternal dosage and timing in relation to birth.

†The cord level indicates the amount of medication that is in the baby's bloodstream as compared to that in the woman's.

Possible Risks and Side Effects for Woman	Possible Risks and Side Effects for Baby*
Slow down labor if given too soon. Disorientation. Drowsiness. Lowered blood pressure.	Accumulation in tissues. Respiratory depression. Decreased sucking ability. Cord level: 70%.[†]
Drowsiness. Confusion. Blood pressure change. Heart rate change.	Heart rate change. Decreased sucking ability. Decreased muscle tone. Lowered body temperature. Decreased attention, increased restlessness. Increased jaundice. Cord level: 95%–100%.
Dizziness. Dry mouth. Euphoria. Nausea. Respiratory depression. Lowered blood pressure. Drowsiness and possible difficulties concentrating on breathing or pushing if dose too large. Sleepiness during delivery.	Depressed respiration. Decreased sucking ability. Altered behavioral responses for several days or weeks. Cord level: Demerol, 80%–130%. *FDA requires Demerol to carry warning label that it may have adverse effects on infant.*
Rapid heart rate. Elevated blood pressure. Nausea and vomiting. Sweating. Trembling. Return of pain. Withdrawal symptoms if woman is addicted to narcotics.	Same as to mother. Severe seizures if mother is addicted to narcotics. Little is known about long-term effects. Effects of antagonists are shorter than those of narcotics, and depression may recur.
Lowered blood pressure; anxiety; increased heart rate; edema; water intoxication. Tetanic (very strong) contractions or rupture of uterus. Increased desire for pain medication. Increased need for coaching and support. Ergotrate or methergine given postpartum can increase blood pressure or cause severe "afterpains." *FDA warns that oxytocin should not be used for elective induction for convenience of doctor or woman.* *Oxytocin is released naturally during breastfeeding.*	Heart rate change. Fetal asphyxia due to tetanic contractions. Increased jaundice.

Type	How Given	When Given	Uses and Benefits
Regional anesthesia (uses local anesthetics or "caine" drugs such as procaine, bupivacaine, lidocaine, or ropivacaine)	See below	See below	Does not affect alertness. Does not affect cough reflex—less danger of aspiration if vomiting occurs. Does not affect labor partner's participation in labor and birth.
Local infiltration	Injection into perineum	Second stage Prior to perineal repair	Numbs perineum for repair of episiotomy or lacerations. Response time: 3–4 minutes. Duration: 1–2 hours.
Pudendal block	Injection into pudendal nerves via vagina	Second stage	Numbs birth canal and perineum for forceps delivery, episiotomy, or repair. Response time: 2–3 minutes. Duration: 1 hour.
Epidural (uses either "caine" drug; narcotic such as morphine, Demerol, fentanyl, or sufentanil; or combination of the two)	Continuously through catheter inserted into epidural space (low spinal area)	Active labor Second stage Prior to cesarean birth	Completely or partially relieves pain from uterine contractions, birth, and repair, depending on dose. Avoids spinal headache if done correctly. Response time: 10–15 minutes. Duration: continuous.
Spinal (intrathecal) *Saddle block (low spinal)*	Single injection into spinal fluid	Labor Second stage Prior to cesarean	Pain relief during labor. Woman can walk. Numbs pubic area to toes for forceps delivery. Numbs area from above navel to toes for cesarean delivery. Requires small dose. Response time: 1–2 minutes. Duration: 3–10 hours for labor (narcotic). 1–3 hours for delivery ("caine" drug).

Possible Risks and Side Effects for Woman	Possible Risks and Side Effects for Baby*
See below.	See below.
Burning or stinging upon administration.	Decreased muscle tone.[7]
Blocked urge to push—coaching needed during birth. Possible toxicity caused by required large dose.	Fetal depression caused by required large dose.
Possible ineffectiveness—technical difficulty may cause it not to work or to take on only one side. Prolonged labor. Lowered blood pressure. Increased maternal temperature, resulting in treatment for nonexistent infection. Increased need for medical supervision and interventions (IV, fetal monitor, urinary catheter, Pitocin). Relaxation of pelvic floor muscles along with diminished urge and ability to push, prolonging second stage and increasing need for forceps or cesarean delivery. Backache, either short or long term.[8] Increased chance of cesarean delivery.[9] Difficulty urinating.[10]	Decreased oxygen and lowered heart rate if mother's blood pressure drops. Subtle behavior alterations. Reduced muscle tone. Testing to rule out infection if mother or baby ran a fever. Nursing difficulties.
Nausea, vomiting, itching, prolonged labor, and respiratory depression if narcotic is used (labor). Lowered blood pressure. "Caine" drugs cause urge to push to be lost. Spinal headache. Difficulty urinating.	Decreased oxygen and heart rate if mother's blood pressure drops.

Type	How Given	When Given	Uses and Benefits
General anesthesia (unconscious) For example: Sodium pentathol (IV) Nitrous oxide (gas) Isoflurane (gas)	IV Via tube inserted into windpipe	Prior to cesarean birth	Emergency cesarean when time is too short to administer regional anesthetic.
Postpartum analgesics For example: Acetaminophen (Tylenol) Ibuprofen (Advil, Motrin) Darvocet Tylenol With Codeine Percocet, Tylox	Orally	Postpartum	Oral medication reduces pain from episiotomy, afterpains, hemorrhoids, and cesarean. Compatible with breastfeeding.
Demerol Morphine Duramorph Fentanyl	IM IV by patient controlled analgesia (PCA)—woman pushes button to release small dose into IV Epidural catheter	First 12 to 24 hours after cesarean	Epidural narcotics give good pain relief for up to 24 hours after cesarean without additional medication. Does not affect mobility.

Possible Risks and Side Effects for Woman	Possible Risks and Side Effects for Baby*
Nausea, vomiting, aspiration of vomitus if intubated incorrectly. Deep anesthesia produces: Skeletal muscle weakness. Depression of central nervous system—requires constant supervision. Cardiac and respiratory depression, irregular heart pattern, lowered blood pressure. Depression of liver, kidney, and gastrointestinal tract function. Incompatibility with prepared childbirth. Labor partner often not allowed to be present.	Crosses placenta rapidly. Effects of deep anesthesia are same as for mother. Cord level: up to 85%.
Drowsiness. Codeine and Percocet can decrease motility of bowels (increase gas pains).	Percocet has been found in moderate amounts in breast-milk—has insignificant effect on full-term infant, but very preterm or ill newborn should be observed for sedation and lowered respirations.
Repeated IM injections are painful. IM and IV medications cause drowsiness and give intermittent relief. Narcotics via epidural can cause itching. All narcotics can cause nausea, vomiting, and depressed respirations.	Insignificant in normal infants. At high maternal IV or IM doses, infant should be monitored for sedation, poor feeding, and respiratory depression.

newborns develop fevers. This may lead to admission into the intensive care nursery for diagnostic procedures, including a spinal tap and blood cultures to determine if there actually is an infection in the infant. It also results in prolonged hospitalization of the mother and baby for treatment with antibiotics for a possibly nonexistent infection.[11]

More severe, but extremely rare, complications include an allergic reaction to the medication, convulsions from an overdose, and numbness in the chest that makes breathing difficult. Rarely, a woman must be placed on a respirator until the effects wear off.

The cost of an epidural is anywhere from $500 to $2,500. In an uncomplicated delivery, the charge is not always covered by insurance.

Before deciding on an epidural, you should also consider how it might affect your perception of your role in giving birth. Some women report that rather than being an active participant in the birth, they were an observer because of the epidural. While many people assume that labor is always painful and requires relief, others view birth as a normal function in which pain can be minimized or relieved by other measures. In many cases, the discomfort of labor causes a woman to find a more comfortable position, and this new position actually facilitates labor. As one anesthesiologist stated, "The practice of obstetric anesthesia is unique in medicine in that we use an invasive and potentially hazardous procedure to provide a humanitarian service to healthy women undergoing a physiological process."[12] Even though the incidence of severe side effects is low, every woman should carefully weigh the benefits and risks before deciding on an epidural or any medication.

Spinal (Intrathecal) Analgesia and Anesthesia

Spinal, or intrathecal, anesthesia uses "caine" drugs to provide complete loss of sensation and movement. A low spinal, known as a saddle block, can be used for a vaginal delivery, and a higher spinal can be used for a cesarean. Now, anesthesiologists are administering a narcotic into the spinal fluid for labor. (See Figure 7.2 on page 151.) This provides a rapid onset of pain relief with no loss of motor control for 3 to 10 hours, depending on the medication used. The benefits of this method over an epidural are that the onset is faster and that it does not give one-sided or patchy relief. Also, the dose of medication is very small to reduce the risk of toxicity. The side effects of narcotics include nausea, vomiting, urinary retention, itching, prolonged labor, and respiratory depression. A spinal headache may also occur.

Combined Spinal/Epidural Analgesia

During the administration of a combined spinal/epidural, the anesthesiologist first inserts an epidural needle. Through the epidural needle, he guides a thinner, but longer, spinal needle past the epidural space and dural membrane, and into the spinal fluid. A small dose of narcotic is given, and the spinal needle is withdrawn. An epidural catheter is then threaded into place, the epidural needle is withdrawn, and the catheter is taped to the woman's back.

As the spinal begins to wear off, the anesthesiologist can provide continuous medication through the epidural catheter. As long as the medication used is a narcotic, the woman will retain muscle control and can walk. A "walking epidural" does not provide as deep a level of pain relief, and the woman can perceive the pressure of the contractions. This can be especially beneficial

Hints for the Labor Partner

Prior to labor:

❏ Discuss your feelings with your partner about using or not using medication as a labor tool.

❏ Share your desires/birth plan with your partner's caregiver.

❏ Learn all you can about the options available if your partner's labor does not progress as expected.

❏ Make sure you understand the risks and benefits of epidurals and the medications used during labor.

during the second stage of labor. If deeper anesthesia becomes necessary, "caine" drugs can be added to the epidural.

SPECIAL SITUATIONS

In a labor that is out of the ordinary or involves complications, medication may be required for medical reasons. These special situations include preterm labor, pregnancy-induced hypertension, and post-term pregnancy.

Preterm Labor

Women who go into preterm labor may be hospitalized and given a tocolytic medication to relax the uterine muscles and stop the contractions. The most common tocolytic medications are terbutaline sulfate (Brethine) and ritodrine hydrochloride (Yutopar). The side effects of these drugs are rapid heart rate, anxiety, nausea, vomiting, tremors, and insomnia. While on these medications, women are carefully monitored, as they can develop complications such as chest pain, palpitations, high blood pressure, and pulmonary edema. Other medications that may also be used as tocolytics are magnesium sulfate, indomethacin, and nifedipine. These medications are given subcutaneously (under the skin) with a pump, intravenously, or orally.

If the preterm labor does not stop, the woman may be given steroids to prevent or decrease the severity of hyaline membrane disease (respiratory distress syndrome) in the premature infant. Steroids stimulate the production of surfactant in the infant's lungs. However, they must be given 24 to 48 hours before delivery to be effective. If the preterm labor was a result of an infection, the woman will also be treated with antibiotics.

Pregnancy-Induced Hypertension

PIH places both the woman and baby at risk. The treatment for PIH is bed rest and delivery of the baby when mature. If untreated, PIH can progress into preeclampsia (elevated blood pressure, protein in the urine, and excessive swelling) and eclampsia (seizures, stroke, and kidney failure). The most common medication used for preeclampsia is magnesium sulfate, which prevents seizures and also helps lower the blood pressure. It is given intravenously

Hints for the Labor Partner

During labor:

❏ Ask a nurse about your partner's progress before requesting medication or an epidural for her.

❏ Suggest first trying a nondrug pain reliever such as changing position, emptying the bladder, massage, and laboring in a tub or shower.

❏ Ask the nurse if your partner is allowed to get up and walk around. If yes, help your partner to do this.

❏ Tell your partner that she is doing great.

How Can I Get Labor Started?

If a woman goes past her due date, she may wonder how to self-induce labor. One of the most popular methods is to drink an ounce of castor oil in orange or grapefruit juice. Grapefruit juice is preferable because of its tartness. Before drinking, apply a thick layer of lipstick to your lips. Quickly stir the castor oil into the juice, and drink. Wipe off the lipstick. This prevents an oily residue on your lips from the castor oil. Then follow with a glass of plain juice.

Another popular method to stimulate labor is to have sexual intercourse. This should not be performed if your membranes have ruptured. The semen that is deposited contains prostaglandins, which can cause contractions. Nipple stimulation releases oxytocin, which can also cause uterine contractions. This can be done by you or your partner. In addition, your partner can stimulate specific acupressure points to induce labor.

Other women may encourage you to eat certain foods or to dine at a certain restaurant that is known for putting women into labor. Usually, the meal consists of something that will increase movement of the intestines or cause loose bowel movements. While these methods may help to initiate labor, if your baby is not ready to be born, there is no guarantee.

prior to labor, during labor, and for 24 hours after delivery. The blood pressure, reflexes, respiratory rate, and urine output of a woman on this medication are closely monitored.

Post-Term Pregnancy

At 42 weeks, a pregnancy is considered to be post-term. Since the incidence of stillbirth is higher after this time, many doctors induce labor. Prostaglandin gel (Prepidil or Cervidil) may be applied in or around the cervix before labor is induced to help "ripen" (soften) the cervix, or a pill of misoprostol (Cytotec) may be crushed and placed on the cervix. This increases the success rate of labor induction and reduces the need for a cesarean. (For a discussion of the self-induction of labor using natural methods, see "How Can I Get Labor Started?" on page 159.)

CONCLUSION

While certain women will require medication and anesthesia during labor and delivery for medical reasons, the majority of pain relief is elective. As with any choice, if the benefits outweigh the risks, you may want to accept the medication. But if you accept the medication without informed consent or the knowledge of how your labor is progressing, you may regret your decision. Know your choices and make decisions based on the facts related to your labor and delivery.

Chapter Eight

Variations and Interventions

or Any Which Way You Can

The type of labor that you experience may be considered normal and yet not progress exactly "by the book." Each woman's labor is unique, and you need to be prepared for any situation that might arise. You may need to modify or adjust the techniques that you learned. Your caregiver may feel that additional measures are necessary. The following discussion of some possible variations and interventions should provide you with further tools and thus enhance your preparation.

FETAL PRESENTATION AND POSITION

At term, most babies lie in the uterus upside down and facing the woman's spine. Several variations are possible, however, and help determine whether any interventions, including a cesarean, will be needed.

Presentation

The term *presentation* refers to the way the baby is situated in the uterus. The part of the baby that is closest to the cervix is called the presenting part. As already discussed, in a normal birth, the head is lowest in the uterus and therefore is the presenting part. (See Figure 8.1.) This type of presentation is called a cephalic presentation. More specifically, if the top of the head is felt at the cervix, it is called a vertex presentation. The brow or face can also be the presenting part, but are much less common and can cause difficulty at delivery.

A very small percentage of births involve a transverse lie, or shoulder presentation. The baby lies sideways in the uterus with his shoulder as the presenting part. (See Figure 8.2.) With a transverse lie, cesarean delivery is mandatory.

Another presentation is breech, in which the buttocks present first. Breech presentations account for 3 to 4 percent of all deliveries. Labor may be longer than with a vertex presentation because the buttocks are not as efficient a dilating wedge as the top of the head. The most common varieties of breech presentation are the complete breech, in which the fetus sits cross-legged in the bottom of the uterus (see Figure 8.3 on page 162), and the frank breech, in which the fetus has his legs straight up, with his feet near his face (see

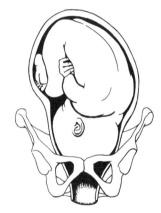

Figure 8.1.
Cephalic presentation.

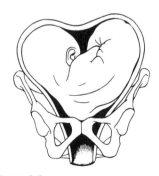

Figure 8.2.
Shoulder presentation,
or transverse lie.

Hints for the Labor Partner

If the baby is breech:

❑ Place your head near your partner's pubic bone when you talk to the baby.

❑ Use a flashlight to encourage the baby to "move to the light."

❑ Encourage your partner to assume the tilt position.

Figure 8.3.
Complete breech presentation.

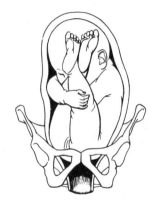

Figure 8.4.
Frank breech presentation.

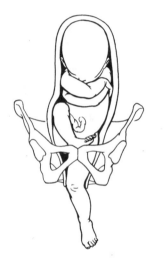

Figure 8.5.
Footling breech presentation.

If your baby is in a breech position, lie on your back with your pelvis elevated to encourage him to rotate.

Figure 8.4). Less common is the footling breech, which is similar to the complete breech, but in which one or both feet present first. (See Figure 8.5.) In the knee breech, the rarest form, the knee, instead of the foot, presents at the cervix.

The risk to the baby is increased in a breech delivery, thus increasing the possibility of obstetrical intervention. Most doctors routinely perform a cesarean in the case of a breech presentation. While the baby's buttocks may pass easily through the pelvis, his larger head may cause problems. When determining method of delivery, the doctor takes into account fetal size, type of breech presentation, the woman's pelvic dimensions and architecture, and progress in labor. He also factors in his own experience in handling vaginal breech deliveries.

The doctor may not realize before labor begins that the fetus is in a breech presentation. If he discovers this during labor, he may order X-ray pelvimetry to determine whether the woman's pelvic measurements are adequate. If there are no other complications, such as a prolapsed cord, the woman may be able to give birth vaginally. Effective pushing is most helpful in delivering a breech baby. Some doctors use forceps if the second stage is prolonged.

Prior to 30 weeks, a baby has plenty of room to turn around in the uterus and his position is insignificant. If your caregiver discovers that your baby is breech after 30 weeks, you may be able to rotate him into a vertex presentation by doing the following exercise. Lie on your back with your knees bent and your feet flat on the floor. Position several pillows beneath your lower back and buttocks to elevate your pelvis 9 to 12 inches. You can also use an ironing board elevated at a 45-degree angle. Stay in this position for 10 to 15 minutes, three times a day, preferably before meals for the greatest comfort. Continue the routine until the baby rotates. When the baby turns, stop doing the exercise or he may return to breech. Once he has turned, walk a lot to help him settle further down in the pelvis. Be sure to check with your caregiver to confirm the baby's change in presentation. In one study, an 88.7-percent success rate was reported with this technique.[1] The exercise is also effective in rotating a baby who is lying transverse in the uterus. Check with your caregiver prior to beginning the exercise to make sure there is no medical reason why you should not do it.

In addition to using this position, you may want to visualize the baby turning in the uterus. Relax your body to decrease the abdominal muscle tension. Some women have reported success in turning a breech by placing headphones on the lower abdomen and playing soft music. This can be done in combination with or separate from the exercise. These women felt that their babies turned to get closer to the music. When your partner talks to his baby, he should position his head low on the abdomen. Other women have used flashlights, pointing the beam at the top of the uterus and slowly moving it down the abdomen. These women believed that the baby may have tried to follow the beam of light. While these methods are anecdotal, they involve minimal risk and may increase the chance of success.

It is also possible to turn a baby from a breech or transverse lie by using external version. This procedure is usually performed in the hospital using the visual guidance of ultrasound. The woman may be given medication to relax the uterine muscle. This makes it easier for the doctor to manipulate the baby into a head-down position, which is done by applying gentle, yet firm, pressure to the woman's abdomen, pressing on the baby's head and hip. External version is usually performed at 37 weeks of pregnancy. Prior to this time, the baby's lungs may not be mature enough if an emergency cesarean needs to be done. After 37 weeks, the doctor is less likely to be able to rotate the baby because of reduced amniotic fluid. In addition, the baby is larger and may have settled into the pelvis. This procedure may even be attempted if the breech is not diagnosed until labor. The risks associated with external version include initiation of labor, soreness to the woman's abdomen, and, on rare occasions, shearing of the placenta from the uterine wall, which would necessitate an emergency cesarean. The technique should be performed only by a doctor experienced in it.

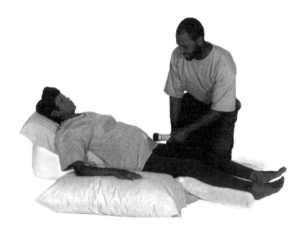

This couple is hoping that their breech baby will follow the beam of light from the flashlight and turn before labor begins.

Position

Position, as used in obstetrics, refers to the relation of the baby's presenting part to the woman's pelvis. In a vertex presentation, the baby's occiput, or back of the head, is the point of reference. The most common position during labor is the anterior position, in which the back of the baby's head is toward the woman's abdomen. (See Figure 8.6.) A less common position is the posterior position, in which the baby's occiput is against the woman's spine. (See Figure 8.7.) A posterior position often results in a prolonged labor accompanied by a great deal of back discomfort. (For a discussion of this labor variation, see "Back Labor" on page 165.)

Your caregiver may use letters—such as ROA, LOT, ROP, or OP—to identify your baby's position. The first letter designates your *r*ight or *l*eft hip. The letter *O* refers to the baby's *o*cciput, and the last letter can be either an *A* for *a*nterior position, a *P* for *p*osterior position, or a *T* for *t*ransverse position. (In the transverse position, the back of the baby's head is toward your side.) For example, if your caregiver says that the position of the baby is ROA, the back of the baby's head is toward your abdomen, but slightly toward your right side. In an OP position, the back of the baby's head is directly against your

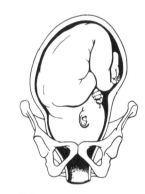

Figure 8.6.
Anterior position.

Figure 8.7.
Posterior position.

Hints for the Labor Partner

❏ Understand the risks and benefits of the various procedures.

❏ Discuss the options during pregnancy.

❏ Be prepared that the birth plan may need to be altered.

❏ Learn the signs of preterm labor and watch for them.

❏ If your partner is experiencing signs of preterm labor, assign others the household chores so that she will not feel guilty while she is on bed rest.

spine, and your baby is "sunny side up." A normal labor begins with the baby entering the pelvis in a transverse position and then rotating to an anterior position.

CARDINAL MOVEMENTS OF LABOR

The cardinal movements of labor are the rotations of the baby as he moves through the pelvis. During labor, the baby must make specific rotations so that the widest diameters of his head and shoulders will match the widest diameter of the pelvis. The uterine contractions move the baby down the pelvis as he follows the path of least resistance. When the baby enters the pelvis, his head faces sideways in the pelvis. As he moves down the pelvis during labor, his head turns so that by the time you are ready to push, he is looking at your back. This also places his shoulders in correct alignment to enter the pelvis. After the baby's head is delivered, his head rotates again to look at your thigh so that his shoulders are lined up to come under the pubic bone.

LABOR VARIATIONS

Even though all labors are different, the majority of labors follow somewhat of a pattern. However, four types of labor that vary significantly from the "norm" are preterm labor, precipitate labor, prolonged labor, and back labor.

Preterm Labor

A preterm labor is a labor that begins before 37 weeks gestation. Preterm labor is a concern because babies born prior to 37 weeks may not be mature and may require intensive nursing care to survive. Your physician will attempt to stop preterm labor. This may be accomplished by bed rest, home monitoring, medication, or hospitalization. For a complete discussion of this labor variation, see "Preterm Labor" on page 36.

Precipitate Labor

A precipitate labor is a labor that lasts 3 hours or less. This short duration may sound appealing, but it presents its own special problems. The contractions in a precipitate labor are usually quite intense and may be misinterpreted as a very difficult early labor. Because the contractions may be hard to control, the labor partner should remain with the woman at all times and use all the comfort measures at his disposal. If left alone, the woman may experience confusion and fear because of lack of knowledge about her labor's progress. These feelings can be complicated by the rushing around of the hospital staff upon discovery of the labor's advanced state.

If you suspect you are having a precipitate labor, you must trust your own feelings about your body. Be sure to request a vaginal examination as soon as you are admitted to the hospital to determine your progress. Your own control and the directions of a good labor partner are crucial. You will need to concentrate on relaxing, even though it may be difficult. In addition, before requesting medication, begin using comfort measures and try accelerated-decelerated breathing, along with changing your position and emptying your bladder. Your labor is almost over!

In some cases, labor progresses so rapidly that the woman does not have

Hints for the Labor Partner

If your partner is having a precipitate labor:

❏ Remain calm.

❏ Drive carefully to the birth facility.

❏ Encourage her to do her relaxation and breathing techniques.

❏ Remind her that the labor is almost over.

❏ Tell her that she is doing great.

enough time to get to the hospital. If this happens to you, follow the instructions in "Emergency Childbirth" on page 175.

Prolonged Labor

A prolonged labor is a labor that lasts 24 hours or more. Some of the causes of this type of labor are ineffective contractions, breech presentation, posterior position, large size of baby, small pelvis, extreme tension, large amounts of medication, early administration of an epidural, fasting during labor, and malnutrition during pregnancy.

Considerable patience is required during a long labor, along with creativity in the use of breathing techniques, comfort measures, and relaxation. Fatigue is difficult to combat, and dozing between contractions may make it even harder to be ready for the next contraction. If you experience a prolonged labor, you and your partner must work together, using all the techniques and comfort measures you can to avoid discouragement, tension, and fatigue. Encouragement is essential. You need to relax as much as possible to conserve your energy. Labor in a tub of warm water if you become fatigued and are tense. Walking often helps to speed up labor. If you have been confined to bed, ask to be allowed to walk around. Also, stimulating your nipples will release oxytocin into your system and may help to strengthen the contractions.

During a prolonged labor, the fetus's condition must be monitored carefully by a nurse or a fetal heart monitor. You will probably receive IV fluids for nourishment and to prevent dehydration if you have not been allowed to eat or drink. Pitocin is usually administered to increase the strength of the contractions.

When a woman has a history of sexual abuse, her labor can be adversely affected. Her emotions can release stress hormones that may slow and alter her labor. It is important that her caregiver be aware of the history and also be familiar with the phrases or words that trigger the memory. These are usually the same words that her attacker used during the abuse. Some of these phrases may be commonly used during childbirth. Certain touches may also be upsetting. During the second stage, the woman may experience difficulty in pushing or may even refuse to bear down. A woman with this type of history will need to be shown patience and understanding during her labor. A female support person or caregiver may be beneficial.

If your labor is prolonged or extremely difficult, make sure that you understand your situation—what is happening to you, suggested procedures, and diagnosis. If you have questions, ask your caregiver. And remember, labor is not an endurance contest. If you become too fatigued and can no longer cope with the more powerful Pitocin-augmented contractions, consider medication or an epidural.

Back Labor

A back labor is a labor that is felt primarily in the back or hips, producing extreme discomfort during and often between contractions. About one out of four women experiences back labor to some degree. Back labor is usually caused by a posterior position of the baby, but can also be caused by a breech presentation, tension, variations in anatomy, or laboring on the back.

Because discomfort is also felt between contractions, rest and relaxation are more difficult to achieve with a back labor. In addition, the labor may last

Prolonged labor.

Hints for the Labor Partner

If your partner is experiencing a prolonged labor:

❑ Encourage her to walk.

❑ Provide light snacks and encourage her to drink fluids.

❑ Have her change position.

❑ Rub her back.

❑ Assist her in getting into the tub or shower.

❑ Try nipple stimulation.

❑ Use acupressure.

❑ Stay positive.

"Dancing" through a contraction can help ease the pain of back labor.

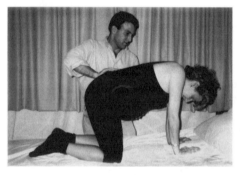

If you experience back labor, kneel on all fours and do the pelvic rock.

longer. If you have a back labor, take the contractions one at a time and experiment with the following comfort measures.

Get the baby off your back. Do not lie or sit in any position that places the weight of the baby on your spine. Get into a position that will encourage the baby to rotate. The most effective positions are ones in which you are upright because they give you the advantage of gravity. You can walk between contractions, and when a contraction begins, use your partner or the back of a chair for support and sway your hips as if dancing. Perform the lunge, or have your partner do the double hip squeeze. (For instructions on how to do the double hip squeeze, see "Counterpressure" on page 101.) Get into the shower and have your partner direct the spray at your lower back.

You may want to try sitting backwards and straddling a chair, using pillows for support. Or, sit forward on the edge of the chair and lean against your partner, kneeling in front of you, for support. If you are in bed, sit on the side of the bed, put your feet on a chair, and lean on the over-the-bed table or a pillow positioned on your lap.

Several kneeling positions are very comfortable. Try the pelvic rock on all fours. You can also try kneeling on the floor, using the seat of a chair as your upper-body support. If you are in bed, kneel on all fours, kneel against the raised head of the bed, or kneel with your upper body elevated on pillows.

Side-lying while in bed or in a tub may be a comfortable position. If in bed, make sure that you are well supported by pillows under your head, uterus, and upper leg. You may want to try changing position from side-lying to kneeling on all fours to side-lying on the opposite side. Repeat this sequence, remaining in each position for 15 minutes.

Another position that may be uncomfortable for the baby and encourage his rotation is to lie on your back with a rolled-up blanket tucked beneath the small of your back to increase the angle of your spine. Alternate this position with side-lying every 15 minutes. If your baby does not rotate, however, and is still posterior when you begin pushing, you can also push in this position to encourage rotation. Your partner can hold up your legs, or you can bend your knees slightly and rest your heels on the bed. Once the baby has rotated, you can continue pushing in a more comfortable position.

The best position for pushing if your baby is in the posterior position is the squat. This position increases your pelvic capacity by as much as 30 percent.[2] You can also try the dangle position. To get into the dangle, have the nurse remove the bottom third of the birthing bed and insert the foot rests. Your partner can sit on the edge of the bed with his feet on the foot rests. Then stand between your partner's legs with your back toward your partner. During the contraction, rest your forearms on your partner's thighs, bend your knees, and perform a partial squat. Other pushing positions that you may want to try if your baby continues to be posterior are side-lying and kneeling. A variation of the kneeling position places one knee on the bed and the sole of the other foot on the bed. During the contraction, you can lunge in this position to expand the pelvis.

In addition to changing position frequently, many women want their partner to perform counterpressure or acupressure. Several methods have been used with success. Try having your partner press the heel of his hand or his fist against the area of greatest discomfort, using as much force as is comforting to you. Your partner can also kneel on the bed with one knee pressed against your lower back as you lie on your side. Or, try lying on your own fists or on a roll of toilet tissue or several tennis balls tied in a sock. These last suggestions can be especially helpful during vaginal exams, when you may need to be on your back. Having your partner massage your lower back with lotion or oil may also be effective.

You may find it comforting to have your partner apply warm or cold compresses to your back. While at home, you can use a hot water bottle. In the hospital, you can soak washcloths in hot water and apply them. Try laboring in a warm tub or shower. You can make cold compresses from ice packs, "blue ice," or frozen juice cans wrapped in towels. In addition, try a Tupperware rolling pin filled with cold water or crushed ice, or washcloths soaked in ice water.

Other measures that might help include slow, deep breathing between contractions, which promotes relaxation, and touch relaxation. Or, move on to the more advanced breathing techniques sooner than you planned. Finally, an encouraging and supportive labor partner is the best tool for handling this kind of labor.

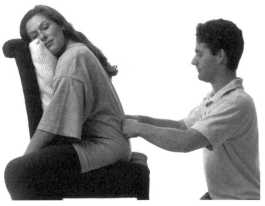

Counterpressure can ease the pain of back labor.

INTERVENTIONS

Your caregiver has various procedures at his disposal to obtain diagnostic information, prevent complications, and even alter the course of labor. Any intervention carries with it some degree of risk and therefore should never be used unless medically necessary.

You need to discuss the various interventions with your caregiver prior to labor, letting him know your desires concerning their possible use and having him tell you at what point he feels they are indicated. If you are clear on his intentions in advance, you will avoid misunderstandings later, during labor.

Become familiar with all the possible interventions and their purposes. Among the more common are IVs and the electronic fetal monitor.

Intravenous Fluids

An intravenous fluid (IV) is a solution that is fed into the body through a vein. It may be indicated in a prolonged labor to prevent dehydration. It is also used during induction of labor because it provides the most accurate administration of Pitocin. (For a discussion of induction, see "Induction and Augmentation of Labor" on page 171.) Prior to an epidural, IVs expand the blood volume to reduce the risk of a drop in the woman's blood pressure. They are also an easy access for medication or blood, if needed. Some doctors routinely use IVs "just in case" a problem arises. During a cesarean birth and the immediate postsurgical period, an IV is important for supplying fluids and administering medication.

To start an IV, a nurse inserts a needle into the patient's vein. Next, a thin plastic catheter is threaded through the needle into the vein, and the needle is withdrawn. The catheter is securely taped into place. Generally, an IV is placed into the hand or forearm. Ask the nurse to use your nondominant arm. Once the IV is started, a solution of water, normal saline, or Lactated Ringers

Prophylactic Antibiotics

If you have a history of mitral valve prolapse or have a positive group B strep culture, IV antibiotics may be administered during labor.

(a solution of sodium chloride, sodium lactate, potassium chloride, and calcium chloride), with or without dextrose (sugar), is continuously infused into the vein.

If you are well hydrated and allowed to drink, and your labor is progressing normally, you probably will not need IV fluids. Normal, healthy women at term store up to 1 to 2 liters of body water. They also experience dependent edema, which adds to their store of fluid. This fluid is readily available for use by the laboring woman. IVs restrict mobility and hamper effective relaxation. If you do have an IV and you would like to walk around during labor, ask for a moveable pole. Or, you could request a heparin lock or a saline lock, in which the catheter is flushed with either a heparin solution or saline to keep the vein open, and the bag of fluid can be disconnected.

Complications that can result from IV use include infiltration (leakage of fluid into surrounding tissues) and phlebitis (inflammation of a vein). You may also experience some discomfort during the insertion of the needle. A more serious complication, water intoxication, can occur from the use of electrolyte-free IV fluids, such as 5-percent dextrose in water (D_5W). Water intoxication can result in vomiting, convulsions, and pulmonary edema in the woman. Therefore, the use of D_5W should be limited to 1 liter during labor. Another problem associated with the administration of a dextrose solution is the higher level of glucose in the woman's system. This, in turn, increases the fetus's sugar level (hyperglycemia), which can rapidly drop and become too low (hypoglycemia) in the newborn period. This is most common when the infusion lasts for longer than 4 hours.[3]

Electronic Fetal Monitor

An electronic fetal monitor (EFM) is a device that measures and records the intensity, frequency, and duration of the uterine contractions as well as the baby's heart rate. Of special interest to the caregiver is the way the baby's heart rate is affected during and immediately after contractions. A normal fetal heart rate is between 120 and 160 beats per minute. Recurrent deviations from this range may indicate that the baby is in distress.

Monitoring can be done either externally or internally. External monitoring is used more frequently, as it is noninvasive and easy to apply. Internal monitoring provides more accurate information. The internal monitor is inserted through the vagina, and it requires that the membranes be ruptured. In both types of monitoring, the leads are connected to a bedside unit that records and prints out the information on graph paper. The information is also relayed to monitors at the nurses' station.

The baby's heart rate can be monitored externally by securing an ultrasound transducer on the woman's abdomen with an adjustable belt. A more accurate method monitors the fetal heart rate internally by inserting an electrode through the vagina and partially dilated cervix, and placing it beneath the skin of the baby's head or buttocks using a spiral projection. A small percentage of babies have developed scalp abscesses from the use of an internal electrode.

The most common method of measuring uterine contractions is to apply a pressure sensitive transducer to the woman's abdomen using an adjustable belt. When the uterus hardens, the transducer picks up the muscle contraction, and

The contractions and the baby's heart rate are being monitored with an external fetal monitor.

a corresponding wave appears on the graph paper. If a more accurate determination of the contractions is needed, an intrauterine pressure catheter (IUPC) may be inserted through the cervix and into the uterus. An IUPC measures the exact amount of pressure exerted by the contractions and may be indicated in a labor involving the use of Pitocin. The IUPC can also be used to infuse saline into the uterus to increase the volume of fluid. This is called amnioinfusion and can be helpful if the baby is showing signs of fetal distress caused by compression of the cord. A low level of amniotic fluid does not provide buoyancy, and the cord can become compressed during contractions. Also, if the amniotic fluid is heavily stained with meconium, additional saline can thin the meconium and reduce the risk of the baby aspirating thick meconium.

EFM use is indicated for pregnancies that are considered "higher risk." An EFM is also used if labor is induced or stimulated with Pitocin, to determine how well the baby is handling the stress of labor and to assess the strength and duration of the contractions. Some doctors feel that monitoring even low-risk women is beneficial in determining fetal well-being or distress. Others monitor all patients because they fear a lawsuit if a problem arises and the monitor was not used. It is also believed that the documentation provided by the monitor will be beneficial in a potential lawsuit. But, because monitor strips are open to interpretation, litigants can often find an "expert" to state that any decelerations (decreases in the baby's heart rate) can cause permanent brain damage. Rather than a benefit, the documentation can become a detriment to many hospitals and caregivers.

Experts are continuing to debate the need for monitoring low-risk labors that are progressing normally. Electronic fetal monitors were introduced into practice in the late 1960s before controlled randomized studies were performed to determine their efficacy and safety. A major controversy concerns the accuracy of the results obtained from monitors, especially from the external type. Many authorities feel that external EFMs show only that the baby is doing well. The information on the printout is open to misinterpretation by the medical staff. Sometimes the monitor picks up the woman's heartbeat, or stomach and intestinal sounds, rather than the baby's heartbeat.[4] Many doctors consider late decelerations of the heart rate (slowdown of the fetal heartbeat at the end of each contraction) as a sign that the baby is in distress. However, several studies have shown that up to 60 percent of fetuses exhibiting late decelerations were not in distress at birth.[5]

Additional studies have concluded that "a specific pattern, or group of patterns, of fetal heart rate monitoring that may predict brain damage is not available for use by the clinician today."[6] If fetal distress is suspected during labor, the physician may take a sample of the baby's blood to check the pH. This test is called a fetal scalp sampling and may be used to determine if the baby is truly in distress and immediate delivery is necessary. This procedure is not available in all hospitals.

Skyrocketing cesarean birth rates have also been associated with increased use of EFMs. In one study involving 690 higher-risk women, monitoring did not improve perinatal outcome, but did result in a threefold increase in cesareans. Dr. McFee, one of the researchers, feels that his results refute the contention that monitoring should be universal. He showed that listening frequently (every 15 minutes during the first stage of labor and every 5 minutes during the second stage) with a fetoscope by expert nurses is as dependable as EFMs in "recognizing continuing abnormal fetal heart rate patterns ominous

Hints for the Labor Partner

If your partner is wearing a fetal monitor:

❏ Encourage her to change position (never let her lie flat on her back).

❏ Have her sit in a chair or stand next to the bed.

❏ Pay attention to her, not the monitor.

❏ Ask to turn down the sound if the "beeping" noises are distracting.

enough to mandate immediate delivery."[7] In 1988, the American College of Obstetricians and Gynecologists supported Dr. McFee's statement, yet the majority of hospitals continue to monitor, citing liability or the lack of adequate staff as their reason. Out-of-hospital birth centers and nurse-midwives use a fetoscope or hand-held doptone to monitor the baby at regular intervals.

A recent analysis done by Dr. Stephen Thacker and colleagues at the Centers for Disease Control (CDC) in Atlanta on twelve controlled randomized studies on EFM use published between 1966 and 1994 agreed that routine EFM use resulted in no significant decrease in maternal or infant morbidity (illness) or mortality (death).[8] Additionally, EFM use has not decreased the incidence of cerebral palsy. The rate of cerebral palsy has remained the same for the past 40 years and is more likely to be the result of prenatal influences such as genetics, toxic exposures, and infection.[9]

Another growing concern is that nurses and doctors are losing the ability to evaluate patients without referring to the "machine." They pay more attention to the monitor tracing than to the woman and her perception of the labor. Many labor partners even become entranced by the beeps and the readout, and forget their main purpose—to support and encourage their partners during labor.

Most women who labor with an electronic fetal monitor are confined to bed. Bed rest increases the length of labor and the need for medical intervention. The woman's perception of pain is altered, her stress level is increased, and medication is accepted more frequently. Medication can adversely affect the woman and fetus. Women who have to remain in bed because of the monitor cannot receive the benefits of walking or laboring in water, or the benefits from the personal attention that would be provided by a nurse actually listening to the baby's heartbeat.

Laboring With a Fetal Monitor

A Hint for the Mother-to Be

❑ Ask if your hospital has telemetry units so that you can walk during labor while still being monitored.

As already discussed, a woman's mobility and position during labor can significantly affect her labor's progress. Therefore, if you choose or are required to be monitored during labor, change position frequently, about every 20 to 30 minutes. The monitor may need to be repositioned to pick up the baby's heartbeat each time you move, but your mobility and comfort are extremely important. You can also request to be monitored while out of bed. You may be able to stand or walk around next to the bed. Or, you can sit in a chair or rocker close to the monitor.

Do not let anyone tell you that you must stay on your back. This position can cause hypotension and lead to fetal distress, the very problems the monitor was designed to protect against. In addition, the longer you can stand and walk during labor, the more efficient your contractions will be. An upright position promotes descent of the baby and dilation of the cervix. It also helps the uterus to work at maximum efficiency.

If the concept of routine monitoring disturbs you, discuss with your doctor the possibility of limiting your time on the monitor. Your doctor may agree to monitor you intermittently—for example, for 15 minutes of every hour or 30 minutes of every 2 hours. Even just waiting until active labor is well established will give you more time to move about and be comfortable. If an internal monitor is used, it can be disconnected every few hours to allow you to stand up and move around. Some facilities have telemetry units, which allow women to walk around freely.

If you find that the beeping noises coming from the machine are distracting or annoying, ask the nurse to turn down the volume. You could also ask her to reposition the machine so that the readout is not in your constant view.

Note to the labor partner: Remember to continue your active coaching and support measures. Machines do break and malfunction, and leads can be positioned incorrectly. If your partner says that her contractions are becoming more intense, she knows what she is talking about.

INDUCTION AND AUGMENTATION OF LABOR

Occasionally, the labor itself needs assistance, either in getting started or in progressing. There are several commonly used methods for each.

Induction

An induced labor is started artificially, by either chemical or physical stimulation. Induction is medically indicated in situations where continuing the pregnancy would adversely affect either the woman or baby. Such situations include preeclampsia, diabetes, postmaturity, Rh sensitization (incompatibility), prolonged rupture of the membranes with no labor starting, and fetal death.

When the amniotic sac breaks prior to labor, it is known as premature rupture of the membranes (PROM). In many cases, the cause of PROM is unknown, but research indicates that PROM may be caused by an infection, such as group B strep. Whether or not you are induced depends on the week of gestation during which PROM occurs. At term, most labors will naturally start within 6 to 12 hours. If not, most caregivers will want to induce labor to prevent infection. Some studies indicate that women can safely wait for labor to begin even after 24 hours of the membranes rupturing, provided that no vaginal exams are performed and that the woman is monitored for infection.

If PROM occurs between 24 and 33 weeks gestation, the physician will need to weigh the risks of infection and prematurity. Women are usually placed on bed rest and closely monitored for infection. The fetus is evaluated for lung maturity, and steroids are usually administered to the woman to promote fetal lung development. Labor can be induced either when the fetus is mature enough for delivery or if the woman shows clinical signs of infection. Amnioinfusion can be performed during labor to provide additional fluid in the uterus.

Caregivers use a number of techniques to induce labor. The simplest technique is called stripping the membranes and is done by the caregiver during a vaginal exam. He inserts his fingers between the partially dilated cervix and the amniotic sac, which irritates and loosens the sac from the uterine wall. This causes a release of prostaglandins. Some women feel a burning or stinging sensation or even pain when this is done. However, unless labor is imminent, this procedure does not initiate true labor, although it may cause contractions for a time.

Another physical method of inducing labor is amniotomy, the artificial rupture of the membranes. This is done by inserting an amnihook, a long hooklike instrument, through the vagina and partially dilated cervix, and making a tear in the amniotic membranes. The procedure is no more painful than a vaginal exam because the membranes do not contain any nerves, but it does present some risks. If labor does not begin, both the woman and baby are exposed to an increased chance of infection and to the use of Pitocin. If

Hints for the Labor Partner

If your partner is induced:

❏ Expect stronger contractions.

❏ Be an active coach.

❏ Prepare her for the next contraction by watching the monitor and alerting her when the contraction begins.

❏ Do not leave her alone.

Pitocin does not produce results within 24 hours, a cesarean delivery is usually performed.

Prostaglandin applied either in or on the cervix helps to ripen the cervix and increase the success of an induction. However, it can also cause strong contractions, nausea, vomiting, diarrhea, fever, and chills. Prostaglandin gel is not recommended for use with women who have a fundal scar, history of asthma, or glaucoma.[10]

Caregivers most frequently induce labor through the use of Pitocin. Pitocin, a synthetic form of the hormone oxytocin, should always be administered through an intravenous drip that is electronically monitored. Some doctors also place a pressure catheter inside the uterus to determine contraction strength.

Labor should never be induced simply for convenience because induction increases the risks to both the woman and the fetus. For this reason, the FDA's Obstetric-Gynecologic Advisory Committee voted to withdraw FDA approval of the use of oxytocic drugs for elective induction of labor. Interestingly, since the late 1980s, weekend births have declined with a corresponding increase during the week. A 3-year investigation of birth certificate records showed that this increase was a result of an increased number of inductions. In addition, the number of cesareans because of failed inductions also increased.[11]

In a natural labor, the oxygen supply to the fetus is decreased during each contraction. The long, intense contractions of an induced labor can deprive the fetus of even more oxygen, resulting possibly in fetal distress and a cesarean birth. An overdose of Pitocin, resulting in tetanic or continuous contractions, can cause premature separation of the placenta from the uterus or even uterine rupture. These conditions could disrupt the oxygen supply to the fetus and lead to an emergency cesarean delivery if a vaginal birth cannot be effected immediately. Other maternal side effects include lowered blood pressure, rapid heart rate, anxiety, and swelling. Also associated with the use of Pitocin is increased jaundice in the newborn.

Induced contractions tend to start out much stronger than natural contractions. The gradual buildup of labor is not present. Induced contractions come more frequently, last longer, and often peak immediately rather than in the middle of the contraction. They make labor much more difficult to manage. If your labor is induced, you must stay on top of the contractions from the very beginning or you may lose control. Your partner is extremely important in this kind of labor. He can watch the monitor to observe the contractions so that he can prepare you for the start of each contraction. If a contraction lasts longer than 2 minutes, he must immediately alert the nursing staff. His encouragement and support are essential. You should not be left alone because panic and loss of control usually result. If your partner must leave you to use the bathroom or get something to eat, ask a nurse to stand in. Because of the strength of the contractions, you may need to use advanced breathing techniques sooner and for a longer time, which can be very tiring. Your partner's assistance in keeping you comfortable and relaxed will help you to conserve the energy that you will need for birth.

Augmentation

If your caregiver feels that your labor is not progressing normally, he may decide to augment it (speed it up). The timetables used to determine "normal" labor are based on averages, and very few women are "average." Before you

A Hint for the Mother-to-Be

❑ Labor should *not* be induced for your or your doctor's convenience.

"So I am post-term. It's still nice and cozy in here!"

agree to any kind of intervention, ask for a little more time and try some non-invasive techniques. Some popular natural techniques to speed up labor are walking, a warm shower or bath, changing position, acupressure, loving support (including hugs, caresses, and words of encouragement), and nipple stimulation to release natural oxytocin. If anyone in the room is causing you stress, ask that person to leave.

If natural measures do not speed up your labor, your caregiver may want to perform an amniotomy. Amniotomy to augment labor carries the same risks it does when used to induce labor. In addition, it removes the protective buffer of fluid between the baby's head and the cervix. As a result, babies who go through labor for an extended period of time with the membranes ruptured experience more head molding and caput succedaneum (swelling of the soft tissues of the scalp), as well as possible cephalhematoma (a lump or swelling on the scalp that is filled with blood). None of these are dangerous, although a caput succedaneum normally takes several days to subside, while a cephalhematoma may take months to reabsorb.

Some studies show that amniotomy does not significantly affect the progress of labor.[12] The contractions often increase in intensity and duration for a while after the procedure is performed, but the average difference in the length of labor is only 50 minutes.[13] In addition, the labor may become uncomfortable and more difficult to control. A drop in the fetal heart rate is also associated with the procedure.

If your caregiver suspects fetal distress, he will need to perform an amniotomy to insert an internal fetal monitor or to obtain a fetal blood sample to measure the pH of the infant's blood. He may also want to check for the presence of meconium in the fluid. Otherwise, you have the right to reject this procedure.

If you have an amniotomy done, but it does not speed up your labor, your caregiver may start a Pitocin IV drip to stimulate your uterus to produce more efficient contractions. Be prepared for stronger and more frequent contractions, the same as in an induced labor. You may need to begin using advanced breathing techniques to stay on top of the contractions. The risks associated with the use of Pitocin are the same for augmentation of labor as they are for induction of labor.

ACTIVE MANAGEMENT OF LABOR

Some physicians routinely practice active management of labor to ensure that labor will be completed within 12 hours. The standard, which originated in Ireland, waits for the woman to be in active labor before initiating this practice. Once active labor is determined, the caregiver performs an amniotomy. If the woman does not progress 1 centimeter per hour, a high dose of Pitocin is started to augment labor. Another important component of this practice is to have a personal nurse provide continuous emotional support for the laboring woman.

Currently, many physicians use this technique, but employ it before active labor. Also, few women are fortunate enough to have a nurse provide continuous support throughout labor. If your physician actively manages labor, you may want to hire a doula to provide this important support. You may also want to discuss with him when he initiates this protocol. Or, you may choose not to have your labor actively managed, but rather, to allow labor to progress at its own pace.

EPISIOTOMY

An episiotomy is a surgical incision made from the vagina toward the rectum to enlarge the vaginal outlet. The incision is usually midline (straight), but can be mediolateral (angled to the side). (See Figure 8.8.) Caregivers most often perform episiotomies when the baby's head begins to stretch the perineum. At this time, a natural anesthesia is in effect, and the woman may not feel the incision. However, a local anesthetic is necessary for the repair of the episiotomy following delivery. Most caregivers give the local prior to making the incision.

Caregivers perform episiotomies to expedite birth in cases of fetal distress or during a prolonged second stage if the woman is exhausted and the perineum is taut. Some doctors do them routinely because they feel that a straight incision is easier to repair and heals better than a jagged tear. Recent studies refute these sentiments, however. While women who deliver with intact perineums recover the fastest, those who have episiotomies heal just about the same as women with spontaneous tears.[14] Also, some doctors feel that an episiotomy prevents tearing, but once a cut is made, the incision is more likely to tear further.[15] In addition, if an episiotomy is not performed and tearing occurs, the tearing may be superficial in nature, whereas an episiotomy cuts into muscle. For these reasons, the American College of Obstetricians and Gynecologists does not recommend episiotomies in uncomplicated deliveries.

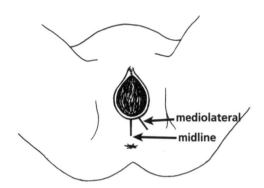

Figure 8.8.
The two types of episiotomy are midline and mediolateral.

Another reason many doctors offer for performing an episiotomy is to avoid loss of vaginal tone and control, which could result in prolapsed organs and a decrease in sexual pleasure for both partners. Other caregivers say that practicing Kegel exercises during pregnancy and following birth strengthens the vaginal muscles and eliminates this problem naturally. Additionally, some experts feel that severing of the perineal tissue during an episiotomy permanently weakens it.

Occasionally, caregivers overstitch the repair to "tighten up" a woman. This overstitching is also known as the "honeymoon stitch." However, stitching too tightly can result in painful intercourse.

You can decrease your chances of having an episiotomy in several ways. Most importantly, talk to your caregiver about your desire not to have one. Performing perineal massage beginning around the thirty-fourth week of pregnancy may also help. (For instructions, see "Perineal Massage" on page 75.) Many caregivers feel that perineal massage not only stretches the perineal tissues, but also prepares a woman emotionally for some of the physical sensations of birth. While you are pushing during delivery, some caregivers perform perineal massage and apply hot compresses to stretch the perineal tissues. Listen to your caregiver's directions and push gently to allow the baby to slowly stretch the birth canal. Avoid the lithotomy position during delivery. With your legs apart and your feet in stirrups, your perineum is taut and is more likely to tear.

An episiotomy takes several weeks to heal. You may experience soreness and itching. Try sitting on pillows or air rings, taking sitz baths, and applying anesthetic pads, creams, and sprays to help alleviate some of the discomfort.

ROTATION AND EXTRACTION

Forceps and the vacuum extractor are two obstetrical tools that are used to rotate a baby to a more advantageous position for birth and to help a baby move down the birth canal. They are used when the baby's head resists rotating from a posterior or transverse position, when a woman's pushing ability is diminished because of anesthesia or fatigue, or when a baby is in fetal distress. Before employing either of these instruments, many doctors administer a regional anesthetic and/or perform an episiotomy.

Forceps.

Forceps

Forceps are large, curved metal tongs whose two blades are inserted into the vagina and placed on either side of the baby's head. The blades are then locked into place and used to manipulate or extract the baby. Forceps can bruise a baby's soft head and facial tissue, but they can be an alternative to cesarean section if birth is imminent.

The dangerous high forceps procedure, in which the forceps are applied before the baby's head is engaged in the pelvis, is not used today, replaced by cesarean delivery, which is safer for both the woman and the baby. The midforceps procedure, in which the forceps are used at zero to above plus-two station, presents some risk to both the maternal tissue and the baby, and should be performed only by an experienced doctor. Low forceps are used when the head is felt at plus-two or more station and the head is not rotated more than 45 degrees past the midline. Outlet forceps, the most common procedure, are applied when the scalp is visible between contractions. They are used to aid in the final expulsion of the baby, and they carry the least risk to the woman and baby.

Cap of vacuum extractor.

Vacuum Extractor

A vacuum extractor is a caplike device that is attached to the baby's head using suction. The suction cup fits over the top portion of the baby's head and helps ease the infant out through the contours of the birth canal. The doctor can adjust the amount of suction that he uses. As a safety factor, the suction is released from the baby's head if the doctor applies too much tension. The use of a vacuum extractor could result in caput succedaneum, a cephalhematoma, lacerations, or abrasions of the scalp.

The advantages of the vacuum extractor over forceps include less trauma to the bladder and vaginal tissues, and lowered risk of extending an episiotomy. The use of anesthesia is not always necessary with the vacuum extractor. In rare cases, the vacuum extractor can be applied before the cervix is completely dilated to avoid a cesarean section if fetal distress indicates the need for immediate delivery.

EMERGENCY CHILDBIRTH

If your labor progresses very rapidly or you fail to recognize that you are in the final phase of labor, you may give birth at home or on the way to your intended place of birth. In most cases, such a birth is uncomplicated, and the baby is born healthy and vigorous. Since you were not medicated or anesthetized, the baby usually breathes immediately and is very alert.

Nevertheless, both you and your labor partner may feel some uneasiness

*"Okay, honey,
I'm ready to deliver now!"*

Hints for the Labor Partner

If your partner is at home and having a precipitate labor:

❑ Remain calm.

❑ Call 911.

❑ Make her comfortable.

❑ Get out the emergency birth kit.

❑ Place a pad under her to absorb the fluid.

❑ Assist in the delivery.

❑ Have her pant or blow as the head is delivered.

❑ When the baby's head is out, lift the cord over the head if it is around the neck.

❑ Support the baby's head as the shoulders and body are delivered.

and fear about handling such a situation. This section is therefore directed toward the labor partner, to give him support and confidence should he find himself in the position of being your caregiver.

For the labor partner: The woman will almost always know if birth is imminent. Take her word for it. She may feel the baby's head coming down the birth canal, feel a strong urge to push, or feel a burning pressure. If you are in the car when this happens, resist the temptation to drive fast or to take chances to reach the hospital or birth center. When it is safe to do so, pull off the road, put on the emergency flashers, get out the emergency birth kit (see page 119), and assess the situation. If this is the woman's first baby and the baby's head is not yet visible at the vaginal opening, you probably have time to get to the birth facility if you are within 15 to 20 minutes driving time. If this is not the first baby or if the baby's head is visible, you are better off staying where you are. If you have a mobile phone, call 911. Help your partner get comfortable in the back seat and then let the baby be born. Make sure the baby is breathing well before you continue on to your birth facility.

If you are home, call 911. Emergency medical personnel are trained to handle this kind of situation. Wash your hands and arms. Help your partner get into a comfortable position on the bed. Place a crib pad, newspapers, blankets, or towels under her buttocks to protect the mattress. Do not leave her alone. She will need your calm support to keep from panicking.

Whether you are at home or in a car, let the uterus do all the work. Once the baby's head is visible at the vaginal opening, coach your partner to pant until the head is born. A slow, controlled birth will reduce the chance of tearing the perineal tissue. As the baby's head begins to emerge, support the woman's perineum with your hand wrapped in a clean handkerchief. If the membranes are still covering the head, break them with your fingernail and pull them away from the face to allow the baby to breathe. You can wipe off any mucus and fluid with a cloth. Check to see if the cord is around the baby's neck. If it is, gently lift it over the head before the rest of the body is born.

When the baby's head rotates to face his mother's thigh, the shoulders are ready to be delivered. Support the baby's head with your hands as your partner bears down lightly with the next contraction. Do *not* pull on the baby's head—this could permanently injure the baby's spinal cord. Once the shoulders are born, the rest of the body will slide out easily. When delivery is complete, place the baby on his mother's abdomen with his face down, dry his skin, and cover both mother and baby with a blanket. The facedown position will help the baby cough up or drain out any mucus that is in his nose or throat. You can further help the baby by gently wiping out his mouth with a clean handkerchief or gently suctioning it with a soft rubber syringe. If using a syringe, make sure that you compress the bulb before insertion into the mouth or nose, and release the pressure gently.

If the baby does not breathe right away, vigorously rub his back or the soles of his feet. *Do not panic.* If the placenta is still attached, the baby is continuing to receive oxygen via the umbilical cord. However, if the baby does not begin breathing within 1 1/2 minutes, you will need to give him artificial respiration. To do this, place him on his back with his head slightly tilted back, cover both his nose and mouth with your mouth, and place your fingers on his chest. Gently breathe out with only the air in your mouth. You will feel the baby's chest rise slightly. Do not blow hard because forcing too much air into his small lungs could cause them to rupture. Repeat the breaths at the rate of one every 3 seconds until the baby responds. (For detailed directions for performing this lifesaving technique, see "Cardiopulmonary Resuscitation" on page 224.)

Do not worry about cutting the cord. It can be cut when you reach your birth facility or when the paramedics arrive. If the cord is long enough, help the mother put the baby to her breast as soon as he is breathing well. His sucking will stimulate the uterus to continue contracting and to expel the placenta. It will also prevent hemorrhaging. In addition, the colostrum the baby receives will help remove the mucus from his digestive tract. When the cord stops pulsating, tie it with a shoestring.

Do not pull on the cord in an attempt to deliver the placenta. When the placenta is ready to be expelled, you will notice the cord lengthening and the woman may feel pressure and the need to push. If the placenta is expelled before help arrives, place it next to the baby in a bag or wrap it up with him to give him extra warmth. The placenta should be taken to your birth facility with the baby because your caregiver will need to examine it.

Some bleeding is normal while the placenta is delivering and right afterwards. Nursing the baby immediately after birth is usually sufficient stimulation to keep the uterus firmly contracted. The uterus should feel as firm as a grapefruit at the level of the woman's navel. If the bleeding seems excessive—that is, more than 2 cups worth—massage the woman's abdomen at the navel using a deep circular motion to encourage contracting. If the baby refuses to nurse, you can stimulate the release of oxytocin to encourage contractions of the uterus by gently massaging the woman's nipples.

If the baby was born in the car, you can now resume driving to the hospital or birth center. If the baby was born at home, wait for assistance to arrive, or call your caregiver and follow his instructions.

When you arrive at the hospital for the mother and baby to be examined, you may want to request immediate rooming-in to prevent isolating the baby, which many hospitals do routinely with babies born outside the facility. If all is well, the woman may feel like returning home within a few hours. She also has the option of staying 1 or 2 days for observation.

GENTLE BIRTH

The concept of gentle birth considers what birth is like from the baby's point of view. It attempts to minimize the stress and trauma experienced by the infant as he passes through the birth canal and thus make his entry into the world more pleasant. Types of gentle birth include Leboyer delivery, underwater birth, and birth without interventions.

Leboyer Delivery

A Leboyer delivery incorporates several techniques that make birth a more soothing experience for the infant. This type of delivery was devised by Frederick Leboyer, a French obstetrician, and popularized in his book *Birth Without Violence*. Dr. Leboyer originated the concept of gentle birth. He felt that birth is a traumatic experience for the newborn and that certain routine delivery procedures increase the trauma. Otherwise, why do babies cry and look so unhappy at birth? In his view, the infant moves from a peaceful womb through the "assault" of labor into a world of bright lights and loud voices. He

---

Hints for the Labor Partner

If your partner gave birth at home:

❑ Place the baby face down on his mother's abdomen and dry him off, which will help stimulate him to breathe.

❑ Wipe or suction the mucus from the baby's mouth.

❑ Keep the baby warm by covering him, as well as his mother, with dry blankets.

❑ Put the baby to her breast as soon as he is interested.

❑ Tell her how proud you are.

❑ Congratulate yourself on a good job.

is held upside down, his cord is cut, and he is immediately removed from his mother. Dr. Leboyer stated that a newborn's senses are very acute and that he perceives the intense sensations of birth, often very vividly.

Even if your caregiver does not "practice Leboyer techniques," he may agree to incorporate some of the aspects that appeal to you. Following is a description of a gentle birth:

> The room is dimly lit, allowing the baby to adjust slowly to the light. The bright lights that are normally used in delivery rooms are blinding to the eyes of a baby who has been in semidarkness for 9 months. Think about what it is like to be in a dark room for a while and then to suddenly have bright lights directed at your face. It is no wonder that babies shut their eyes tightly.

> To keep the baby from becoming chilled, the temperature of the birthing room is adjusted for the baby's needs, rather than for the hospital staff's comfort. Talking is kept to a minimum or a whisper. Loud voices and exclamations may seem deafening to the new baby's ears.

> As the baby emerges from the birth canal, he is gently lifted up and placed onto his mother's bare abdomen for skin-to-skin contact. He is not held upside down by his feet, which would straighten his spine, a position exactly opposite of the one he had in utero. He is not stimulated to cry, but allowed to begin breathing spontaneously. His mother can gently soothe him through massage or stroking. His nose and mouth are not suctioned unless they need to be.

> The cord is not cut until it stops pulsating. This allows the baby to continue receiving oxygen-carrying red blood cells, which decreases his chance for anoxia. The cord is also not clamped immediately after birth, which means that the baby does not have to be rushed into breathing, since he is still receiving oxygen from his mother via the cord. The transition from intrauterine life to breathing on his own is much easier for the baby.

> The baby is then given to the father, who can place him in a warm bath to simulate a return to the security of the womb. Many babies completely relax and stop crying while they gently float in the water. The baby is then dried, wrapped, and given to his mother.

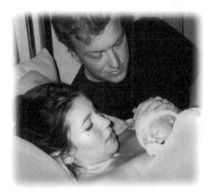

This new mother, father, and baby take a well-earned rest after birth.

Some of the arguments against Leboyer delivery are that the baby is allowed to be cold, that the inadequate lighting interferes with the assessment of the baby, and that the father may inadvertently drop or drown the baby in the bath water. Opponents of delayed cord cutting argue that the baby receives extra red blood cells, which causes increased jaundice. However, unless the newborn is held below the level of the placenta or the cord is "milked" (compressed and stroked toward the baby), equal amounts of blood enter and leave the baby while the cord is pulsating.

Caregivers who specialize in Leboyer deliveries and have kept statistics have found no increase whatsoever in infection, heat loss, undetected distress, or other complications attributed to gentle-birth procedures.[16] Since the parents are intimately involved during this type of birth, bonding may be encouraged more than in a non–Leboyer birth, and the parents' competence at caring for their new baby may be enhanced.

Interestingly, many of Leboyer's techniques are slowly being incorporated into regular birthing room routines. For example, caregivers no longer hold babies upside down by their feet, but instead, deliver the infant up onto the mother's abdomen. Babies are being born more alert, since women are taking less medication. These alert babies do not need to be stimulated or "spanked" at birth. Most babies today are being welcomed into the world more gently, with their comfort in mind.

Underwater Birth

Some women have taken the concept of gentle birth one step further by choosing to deliver their babies underwater. Just as laboring in warm water has been found to promote relaxation, making the contractions less painful and more efficient, delivering while still in the water can reduce the stress of birth, making it easier for both mother and baby.

Waterbirth allows the infant a very gentle entry into the world.

In this type of birth, the woman rests in a tub of water heated to around 98°F. After the baby is born, he is gently lifted from the water and handed to his mother, or he is lifted out of the water by the mother herself. According to proponents of this method, the physiological mechanism that causes the baby to breathe is not stimulated until the baby's skin is exposed to changes in temperature and air pressure. Therefore, the baby does not take his first breath until after he is removed from the water. He continues to receive oxygen from the placenta through the umbilical cord.

The concept of birthing underwater originated in France, at the Pithiviers Maternity Unit, headed by Dr. Michel Odent. After learning of Dr. Leboyer's techniques, Dr. Odent created an atmosphere in which a gentle birth could be accomplished. Women could labor and deliver however they felt most comfortable. He began by gradually removing the traditional obstetrical technologies, which he felt created barriers between the parents and child. He incorporated the use of dimmed lights and reduced noise, and had the staff remain out of the way unless needed. In finding their most comfortable labor and birthing positions, women began opting to get into the tub of water provided for them. Underwater birth became a natural outgrowth of these efforts. Dr. Odent saw that delivering in this manner reduced the trauma of birth to its minimum, and he began actively promoting birth underwater. Over the years, his name has become almost synonymous with underwater birth.

According to Barbara Harper, RN, an author and expert on underwater birth, being in water helps some laboring women to relax so much that fear and resistance are almost totally eliminated, allowing for the easiest delivery possible.[17] Sometimes, women get into the tub just to labor and the birth happens before they can get out. Another benefit of waterbirth is that it causes the perineum to be more elastic, reducing the chance of tearing and the need for episiotomies. Dr. Odent reported that in 100 waterbirths he attended, there were no episiotomies and only 29 cases of superficial tearing.[18]

Women who experienced birthing underwater felt that it allowed them to be more in tune with their bodies and to work with the labor process more effectively. They stated that delivering in this manner gave them the opportunity to really "give birth," rather than "being delivered."

Many doctors feel that the risks of waterbirth are too great. They state that the chance of a baby drowning, however slight, prevents this from being an acceptable procedure.

Waterbirth is available in certain areas in the United States. If you are interested in this type of delivery, begin by checking with the nearest birth center. The Global Maternal Child Health Association is a group that provides practitioner referrals, information, book and video sales, and tub rentals and sales. Call them toll-free at 800–641–BABY (800–641–2229), or write to them at P.O. Box 366, West Linn, Oregon 97068.

Birth Without Interventions

Have It Your Way

If you want to have a gentle birth, begin your search for an accommodating caregiver and birth facility early in your pregnancy.

A birth without interventions, one in which the woman is allowed to do whatever feels best during labor and delivery, is a truly natural birth. In other words, the woman acts instinctively to birth her baby. For example, she may instinctively choose to kneel on all fours during parts of her labor and to squat while pushing the baby out. Because there are no interventions (other than listening to the baby's heart rate with a fetoscope or doptone), her positions and movements are not restricted by any tubes, wires, or medications. The woman feels free to make whatever noise is comforting to her, and she is not rushed by anyone's schedule to "get the baby out."

Because doctors are trained in a medical setting, the majority of them have never witnessed a natural birth, one without any interventions. They are trained to see birth as a medical event, something that requires managing and regulating. Women who experience a birth without interventions usually do so with a midwife, either in a birth center or at home.

Most advocates of natural, or "instinctive," birthing do not teach a method of childbirth, such as patterned breathing techniques. Instead, they encourage a woman to look within herself for the resources to cope with labor. Dr. Michel Odent has stated that when laboring women follow their instincts, there is "almost nothing to teach."[19] In his words, "One simply cannot help an involuntary process; one can only disturb it."[20]

The books *Active Birth* by Janet Balaskas and *Birthing Normally* by Gayle Peterson provide more in-depth discussions of this type of birth.

UNEXPECTED OUTCOMES

This chapter has presented variations in the usual progression of labor and the possible medical interventions that could result. The next chapter discusses cesarean birth. If you are like most expectant parents, you are probably saying, "These situations don't apply to me." But the reality is that every labor and birth is unpredictable, and yours may not be the "ideal" experience that you have been hoping for. It is important that while you are designing your birth plan, you discuss all the possibilities and try to conclude how you would respond if confronted with an unexpected outcome.

Any variation from your birth plan is an unexpected outcome. While a labor that goes faster or easier than you planned is an unexpected outcome, most women have positive feelings after that type of experience. When the outcome is not as planned and is very sad or upsetting, you may require help in dealing with your feelings.

An unexpected outcome may be a cesarean delivery when you had planned on having a vaginal birth. It could also be accepting an epidural when you wanted an unmedicated birth. Occasionally, women feel as if they were told one thing by their caregiver before labor and then were treated differently or without regard to their desires once they were admitted to the hospital. They may have felt rushed or pushed into accepting procedures they did not want.

Women who plan to deliver at a birth center and then require a transfer to a hospital often have to deal with their own feelings while dealing with the questions and comments from family and friends. An unexpected outcome could also be baby-related. The infant may be premature, require treatment in the intensive care nursery, or have a deformity.

At the very least, you can expect to have feelings of disappointment. Get adequate rest and try not to be Superwoman to compensate. Accept offers of help. Guilt and anger are also common emotions at this time. These feelings are normal and should not be minimized. You and your partner should share your feelings with each other. If they persist, attending a new parents' support group may prove helpful. Get a copy of your medical record. This may give you additional information on the course of your labor. It may also provide you with the knowledge to avoid repeating this experience with a subsequent pregnancy. You may want to avoid certain interventions next time, or change caregivers or place of delivery. And you should eventually come to the realization that, while you may influence, you cannot control all the circumstances during labor.

The ultimate unexpected outcome is the stillbirth or death of a baby, either before, at, or shortly after birth. No amount of preparation can prepare you for dealing with this type of devastating event. It is very important that you express your feelings of grief and be allowed to mourn the loss of your child.

The following are suggestions from parents who have experienced a stillbirth or infant death. They may help you in coping if you have this type of loss. The suggestions are:

❏ Give your baby a name. It affirms that you are a parent and that there was a life lost for which you are grieving.

❏ Hold and touch your baby. Remove the blanket so you can count the fingers and toes, and get a full image of your child. If you have other children, they and the grandparents may also want to see and hold the baby. This enables all of you to say hello and good-bye, and to acknowledge that you really did have a baby.

❏ You may also want to get a lock of the baby's hair, and have handprints and footprints made.

❏ Have a photo taken of your baby, even if he has a physical deformity. If you are not sure that you want to have a picture, have a friend or relative keep the photo until you ask for it.

❏ You may want to hold a memorial service with family and close friends. This gives you an opportunity to affirm that this child was born into the family, and it allows others to share in your sorrow and grief.

It goes without saying that you will grieve for the loss of your child. It is very important that you and your partner share your grief openly with each other. Women usually grieve more intensely and for a longer time than men. This is understandable because the woman carries the baby and begins to bond with him long before birth.

You can expect to experience a number of emotions as you go through the process of grieving. Initially, you may be in a state of shock, which is nature's coping mechanism. This is often followed by denial. Feelings of anxiety and/or depression can be felt for some time after the death. Anger that this could have happened to you is a very common feeling at this time. Feeling guilty and blaming yourself or others for causing the death are normal. Experiencing some jealousy when you see babies and other pregnant women is not unusual. Some women have difficulty attending baby showers or being around pregnant friends. A future pregnancy may also revive these feelings of sadness and vulnerability. While others may assume that you are happy about being pregnant, it is not unusual for women who have lost a child, either through miscarriage in early pregnancy or a loss in late pregnancy, to experience recurring periods of grief.

Obviously, grieving takes time. For many women, it can take 6 months to a year to reach a point of acceptance that allows them to move forward with their lives. The more open you can be about your feelings, the quicker you will heal. Let others know that it is okay to talk about the baby. You may also find it helpful to join a support group for bereaved families, such as Compassionate Friends or Resolve Through Sharing. Professional counseling or talking to a member of the clergy may also be beneficial. Some families choose to remember the anniversary by donating to a favorite charity in memory of the baby, planting a tree, or just talking about the event. Some excellent books on the subject of bereavement include *Empty Arms* by Sherokee Ilse, *Silent Sorrow* by Ingrid Kohn and Perry-Lynn Moffitt, and *When Pregnancy Isn't Perfect* by Laurie A. Rich.

CONCLUSION

If you end up experiencing a labor that varies from the norm or that requires some type of intervention, it does not mean that you have "failed." Giving birth is not a performance, and the only real goal is a healthy baby. If you know that you did the best that you could, accept the fact that circumstances were out of your control. You can be grateful for the technology and the medical knowledge that made available the necessary procedures or interventions that assisted you in birthing your baby.

Cesarean Birth
or I Wish I Had a Zipper

A cesarean birth is one in which the baby is delivered through incisions in the abdominal wall and uterus, instead of through the vagina. The medical term for this type of birth is *cesarean section*, which is often shortened to *c-section*. Cesarean sections occur in approximately 21 percent of all births. Therefore, you need to understand the procedures and options for delivering in this manner. You also need to know which factors increase your chance of having a cesarean, as well as ways to avoid having one unnecessarily.

Julius Caesar is usually credited with being the first baby delivered by cesarean section and for having the procedure named after him. Actually, it is unlikely that he was delivered by c-section, since during his time babies were delivered surgically only if the woman had died, and documents indicate that Caesar's mother was alive for many years following his birth. The term *cesarean section* probably comes from the Latin word *caedere*, which means "to cut." Hundreds of years before Caesar, a Roman law, *lex caesarea*, stated that a dying woman should be operated on to save the infant.

The first successful cesarean (meaning that the woman survived) was recorded in 1500. In 1882, Dr. Max Sanger was the first doctor to suture the uterus instead of removing it. Over the years, advances in anesthesia, antibiotics, surgical techniques, and pain medication have increased the safety of the procedure tremendously.

Since many cesarean births are not planned, you should read this chapter carefully to become familiar with the standard procedures and possible options in case you need a c-section. Cesarean delivery is covered in most childbirth preparation classes. In addition to providing a discussion about the actual procedure, the classes should also include ways to decrease your chance of having a cesarean. If your cesarean is planned, special classes are offered by some hospitals and may be a prerequisite for participation by your support person. These cesarean birth classes may also provide specialized instruction on exercises and postpartum care, as well as breastfeeding hints geared to the cesarean mother. Additionally, even though cesarean section is major abdominal surgery, proper preparation can make it a satisfying birth experience for the entire family.

FAMILY-CENTERED CESAREAN BIRTH

A cesarean section is more than an operation. It is the birth of a baby. The way a father and mother feel about their childbirth experience may affect their ability to bond with their newborn. Seeing, touching, and comforting the baby immediately after birth begins the bonding process that is so important to the fostering of maternal and paternal feelings. Therefore, many cesarean couples desire to share in the miracle of birth just as they would if it were a vaginal delivery. George Nolan, MD, of Women's Hospital, University of Michigan Hospital, reported in "Family Centered Cesarean Maternity Care Policy" that 100 percent of parents who attended the cesarean births of their babies indicated that they would prefer being together for future cesarean births. He also noted that 50 percent of parents separated at the time of cesarean delivery expressed a desire to be together for future cesarean births.[1]

Many fathers wish to participate in the cesarean delivery of their children to comfort and support their partners and also to witness the birth. Most hospitals permit labor partners to attend cesarean deliveries as long as regional anesthetics are used. If general anesthesia is necessary, couples need prior permission from the obstetrician and anesthesiologist. Some doctors feel that the labor partner does not need to be present when general anesthesia is used because the woman is asleep and unaware of any emotional support. They also fear that the woman's unconscious appearance may be upsetting to the labor partner. If you would like your labor partner to be present while you are under general anesthesia so that he can later describe the birth to you, talk to your doctor. If a true emergency exists, however, this option may not be available. Also, if more than one support person is present during labor, only one may be allowed to attend the cesarean because of space limitations.

A cesarean couple needs to find a pediatrician who is flexible and open to their desires. They should discuss with him their wish to touch, hold, and breastfeed their newborn as soon as possible, even in the delivery room or recovery room, if the baby's condition is good. Of course, if complications arise and the baby needs special care, even the most flexible pediatrician will delay bonding and breastfeeding.

If you give birth by cesarean, ask your pediatrician to evaluate your baby as an individual and, if the baby's condition is good, to admit him to the regular newborn nursery instead of to the special care nursery. This will allow you contact with your baby sooner.

During the birth of a baby, whether the birth is vaginal or by cesarean, a couple needs each other's emotional support. Some couples experience an emotional climax at the moment of birth—a feeling that should be shared. During a cesarean delivery, your partner can hold your hand, wipe your forehead, and talk to you. His emotional support can be invaluable. Your attitude may become so much more positive that you relax better and recover faster. Many fathers like to take photographs or videos during and after the cesarean delivery. Your partner may even be able to take his equipment into the nursery to film the baby's admission bath and procedures. This is a good opportunity to record the events that you are unable to view.

Couples who are not allowed to share in a cesarean birth may instead end up sharing feelings of resentment and disappointment. It is even more necessary for a couple such as this to bond with their baby as soon as possible and to talk to each other about their feelings.

Another option that should not be affected by the method of delivery is rooming-in. With help from her labor partner, a cesarean mother can enjoy all the benefits of having her baby with her. For the first 1 or 2 days, however, she may wish to delay rooming-in, or to limit it to times when help is available. If she is in a private room, her partner can have unlimited visitation and provide the needed assistance, day and night.

If the possibility exists that you will be delivering by cesarean, you need to participate actively with your doctor, anesthesiologist, and pediatrician in planning your birth. You should have your partner join you for several of your doctor's appointments and talk with him about the surgery, anesthesia, and postpartum period to make sure he knows your desires. Do not take anything for granted or you may be disappointed. Your requests, of course, must be reasonable because a cesarean section is major surgery and involves risks to you and your baby. However, having a doctor who strongly believes in the benefits of family-centered maternity care will increase your chances of having the type of birth you desire.

Another good source of help is your local cesarean support group. The members of a group such as this can give you additional emotional support after your birth. Many cesarean mothers find it helpful to talk to someone else who had a c-section and who knows what the mother is going through.

INDICATIONS FOR CESAREAN BIRTH

Cesarean deliveries are performed for many reasons. Because opinions vary concerning these reasons, you might want to get a second opinion if you are told that you need a c-section.

Over one-third of the cesareans that are performed in the United States are done because of previous cesarean birth. In 1988, the American College of Obstetricians and Gynecologists issued the statement that in the absence of medical complications of pregnancy, women who previously had a cesarean should be encouraged to attempt a vaginal birth. As more and more doctors incorporate this philosophy, the outdated practice of "once a cesarean, always a cesarean" will continue to decline.

Cephalopelvic disproportion (CPD) occurs when the baby's head does not fit through the woman's pelvis. This diagnosis is also often used to indicate a labor that fails to progress. Failure to progress may refer to a prolonged labor with no change in cervical dilation or station of the baby, an extended period of time since the rupture of the membranes, or weak and ineffectual uterine contractions. This is the most common indication for a cesarean occurring during labor.

Fetal distress is a condition in which the baby is not receiving enough oxygen. It may be indicated by an abnormal fetal heart rate pattern or low fetal blood pH. Meconium-stained amniotic fluid, which is greenish in color, may also be associated with the condition. Another condition is fetal intolerance of labor. This means that even though the baby is not currently in distress, the fetal heart rate pattern observed on the electronic fetal monitor is somewhat questionable. If the woman is not close to delivery, the doctor may decide to perform a cesarean rather than to wait and see if the fetus has distress. If the amount of amniotic fluid is too low, fetal distress may be noted when the umbilical cord becomes compressed during contractions. The volume of amniotic fluid may be increased by a saline solution that is infused into the uterus. The infusion process is called amnioinfusion and may be a way of

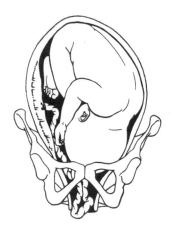

Figure 9.1.
Prolapsed cord.

allowing labor to continue when a cesarean would otherwise be necessary.

If the baby is in an abnormal presentation within the uterus, a cesarean may be indicated. One example is a transverse lie, in which the baby is lying sideways in the uterus and a vaginal delivery is impossible. A baby who is in a breech presentation may be delivered either vaginally or by cesarean section, depending on several factors. If the doctor is experienced in delivering breech babies, he may more readily agree to a vaginal birth. He will need to make sure that the woman's pelvis is adequate and that the baby is not too large. He will also need to determine the type of breech presentation, including the position of the baby's head, and will need to confirm that the labor is progressing normally. Many newer doctors are not trained in the vaginal delivery of breech babies. Others feel that the additional risks involved do not warrant attempting a vaginal breech delivery and deliver all breech babies by cesarean. With both a transverse lie and breech position, the physician may attempt an external version prior to or even during labor.

In abruptio placentae, the placenta partially or completely separates from the uterine wall before the baby is born. An immediate cesarean is necessary in this emergency situation because the woman may hemorrhage and the baby may lose all or part of his oxygen supply. This condition is rare in low-risk women.

A prolapsed cord occurs when the umbilical cord protrudes into the vagina ahead of the baby. (See Figure 9.1.) This usually happens after the membranes rupture and the baby is in a breech position or his head is not well engaged in the pelvis. The baby's oxygen supply is cut off as the presenting part compresses the cord. If you feel that this may be happening to you while you are still at home, immediately get down on your hands and knees, and position your hips higher than your head to relieve the pressure on the cord.

Knee-chest position
for prolapsed cord.

Call 911 and *remain in the knee-chest position* until help arrives. If the cord is protruding from your vagina, place a wet cloth on it to keep it moist. However, do this only if you can accomplish it without leaving the knee-chest position. When you arrive at the hospital, your doctor will perform an immediate cesarean.

Placenta previa is a condition in which the placenta partially or completely covers the cervix. The degree of severity determines whether or not a cesarean is necessary. If the cervix is completely covered, a cesarean is mandatory because the placenta would deliver first and the baby would lose his oxygen supply. This is usually identified prior to labor by an ultrasound.

When preeclampsia (severe PIH) is present, the woman may have a stroke or kidney failure. The treatment for preeclampsia is delivery. PIH affects the welfare of the fetus as well as that of the woman, thereby necessitating delivery, either by induction or cesarean.

If the woman is diabetic, early delivery is necessary for the baby's sake. The placental blood flow may be poor, the baby may be excessively large, or he may respond poorly to the stress of labor. If induction is unsuccessful, a cesarean will need to be performed.

When an Rh-negative woman has been sensitized by Rh-positive blood, her baby may develop erythroblastosis fetalis. During the pregnancy, antibodies may pass through the placenta and attack the Rh-positive baby's blood cells, leading to anemia and other problems that necessitate delivery. With the advent of Rh-immune globulin (RhoGAM), which can be given to the Rh-negative woman during pregnancy and after every birth of an Rh-positive infant, as well as after miscarriage, abortion, amniocentesis, and chorionic villus sampling, erythroblastosis fetalis is now rare.

A woman who has an active herpes simplex virus II (HSVII) infection on her vulva and/or vagina at the time of birth needs a cesarean section to prevent infecting the baby. HSVII can be transmitted to the baby if he comes in contact with an active lesion or even if the membranes have ruptured. It is an untreatable illness that causes death in 50 percent of the infants infected.

Some doctors schedule a cesarean if they feel that the baby's size is excessive (macrosomia). They are concerned that the baby's shoulders would become stuck (shoulder dystocia), which can be a serious complication. Since the methods of determining a baby's size are inaccurate, many doctors observe the woman's progress during labor and while pushing to determine whether a cesarean is necessary.

FACTORS CONTRIBUTING TO THE HIGH CESAREAN RATE

The United States' cesarean birth rate skyrocketed from 4.5 percent in 1965 to a high of over 24 percent in 1988. This has decreased slightly to the current rate of approximately 21 percent. This decrease was the result of a concerted effort to reduce the high rate of cesarean deliveries. Among the factors that contributed to the reduction is the increase in vaginal births after a cesarean. The U.S. Public Health Department and the World Health Organization have called for a cesarean rate of 15 percent by the year 2000, although many experts doubt that this goal is attainable.

Many factors contribute to the high cesarean rate. One reason given by some doctors is the threat of a malpractice suit if a cesarean is not done and a "less than perfect" baby results.[2] At least 79 percent of obstetricians have been sued at least once. About 80 percent of these lawsuits involve a claim that a cesarean was not done or was not done soon enough.[3]

The training that obstetricians receive is changing. Because of the risks involved in the use of forceps, doctors now receive less training in managing difficult deliveries (breech births and fetal distress) using this tool. High forceps deliveries have been completely replaced by cesarean sections, and some doctors now also substitute surgical intervention for the difficult midforceps delivery.

Obstetrical training revolves mostly around handling complications. As a result, many doctors treat all laboring women as potentially high risk and rely on sophisticated equipment such as electronic fetal monitors and on the routine use of IVs. A dramatic increase in the use of epidurals for labor may also be contributing to the high rate of cesareans.

The increase in women over 30 years of age giving birth is another factor in the high cesarean rate. They are at increased risk for complications, and physicians may be more likely to perform cesareans if they perceive that an adverse outcome may result. Also, multiple births have increased dramatically in the past 20 years, and these infants are more likely to be delivered by cesarean, especially if one of the babies is in an abnormal presentation.[4] Additionally, c-section is often used for very low birth weight babies.

Some professionals feel that at least a small percentage of the increase in cesareans is due to the convenience and increased income the procedure offers doctors. Higher fees result from the surgical procedure, the longer hospital stay, and the guaranteed insurance coverage.

AVOIDING AN UNNECESSARY CESAREAN

*Hints for
the Mother-to-Be*

To avoid a cesarean:

❑ Select a caregiver with
a low cesarean rate.

❑ Hire a doula.

❑ Have a supportive
labor partner.

❑ Avoid Pitocin and
elective induction.

❑ Walk during labor.

❑ Avoid an epidural
and medication.

❑ Request that monitoring
be done intermittently.

A cesarean delivery may be necessary to save the life of the woman or baby. But an unnecessary cesarean should be avoided at all costs, as there are risks involved. Cesarean section is major abdominal surgery, and, as does any surgery, it carries with it the risk of infection, hemorrhage, pneumonia, blood clots, and anesthesia-related complications, along with increased financial costs, additional discomfort, and longer recovery. A cesarean baby is at a higher risk than a baby delivered vaginally. He is more likely to suffer from premature birth, asphyxia, or a breathing disorder.[5] The resulting problems, intensive care, and financial costs can be overwhelming.

The chances of having a cesarean delivery can be affected by certain hospital practices during labor and even by the choice of caregiver. Selecting a midwife or doctor who favors family-centered childbirth and has a low cesarean rate will decrease the chances of having a cesarean. Women who have a certified nurse-midwife as their caregiver have the lowest rate of cesarean deliveries. This is because these practitioners treat mainly low-risk women and are less likely to use interventions or epidurals during labor. Women are more likely to walk during labor, and they benefit from the one-on-one personalized care given by the nurse-midwife.

Having continuous support from a labor partner can also lessen the chances of a cesarean. The use of a doula can reduce the chances even further. A doula's presence provides a supportive atmosphere and is often accompanied by a dramatic reduction in interventions.[6]

The use of Pitocin or artificial rupture of the membranes to induce labor can change the type or the force of the labor contractions, can precipitate fetal distress, and can create potential hazards for the woman and baby.[7] Failure of induction is a common reason for emergency cesarean section.[8] Labor should be induced only if a medical reason exists. Since the 1980s, there has been a steady increase in the number of births occurring during the week and a corresponding decline in the births on weekends. This concentration of births during the week is caused by an increase in the number of inductions of labor. Cesarean sections as a result of failed inductions have also increased.[9]

In a normal labor, early intervention (such as amniotomy, Pitocin, pain medication, or epidural anesthesia) may lead to complications that indicate a cesarean delivery. The rule that every baby should be delivered within 24 hours after rupture of the membranes or within a specific amount of time after the onset of labor increases the chance of a cesarean section. Some doctors closely monitor a laboring woman for signs of infection by keeping track of her temperature and blood count instead of routinely performing a cesarean after 24 hours with ruptured membranes.

A woman's position during labor can affect her need for a cesarean delivery. Walking can assist the normal progression of labor. Walking has been shown to improve the quality of contractions, to shorten labor, and to improve the condition of the baby during labor and delivery. Lying flat on the back can cause supine hypotension and fetal distress.

An electronic fetal monitor may be indicated and beneficial for a higher-risk woman, but when it is used routinely for a low-risk woman, it can increase her chance of having a cesarean delivery.[10] For example, insufficiently trained personnel may misinterpret its readings. They may overreact to abnormalities in the fetal heart tracings, which may just *appear* to indicate fetal distress. If dilation is sufficient, an internal monitor should be applied to verify any readings of problems by an external monitor.

Abnormalities in the fetal heart rate tracings can also be confirmed by a fetal blood test. A blood sample can be taken from the baby's scalp to measure the pH. Not all hospitals are equipped to do this, however, and not all doctors take advantage of it, perhaps because of a lack of knowledge or skill in this area.[11] The equipment needed for this test is very sensitive and must be maintained and operated by a skilled technician to ensure accurate results. Utilization of this test may help to avoid many unnecessary cesarean births.

The electronic fetal monitor also limits mobility during labor. Some nurses insist that a monitored woman lie on her back to ensure a good tracing. Lying flat on the back can lead to supine hypotension and fetal distress.

Epidural anesthesia can inhibit the force of contractions and prolong the second stage of labor, affecting the urge to push and the effectiveness of the pushing. An epidural can complicate a potentially normal labor and delivery, decreasing the baby's oxygen supply because of low maternal blood pressure and therefore increasing the likelihood of a cesarean delivery.[12] An epidural may also relax the pelvic muscles and thus affect the rotation and descent of the baby.[13]

Analgesics and sedatives can slow labor, inhibit the force of contractions, or depress the baby's heart rate, thereby indicating the need for a cesarean section.

PLANNED AND UNPLANNED CESAREANS

There are two types of cesarean births—planned and unplanned. Most primary (first-time) cesarean births are unplanned. Many of the same routines are followed for both types of cesareans, although they might be done in a different order and often somewhat more hurried in an unplanned cesarean. When dealing with an emergency cesarean, more stress is involved, since the woman has not had adequate time to prepare emotionally. If she is separated from her labor partner during delivery, the trauma of the experience is intensified.

A planned cesarean birth is usually scheduled to occur just prior to the anticipated due date. Early confirmation of pregnancy and accurate documentation of fetal growth are essential for determining the date precisely. Because the due date is only an estimate, prematurity is a risk. Premature babies are more likely to develop respiratory distress syndrome (RDS) and are generally less able to handle life outside the uterus than full-term babies. They are therefore more likely to be kept in the hospital for an extended period of time, separated from their mothers and fathers. This increases the new parents' anxiety about the birth experience and inhibits bonding with the baby.

If you will be having a planned cesarean, request permission to go into labor spontaneously. Labor is the best indicator that a baby is adequately mature and ready to be born. RDS has been found to be "four times less frequent in babies that were delivered after labor had commenced than in those that experienced no labor."[14] Labor contractions stimulate the baby's body, better prepare his lungs for breathing, and reduce his chance of respiratory difficulties. Since the contractions also draw up and shorten the cervix, many doctors feel that an incision made in this area is the strongest one possible and offers less chance of rupture if a vaginal delivery is attempted in the future. When labor begins, call your doctor at once. *Do not labor at home.*

Doctors can perform several tests to help determine fetal maturity and

A Hint for the Labor Partner

❏ If a cesarean is planned, attend cesarean preparation classes with your partner.

therefore lessen the risk of delivering prematurely. Your doctor might choose to do a sonogram in order to measure the biparietal (ear to ear) diameter of the baby's head. With this measurement, the doctor can estimate gestational age. The accuracy of the test depends upon when it is done. It is most accurate when performed early in pregnancy.

Some doctors also perform amniocentesis to assess the maturity of the baby's lungs. This test evaluates the amniotic fluid for the proportions of lecithin and sphingomyelin, substances that are produced by the lungs. The proportion of lecithin to sphingomyelin is called the L/S ratio. This ratio changes toward the end of pregnancy, with a sudden increase in lecithin occurring after 34 weeks. A ratio of two to one or greater indicates lung maturity in the baby. A sonogram should be done in conjunction with amniocentesis to locate the placenta and the baby.

In certain high-risk conditions, such as diabetes and PIH, the placenta begins to deteriorate prior to term. In these cases, serial estriol levels can be measured to determine placental function and fetal well-being as an indicator of the best time for delivery. The biophysical profile is a more recent test used for determining optimum time for delivery.

Since the American College of Obstetricians and Gynecologists has recommended that all women without medical contraindications attempt a vaginal birth after a cesarean, the number of planned cesareans is decreasing.

PREOPERATIVE PROCEDURES

If you are having a planned cesarean, you have the choice of entering the hospital the day before the surgery or on the morning of the baby's birth. Some women choose the second option because it gives them one more night at home with family members. This can be important, especially if small children are involved. It also allows the woman to get a more restful night's sleep in a familiar environment.

Though every doctor and every hospital follow a different set of procedures, certain procedures are standard almost everywhere. You will be instructed to take in nothing by mouth (NPO) for 8 to 12 hours before surgery to prevent aspiration of stomach contents if general anesthesia is needed. If you elect to spend those hours at home, it is your responsibility to refrain from eating. Most doctors also recommend a light, bland dinner the night before surgery.

You will need to have blood drawn for several tests and for typing and cross matching. Most doctors also require a urinalysis. Some may request a chest X-ray and respiratory function tests if you are a smoker or are congested. You can have all of these tests done on an outpatient basis.

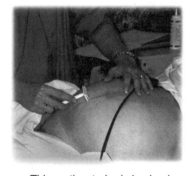

This mother-to-be is having her abdomen shaved in preparation for the cesarean birth of her baby.

In the hospital, a nurse will shave your abdomen in preparation for the surgery, but the area she shaves may vary. If you are given a partial prep, your hair will be removed from your abdomen down to your pubic area. A small amount of hair may remain visible when you hold your legs together. If you are given a complete prep, you will be shaved from beneath your breasts down to and between your legs and up to your tailbone. Many doctors today feel that the extensive shaving of a complete prep is unnecessary and adds to postpartum discomfort.

Your doctor may also order an enema before surgery. Discuss this with him beforehand. He may allow you to give yourself the enema at home.

A hospital representative will ask you to sign a consent form for the surgery and the anesthesia, and will ask if you have a living will. Read all documents carefully before signing them.

The anesthesiologist will visit you prior to surgery to discuss preoperative medication and surgical anesthesia. Tell him about any allergies or sensitivities that you have to medications, and discuss with him your preferences.

If you enter the hospital the night before surgery, you may be offered a sedative or sleeping pill. The decision whether to take it is yours. If you have difficulty sleeping, you may need it. On the other hand, it may make you feel groggy, rather than rested, in the morning.

Whether your cesarean is planned or unplanned, you may be offered a sedative or tranquilizer prior to surgery. Prepared women often feel that they do not need anything, choosing instead to rely on relaxation techniques. A sedative or tranquilizer can make both the woman and baby sleepy at the time of birth. Many physicians also routinely order a shot of atropine before surgery to dry up secretions. Unless you choose general anesthesia, you may not need this medication.

The two types of anesthesia that are used for a cesarean birth are regional and general anesthesia. Most women and doctors prefer regional anesthesia because it allows the mother and father to actively participate in the birth and does not depress the baby. Unless an extreme emergency exists, adequate time is available for regional anesthesia to be administered.

Regional anesthesia includes spinals and epidurals, with epidurals being more common. They produce similar effects, although spinals provide deeper anesthesia. When the anesthesia is administered, you will feel warm, then tingly, and finally numb. With an epidural, you may still experience some physical sensations such as tugging and pulling as the baby is born. Some women feel that this allows them to experience the baby's birth more completely. Because an epidural is usually administered through a catheter, it can be continuously dosed to give you comfort during the bonding period, and it can continue to provide pain relief for the first 24 hours after surgery. A spinal is administered in one injection. Because of this, a general anesthetic is sometimes required for the repair work if the surgery took longer than expected and the effects of the spinal have begun to wear off.

When the health of the woman or baby demands immediate delivery, general anesthesia is used. Because the woman is unconscious, the labor partner usually is not permitted to participate in the birth. However, some doctors allow the husband to be present to permit him to bond with the baby and to later tell his wife the story of the birth.

If you need general anesthesia, you will first be put to sleep with an injection of medication into your IV. Next, a medication will be given to relax your muscles, and a tube will be inserted into your trachea (windpipe). A mixture of oxygen and a gas will be administered via the endotracheal tube to maintain breathing and keep you unconscious throughout the surgery.

SURGICAL PROCEDURE

Depending on the hospital, your delivery will take place either in the labor and delivery area or in a surgical operating room. The location might be a factor in your partner's participation. Some hospitals have a policy of not allowing any relatives in the operating room.

Hints for the Labor Partner

If your partner is having a cesarean:

❏ Stay with her during the surgery.

❏ Hold her hand and reassure her during the surgery.

❏ Take videos and photos of the newborn.

❏ Go with the baby to the nursery and film the events (weighing, measuring, bath).

Whether your cesarean is planned or unplanned, you may feel apprehensive as you are being wheeled in for surgery. You can minimize this with advance preparation and the use of relaxation techniques. If your partner plans to be present for the birth, he will change into scrub clothes (a mask, scrub suit, cap, and shoe covers) while you are being taken to the delivery room. Unless you have made prior arrangements with your doctor, your partner will not rejoin you until the surgical team is ready to begin the operation.

Once you have been placed on the table, an IV will be started in one of your arms, if you do not already have one. That arm will then be strapped to a board. A blood pressure cuff will be put on your other arm, and electrocardiogram leads will be attached to your chest. If you would like to hold your partner's hand during surgery and touch your baby once he is born, you will need to request that one arm be left free.

Next, the anesthesiologist will administer the chosen regional anesthesia. He may also offer you oxygen, which you can breathe through a mask until

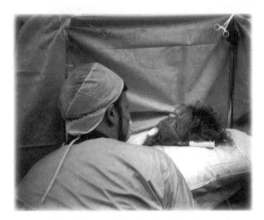

the baby is born. A nurse will insert a urinary catheter to drain your bladder. She will probably do this after the regional anesthetic has taken effect to minimize the discomfort. Because of its location, the bladder must be kept flat and out of the way to avoid being damaged during the surgery. Your abdomen and thighs will be scrubbed with a reddish orange antiseptic solution, a screen will be placed across your shoulders, and sterile drapes will be adjusted to cover everything. Because of the screen, you and your partner will not see anything you do not wish to see. If you would like to see the baby emerge, talk to your doctor about having a mirror in the room or the screen lowered at the moment of birth. When everything is set up and the doctor is ready to begin the surgery, your partner will be brought into the room and seated next to your head. If general anesthesia is used, it will not be administered until this time to decrease the amount of anesthesia that gets to the baby.

Her labor partner's emotional support is invaluable to this mother-to-be as she awaits the cesarean birth of her baby.

The type of skin and uterine incisions that your doctor will use will be influenced by his preferences, the baby's position, your desires, and the speed with which the baby must be delivered. (For a discussion of the incisions used for cesareans, see "Skin and Uterine Incisions.") If your physician uses a cautery to stop the bleeding from small blood vessels during the surgery, a burnt odor may be noticed. After he makes the incisions, the doctor will suction the amniotic fluid, which you may hear. Within a few minutes, you may feel a tugging or pulling sensation as your baby is born. If your doctor uses fundal pressure (downward pressure on the top of your abdomen) to assist the delivery, you may feel a great deal of pressure. The doctor will then lift the baby out, using either his hands, forceps, or a vacuum extractor. If you feel discomfort from this, try slow paced breathing. Within moments, you will hear your baby's first cry. The cord will be clamped and cut, and the baby will be handed to the pediatrician or nursery nurse. You will be shown your new son or daughter, and then the baby will be examined. A nurse will perform routine identification procedures. (For a discussion of the routine followed at most hospitals and birth centers, see "Care Given to the Baby at Birth" on page 202.) These exams can usually be done within your view to help relieve any anxiety that you may have about your baby's condition.

Your doctor will also deliver your placenta through the incision and will give you Pitocin through the IV to help your uterus contract. He will examine your uterus, ovaries, and tubes, then repair the uterus, abdominal muscles, subcutaneous tissues, and skin. Some doctors use clamps or staples to close the skin incision. The repair work normally takes about 45 minutes. If you feel nauseated or experience any other sensations, tell the anesthesiologist.

While the repair work is being completed, you can ask to touch and hold your baby. If your arms are strapped, your partner may be allowed to hold the baby next to your cheek. Since the operating room will be cold, your baby and partner will leave during the repair, and your partner can stay with the newborn in the nursery. When you are moved to the recovery room, your partner and newborn can be reunited with you. If your partner was not present for the delivery, the baby can be brought out to him immediately after the birth. Seeing the baby will help to relieve your partner's anxiety about your condition and that of the baby.

SKIN AND UTERINE INCISIONS

A cesarean delivery requires two incisions—one in the skin and one in the uterus. Both can be done either vertically or horizontally. Most commonly, both incisions are made horizontally. If a woman has had previous abdominal surgery, the doctor will remove the old scar and use that area for the skin incision. Therefore, if the scar was vertical, the skin incision may not match the uterine incision. The incision in the skin is usually chosen for cosmetic reasons, while the one in the uterus is chosen for medical reasons.

The low transverse skin (Pfannenstiel) incision is made crosswise along the pubic hairline. (See Figure 9.2.) This "bikini cut" is preferred for cosmetic reasons because the scar is barely noticeable. However, the incision takes longer to do and gives the doctor limited space in which to work. Therefore, it is not used in an extreme emergency. On the plus side, discomfort during recovery is less, and the wound heals more quickly. A vertical skin incision is faster to make and gives the doctor more room in which to work. (See Figure 9.3.) Hence, it allows for a quicker delivery in an emergency situation.

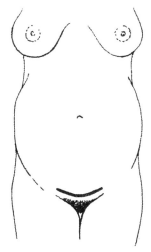

Figure 9.2.
Low transverse skin incision.

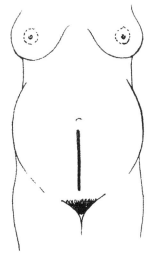

Figure 9.3.
Vertical skin incision.

Figure 9.4.
Low transverse cervical incision.

Figure 9.5.
Classical uterine incision.

The most common uterine incision is the low transverse cervical incision. It is made horizontally in the cervical area. (See Figure 9.4.) Because it is not in the contractile part of the uterus, it forms the strongest scar with the least danger of rupture and fewest postoperative adhesions. The incision is smaller and is thought to heal more quickly. It is the only incision that doctors will accept for a vaginal birth after a cesarean (VBAC).

A classical uterine incision is made vertically in the fundal area and gives the doctor more working room. (See Figure 9.5.) It is done when the baby is large, when the baby is in a transverse lie, when adhesions or scar tissue from previous cesareans are a problem, or when the baby must be delivered immediately. A classical incision forms the weakest scar and heals the slowest. You may not attempt a VBAC with this incision.

RECOVERY ROOM

Once the repair work is completed, you will be taken to the recovery room. You will stay there until the staff feels that you are stable, usually about 1 to 2 hours. During this time, a nurse will check your blood pressure, temperature, pulse, respiration, and vaginal and incisional bleeding. If your uterus becomes soft, she may massage it to prevent bleeding. If you feel any discomfort, use your breathing and relaxation techniques. You can also request pain medication. If you had an epidural, the pain medication can continue to be administered via the epidural catheter. You will thus be able to bond with your baby and initiate breastfeeding with minimal discomfort.

The nurse may ask you to breathe deeply and cough. This is to help prevent pneumonia. Splint your incision by holding a pillow firmly against your abdomen and "huff" if coughing seems difficult at first. (For instructions for huffing, see "First Day" on page 197.)

If you had a regional anesthetic, you will notice the feeling returning first to your toes and feet, and then progressively up toward your abdomen. Medication given continuously through the epidural catheter, if you have one, will give you good pain relief while you regain movement in your extremities. In some hospitals, prior to leaving the operating room, a single injection of morphine is given through the epidural catheter, and then the catheter is removed. This also provides good pain relief for the next 24 hours. If you had general anesthesia, you may be groggy or nauseated upon awakening and feel the need for pain medication.

Many hospitals will allow your partner to stay with you if you recover in the maternity recovery room. Your pediatrician may permit you some bonding time, providing the baby's condition is good. Bonding is just as important for cesarean parents as it is for couples who experience a vaginal birth.

THE CESAREAN BABY

No two babies are alike, cesarean babies included. One noticeable difference between vaginally delivered and planned cesarean babies is that the head of a cesarean infant is nicely shaped because it was not molded by the birth process. If you were in labor for many hours prior to the cesarean, some molding may be noticeable. Because a cesarean baby experienced a surgical delivery, he may need to be more closely observed. Some hospitals require all cesarean babies to spend a certain amount of time in the special care nursery. Since a cesarean baby did not pass through the birth canal, which compresses the amniotic fluid from his lungs, he may have more mucus or may have retained more amniotic fluid in his lungs. This is lessened if the mother experienced some labor. If the mother was given medication or general anesthesia, the baby may be drowsy.

If your baby's condition is good, ask to have him placed in the regular nursery so that you can have earlier contact with him. If your baby was in distress at birth, however, he may be immediately placed in the intensive care nursery. As soon as you feel able, you can visit him in the nursery. Your partner can push you there in a wheelchair.

If the baby is unable to nurse, you should pump your breasts to provide him with your colostrum and milk. Even if he is not allowed out of his isolette, your baby needs you to touch him and talk to him.

POSTPARTUM

The average stay in the hospital after a cesarean is 3 to 4 days. The IV and catheter will remain in place for approximately 24 hours following the surgery. The IV will provide you with nourishment and adequate fluids until your intestines begin to function again. The catheter will give your bladder time to recover from the surgery and keep it empty until you are able to walk to the bathroom yourself. If you are given narcotics through the epidural catheter, you may have a device attached to your finger known as a pulse oximeter. This device measures the amount of oxygen in your blood to ensure adequate levels, since narcotics can decrease your respirations.

Your diet at first will consist of liquids and will be gradually increased to a regular diet. Adequate intake of fluids is important to ensure proper kidney function, to prevent dehydration and fever, and to build an adequate milk supply.

You will be encouraged to get up and walk around 12 to 24 hours after your surgery. Walking promotes good circulation, which reduces the chance of blood clots, and it also helps relieve gas. Your first attempt at walking will be the most difficult, but each successive attempt will be easier. Some doctors order support stockings or an abdominal binder for their patients.

Even though you will have given birth by cesarean, you will still have a vaginal flow. You can use beltless pads, placing them in your underwear or in mesh panties provided by the hospital.

You may feel discomfort in one or both of your shoulders as a result of a collection of blood and air under your diaphragm. The pain is felt in the shoulders because of nerves that connect with the diaphragm. If you had general anesthesia, you may have a sore throat because of the tube inserted down your throat.

You will have abdominal pain for several days following the surgery. If you had an epidural, you may have been given a single dose of a narcotic injected into the catheter prior to its removal in the recovery room, or you may receive a continuous infusion of a narcotic via the epidural catheter. If you had general anesthesia, pain medication can be provided by a patient controlled analgesia (PCA) device. The narcotic is given through the IV tubing and is controlled by the patient intermittently pressing a button for a small

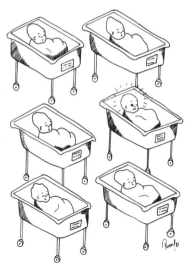

"Can't you tell I'm the cesarean baby?!"

Hints for the Labor Partner

If your partner had a cesarean:

❑ Take the baby to see her in the recovery room, if possible.

❑ Help her position the baby at her breast.

❑ Stay with her overnight in the hospital to help with the baby.

❑ Reassure her that she did well and that sometimes events happen that cannot be controlled.

❑ Help her find relief from gas pain by encouraging her to walk, giving her warm liquids to drink, and urging her to avoid carbonated beverages.

❑ Make sure she has help at home.

dose of medication. Or, your doctor may order intramuscular injections of medication every 3 to 4 hours.

Once the epidural or IV is out and you are taking fluids orally, you will be given pain medication in pill form. You will most likely need it to be able to interact comfortably with your baby. Also, use your relaxation techniques to maximize the effect of the medication.

As your intestines begin to function again, you may experience sharp gas pains. Avoid apple juice and carbonated beverages, which can increase gas. Hot tea and lemon water will be more soothing. Use a heating pad while in bed, and begin walking to help the gas to pass. Some doctors order medication to aid digestion.

As your incision heals, it will probably itch, possibly for several months. Wear cotton panties rather than nylon during this time. Your doctor will remove the clamps or staples from your incision before you leave the hospital and place strips of tape (Steri-Strips) over the incision to keep the edges together. This tape will peel away and fall off during the next week. You and your partner may want to look at the incision together before going home.

When breastfeeding after a cesarean, use the football hold to reduce the pressure on your incision.

Rooming-in is especially important for the cesarean couple to help them develop feelings of attachment to their baby. You will need assistance, however, since you will have difficulty moving around for several days. Do not hesitate to ask for help from the nursing staff. If you have a private room, your partner will most likely be welcome to stay with you around the clock. Rooming-in will also help you to get breastfeeding off to a good start. For comfortable nursing positions for cesarean mothers, see "Breastfeeding Following a Cesarean Delivery" on page 264.

Once you arrive home, you will need household help for the first few weeks. Housework should not be one of your priorities at this time. Setting reasonable goals and expectations for yourself and your baby will make life much easier for all concerned. Take time to relax, and nap when the baby does.

Your recovery will be more rapid if you concentrate on your health and the baby's welfare, rather than on entertaining visitors or cleaning the house. Continue taking your prenatal vitamins and maintain a high level of protein in your postpartum diet. A healing wound requires lots of protein, just as a growing fetus does during pregnancy. Nutrition plays an important part in how strongly your incision heals.

The correct time to resume sexual relations is different for every couple. Your decision should be based on whether the placental site has healed, which is signaled by cessation of vaginal discharge, and on the amount of abdominal discomfort you are experiencing. Your doctor's advice and your own desire for sex are also important factors.

While you are not dealing with an episiotomy, you are coping with an abdominal incision, which is even larger and more painful than an episiotomy. During sex, you may find some of the positions that you used during the last months of pregnancy to be most comfortable. (For a discussion of sexual relations following birth, see "Postpartum Sex" on page 291.) Many women experience a changed body image. Because of their incision, they worry that they are no longer attractive to their husbands. You may need lots of reassurance that you are still appealing.

Your emotional recovery from your cesarean birth can take from 2 to 6 months. Your feelings may vary from relief that it is over to painful depression. You may find that you need to be reassured that you did nothing wrong and that you are not inadequate or a failure. Cesarean delivery is simply another way to give birth safely. Contact your local cesarean support group for help and information.

EXERCISE AFTER A CESAREAN

Because having a cesarean involves major surgery, you will be sore afterwards and will require longer to fully recover than if you had delivered vaginally. Postpartum exercises will need to be delayed for a couple of weeks, and you will need to check with your doctor before beginning them. However, you can start some simple exercises immediately. These will help your body get back to normal more quickly.

First Day

Since you may spend the first 24 hours in bed, you should begin doing ankle rotating and foot flexing and stretching as soon as possible after surgery—in the recovery room when sensation returns after regional anesthesia or as soon as you are alert after general anesthesia. (For complete descriptions of these and any of the following exercises, see "Postpartum Exercises" on page 285.) These two exercises stimulate circulation and decrease the chance of blood clots and dizziness.

You will also need to begin deep breathing to expand your lungs. In the recovery room or as soon as you wake up, take 10 slow deep chest breaths. Repeat once an hour to loosen any phlegm and mucus that may have collected in your lungs during surgery. This deep breathing is important to prevent pneumonia. Along with deep breathing, "huff" to bring up phlegm. To huff, hold your incision with both hands, take in a deep breath, and breathe out with a short, sharp "ha" sound. Huffing is not as uncomfortable as coughing and will be very effective if you take in enough air first. Do not worry about your stitches breaking. Stitches are done in a number of layers and are very strong.

To relieve gas and help the incision heal, practice abdominal tightening. While sitting, lying down, or standing, slowly tighten your abdominal muscles as you exhale and hold them tight for 1 to 2 seconds. Gradually increase the holding time to 5 seconds or more. Doing

Log rolling.

this exercise may be difficult at first, but the increased circulation will help the incision heal, and the muscle contractions will actually draw the ends of the incision closer together. The first few days that you do this exercise, support the incision with your hands for added comfort.

Proper body mechanics can help ease the strain on your abdomen as you roll over and sit up in bed. To turn to your left side, bend your right knee and bring it over your straight left knee. As you turn your body, reach for the left side of the bed with your right arm. This maneuver is called log rolling. If you want to turn to your right, reverse the procedure. If you want to sit up, you can easily raise yourself using your arm and shoulder muscles, swinging your legs over the side of the bed, without putting undue strain on your abdomen.

Knee reaching.

Second Day

If you are still in bed most of the time on the second day, continue doing your ankle rotating and foot flexing and stretching. You should also continue huffing until your lungs are clear.

Deep breathing along with the pelvic tilt and Kegel exercises will stimulate intestinal activity and reduce the discomfort from gas. To do the pelvic tilt, lie on your back or side with your knees bent, and gently rock your pelvis backwards and forwards using your abdominal and buttocks muscles. Begin doing super Kegels, contracting the muscles of your pelvic floor for 20 seconds. Do 1 super Kegel ten times a day.

To begin strengthening your abdominal muscles, practice knee reaching. Sit semireclined (at a 45-degree angle) with the bed raised or your back and head supported by pillows. Breathe in deeply, then exhale, tucking in your chin and reaching for (but not touching) your knees with both hands. Breathe in again, lowering your head to the pillow, and relax. Repeat several times. Start slowly and gradually increase to 10 repetitions. If necessary, support your incision as you raise your head.

Before you go home, check for separation of the recti muscles. (For instructions, see "Third Day" on page 287). You must restore the separation to normal before you do any further abdominal strengthening exercises.

Progress at your own pace with postpartum exercising when your doctor gives his permission. Avoid lifting, straining, and unduly exerting yourself. Be sure to get plenty of rest to speed your recovery.

VAGINAL BIRTH AFTER CESAREAN

In most countries of the world, a vaginal birth following a cesarean is not unusual. The past 15 years have witnessed a surge of new information in this country strongly supporting the position that the majority of women can have a vaginal birth after cesarean (VBAC, pronounced *VEE back*). In the United States, the VBAC rate rose from 3.4 percent in 1980 to 28.4 percent in 1996. The national health objective for the year 2000 is a VBAC rate of 35 percent. According to Dr. Sidney M. Wolfe, of the Public Citizen Health Research Group, this number is still low, considering that approximately 80 to 90 percent of all women with a cesarean history should be candidates for VBAC.[15]

If you had a transverse uterine incision, you may be a candidate for a future vaginal birth. The major concern is the rupture of the scar while you are in labor. Yet the risk of scar rupture is only 0.2 percent with this type of incision.[16] This risk is thirty times lower than that for any other unpredictable childbirth emergency, such as acute fetal distress, premature separation of the placenta, and prolapsed umbilical cord.[17] Because women who are having a VBAC are not considered to be at any greater risk than other low-risk women, they may even deliver in birth centers, if emergency care can be initiated within 30 minutes of the recognition of a problem.[18]

As long as the indication for your previous cesarean does not recur and no new indications appear, your chances for a vaginal delivery are quite good. Your choice of caregiver is an important factor. You need to discuss with him his criteria for permitting a trial of labor. Studies show that a successful vaginal birth is possible if the original cesarean was performed for one of the following nonrecurring reasons—multiple birth, cephalopelvic disproportion, abruptio placentae, failed induction of labor, fetal distress, placenta previa, PIH, abnormal presentation, failure to progress, or abnormal labor.

In 1988, the American College of Obstetricians and Gynecologists released a statement supporting VBAC. Even so, many physicians still continue to perform routine repeat cesareans. They caution about the dangers of uterine rupture to the woman and the baby. However, they neglect to mention the dangers of a repeat cesarean, when in fact a c-section can be more risky than a vaginal birth. Possible complications include surgical damage to the bowel and bladder, hemorrhage, infection, poor wound healing, blood clots, and anesthesia-related problems.

Furthermore, a woman who has given birth surgically is more likely to experience depression, feelings of failure, and other negative emotions.[19] Her feelings of inadequacy are greater when she believes that the surgery was performed unnecessarily. After having a VBAC, many women report that they feel "complete," even if they had accepted the fact that the previous cesarean was justified.

Women planning a VBAC require good emotional and physical support, since they may receive many negative comments from lay persons as well as professionals. A good source book is *Birth After Cesarean: The Medical Facts* by Bruce Flamm. This book provides important medical facts to support the decision for a VBAC and helps the expectant mother to attain her goal. It is "must reading" for cesarean prevention.

CONCLUSION

Having a baby by cesarean can be a rewarding, family-centered experience. And, in those rare cases in which an emergency situation exists, it can be the only avenue to a healthy baby. However, because a cesarean involves major surgery, with risks to both you and your baby, you should make every effort to avoid an *unnecessary* one.

Your best bet for reducing your chances of a cesarean is your careful choice of a caregiver. Another important factor is making sure you have continuous support from a caring labor partner. The presence of a doula further reduces your chances. Allowing your body to labor naturally without interventions is another important element. It is particularly crucial to avoid interventions such as Pitocin or an epidural in early labor. Walking during labor and utilizing upright laboring positions also help to encourage a vaginal delivery.

Last, but very important, is your trust in your body's ability to give birth. Our society has come to accept a 21-percent cesarean rate as normal, implying that over one fifth of women's bodies do not function properly. We need to reverse this trend by realizing and demonstrating that birth is a natural, normal event. Use your visualizations to "see" yourself giving birth, knowing that your body was designed to give birth vaginally. Use your relaxation techniques to get in touch with your body, and realize that, in most cases, babies will be born healthy on their own, without any help or interventions. Having complete confidence that your body will know how to carry out this age-old process can be the key that ensures you a vaginal delivery.

Chapter Ten

The Newborn
or There Will Be Some Changes Made

*C*hange is a keyword when it comes to babies. Not only do newborns change the lives of their parents and siblings, they also change physically, almost on a daily basis during the first few months. This chapter focuses on the changes connected with a baby—the physical changes that begin at the moment of birth, the changes in health that may or may not be signals for concern, and the changes that you must make to your home and lifestyle. This chapter also discusses some of the new things that you must learn to take care of a baby (such as making many diaper changes), as well as the basic things that you may need to keep him fed, clothed, and happy.

THE BABY'S APPEARANCE AT BIRTH

The first questions that most parents ask after confirming or learning the sex of their baby are, "How much does he weigh and how long is he?" Babies weigh an average of 7 to 8 pounds and are from 19 to 21 inches in length. A newborn can lose up to 10 percent of his birth weight. This weight loss is normal, and the weight is usually regained within 2 weeks.

Most people do not know what newly born babies look like and expect them all to resemble the Gerber baby. You may be surprised or even concerned over your baby's appearance upon delivery. Immediately after birth, your baby may appear bluish or gray. Once he starts to cry or begins to breathe, he will become pink. However, his hands and feet may remain slightly bluish for a few hours or even days, and it is more noticeable when he is chilled. Your baby's head may be misshapen and elongated due to molding that took place during birth. (See Figure 10.1.) This molding is a result of the skull bones overlapping, which eases the passage of the baby's head through the birth canal. The head may take a couple of days to become rounder. The baby's head may also exhibit swelling, or caput

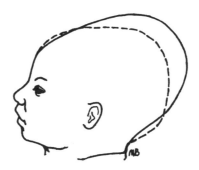

Figure 10.1.
The solid line indicates what a newborn's head may look like if it was molded during the birth process. The dotted line indicates the normal shape of an infant's head, which most newborns attain within a few days.

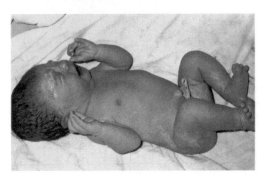

Your newborn's head may be molded from going through the birth process.

succedaneum, which could last for several days. If the doctor used a vacuum extractor during birth, the swelling will be accentuated.

Your baby's face and genitals may appear swollen or puffy. This swelling will also subside in 1 or 2 days. His nose may be flattened and his ears pressed to his head.

A cheeselike coating called vernix caseosa may cover your baby's body. You may notice this coating only in the creases of his skin or under his arms. The closer to term your baby is delivered, the less vernix he will have. This "baby cold cream" protected his skin while he floated in the amniotic fluid. Some mothers prefer to massage the vernix into their baby's skin to serve as a natural skin conditioner, rather than having it washed off. Your baby may also have some blood on his body. The amount of blood varies from baby to baby.

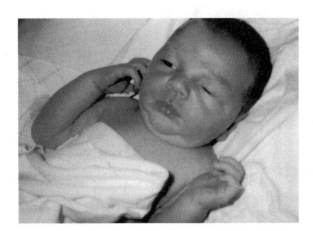

This newborn's eyes are puffy from birth.

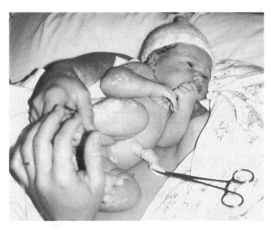

Many babies are born with a protective cheeselike coating called vernix caseosa.

PHYSIOLOGICAL CHANGES AT BIRTH

Your baby's circulatory system will change at the moment of birth. While he is in your uterus, your baby receives his oxygen from your red blood cells via the placenta. At birth, he will begin to expand his lungs and breathe on his own. Your caregiver may suction his nose and mouth to remove any mucus that may be present and hampering his breathing. The baby's heart will begin to pump blood to his lungs to pick up the oxygen that he will now be breathing in. After the umbilical cord is cut, certain internal blood vessels that carried blood to and from the cord will no longer be needed and will become ligaments.

CARE GIVEN TO THE BABY AT BIRTH

Your baby will be given his first exams in life at 1 minute and 5 minutes after birth. This two-part evaluation is called the Apgar score and is designed to show how well the baby handled labor and delivery, and how he is adjusting to

APGAR SCORING CHART

Characteristic	0	1	2
Color	Blue pale	Body pink Extremities blue	Body completely pink
Respiratory Effort	Absent	Slow, irregular weak cry	Strong cry
Heart Rate	Absent	Less than 100	More than 100
Muscle Tone	Limp	Some flexing of extremities	Active motion
Reflexes	Absent	Grimace, some motion	Cry

Figure 10.2.
Babies are evaluated at 1 minute and 5 minutes after birth using the Apgar Scoring Chart to determine how well they handled delivery and are adjusting to extrauterine life.

life outside the uterus. (See Figure 10.2.) The scoring system was developed by an anesthesiologist, Dr. Virginia Apgar. A score of 8 to 10 at 1 minute of life means that the baby's condition at birth is good. A low Apgar rating alerts the staff that the baby is in distress and needs assistance, and that he will require continued observation. The rating at 5 minutes indicates the baby's adjustment to extrauterine life. You can ask your caregiver what Apgar score he gave your baby. (For the criteria that must be met for a baby to be sent home, see "Criteria for Newborn Discharge From the Hospital" on page 204.)

After you have had an opportunity to hold and soothe your newborn, the nurse may "borrow" him to perform admission and identification procedures. Since the birthing room will probably be about 20°F cooler than body temperature, your baby must be kept warm. During the procedures, therefore, he will

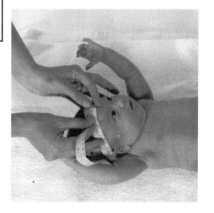

Measuring the head is part of the admission procedure following birth.

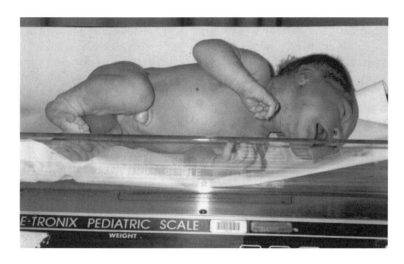

This baby boy weighs in during the admission procedure after birth.

Criteria for Newborn Discharge From the Hospital

In October 1995, the American Academy of Pediatrics issued the minimum criteria that should be met before a baby is discharged from the hospital. These criteria included:

❏ An uncomplicated pregnancy and vaginal delivery.

❏ The baby is an appropriate weight for term, with good vital signs.

❏ The baby has completed at least two successful feedings, has urinated, and has passed at least one stool.

❏ No evidence of jaundice in the first 24 hours.

❏ The mother has received adequate training to care for the newborn.

❏ A plan is in place for follow-up and support, including a physical examination by a nurse.

If risk factors—such as substance abuse by the mother, a family history of domestic violence, or child abuse or neglect—are present, the discharge should be delayed until a solution to the problem is available. The committee did not believe that the criteria could be accomplished in less than 48 hours.[1]

be placed under a warming light. When he is with you and covered with a blanket, he will not need a light because mothers are the best baby warmers!

The nurse will record your fingerprint and your baby's footprints on the proper documents. Ask her to record the baby's footprints in your baby book, too, if you brought it with you. The nurse will also give both you and the baby identification bracelets, which will be checked throughout your hospital stay. These bracelets are intended to prevent nursery mix-ups. Interestingly, mothers who are awake and bond with their babies right after birth rarely look at the identification bracelets because they know their babies by sight. In some facilities, the father also receives an identification bracelet to allow him to retrieve the baby from the nursery. (For a discussion of how to choose a name for your baby, see "Naming Your Baby.")

All states have a law requiring that an antibiotic ointment or silver nitrate drops be placed in a baby's eyes soon after birth. The purpose of the medicine is to prevent blindness in the baby if the mother has gonorrhea. It also prevents other bacterial eye infections. You can ask the nurse to delay administering the ointment or eye drops until after the bonding period, since eye-to-eye contact is an important component of the bonding process. The antibiotic ointment is less irritating to the eyes than the silver nitrate drops and is used more commonly.

Your baby will also receive an injection of vitamin K while he is still in the birthing room or upon his admission to the newborn nursery. Vitamin K is an important factor in blood clotting and is manufactured by the body in the intestines once certain normal bacteria are present. Babies are all deficient in vitamin K, however, as their normal flora, or bacteria, is inadequate. In some areas, vitamin K may be available in oral form.

Between the first and second hour after birth, your baby may have his heel stuck for a drop of blood to check his glucose level. If this level is low, he may be given sugar water and also be stuck several more times to recheck the blood sugar. To prevent low blood sugar, nurse your baby as soon after the delivery as possible, especially before sending him to the nursery if required.

Within the first week of your baby's life, he will have his heel stuck to send several drops of his blood to a laboratory. This is called the infant screening test, and it checks for several rare inherited metabolic diseases. Some of them can be managed with diet or medications. Others require close management

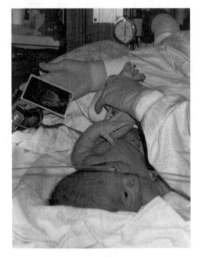

A baby's footprints are recorded as part of the identification procedure following birth. If you bring your baby book to the hospital or birth center, you can also have the footprints recorded there.

to prevent complications. Through early screening, your baby can be saved from serious problems, including mental retardation or death. Among the diseases for which your baby may be tested are phenylketonuria (PKU), hypothyroidism, galactosemia, sickle cell anemia, congenital adrenal hyperplasia, and thalassemia. The diseases that are screened vary from state to state. The test is not valid until the baby has received at least 24 hours of breast or formula feeding. It is usually considered valid after 48 hours of age. If you are discharged from the hospital prior to that time, the test will be performed anyway and you will be instructed to return for a repeat test.

NEWBORN CHARACTERISTICS

At first glance, your baby's head may appear to be too large for his body. It will be about one quarter his body size. If your baby's head is average in size, its circumference will be about 13 to 14 inches. Your baby's neck muscles will be weak, so you must support his wobbly head at all times.

You may be concerned about the two fontanels ("soft spots") on your baby's head. These are areas where the skull bones have not yet joined, but

Naming Your Baby

The ritual of choosing a name for your baby is an important one for you as expectant parents. Not only is it an activity that you can do together, it is also one that helps you prepare for the reality of parenthood. Numerous books have been written on this subject, so there are many resources available to assist you if you have not yet decided on a name. Check your local library or bookstore.

Some parents decide on a name months before their baby's birth, once they are certain of the baby's gender. This may even aid in the bonding process because they can then refer to their child by name before they have actually met him. Others, while possibly narrowing their list to three or four names, prefer to wait to name their baby until after he is born and they can choose whichever name seems to fit their particular baby.

Many couples find the task of choosing a name easy because they have decided to honor a parent, grandparent, or other relative by using that person's name for their child. Others search for something unique or for a name that has special meaning for them. Popular names seem to run in cycles. Every decade sees the emergence of certain names, often because of well-known national figures or even soap opera stars who are popular at that time. Many of today's new parents were named Kimberly, Jennifer, Scott, or Brian. They are now choosing names like Ashley, Lindsay, Tyler, and Nicholas for their offspring. Classic names, such as Mary, Elizabeth, Michael, and David, have remained popular over the years. An analysis done by the Bureau of Vital Statistics in Colorado in 1989 found that 40 percent of boys and 30 percent of girls were named from a list of only twenty-five boys' names and twenty-five girls' names.[2]

If you are debating between a traditional name and an unusual name, be aware that the number one reason given by parents for staying with a traditional name is that most people will find it acceptable. When considering an unusual name, you need to ask yourself if that name will be appropriate as your child grows older and becomes an adult.

You should also keep in mind any stereotypes that may be associated with certain names. Unfortunately, some people expect a certain type of behavior or appearance from a person based simply on his or her name.

Other questions you should consider as you evaluate options include:

❑ How does the full name flow?

❑ Do the initials form a word that could be embarrassing to your child?

❑ What are the possible nicknames for the name?

❑ Is the name appropriate for the child's gender?

Several authors caution against using the diminutive or nickname for your child's legal name—Billy Joe instead of William Joseph, for example. Such a name may not be considered appropriate when your child becomes an adult.

In the final analysis, it is most important that you decide on a name that you think will please both you *and* your child for a lifetime.

instead are held together by membranes. They facilitate the molding necessary during delivery and allow for further growth of the skull after birth. The posterior (back of the head) fontanel is triangular shaped and will close by around 6 weeks of age. The anterior (top of the head) fontanel is diamond shaped and will close by about 18 months of age. You should not worry too much about harming the baby in these areas because the fontanels are covered with a tough membrane called the dura.

A cephalhematoma may appear on the head during the first few days as a result of pressure. This collection of blood is noticed as a bump under the scalp. It gradually increases in size and may take months to reabsorb and disappear. It can be caused by the use of a vacuum extractor, the application of forceps, or the baby's head pressing against the pelvic bones during labor or birth.

Some babies are born with a full head of hair. Others are bald. If your baby is born with hair, he will probably lose at least some of it and possibly even all of it.

You may notice milia (little whiteheads) on your baby's chin, nose, and cheeks. These are immature oil glands and will go away without any treatment when the glands begin to function. Do not attempt to remove them.

A Caucasian baby's eye color is usually blue at birth, while a non-Caucasian baby's eye color is generally brown. Your baby's permanent eye color will probably be determined by 6 months of age, although it can change for up to a year.

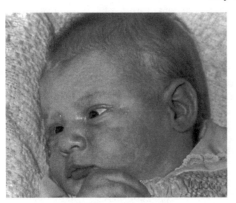

Don't worry if your baby's eyes are crossed at birth. The eye muscles are still developing, and the eyes should focus together by around 6 months of age.

Your baby will blink at bright lights and may not nurse well or look at you if a light is shined directly in his face. In addition, he may appear cross-eyed when he looks around. This is because his eye muscles are not well developed. By 6 months of age, his eyes should be focusing together. If not, your pediatrician will refer you to an ophthalmologist (a medical doctor who specializes in eye disorders).

Tearless crying is common in newborns, as the lacrimal glands that produce tears are not completely functional. It could be many months before your baby begins to cry real tears. You might notice some swelling if silver nitrate was placed in your baby's eyes after birth. If a discharge is present, your pediatrician should be notified, as this may indicate that the tear ducts are blocked. He may order an antibiotic ointment or instruct you in a massage technique designed to open the ducts.

The whites of your baby's eyes may display small hemorrhages caused by pressure during birth. These hemorrhages could take several weeks to disappear.

For years, mothers were told that their babies could not see until they were several weeks old, but many mothers continued to feel that their babies did indeed look at them. Research has proven that even though their vision is not perfect, babies *are* able to see, and their best vision is at a distance of 8 to 10 inches.

Even before birth, a fetus exhibits sensitivity to sound. Hearing becomes more acute within several days following birth as the amniotic fluid is absorbed. Loud noises will be disturbing to your newborn, while soft, soothing voices or sounds will quiet him. Many babies react positively to their parents' familiar voices.

The senses of taste and smell will be well developed in your newborn. Your baby may react negatively to someone wearing heavy perfume or smoking. Research has shown that by the age of 6 days, a baby can recognize the smell of his own mother.[3]

You may notice clusters of small capillaries on the nape of your baby's neck, on his eyelids, or on the bridge of his nose. They are minute blood vessels close to the skin. These "stork bites" or "angel kisses" are more obvious when the baby cries. They usually fade by 9 months of age.

Your newborn's skin will be very sensitive. If he becomes chilled, his skin will appear blotchy and skin capillaries may be apparent. His hands and feet may become slightly bluish. If he is overdressed or wearing irritating clothing, he may develop a rash. Another harmless rash, known as erythema toxicum, may also appear during the first days after birth. This rash resembles a heat rash—red splotches with small yellowish white bumps in the center. It does not appear on the extremities and has no known cause. It will disappear without treatment in a few days.

Your baby may be covered with fine downy hair called lanugo. Lanugo is seen more frequently on preterm babies and less frequently on those born past their due date. It usually disappears within a few weeks. Your baby may also have dry, scaly skin, most noticeably on his hands and feet, with some peeling occurring 1 to 2 weeks after birth. Avoid using lotion or oil, especially if the skin is cracked.

Dark- or olive-skinned babies may have purplish brown discolorations on their lower back. These are called Mongolian spots and fade by 1 year of age.

Your baby's breathing will be fast (20 to 60 breaths per minute), irregular, shallow, and abdominal in nature. It may be noisy at night. The hiccups you may have felt during pregnancy will continue until the baby's diaphragm matures. The baby's heart rate will also be rapid, between 100 and 160 beats per minute. When the baby cries, his heart rate may accelerate to 180 to 200 beats per minute.

Both newborn boys and girls may have enlarged breasts due to hormones that crossed the placenta while the baby was still in utero. They may even secrete some milk ("witch's milk") within the first 2 weeks of life. Female babies may also have some vaginal bleeding, or "false menstruation," due to these hormones. The genitals of both sexes may be enlarged or swollen, with a little girl's clitoris and labia possibly large enough for her to be mistaken for a boy at quick glance. Your son's scrotum may be swollen and darker in color. His testes may move in and out of the scrotum. They may retract as far as to the crease at the top of the thigh. As long as they are located in the scrotum most of the time, they are normal.

The umbilical cord stump will dry up and fall off in 1 to 2 weeks. His abdomen will be round and protruding. This is due to poor abdominal muscle tone, relatively long intestines confined to a small area, and, possibly, to swallowed air.

Your newborn's arms and legs will be proportionately short for his body. He will tend to hold his arms bent and close to his chest, with his hands clenched in fists. He will hold his legs, which may appear bowed, in a position that is probably similar to what he had assumed in utero. His nails may be very long at birth and need cutting. They will be soft and pliable, and should be filed for the first few weeks to prevent bleeding. After that, you will be able to trim them with baby scissors or clippers. You may find it easiest to do this while the baby is sleeping.

Certain reflexes will be present in your newborn at birth. Some of these will be vital to his survival. All are signs of gestational maturity. Many he will have "practiced" while in utero.

Not to Worry

The following are common, normal newborn variations that may surprise you:

❏ Hiccups are common until the baby's diaphragm matures.

❏ Newborns sneeze to get rid of mucus.

❏ Both male and female babies have swollen breasts from the mother's hormones.

❏ A newborn's nails may be so long that he scratched himself in utero.

❏ Babies can be born with blisters or bruises from sucking on their hands and wrists.

Keep in mind that this list is not inclusive. Your newborn may display a variation that is not noted here, but that nevertheless is common and normal. Talk to your pediatrician if you have any concerns.

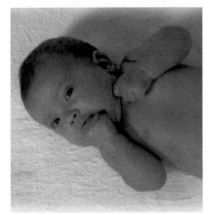

Sucking reflex.

Your baby's sucking reflex will be very strong soon after birth. Any stimulation of his lips will elicit sucking motions. It is not unusual to see a newborn sucking on his thumb, fingers, or fist. This is just a continuation of what he did before delivery. You may even see bruises on his hands or arms from sucking in utero. The swallowing reflex is also present prior to birth, since the fetus swallows amniotic fluid and then urinates into the fluid in the amniotic sac. If you stroke your baby's cheek or lips, he will turn his head in that direction and open his mouth. This is called the rooting reflex.

Several protective reflexes are also apparent at birth. These include the gag reflex, which prevents choking, and the cough reflex, which gets rid of mucus. Even a newborn instinctively attempts to protect himself. If his face becomes covered with a blanket, he will flail his arms and move his head to remove the cover. If a limb is exposed to cold, he will draw it close to his body to warm it. If he is pinched or stuck with a pin, he will quickly withdraw.

If you place your fingers in your baby's palms, he will grasp them tightly. This is the grasp reflex. Your baby's grasp may even be strong enough to

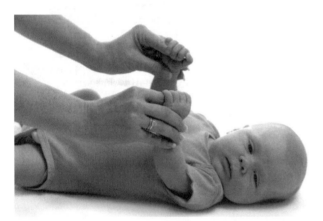

Grasp reflex.

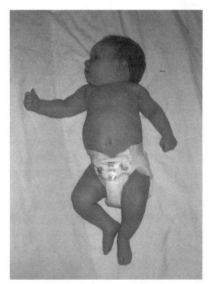

Tonic neck reflex.

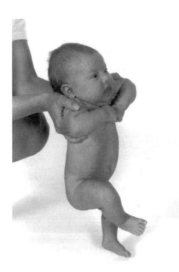

Stepping reflex.

Moro reflex.

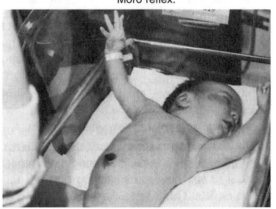

allow you to raise his body up. (Do not try this, however, because he may let go and fall.) If held under his arms in a standing position, he will make walking motions. This is the stepping reflex. When your infant is lying on his back, he may assume a "fencing position" with his head turned to the side. The arm on that side will be extended, and that leg flexed. This is called the tonic neck reflex. If the baby is startled, he will thrust out his arms as if to embrace you in a movement that is called the Moro reflex.

Two reflexes can be observed involving the soles of the infant's feet. The plantar toe reflex causes the toes to curl if you press your finger at the base of the toes. If you stroke the sole from the heel to the toes, you will notice that the foot hyperextends and the toes fan outward. This is called the Babinski toe reflex.

Plantar toe reflex.

COMMON CONCERNS OF NEW PARENTS

Most new mothers and fathers express some concern over their newborn's appearance or the care involved with a new baby. If you are a first-time parent, you may feel unsure of yourself and wonder what to do with this little person. This section discusses those topics that new parents have many questions about.

Cord Care

The most common concern of new parents is how to care for the umbilical cord stump. If the umbilical cord was clamped at birth, the clamp is usually removed within 48 hours. If the cord was tied off, the tie will remain on the stump until the stump falls off. The stump will dry up and fall off in 1 to 2 weeks. Some pediatricians tell parents to give their babies only sponge baths until the cord falls off. Others allow tub baths right from birth, citing studies that show no increase in infection. Whether you give your baby tub baths or sponge baths, keep his cord dry between baths by folding the top of the diaper to a level below his navel and by wiping the cord with alcohol three to four times a day. If you notice a foul odor, redness, or discharge, notify your pediatrician. You might find some blood when the cord finally does fall off. This is normal.

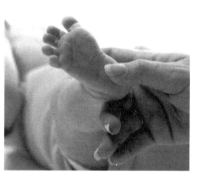

Babinski toe reflex.

Jaundice

Normal physiologic jaundice is a condition that affects 50 percent of all newborns. A fetus has a large number of red blood cells (RBCs) to carry oxygen to handle the stress of labor. After birth, the extra RBCs are not needed and begin to deteriorate. A product of this breakdown is bilirubin. Bilirubin is normally detoxified by the liver and excreted by the bowel. However, because a baby's liver is immature and unable to handle the bilirubin, the excess may cause jaundice, which is marked by a yellow discoloration of the baby's skin, mucous membranes, and whites of the eyes. Physiologic jaundice usually appears on the second or third day of life and disappears within a week. Your pediatrician may test your baby's blood to determine the level of bilirubin. Treatment is usually not necessary, as jaundice is a normal condition found in newborns.

Certain factors such as delayed or poor feeding, first stool after 24 hours, Oriental race, maternal diabetes, bruising, use of Pitocin during labor, or polycythemia (high RBC count) can increase the chances of a full-term infant developing jaundice.[4] Babies who begin nursing soon after birth or who room-in with their mothers, thereby enjoying frequent nursings of every 2 to 3 hours, are less likely to develop jaundice. Early breastfeeding stimulates the passage of meconium, which contains a high level of bilirubin. This decreases the reabsorption of the bilirubin through the intestinal wall. Also, the protein in the colostrum binds with the bilirubin, which can then be excreted with the bowel movements. Supplemental feedings of water have not been proven to decrease bilirubin levels and should be avoided. If your pediatrician encourages you to give your baby supplemental feedings, nurse more often. If your baby nurses poorly, you can pump your breasts and give him this additional breastmilk between feedings, preferably with an eye dropper to avoid nipple confusion.

Phototherapy is another formerly popular corrective therapy for normal physiologic jaundice that is no longer recommended for healthy term infants.[5] Phototherapy uses light energy in the blue-to-white range to break down the bilirubin through the skin. While under "bili-lights," an infant's eyes must be protected to avoid damage. Because phototherapy can cause dehydration and results in the separation of the mother and baby, it should be avoided if the bilirubin level is not significantly elevated, is not pathologic (abnormal) in nature, or is observed in a baby who is otherwise healthy and vigorous.

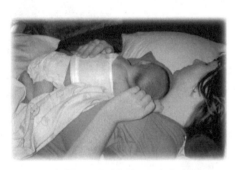

A fiberoptic blanket can help correct jaundice without glaring bili-lights or separation of mother and baby.

Feeding the baby frequently and placing him in front of a sunny window are methods for helping the bilirubin level return to normal without the trauma of prolonged separation. In addition, many areas offer home phototherapy in the form of either bili-lights or a fiberoptic blanket that is wrapped around the baby. A home health nurse comes to the parents' home to set up the equipment, perform the blood tests, and also provide reports to the pediatrician.

Some pediatricians encourage nursing mothers to eliminate several feedings if their baby's bilirubin level is elevated. A high bilirubin level is not an indication to stop nursing or to give supplemental water or formula. Frequent nursings provide sufficient fluid. While some mothers' milk contains a factor that tends to prolong jaundice, true breastmilk jaundice is rare. It does not appear until after the third day of life and may peak between the fifth and the fifteenth days.[6]

Your pediatrician will observe your infant closely and may order blood tests to determine whether his jaundice is normal or pathologic in nature. Pathologic jaundice usually occurs within the first 24 hours after birth. It may be due to a blood-type or Rh-factor incompatibility. This type of jaundice is cause for more concern because a high bilirubin level can prompt irreversible brain damage. Preterm infants are also at greater risk. Treatment in these cases may include frequent feedings, phototherapy, or blood transfusion.

Circumcision

Circumcision is a surgical procedure in which the foreskin is removed from the head of the penis. Traditionally, in the United States, this procedure is performed within the first week of life, usually prior to discharge from the hospital. Experts at one time thought that removal of the foreskin promoted health and cleanliness, and prevented masturbation. However, studies have shown that circumcision is not necessary for good health or hygiene, and that it does not affect the desire to masturbate. One argument still used for routine circumcision is that it prevents cancer of the vagina or cervix in the female sex partners of these men, but little evidence exists to support this.[7] The United States remains the only country that practices nonreligious circumcision almost routinely.

Unless you are sure your baby is a girl, you should decide before your due date whether you truly wish to have your son circumcised. In 1989, the American Academy of Pediatrics stated that newborn circumcision has potential medical benefits as well as risks. This was a modification of an earlier statement that routine circumcision has no medical benefit. The change was prompted by a task force that looked into the benefits and risks of circumcision. According to one study, uncircumcised male infants have an increased rate of urinary tract infections. The task force also took note that cancer of the penis almost always occurs in uncircumcised men, though this form of cancer is very rare and is also associated with poor hygiene and certain sexually transmitted diseases. In addition, the task force reported that circumcision can prevent phimosis (the inability to pull back the foreskin), paraphimosis (the inability to return the foreskin to its original position), and inflammation of the foreskin and head of the penis.[8] These conditions usually occur after the normally tight foreskin is forcibly retracted. There is some evidence, however, that uncircumcised men have a greater incidence of sexually transmitted diseases, including HIV.

Circumcision is a surgical procedure and can result in bleeding or infection. Ask your pediatrician whether he uses an anesthetic for the surgery. Recent studies have verified that infants who receive local anesthesia for the procedure cry less and have lower amounts of stress hormones in their bloodstreams.[9] Local anesthesia is usually given by injecting the nerves at the base of the penis. Because this method causes discomfort upon administration, physicians who do not use a local anesthetic argue that the pain from the injection is just as bad as the circumcision. Some physicians have started using a topical anesthetic instead of or prior to the injections. A recent study showed that the application of a lidocaine-prilocaine (EMLA) cream to the penis 60 to 80 minutes before circumcision decreases pain and has no adverse effects.[10] This technique is pain-free. EMLA cream is currently approved for use on children over 1 month of age as a topical anesthetic prior to injections, blood work, IV starts, and minor surgery. The disadvantage is that the cream must be applied approximately 1 hour prior to the circumcision.

The decision of whether to circumcise a baby is a personal one and should be made by the parents in consultation with their pediatrician. Some couples decide to circumcise their sons for religious reasons. Other parents choose to have the surgery performed for cosmetic reasons or to keep their child from being different. However, the number of males not circumcised is increasing. Uncircumcised males are no longer so "different." After examining both the benefits and risks, many parents today are deciding against routine circumcision.

If you are considering having your newborn son circumcised, check with your insurance company regarding coverage of the procedure. Some companies no longer pay for routine circumcision of newborns.

If you decide to have your son circumcised, delay the procedure for at least 24 hours to give him time to adjust to extrauterine life. A baby who is born preterm or who has any medical problems should not be immediately circumcised. The procedure should be performed only on healthy, stable infants. After the surgery, watch for bleeding, infection, and discomfort, and notify your pediatrician if they occur. Make sure you receive instructions on the

A Hint for the New Mother

❏ Ask your pediatrician if he uses an anesthetic when performing a circumcision.

proper home care, since this procedure can be done in different ways and each requires different postsurgical care. Placing your baby on his side or back may make him more comfortable. If the procedure was done using a Gomco or Mogan clamp, you should apply petroleum jelly to the head of the penis to prevent the diaper from sticking. When washing your baby, gently pull back the small remaining foreskin to prevent scar tissue from growing between the foreskin and the head. If a Plastibell was used, there will be a plastic ring on the penis that will fall off in 5 to 7 days. You do not need to use petroleum jelly with this type of circumcision.

Do not request a particular method of circumcision. Each physician performs the method he was trained in or the one with which he is most comfortable. Of the procedures in use today, one type does not give better results than another. It is more important to choose a doctor who performs this surgery frequently and is competent in the technique.

The uncircumcised penis requires no extra cleaning. Just wash, rinse, and dry it along with the rest of the baby's bottom. Do not pull the foreskin back over the head of the penis. In a newborn, the foreskin is almost always attached to the head, and forcing it back may cause damage. It may be years, possibly even into puberty, before separation occurs. By 3 years of age, the foreskin can be retracted in up to 90 percent of uncircumcised boys. Forcibly retracting the foreskin can cause pain, bleeding, adhesions,[11] and paraphimosis. Once the foreskin is fully retractable, you should pull it back gently to wash the penis and then replace it gently. Your son can learn to do this himself when he bathes.

Skin Care

Hints for the New Mother

❏ Avoid using powder on the baby. It can cake in the creases in his skin, and he can also breathe it into his lungs.

❏ Do not use mineral oil–based lotions. They can rob the skin of vitamins.

Diaper rash is the result of the skin being irritated by urine and stools, the laundry products used on the diapers, or the chemicals used in the disposable diapers. Some babies break out in diaper rash while teething. Breastfed babies are less likely to develop diaper rash, for reasons that are not known.[12] You can prevent diaper rash by changing your baby frequently and washing his bottom with warm water. If the baby has a bowel movement, use soap and water. Always make sure to dry the baby well, especially in the folds of his skin. Apply petroleum jelly or medicated ointment if you desire. If you use cloth diapers, avoid plastic pants. Exposing the irritated area to air is helpful, as is rinsing diapers twice to remove all traces of soap or changing your brand of disposables.

Avoid applying powder to your baby's genitals. It can cake in the creases and irritate sensitive tissues, especially in girls. If you use talcum powder or cornstarch, first pour it in your hand and then apply it sparingly. If you shake powder onto the baby, he may breathe it into his lungs, which could cause irritation.

Baby oil or lotion that has a mineral oil base should not be used on infants. Mineral oil robs the skin of vitamins. A better choice is an unscented, edible nut or vegetable oil, such as almond, sunflower, or safflower oil.

Prickly heat is another type of rash that is common in babies. It usually occurs if the weather is warm or the baby is overdressed. Most new parents tend to overdress their infants. A baby should be dressed just like an adult or older child. If it is 90°F outside, you certainly do not need a sweater and neither does your baby. In addition, you should wash all baby clothes and bedding with special baby detergent before using them for the first time. This is to avoid rashes from allergy to strong detergent or to chemicals in new clothes or bedding. You should also use a softener that is diluted in the rinse water because the softener on dryer sheets is not rinsed out, is usually perfumed, and may cause a skin reaction in the baby.

Cradle cap appears as flakes, scales, or crusts on the baby's scalp or behind his ears. Wash the area daily and brush it vigorously with a baby brush. You may want to apply baby oil to loosen the crusts prior to shampooing. Using oil and *not* washing it out would allow the scales to build up on the scalp. If necessary, ask your pediatrician to prescribe a special soap.

Bowel Movements

Your baby's first bowel movements will be black, tarry, and sticky. They are called meconium and consist of the waste that was in the baby's intestines while he was in utero. During the first 4 to 5 days, the baby's stools will gradually change from tarry black to greenish brown to brownish yellow to greenish yellow. After the transitional period, they will become "milk stools." If you bottlefeed your baby, his stools will be soft and yellow, and will have an offensive odor. If you breastfeed your baby, his stools will most likely be mushy, loose, and not offensive. The number of stools he has can vary from one to eight per day (a small amount with each diaper change). Or, after 1 to 2 months of age, he may have them as infrequently as one every several days or, if he is totally breastfed, even just one a week.

Constipation occurs when the stools are hard, dry, and difficult to pass. It is not related to the frequency of bowel movements. Infants who are totally breastfed and do not receive any supplements of formula or solids rarely become constipated. If you bottlefeed your baby and his constipation becomes severe, you may need to change his formula.

If your baby has diarrhea, he will need medical attention to prevent dehydration. Diarrhea is frequent stools that are watery, green in color, or foul smelling, or that contain mucus. Be prepared to tell your pediatrician the number, color, and consistency of the stools. Remember, the stools of a totally breastfed baby normally are loose and are not considered to be diarrhea unless other signs are present.

Spitting Up

Spitting up is common in the early weeks. The sphincter at the top of the baby's stomach may be immature and, when you burp the baby after feeding him, some milk may escape along with the air. Be prepared by keeping an extra diaper handy. If you give your baby a bottle, hold him at a 45-degree angle while he feeds and burp him often. Try not to overfeed him, since this may cause him to vomit. If you nurse your baby and your let-down (release of milk) is forceful, the baby may choke and gulp air. Gently remove him from your breast until your let-down slows.

If you allow your baby to cry for too long before feeding him, he may gulp large amounts of air, which will cause him to spit up. After you feed your baby, make sure you burp him and place him on his right side to aid his diges-

Hints for the New Father

When the baby gets fussy:

- ❏ Take over for your mate.
- ❏ Take him for a walk while your mate cooks dinner or takes a break.
- ❏ Take a bath with him.
- ❏ Lay him skin-to-skin on your chest.
- ❏ Talk or sing to your baby.
- ❏ Turn on the vacuum cleaner. "White noise" often lulls fussy babies.
- ❏ Check for a soiled or wet diaper.
- ❏ Check if he is over- or underdressed.

A calm daddy can be very handy for soothing a crying baby.

tion. As he matures, his sphincter will become stronger and he will stop spitting up.

If your baby frequently vomits forcefully either during or right after a feeding, inform your pediatrician.

Crying

Crying is a baby's only way of expressing his needs. However, trying to cope with a crying newborn can be a very frustrating experience for new parents. Many babies have "fussy periods," usually at the same time each day, commonly late in the afternoon when you are rushing to make dinner. In fact, so many babies become fussy at this time that in earlier days, mothers aptly named it "Grandma's hour"—the time when Grandma could help by rocking and cuddling her grandchild. Do not let anyone convince you that "crying is good for the lungs." A baby's lungs do not need "exercise." Try to approach your crying baby with as much calmness as possible, since he can sense your tension and may become even more irritable.

Is he hungry? If your baby is crying and has not eaten for 2 or more hours, he may be hungry. If the baby is breastfed, he may be trying to build up your milk supply with more frequent feedings. Even if he recently nursed, he may want to breastfeed some more just for comfort. After 3 weeks of age, you can also try giving him a pacifier if he enjoys it and needs more sucking. If you bottlefeed your baby, check the nipple of the bottle to make sure that the milk drips freely.

Is he uncomfortable? If the baby is crying but is not hungry, check him for a loose diaper pin, a soiled or wet diaper, or an irritating diaper condition such as diaper rash or a diaper that is too tight. Is he underdressed or overdressed? Is his clothing too tight or too rough? Is the room too hot or too cold? Any of these conditions can make a baby fussy.

Is he lonely? For 9 months, your baby was safe and snug within your warm body, listening to your heartbeat and other sounds. Then he was delivered and is now expected to be satisfied lying alone in a hard wooden crib. Your baby may just need to be cuddled and held close. You may find a front-pack baby carrier or sling to be of tremendous help. This way, you can make your baby happy by holding him close to you and still have your hands free to do other things.

Is he bored? Some babies need more interaction than others. Change the environment by taking your baby outside or just into another room. Take him on a tour of the house to see what interests him. Try to distract him with a mobile or show him bright objects. Talk or sing to him, or even read him a book. The book does not have to be a child's. Read out loud any book or magazine article that interests you.

Has he been overstimulated? Too much handling by visitors or long periods of wakefulness can exhaust your baby. Try using motion of any kind—a stroller, car ride, baby swing, or walking—to help calm him down. If you are tense, have someone else hold him. Or, try removing all your baby's clothes except for his diaper, laying him on your breast or your husband's bare chest, and lightly massaging him. You can also take the baby into a warm bath. This accomplishes three things—quieting the baby, giving him a bath, and taking a bath yourself. Have someone available to take the baby out of the tub, or carefully place the baby into a towel on the floor while you get out. An infant may also be quieted by swaddling (being wrapped snugly in a blanket).

Surprisingly, the sound of a vacuum cleaner may be just the trick to quiet your little one. The constant hum or "white noise" seems to lull and relax some fussy babies. There are also tapes available that mimic the mother's heartbeat or the sounds that the baby heard inside the womb. These may be used to quiet a young baby.

Colic

Colic is identified as inconsolable crying for 2 to 3 hours a day, three or more times a week. Babies usually have colic at the same time each day. Even the experts disagree on the cause of colic. Some doctors state that it is character-ized by abdominal cramps or spasms, often with some swelling or hardness of the abdomen. The baby may draw up his knees as he cries in pain and may also pass gas. A colicky baby may be milk intolerant and require change to a soy formula. If the infant is breastfed, the mother should cut out all dairy products from her diet to see if the colic improves. While colic is rare among breastfed babies, it is believed that the cow's milk proteins can get through the breastmilk and cause colic in some infants.

Other doctors believe that colic is not a stomachache, but a response to being overstimulated by too much noise, bright lights, and activity. They sug-gest that providing the baby with a quiet, dimly lit environment, especially during feeding, may help. You may even want to place cotton in the baby's ears while you are feeding him if the household is noisy.

Try to soothe a colicky baby by walking him slowly or by rocking him. Do not jiggle or bounce the baby on your knee. He may prefer to be held facing away from you, with your forearm across his belly. The colic hold may also provide relief. To do this, hold your baby by straddling his legs over your arm, supporting his head with your hand. Use your forearm to apply pressure against his upper abdomen and chest. Placing him over your knees with a warm towel under his tummy may also help. You can easily warm a towel by placing it in the dryer. You may also want to try moving his legs as if he were riding a bicycle. Do this gently with the baby on his back. This may help the baby to expel gas. Fortunately, colic usually disappears by 3 months of age.

Crying spells, especially when caused by colic, can make a parent angry and frustrated. If you have tried everything and the baby is still crying, place him in his crib, remove yourself from the room, and close the door. Turn on the vacuum cleaner, put on earphones, take a shower, or go to another area of the house. Give yourself time to calm down so you can better take care of your infant. After 10 to 15 minutes, go back and try to soothe your baby. Never take your anger out on your infant. Shaken baby syndrome and child abuse can result when a parent feels unable to handle the situation. If you are dealing with a colicky infant, do not feel guilty or responsible. Colic is not a result of poor parenting. Talking about it, accepting offers of help, or even laughing about it with your spouse may help you to get past this difficult time. Remember that the baby is not mad at you or doing it on purpose.

Sleeping

Newborns sleep from 12 to 20 hours per 24-hour day. The periods of sleep and wakefulness vary from baby to baby, depending upon individual sleep cycles

Colic hold.

Bicycle exercise for colic.

and eating patterns. Some babies seem to be awake all the time. Most newborns wake up when they are hungry and fall asleep again when they are satisfied. This rhythm usually continues throughout the day, except for that possible late-afternoon fussy period. As a baby grows, his need for sleep lessens. At 9 months, most babies need only a morning and afternoon nap. By 12 to 15 months, they usually take just one nap. Remember, however, that each baby is an individual and establishes his own routine.

Some babies have problems falling asleep. They are not lulled to sleep by sucking and may fuss or cry for a few minutes. If your baby has trouble going to sleep, try rocking him or singing a lullaby to him. You will find that a comfortable rocking chair is a necessity. Do not give your baby any medication to help him sleep. Such drugs are not good for babies and may even be dangerous.

Most babies are very versatile and will sleep almost anywhere. Some sleep in cribs, others in bassinets, and still others in carriages or their parents' beds. One place where a baby should not sleep, however, is in an adult waterbed. An infant can suffocate by sinking into the bed or rolling into the space between the mattress and the frame. You should also be cautious about placing your baby on soft bedding, pillows, sheepskins, and comforters. Infants lying on their stomachs on these surfaces can rebreathe the same pocket of air with decreasing levels of oxygen and can suffocate. In addition, do not place stuffed toys in the bed with your infant. If your infant's face is close to the toy, the same problem can result. Otherwise, personal preferences should guide you in making the sleeping arrangements for your family.

Some people feel that allowing your older baby to sleep in bed with you or a sibling can help make him feel secure. Many adults do not like sleeping alone and understand why a baby feels comforted and sleeps better when in his parents' bed. Your child will not become perverted by sleeping with you. In many cultures, the entire family sleeps together. Our progressive society is the only one that frowns on this custom. You should do what is comfortable for you and your baby. When your child is older, he may prefer sleeping in his own bed and may just return to your bed when he is sick or frightened. A dark, shadowy room can be quite scary to a young child with an active imagination.

In 1992, the American Academy of Pediatrics issued a statement on infants' sleep positions. After reviewing studies from other countries, the Academy determined that the prone (on the stomach) position for sleep was linked to a higher incidence of sudden infant death syndrome (SIDS). SIDS is a medically unexplained death of a baby under 1 year of age. It is most common between 2 and 4 months of age, and during the winter months. About 80 percent of cases are in children less than 6 months old. The actual cause of SIDS is still unknown. Other factors, according to the statement, include overbundling of the infant, smoking, and not breastfeeding.[13] In 1992, the Academy recommended that a baby be placed on his side or back to sleep. It said that no evidence exists that these positions increase the chance of a baby choking from vomiting.[14] In 1996, the Academy altered its original recommendation to state that a baby should be placed only on his back (not on his side) until age 1 or until he can roll onto his back unaided. This is to prevent side-lying infants from rolling onto their abdomens. Since the Back to Sleep program was initiated in the United States, there has been a 30-percent decrease in the number of deaths attributed to SIDS.[15] The SIDS Alliance, while supporting the Academy's findings for normal infants, does not recommend sleeping on the back or side for premature infants or infants with gas-

Sleeping Times Two

Recent studies indicate that twins who sleep together as infants grow faster and are healthier.

Back to Sleep

Placing your baby on his back to sleep reduces the risk of SIDS. Other things that reduce the risk are breastfeeding, not over-wrapping him with blankets, and not smoking in the house.

troesophageal reflux or upper airway anomalies.[16] For further information about SIDS, write to the SIDS Alliance at 10500 Little Patuxent Parkway, Suite 420, Columbia, Maryland 21044; or call its hotline at 800–221–7437.

Babies' Needs

You may be wondering if you are spoiling your new baby by giving him too much attention. Current authorities feel that it is impossible to spoil an infant. Babies need lots of love, warmth, tenderness, affection, and holding. These are very important for their security and development. If you compare a human baby to the offspring of other mammals, you will find that humans are born more immature and remain so for a much longer period of time. Most other mammals are able to walk very soon after birth. Ashley Montagu, a noted anthropologist, said that a human baby's gestational period is only partly completed by the time he is born; the remainder is completed outside the womb. This is necessary because of the rapid brain development that occurs in human infants. If a human baby were not born until he was completely developed, he would not be able to fit through his mother's pelvis. Therefore, the same way that he is carried within his mother's body for 9 months, he needs to be carried and held until he is able to move around on his own, which is at least another 9 months, according to Montagu.[17]

Your young baby is completely ego-centered. He wants his needs met immediately, and if they are not, he lets you know. He really does not plan to fuss or cry as soon as you start to make dinner or sit down to enjoy it, or at any other inopportune time.

Your infant's needs include physical factors (such as food and warmth) and emotional factors (such as comfort and love). Babies who receive only physical care exhibit slower emotional and physical development than do babies who are given plenty of attention and love. Do not listen to people who tell you that you are spoiling your baby by holding and cuddling him a lot. If your baby stops crying when you pick him up, it is because he is happy to see you and needs to be held. Your baby will be tiny for such a short time—enjoy him and give him plenty of love. As he matures, he will cry less frequently and become less demanding because he will know that comfort is coming.

Bathing

Bathing your baby is one task that you do *not* need to do every day. After all, your new baby does not go out and play in the dirt! The only area on his body that you do need to wash daily is the diaper area. Make sure that you thoroughly clean his bottom with soap and water after each bowel movement to prevent diaper rash. If he just urinated, plain water is sufficient. Take care drying the area, especially the creases. If, during a feeding, milk drips into the creases of his neck, you will want to make sure that the area is clean and dry.

When your baby does need a bath, you can take him into the tub with you to combine the chore with fun. You can also use one of the many commercial tubs that have a special hammock in which to place the baby so that you can keep both your hands free. If you wish, you can even use a large sink, but wrap a cloth around the faucet to protect the baby from injury. By cradling the baby in the crook of your arm and holding his arm with your hand, you will have a free hand with which to wash him. Make sure you have all your supplies handy before you start. Never leave an infant alone in a bath, even for a second.

Lots of Lovin'

Infants cannot be spoiled. They *need* to be held in order to thrive.

WHEN TO CALL THE DOCTOR

You should never hesitate to call your pediatrician about your baby if "something is not right." A mother's intuition is often correct when it comes to her child. Your pediatrician may be able to calm your fears or to suggest an appropriate treatment.

A fever is a symptom of an illness, not a disease in itself, and may or may not be a reason to call the doctor. It can be caused by an infection, a virus, an immunization, or teething. (Doctors refute that teething can cause a fever, but mothers see it happen time and again.) Suspect a fever if your baby feels hot, has dry skin and a flushed face, and seems listless. A low temperature may also be a sign of an infection. To take your baby's temperature rectally, dip a rectal thermometer in petroleum jelly or K-Y jelly, and insert it into the rectum just past the silver bulb tip. Hold it in place for 3 minutes, then gently remove it. Keep a towel or washcloth close by for any accidents. To take your baby's axillary temperature, place a thermometer under his arm and hold it in place for 3 minutes. First make sure that the armpit is dry. When reporting the temperature to your pediatrician, tell him also how you took the reading. Tympanic thermometers, which read the temperature in the child's ear, are also available, but studies are questioning their accuracy.[18] If you feel the result is not accurate, recheck with a rectal thermometer. Two other products that should be avoided because of the difficulty in recording accurate readings are the forehead strip, since moisture will affect the result, and the pacifier thermometer, since the infant must continuously suck on the device for 5 minutes for an accurate result.

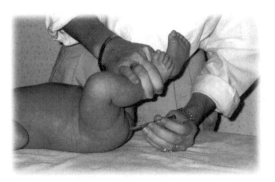

Taking the rectal temperature.

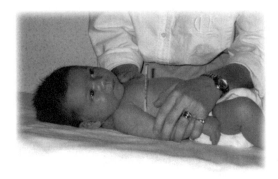

Taking the axillary temperature.

Immediately report to your pediatrician any temperature that is lower than 97°F or higher than 100.2°F in an infant under 3 months of age or higher than 103°F in a child of any age. You should also notify your doctor if a fever lasts longer than 24 hours and is of unknown origin. If the fever is above 101°F and the child is uncomfortable, give him a nonaspirin fever reducer according to your doctor's orders and a 15-minute lukewarm bath. Dress your child lightly; do *not* bundle him up because heavy clothes and wrappers retain heat. If your child has a mild fever, he does not need any medication because a moderately high temperature stimulates the body's protective immune defenses. Never give your child aspirin to reduce a fever because it has been linked to the sometimes fatal disease known as Reyes Syndrome. Alert your pediatrician if the fever does not go down within 24 hours or if your child shows other symptoms.

You should also alert your pediatrician if your baby repeatedly or frequently vomits following a feeding. Also call him if your baby has diarrhea (loose, watery, greenish, foul smelling bowel movements) or bowel movements that contain mucus or blood. Vomiting and/or diarrhea are reasons for concern because they can cause dehydration, often very rapidly in a tiny baby. The signs of dehydration are loss of tears or saliva (dry mouth), sunken eyes, a decrease or absence of urine, the presence of dark amber urine, and/or lethargy. Dehydration is a medical emergency and needs to be treated immediately.

Coughing and a stuffy or runny nose are signs of a cold. Use a cool mist vaporizer to help ease your baby's breathing. If your baby's nose is congested, your pediatrician may recommend that you use normal saline nose drops. To make these nose drops, dissolve 1/4 teaspoon of salt in 8 ounces of water. Hold the baby firmly in your lap on his back and place two drops in each of his nostrils using an eye dropper. Wait a moment, then suction his nostrils with a bulb syringe, compressing the bulb before you insert the tip in his nose. Give your baby nose drops before meals and at bedtime to help him nurse and sleep better. If he has a fever and is also irritable or pulling on his ears, he may have an ear infection, which requires medication. Severe hoarseness, difficulty breathing, or a "barking cough" also need to be reported.

Alert your pediatrician if your baby displays a change in temperament or habits—for example, if he cries excessively, is unusually irritable, is extremely drowsy, has unusual trouble sleeping, is restless, or has a severe loss of appetite.

If your baby has an eye inflammation or discharge, he may need medical attention. A body rash that you cannot cure by any of the methods explained on page 212 may indicate a communicable disease or allergic reaction.

Report any twitching, convulsions, or rigidity at once. Also, if your child appears to be in pain, he may require medical attention.

If your child suffers a head injury, observe him for a change in mental alertness, extreme sleepiness with difficulty waking, vomiting, discharge from the ears or nose, unequal pupil sizes, or skull deformity. Elevate his head and alert your doctor immediately. When a limb is injured, check for and report any deformity, redness, swelling, extreme tenderness, or inability to use the limb. An open wound may require suturing. For cosmetic reasons, some parents prefer a plastic surgeon to repair a facial cut.

In case your child swallows a nonfood substance, immediately call your pediatrician or local Poison Control Center for instructions.

IMMUNIZATIONS

Immunizations are an important part of your baby's health care because they protect him from potentially harmful diseases. Some babies, however, have reactions to the vaccines. The symptoms include pain and redness at the injection site, fever, and irritability. Occasionally, a baby will break out in a rash 6 to 12 days after receiving the measles vaccine. To reduce the fever or pain, give your child a nonaspirin medication, such as acetaminophen, as ordered by your pediatrician. Be sure to call the doctor if your child has a severe reaction.

Table 10.1 on page 220 presents a recommended schedule for immunizations. The schedule for the Hib (*Haemophilus influenzae* type b) vaccine against meningitis depends upon which vaccine is used. Doctors now recommend that all infants be immunized for hepatitis B. If your baby was not given the vaccine in the hospital, he should receive three doses by 18 months of age.

Polio Vaccine

The polio vaccine comes in two types—oral and injectable. The oral vaccine is made from a weakened form of the live polio virus. It is the most common one administered to infants. The benefit of the live vaccine is that it is easy to

When to Call the Pediatrician for Your Newborn

Telephone your doctor if your baby displays any of the following symptoms:

❏ Temperature over 100.2°F or under 97°F (phone immediately if your child is under 3 months of age).

❏ Projectile vomiting.

❏ Severe diarrhea (green, foul smelling, loose bowel movements containing mucus).

❏ Poor appetite or a refusal to feed.

❏ Unusual behavior.

❏ Extreme lethargy (difficulty being roused, floppy).

❏ Inconsolable crying.

❏ Few wet diapers or bowel movements.

Catching and treating a problem early may prevent a more serious condition and possible complications.

Table 10.1. Immunization Schedule

Vaccine	Birth	1 month	2 months	4 months	6 months	12 months	15 months	18 months	4–6 years	11–12 years	14–16 years
Hepatitis B-1	■	■									
Hepatitis B-2		■	■	■							
Hepatitis B-3					■	■	■	■			
Hepatitis B										■ [1]	
Diphtheria, tetanus, pertussis			■	■	■		■	■	■	■	■ [2]
H. influenzae type b (Hib)			■	■	■	■	■				
Polio			■	■	■	■	■	■	■		
Measles, mumps, rubella						■	■		■	■ [3]	
Varicella (chickenpox)						■	■	■		■ [4]	

[1] Only if child was not previously vaccinated for hepatitis B.
[2] Can be given without pertussis.
[3] Only if child was not vaccinated at 4 to 6 years.
[4] Only if child was not previously vaccinated for varicella, and did not or may not have had chickenpox.

administer and is excreted in the bowel movements. Because of this, it is also excellent for providing a booster to adults who have been immunized. The disadvantage of the oral vaccine is that it is the cause of the eight to ten cases of polio that occur in the Western hemisphere each year. There has not been a case of polio from a wild virus (not vaccine related) since 1979. In addition, persons whose immune systems are compromised or suppressed, AIDS victims, and persons receiving chemotherapy can contract the disease after receiving an oral dose or following exposure to the excreted virus.

The injectable polio vaccine is made from a killed virus and is therefore slightly less effective. In addition, it requires an injection, which makes it more expensive.

To reduce the annual number of polio cases, the CDC has recommended that the first two doses of polio vaccine be given by injection using the inactivated virus and that the following two doses be given orally using the live virus. If your child or a family member is immunocompromised, the injectable form of the vaccine should be used.

Chickenpox Vaccine

Chickenpox (varicella) is a common, usually mild, childhood disease that, once contracted, provides lifelong immunity. The most common side effects are itching and a mild fever. Serious complications are extremely rare and include pneumonitis, encephalitis, kidney problems, and bacterial superinfections of the lungs, bones, and skin.[19] Because the disease is easily transmitted, infected children are isolated for approximately 1 week during an outbreak to reduce the spread of the disease.

The advantage of receiving the chickenpox vaccine (varivax) is that it prevents a child from getting chickenpox. This eliminates the aggravation of missing a week of school or daycare for the child, and possibly a week or more of work for the parent (parents with more than one child may miss more than 1 week of work). Some experts are questioning the benefit of giving the vaccine to all children. They state that the main benefit is an economic one for parents who work, since chickenpox is more of an annoyance than a danger to children. Plus, it is unknown how long the immunity to the disease will be with the vaccine.

If a person over the age of 13 contracts chickenpox, the risk of serious complications is greater. It is rarely just a mild disease in adults. The vaccine may require one or more boosters, and compliance to a booster schedule becomes more difficult as children mature. It is recommended that children over the age of 13 who have not had the disease naturally and adults who have never contracted the disease receive two doses of the vaccine. The vaccine is not recommended for immunosuppressed children or adults.

HANDLING EMERGENCIES

Some conditions should be considered emergencies and treated immediately. Following are instructions for handling these life-threatening situations. You should become familiar with these procedures so that they will not be confusing to you if you ever need to use them. All parents should take a course in infant cardiopulmonary resuscitation (CPR) to get firsthand practice on a manikin under the guidance of a certified instructor. Baby sitters, grandparents, and other caregivers should also be trained, as accidents can happen at any time.

Never practice CPR on a living person.

What to Do for Choking

If an infant or small child is choking because his airway is obstructed, you will need to do something to dislodge the obstruction. The signs of obstruction are blue lips, hoarse or crowing breathing, and inability to speak or cough. (If the child can speak or cough, allow him to expel the object on his own. Unnecessary intervention may cause further problems.) Call for help if you can. However, if you are alone, do not take the time to use the phone. You are the lifesaver at this time. *Warning:* Do not sweep your finger blindly in the child's mouth. This could cause further obstruction. Instead, for a child over 1 year old, use the Heimlich maneuver, and for a child under 1 year old, use back blows and chest thrusts. *Never perform abdominal thrusts, such as the Heimlich maneuver, on an infant under 1 year of age because of the risk of injury to the abdominal organs.*

Back Blows and Chest Thrusts

If the baby is *under 1 year old and conscious*, do the following:

Caution:
Tylenol Overdosing

When giving acetaminophen (Tylenol) to your infant or young child, make sure that you give him the proper dose. Overdosing has resulted in death or irreversible liver damage. Because Infants' Tylenol can be up to three and a half times more concentrated than Children's Tylenol, you should always check with your pediatrician for the proper dosage, letting him know which concentration you are using. Then double-check the dosage on the bottle. *Never* give more than the recommended amount. Even small overdoses present the risk of serious health problems.

1. Place the baby facedown over the length of your arm, with his head lower than his chest and supported by your hand.

2. Using the heel of your free hand, give the baby 5 sharp blows on his back between his shoulder blades.

3. Turn the baby onto his back, supported on your arm, with his head lower than his chest. Give him 5 chest thrusts, compressing his breastbone quickly and firmly one finger-width below the nipple line, using two fingers of your free hand. (This step is the same as the Cardiac step in infant CPR.)

Repeat these steps until the object is expelled or the infant loses consciousness.

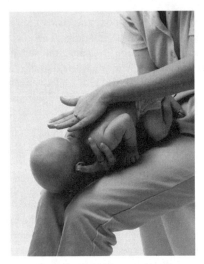

Back blows for a conscious infant.

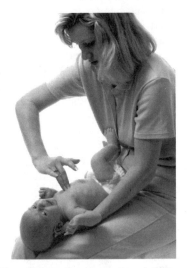

Chest thrusts for a conscious infant.

If the baby is *under 1 year old and unconscious* or lost consciousness while you tried to unblock his airway with the preceding steps, do the following:

1. Call out for help. If an extra person is available, have that person call 911.

2. Place the baby on his back and kneel next to him.

3. Open the baby's mouth, using your thumb on the tongue to lift the jaw, and look for the obstruction. If you see it and can easily access it, remove it.

4. If the obstruction is not visible or is inaccessible, open the baby's airway by tilting his head back, lifting his chin up gently with one finger, and pushing his forehead down with your other hand. Cover his nose and mouth with your mouth and breathe out twice slowly and gently, using just enough force to make his chest rise and fall as in normal breathing. Reposition his head and repeat the breaths if they were unsuccessful the first time.

Perform steps 1 through 3 for a conscious infant (back blows and chest thrusts), followed by steps 2 through 4 for an unconscious infant (obstruction check and rescue breathing) until the obstruction is dislodged or medical help arrives. If you are alone, call 911 after 1 minute of effort.

Obstruction check for an unconscious infant.

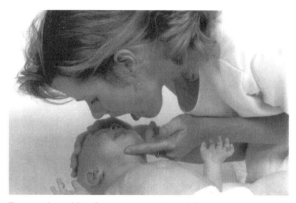

Rescue breathing for an unconscious infant.

Heimlich Maneuver

Choking in older babies and children can be treated the same as in adults. If the child is *over 1 year old and conscious*, use the Heimlich maneuver:

1. Stand behind the child and wrap your arms around his waist between his navel and rib cage.

2. Make a fist with one of your hands and grasp that fist with your other hand. With your fist, make a quick upward thrust into the child's abdomen to force air up through his windpipe.

Repeat these steps as necessary until the obstruction is expelled.

If the child is *over 1 year old and unconscious* or lost consciousness while you tried to unblock his airway with the preceding steps, do the following:

1. Call out for help. If an extra person is available, have that person call 911.

2. Place the child on his back and kneel next to him.

3. Open the child's mouth, using your thumb on the tongue to lift the jaw, and look for the obstruction. If you see it and can easily access it, remove it.

4. If the obstruction is not visible or is inaccessible, open the child's airway by tilting his head back, lifting his chin up gently with the fingers of one hand, and pushing his forehead down with your other hand. Pinch his nostrils closed, cover his mouth with your mouth, and breathe out twice slowly and gently, using just enough force to make his chest rise and fall as in normal breathing.

Heimlich maneuver for a conscious child over 1 year old.

5. If the child's airway is still obstructed, kneel at the child's feet or straddle his thighs, depending on his size. Place the heel of one of your hands on the child's abdomen midway between his navel and rib cage. Place your other hand directly on top of the first and make 6 to 10 quick upward thrusts into the child's abdomen to force air up through his windpipe.

If you are alone, call 911 after 1 minute of effort. Then repeat steps 3 through 5 for an unconscious child (obstruction check, rescue breathing, and abdominal thrusts) until the obstruction is dislodged or medical help arrives.

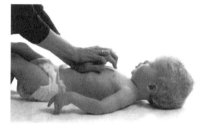

Abdominal thrusts for an unconscious child over 1 year old.

How to Prevent Choking

The best way to save your child from choking is to take precautions beforehand. Although most people realize that small objects such as buttons and coins can be dangerous to babies and young children, many parents are not aware that some foods also pose hazards. The following foods are the most frequent causes of fatal choking in children under 5:

❑ Hot dogs and sausages.

❑ Round candy.

❑ Peanuts and other nuts.

❑ Whole grapes.

❑ Hard cookies and biscuits.

❑ Meat chunks and sticks.

❑ Raw carrot slices and sticks.

❑ Peanut butter and peanut butter sandwiches.

❑ Apple pieces.

❑ Popcorn.

Never leave a baby alone while he is eating and always make sure that a small child is adequately supervised at mealtime. Children can also choke when a bottle is propped. Many children choke when they run or play with food in their mouths, or when they talk and laugh while eating.

Cardiopulmonary Resuscitation (CPR)

If your child stops breathing, he is not receiving the oxygen he needs to maintain life. If his breathing has stopped, his heart may also soon stop. (Other causes of cardiac arrest are electric shock, drowning, and sudden infant death syndrome.) You must act immediately to breathe for him, possibly pumping his heart.

While you tend to your child, have someone else call for a rescue unit. If you are alone, perform CPR for at least 1 minute before quickly calling the emergency squad yourself.

To perform CPR on a baby under 1 year old, remember your ABCs:

1. *Airway.* Gently tap or shake the baby's shoulder to gauge his responsiveness. Place the baby on his back and kneel next to him. Tilt his head back by gently lifting his chin up with one of your fingers while pushing his forehead down with your other hand. His head should be positioned as if he were trying to sniff something. *Warning:* Do not exaggerate the tilt, as this may close the airway completely.

2. *Breathing.* Place your ear over the baby's mouth, your face pointing toward his chest, to look, listen, and feel for breathing. If all the signs of breathing are absent, cover the baby's nose and mouth with your mouth and breathe out twice slowly and gently, using just enough force to make his chest rise and fall as in normal breathing. *Warning:* Do not blow hard. Blowing too hard can injure the baby's lungs. However, blowing too softly will not give the baby enough oxygen. When blowing, you should make each inflation 1 to 1 1/2 seconds long.

Next, check to see if the baby's heart is beating by placing the tips of your

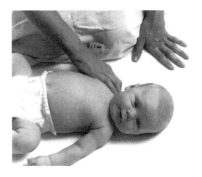

Gauge the baby's responsiveness.

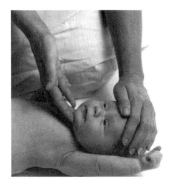

Tilt his head back *slightly*.

Look, listen, and feel for breathing.

Check for a pulse.

Imagine a line between the nipples.

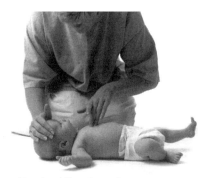

Do chest thrusts and rescue breathing.

Infant CPR

index and middle fingers on the inside of his upper arm, between his elbow and shoulder. Press gently to feel for the brachial pulse. Keep your other hand on the baby's forehead to maintain the position of his head. If you feel a pulse but the baby is not breathing, continue breathing for him at the rate of 1 breath every 3 seconds, or 20 breaths a minute. If you do not feel a pulse, proceed to the Cardiac step, below. If you are alone, continue breathing and performing the heart compressions for 1 minute before phoning for emergency help.

3. *Cardiac.* Imagine a line drawn between the baby's nipples. Place your index finger below the line, with the middle and ring fingers next to the index finger. Lift up the index finger and use the tips of the other two fingers to compress the breastbone (sternum). Make sure that you are not on the tip of the breastbone. Compress the area about 1/2 to 1 inch at a rate of at least 100 times a minute. Use your other hand to maintain the baby's head position. After every 5 compressions, give the baby 1 breath. After 20 cycles, check for a pulse and look for spontaneous breathing. If you do not find a pulse or signs of breathing, continue compressing the chest and giving breaths, rechecking for a pulse and breathing every few minutes until medical help arrives.

For children 1 to 8 years of age, follow the same procedure. However, when breathing for the child, pinch his nostrils shut and cover just his mouth with your mouth. Also, use the heel of your hand instead of the tips of your fingers to depress his sternum. To locate the correct hand position, find the lower tip of the sternum with two fingers and place your hand above this area. Compress the sternum 1 to 1 1/2 inches at the rate of 80 to 100 times per minute. Determine if the heart is beating by checking for a pulse on the carotid artery, located on the side of the neck.[20]

BABY-PROOFING YOUR HOUSE

Before your baby begins to creep or crawl, you must baby-proof your house—that is, make it safe for curious little fingers. It is easy to put this job off, but if you do, you may find that while your baby is rapidly learning to move around, he is getting into *everything*. The best time to make your home safe for your baby is during your last trimester of pregnancy.

To baby-proof your house or apartment, take a crawling tour through every room to get a baby's eye view. Remove anything that looks even remotely enticing or dangerous. As you move these items out of the way, replace them with interesting safe things your baby can play with. A stimulating environment contributes to the development of creativity in a child.

Among the things that you should do to make your house or apartment safe for your baby are:

Send in Those Cards and . . .

Send in the warranty cards you receive with new purchases. If an item is recalled, you will be notified directly.

❏ *House in general*

• Install smoke detectors and carbon monoxide detectors. Check the batteries monthly and change them annually.

• Place fire extinguishers in areas of fire risk. Plan two escape routes and hold periodic fire drills.

• Elevate your gas hot water heater to 18 inches above the floor to reduce the risk of a flash fire in case of a flammable liquid spill. Store all flammable liquids in closed containers.

• Turn the water heater thermostat down to 120°F to protect against scalding.

• Check all your baby furniture for the Juvenile Products Manufacturers Association (JPMA) Safety Certification Seal to make sure that it meets the basic safety standards. Check for the seal before purchasing anything. For a free pamphlet on baby furniture safety, write to the Consumer Product Safety Commission, Office of Information and Public Affairs, Washington, DC 20207.

• Move your furniture away from the windows.

• Move furniture in front of as many electrical outlets as possible to protect against electrical shock.

• Insert plastic covers in all unused electrical outlets and put large boxlike covers over those that are in use. Replace outlet covers with childproof covers.

• Cover all unused telephone outlets with duct tape.

• Hide all electrical and telephone cords, as babies like to chew on them.

• Store your iron out of sight to prevent the baby from tugging on its cord and pulling it down onto his head. Never leave a hot iron unattended.

• Shorten the cords on all blinds and draperies, or cut the loop, to prevent strangulation.

• Replace all vinyl miniblinds that are imported and have a matte finish. These blinds may contain lead. If you are not sure about your miniblinds, check them with a home test kit.

• If your home is over 30 years old or you have secondhand painted furniture, strip and repaint any surface on which your baby might chew. The original paint may contain lead.

• Move ashtrays, pipes, cigarettes, matches, and lighters out of reach. Tobacco can be fatal when eaten by a small child.

• Unload and lock up all guns. Never keep a gun in a bedroom drawer or purse, and never let a small child see you using one.

• If you have any toxic houseplants, hang them out of reach, move them outside, or put them into loving "foster care."

• Set aside a special utensil set for measuring and applying fertilizer to your houseplants. Do not use household utensils for poisons.

• Keep all exercise equipment closed up in a room away from the baby. Do not allow the baby to be near when you exercise.

• Put a safety doorknob cover or a very high lock on every door leading either outdoors or to an unsafe room, such as a sewing room, bathroom, or garage.

• Mark all sliding glass doors with decals and do not allow any heavy toys near them.

• Install a baby gate at the top and bottom of every staircase to prevent climbing and falling. Avoid accordion-style gates, which can trap an arm or leg. Gates with vertical slats or a mesh design are preferable.

❏ *Kitchen*

• Install a gate across the doorway to keep the baby out of the kitchen when you are not there.

• Install safety latches on all cupboard doors that you do not want little hands to open.

• Put all vitamins, medicines, wastebaskets, plastic bags, glassware, knives, and other potentially dangerous items in locked cupboards.

• Move all wines and liquors to a locked cabinet. Do not leave leftover drinks sitting out where a toddler can find and drink them. Alcohol can be toxic.

• Move all household cleaners, detergents, and similar products out of reach.

• Put some safe kitchen items, such as plastic bowls and wooden spoons, in a low cabinet away from the stove for the baby to play with. This is to divert his attention from items that are not as safe and to keep him occupied while you are cooking.

• Tie plastic bags in knots and throw them away after use.

• Remove all tablecloths that toddlers can pull.

• Store appliances away from the edges of countertops. Unplug and wrap the cords.

• If your stove has knobs on a front panel, either remove the knobs or install knob covers when you are not using the stove.

• When the dishwasher is not in use, keep the door latched.

• When filling the dishwasher, position sharp utensils with the pointed ends down. Do not add detergent until you are ready to run the machine.

Hints for the New Father

❏ Attend a baby-care class.

❏ Change your baby's diaper.

❏ Talk and sing to your baby.

❏ Give your newborn a bath, or help your mate do this.

❏ Take the baby into the bath with you.

❏ Rock the baby.

❏ Put the baby to sleep on his back to reduce the risk of sudden infant death syndrome.

❏ Take pictures and videos of the baby.

❏ Attend an infant CPR class with your mate.

❏ Massage the baby.

❏ Play games with the baby.

❏ Carry the baby in a front pack or sling.

❏ Baby-proof your house.

❏ Use a safety seat every time the baby is in the car.

❏ Never place the safety seat or any child in the front seat of your car if you have dual air bags.

❏ Invest in a comfortable rocking chair for the fussy times.

❏ *Bathroom*

• Lock your medicine cabinet or move all toxic and dangerous medical supplies out of reach.

• Move perfumes, cosmetics, and other grooming products out of reach.

• Store all razors out of reach.

• Move the wastebasket out of reach.

• Pad the bathtub faucet to prevent bumps.

• Put adhesive nonskid decals on the bottom of the bathtub to prevent slipping.

• Install a lock on the toilet lid and always keep the lid down and the bathroom door closed. Toddlers can drown in a toilet.

❏ *Nursery*

• Replace the crib if its slats are more than 2 3/8 inches apart or if the rail, when raised, is less than 26 inches above the mattress support when the support is in the lowest position or, when lowered, is less than 9 inches above the mattress support when the mattress support is in its highest position. Cribs manufactured after 1974 meet all these requirements.

• Replace the crib mattress if it does not fit snugly in the crib.

• Position the crib mattress support at the highest position for your newborn. Lower the mattress support as the baby grows. Once the baby reaches 35 inches in height or can crawl out of the crib, put him in a regular bed.

• Be sure the locking latch that holds the side of the crib up is sturdy and cannot be released by a child. Always leave the side up when your baby is in the crib.

• Use a crib bumper when your child is an infant. It should be secured with at least six ties. To prevent strangulation, the ties should be no longer than 6 inches. Remove the bumper, as well as any pillows, when your baby can pull to a standing position.

• Do not leave stuffed animals in the crib when the baby is sleeping.

• Move the crib away from heaters, air vents, and drapery and venetian blind cords. For warmth, put the crib against an inside wall.

• Do not hang glass mirrors or picture frames on the wall above the crib.

• Choose a changing table that is sturdy and has a 2-inch guardrail on all sides and a safety strap.

• Store diaper pins, cotton balls, baby oil, and talcum powder out of the baby's reach. Keep these items away from other young children, as they may try to powder the baby.

❏ *Playroom*

• Move all toys that have small parts or sharp points to a shelf that the baby cannot reach but that your older children can.

• Discard all stuffed toys and dolls that have eyes, noses, mouths, or other features that might come off. Embroidered features are the safest; sewn or glued parts can be pulled off.

• Do not use lightweight hammocks without spreader bars to store toys. They can cause strangulation.

❏ *Garage or workroom*

• Move all pesticides, paints, and petroleum products to a high shelf or locked cabinet. Do not store them in containers such as soft drink bottles or food jars that could cause them to be confused with something else.

• Move dangerous tools out of reach.

• Put small items such as nails, screws, and bolts in closed containers.

• If you have an old automatic garage door opener, replace it with a model that has an electric eye or that is programmed to stop and reverse if the door touches an object before reaching the ground. Test the door by using a roll of paper towels to simulate a small child. The door should reverse within 2 seconds.

❏ *Yard*

• Remove any poisonous plants. These include oleander, daffodils and other narcissuses, caladium, elephant's ear, English ivy, castor bean plants, common lantana, nightshade, rosemary pea, pokeweed, foxglove, Carolina yellow jasmine, jatropha, gloriosa lily, dieffenbachia, hyacinth, holly, mistletoe, Jerusalem cherries, azaleas, angel's trumpets, poinsettias, philodendron, and rhododendron. Your local Poison Control Center can identify other toxic plants for you.

• If you use pesticides or herbicides on your yard, follow the instructions carefully. Do not allow a child on a treated lawn for at least 48 hours.

• If you have a pool, block it off with a tall, sturdy fence with a self-locking gate. Many states require this by law. Hot tubs and spas should be covered when not in use. Also, make sure that you have the proper lifesaving equipment on hand.

• Even if your child is a good swimmer, keep an eye on him when he is in or near your pool or hot tub. Drains and intake valves in pools and hot tubs can draw in water at great pressure, entangling long hair and trapping a child under water. If the drain cover is broken or dislodged, your child could become sucked into or held onto the drain, and trapped under water.

• Use caution when placing your infant in a swimming program that involves dunking or repeated submergence. Swallowing large amounts of water can dilute his blood and cause a life-threatening condition known as water intoxication. Also, infants can develop severe diarrhea from the bacteria in the water from other babies' diapers. Additionally, even if your child has been through a swimming or life-saving program, do not expect him to remember how to swim or "float" from year to year. The techniques need to be reinforced frequently.

• Discard or store out of reach any large containers in which rain or sprinkler water can collect. A child can drown in a 5-gallon bucket.

• Remove any clothes with hoods or strings when your child plays on playground equipment. A hood or string can get caught on the top of a slide or entangled in a swing chain.

• Do not allow your infant or toddler to suck or chew on the bars of playground equipment, which may contain lead. For information about lead, call 800–424–LEAD (800–424–5323).

When you take your child to someone else's house, check for these same hazards.

Bathtub Safety

Do not assume that your child is safe in an infant bathtub seat. A number of children have drowned when left alone in one. According to the U.S. Consumer Product Safety Commission, the seats are safe when used properly. However, if children are left alone in the seats, they can "tip the seats over, slide into the water through the leg openings and climb out of the seats into the water, posing the risk of drowning."

BABY-PROOF HABITS

In addition to baby-proofing your house, you should baby-proof yourself and other family members. Take a look at your habits. Do you do anything automatically that could spell trouble for your baby? What about your spouse, other children, parents, friends, and anyone else that is in your home on a regular basis? Replacing a dangerous habit with a safe practice could avoid a possible life-threatening tragedy.

The following are just a few of the habits that you can correct (or never establish in the first place) to make your child's life safer:

❑ Do not allow smoking in the house. Children exposed to smoke in their homes have more colds and upper respiratory infections, and miss more school than those in nonsmoking households.

❑ Do not drink or pass hot beverages while your child is nearby or on your lap.

❑ Do not leave your baby in a drop-side playpen with the side lowered. He can roll into the space between the pad and the loose mesh side, and possibly suffocate. The best kind of playpen has a firm lower edge in which an infant cannot be entrapped.

❑ Never leave your baby or small child alone in the tub.

❑ Never leave your baby alone on the changing table or on any other high surface.

❑ Do not leave your infant unattended in a bassinet if you have other small children. They could try to pick up the baby or rock the cradle.

❑ Avoid the use of walkers. They can result in serious injuries.

❑ Never drape clothes or blankets over the side of the crib because they can fall or be pulled over the baby's head.

❑ Do not use a cord to tie rattles or pacifiers to your baby's clothes or to tie a pacifier around his neck.

❑ Purchase pacifiers that cannot possibly come apart. Solid, one-piece molded plastic ones are the safest. Check them periodically for deterioration. Never use the top and nipple from a baby bottle as a pacifier.

❑ Never give balloons to a baby or small child. An uninflated balloon or pieces from a popped balloon could get stuck in his throat and choke him.

❑ When you are cooking, turn the handles of your pots and pans toward the back of the stove.

❑ Do not take medication or vitamins in front of your child.

❑ Remove your pet's food dishes from the floor when he has finished eating.

❑ When you have visitors or overnight guests, make sure that their purses and suitcases are locked or out of the reach of curious hands.

In addition to baby-proofing your house and yourself, you should also teach your child as soon as possible what is dangerous and what is not. For example, teach him early on what "hot" means.

Make a list of emergency telephone numbers and keep it near the phone or even taped to it. Include your local Poison Control Center, rescue unit, fire department, and police department. Do not forget your pediatrician. Teach your children about 911 and when to call it.

Finally, buy a bottle of syrup of ipecac to induce your child to vomit if he swallows something poisonous. However, use it only on instruction from your doctor or local Poison Control Center. Not everything should be brought back up again.

AUTOMOBILE SAFETY

Buy a safety seat that is labeled, "Meets Federal motor vehicle safety standards," and begin using it the day you bring your baby home from the hospital. Many hospitals, in fact, do not allow parents to take their baby home until they show a hospital representative that they have a car seat. Continue using a safety seat for your child until he is 4 years old or weighs over 40 pounds, at which time you can switch him to adult seat belts. However, if your 4-year-old does not weigh 40 pounds, he is best protected in a safety seat. Do not put your child in an adult shoulder harness until he is 4 feet in height. You may want to use a booster seat. Every state has a child restraint law. Check with your local Department of Motor Vehicles to learn the restrictions in your state. If your safety seat is secondhand or several years old, you might want to call the National Highway Traffic Safety Administration's Hotline to check if it was recalled. The Hotline number is 800–424–9393. The operator can also give you other car seat information.

Automobile accidents are the leading cause of death in young children. Statistics show that they are way ahead of all other types of accidents, as well as all diseases. In addition, auto crashes are a major cause of epilepsy and paraplegia in children.

In a crash, swerve, or sudden stop, your baby could be thrown into the dashboard, windshield, or another passenger. He could also be thrown out of the car. Although your arms are usually the best place for your baby, they are not when you are riding in an automobile. Tests have shown that volunteers holding 17-pound baby-size dummies were not able to hold onto the "babies" in impacts at 15 miles per hour and 30 miles per hour, even though they were prepared for the crashes. Even a tiny 10-pound infant can be thrown forward with a force of 300 pounds in a 30-mile-per-hour impact. This is equivalent to falling from a three-story building. Putting your baby in the seat belt with you is also not safe because the baby would be crushed by the force of your body.

Infants, as well as babies under 20 pounds and less than 1 year of age, should be placed in a semireclined, backward-facing restraint that you have anchored snugly to the vehicle seat using a lap belt according to both the car and safety seat manufacturers' directions. When your baby is over 1 year of age and at least 20 pounds, he can safely be moved to a securely anchored forward-facing seat. Certain child restraint models are raised to allow the occupant to see out the window, a feature that many older children prefer. If your car has dual air bags, do not place the safety seat, or any child under the age of 13, in the front passenger seat. According to a 2-year study by the National Transportation Safety Board, an air bag can discharge with enough force to cause multiple injuries and even death in children. The study also found that children sitting in safety seats may incur injuries or die if the child restraint is improperly attached.[21]

Infant safety seat.

Newborns with specific risk factors may need to be transported in a special car bed rather than the standard infant seat. These babies include preterm and low-birth-weight infants, infants who have experienced apnea (stopped breathing), and infants with certain genetic disorders (Down syndrome). If your infant falls into any of these categories, check with your pediatrician about the need for a special car bed.

Remember that no safety seat will protect your child from injury unless he is properly secured in it. Take the time to strap him in, even for short trips. Most accidents happen within 25 miles of home. Studies have shown that up to 90 percent of child restraints are used improperly. Read your car owner's manual and the instructions with the safety seat. Check to make sure the seat is properly fastened in the car each time. Do not wrap your child in blankets before securing the straps. The straps should fit snugly against his body.

Never leave your child (or pet) in an unattended car for any amount of time. A car heats up rapidly, even with the windows down. Your child could become overheated, have an accident, be kidnapped, or wander off unnoticed.

BABY EQUIPMENT

When you begin shopping for baby equipment, you may notice that the advertising is designed to appeal to your most tender and protective feelings. Some ads even attempt to arouse guilt and anxiety in you if you choose not to buy the products. You may be tempted to buy everything you see, especially if this is your first child. Resist buying too much too soon.

The needs of a newborn are very simple. In the early weeks, a new baby requires only a safety seat, a few nightgowns, diapers, and a place to sleep. You can add other items gradually.

Babies quickly outgrow newborn-size garments. By 4 to 6 weeks, your baby may wear 3- to 6-month sizes. If friends ask what you could use for the baby, encourage them to buy 12-month or larger size clothing. Otherwise, before you know it, you will have a dresser full of "little" clothes that do not fit and nothing for your baby to wear.

Be sure that all the garments you buy or receive are soft to the touch and easy to put on. Babies dislike having their heads covered for more than a second. Also, choose clothing that has room for growth in the form of extra wide hems, extra long or adjustable straps, and so on.

Front-pack carriers and slings offer babies good transportation plus a warm place to sleep during the first months of life. As your baby reaches 2 to 3 months of age, you may prefer a stroller for shopping trips and other long excursions.

Pediatricians strongly discourage the use of baby walkers. Walkers cause more injuries each year than any other nursery product. They allow infants to be more mobile and more vertical than they normally would be at that age. As a result, unsupervised infants can fall down stairs or reach items on the stove or table tops. Serious injuries can include skull fractures, head injuries, lacerations, and scald burns. In addition, rather than encourage walking, baby walkers can impede a baby's progress in learning to walk. Several companies now make bouncers or "saucers" to be used in place of walkers. These products allow the child to be upright, and they provide activities to entertain the baby without allowing him to be mobile.

You will not need a high chair until your baby is about 6 months old. Before then, your baby's back and neck will not be strong enough for him to remain sitting upright.

Among the items that most parents feel are necessary for meeting an infant's basic needs are the following:

A sling-style carrier.

❏ *Sleeping*

• A sturdy crib with a firm mattress that can be used for at least 2 years. (For some important specifications, see "Baby-Proofing Your House" on page 226.)

• A bassinet to provide the small, confined space that most newborns prefer in the first weeks of life. This, however, is an expensive purchase considering the short time it is used.

• A set of crib bumper pads to protect your baby's head, arms, and legs as he begins to move about in his sleep.

• One to two mattress pads to protect the baby against wetness and to absorb perspiration.

• Two crib sheets, one to use and one to wash. Fitted sheets stay on a mattress better than flat sheets do, and knitted cotton is the softest material.

• Four to five receiving blankets to cover the baby when he is sleeping or when you take him outside on a cool day.

• One to two warm blankets.

*"I'm sorry, dear.
You'll have to take the bus!"*

❏ *Diapering*

• Diapers. Disposable diapers are convenient, but they are also expensive and are detrimental to the environment. The initial cost of cloth diapers may seem high, but the money saved by not buying disposables more than offsets the cost of the fuel, hot water, and soap needed to wash them. Cloth diapers come in two types—flat and prefolded. Flat diapers are less expensive and dry more quickly, but prefolded ones are more absorbent and save time. Preshaped diapers with Velcro tabs are convenient, but expensive. If you use cloth diapers, you need three to four dozen diapers and four to six diaper pins. Most new mothers appreciate the gift of 1 to 2 months of a diaper service. Continued use of the service, however, is expensive and of questionable benefit ecologically if your particular one rinses its diapers five to six times. Do not begin using cloth diapers until your baby's bowel movements have changed from meconium to milk stools. Meconium does not wash out and will permanently stain your diapers.

Most newborns go through about ten diapers a day. If using disposables, you will need to buy about seventy a week. Even if you use cloth diapers, you may want to use disposables for outings and trips. They are available in a range of sizes and absorbencies. If using the new super-absorbent ones, be sure to change your baby just as often as with the less absorbent varieties. Leaving diapers on too long can cause diaper rash.

• Diaper liners to make clean up after bowel movements easier. However, they will also add to your weekly expenses.

• A diaper pail that can hold 2 to 3 days' worth of diapers and water, but that is not too large to carry.

❏ *Clothing*

• Three to six cotton nightgowns that close at the bottom to make diaper changing easier.

• Two to three one-piece stretch sleepers in the 6-month size. These are great for day and night wear as your baby grows and becomes more active.

• Three to six waterproof pants if the baby wears cloth diapers. Choose plastic-coated fabric pants that snap together at the sides to allow air circulation and to lessen the risk of skin irritation.

• Seasonal items, such as several short-sleeve snap-front shirts, a sweater and cap, or a snowsuit.

❑ *Bathing*

• A baby bathtub. The kitchen sink, lined with a towel, works just as well.

• Three to four soft washcloths for bathing and for wiping little bottoms.

• Two to three baby bath towels. Your regular towels will work just fine.

• Mild bar soap or liquid baby soap for cleaning tender skin.

❑ *Traveling*

• A safety seat. (For complete discussions of car seats, see "Buy and Install a Safety Seat" on page 119 and "Automobile Safety" on page 231.) Your community may have a program that rents car seats for a minimal fee.

• A front-pack baby carrier or sling.

• A stroller.

❑ *Optional items*

• A wind-up or battery-operated baby swing to provide movement and diversion for your baby when your hands are busy. Make sure that it is well balanced to prevent tipping.

• A playpen to protect the baby from the activities of older children, but never to "cage" him. If you have baby-proofed your house, you will have little need for one.

• A backpack carrier for shopping trips and excursions when your baby is older.

• A baby monitor so you can hear your baby from another room. *Warning:* Some monitors have been known to overheat and start fires. The Gerry 602 Deluxe model was recalled for this reason.

If you spread out your purchases over an extended period of time, you will not be overwhelmed by their cost. You could also ask friends and relatives who no longer need certain items if they would loan them to you or sell them at a fraction of their original cost. Garage sales and consignment shops are other good sources of "nice as new" furniture, clothing, and toys. Babies do not wear out things the way older children do. However, if you purchase a used crib or other baby furniture, make sure to check for the safety features mentioned throughout this chapter.

PLAYING WITH YOUR BABY

Positive interaction is a crucial factor in the proper mental and emotional development of a baby. Visual, vocal, and tactile stimulation are all valuable aids to learning. Talk to your baby while you change his diaper. Read to him from the time of birth. Even though he cannot understand what you are saying, the sounds of the words will become familiar to him, and it will not be long before he *is* comprehending some of them.

Set aside some time each day to simply play with your baby. He should be wide awake, happy, and well fed. Sing to your baby or recite nursery rhymes

"I wonder how long before they learn to talk!"

to help him gain an awareness of language. You can involve him in clapping and other hand movements to keep him entertained. Some suggestions are "Pat-a-Cake," "This Little Piggy Went to Market," and "Itsy Bitsy Spider." Following are some suggested activities to do with your baby.

Bath Play

Bath time provides a good opportunity for playful interaction. During bath time, you can help your baby learn the names of his various body parts by saying them as you wash them. You can borrow the tune from a song such as "Here We Go 'Round the Mulberry Bush" and substitute verses such as "This is the way we wash your face." As your baby gets older, he will enjoy splashing and playing with bathtub toys.

Toys

You should select toys for your child according to his age and abilities. Toys that are too advanced for him will not only frustrate him, but may also hurt him. For a child under 1 year of age, toys should be large, simple, brightly colored or black and white, and lightweight. In addition, they should not have any small parts that the baby could remove. Household items such as plastic cups and bowls, wooden spoons, and pots and pans are fascinating to little ones. Other good choices are squeak toys with noisemakers molded in; sturdy, nonflammable rattles; washable dolls and stuffed animals with embroidered features; and teethers and other smooth items that can be chewed.

Additional toys that you might want to purchase include the following:

❏ *For a baby under 2 months old*
• A mobile that looks interesting from underneath, which is where the baby will be. Remove the mobile from the crib when the baby is able to pull it down.
• Pictures or decals to decorate the walls of his room.

❏ *For a baby 2 to 4 months old*
• A stainless steel mirror that can be placed about 6 inches from the baby's eyes.
• A cradle gym.

❏ *For a baby 4 to 6 months old*
• Rattles, squeak toys, and teethers.
• Cloth books with colorful pictures.
• Stuffed animals.

❏ *For a baby 6 to 8 months old*
• Balls.
• A box filled with simple objects that the baby can take out and put back.
• Stacking and nesting toys.

❏ *For a baby 8 to 12 months old*
• An activity box for the bathtub.
• Bath toys that pour or float.
• A box of interesting objects that are too large to be swallowed.

Black and White

Black and white designs on toys and walls stimulate the growth and development of the baby's brain. They provide the optimal contrast for the infant's visual development. According to Jeff Marin, PhD, clinical psychologist and neurological psychology specialist, "Looking at black and white designs helps the baby's brain to grow and even helps to increase his powers of concentration and memory. And, it has a soothing and comforting effect on the infant."[22]

Remember that a young baby does not need elaborate toys. Although toys can be useful in helping a baby to learn about his world, no toy is as fascinating to a child as his mother's face and voice. The time that you spend playing with your baby is more beneficial than any toy could ever be. Do not be swayed by advertising claims for expensive or complicated baby toys.

INFANT MASSAGE

Infant massage is another pleasurable way that you can interact with your baby. He needs your gentle touch, and massaging him produces many healthful benefits. It can help calm a crying or fussy baby, as well as relieve gas, reduce colic, improve circulation, stimulate the immune system, enhance neurological development, and tone the muscles. Massage can also promote parent-infant bonding and allow parents to synchronize their body rhythms with those of their baby.

You do not have to be an expert to perform massage on your infant, and it does not have to be complicated. It is a natural extension of the loving touch you give him every day. Many mothers naturally stroke their baby's arms and legs while the baby nurses. Or they rub the baby gently all over with lotion following a bath. Incorporating a daily massage into your routine of caring for your baby should be easy.

When performing massage, it is best to choose a quiet, relaxed location where you can be free from distractions and where the baby is comfortable. You will want the room to be warm so that you can remove the baby's clothing, including his diaper. (Use a waterproof pad under him.) For young babies, cover the infant with a blanket and expose only the area you are working on. The addition of soft music helps to create a calming, pleasurable atmosphere. Soft or dimmed lighting is preferable to bright lights. The use of an unscented, edible light vegetable or nut oil, such as almond, sunflower, or safflower, will reduce the friction between your hands and your baby's skin. Place a few drops of the oil on your hands and rub your palms together to warm the oil before applying it to the baby.

The quality of your touch should be gentle, yet firm. Your baby's smiles, coos, and wiggling will let you know that it feels good to him. Any crying, grimacing, or stiffening would signal that you are hurting him or that he is not enjoying it. Your hands should remain soft and relaxed as they move in a smooth, flowing manner over his body. Keep your movements slow and rhythmic. Avoid abrupt, jerky moves or lifting your hands from his body. Because your baby will not lie perfectly still, you should work with, not against, his movements. Never force an arm or leg to straighten out if it is bent tightly.

A good time for a full body massage is right before a bath. Your baby will already be undressed and in a warm environment. Any excess oil will wash off in the bath. A massage, followed by a warm bath, should ease him into naptime.

Make sure your nails are short and you are not wearing jewelry that could scratch your baby. Wait until he is about 1 month old before beginning the massage routines. Do not massage your baby if he is sick or received an injection within 48 hours. Wait at least 90 minutes after a feeding. It is not necessary to do a full body massage each time; you can just do specific areas. Downward strokes are soothing and calming, while upward strokes are stimulating.

Below is a sample routine for you to begin with. You will soon learn which strokes are the most enjoyable for you and your baby.

❏ *Chest and abdomen*

1. Place your baby on his back with his feet toward you.

2. Place your fingers in the center of the chest and gently stroke outward to the sides, following the ribs.

3. Using a clockwise motion (to relieve gas and improve the digestion), make circles around his belly with your fingers.

4. Gently stroke the sides of the torso.

5. Gently stroke down the torso.

Chest and Abdomen Massage

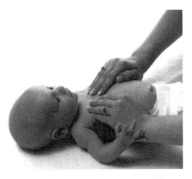

Place your fingers in the center of the chest and gently stroke outward to the sides, following the ribs.

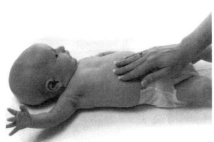

Use a clockwise motion to make circles around his belly with your fingers.

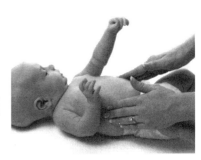

Gently stroke the sides of the torso.

❏ *Arms and hands*

1. With the baby on his back, gently stretch the arms out to the sides to form a cross. Use your thumbs to massage the palms and open the hands.

2. Support one hand and wrist with your hand, and gently stroke up the arm from the wrist to the shoulder.

3. Lightly knead the arm from the wrist to the shoulder.

4. Repeat steps 2 and 3 with the other arm.

Arm and Hand Massage

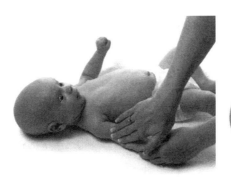

Gently stretch the arms out to the sides to form a cross.

Gently stroke up the arm from the wrist to the shoulder.

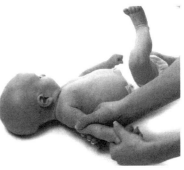

Gently knead the arm from the wrist to the shoulder.

Gently knead the leg, beginning with the fleshy part of the thigh and working down to the ankle.

Supporting the leg with one hand under the knee, stroke the leg from the ankle up the thigh and back down again.

Leg and Foot Massage

Gently smooth the palm of your other hand over the top of the foot to the toes.

Move your thumb in a circular motion on the bottom of the foot.

❏ *Legs and feet*

1. With the baby on his back, support one leg with both your hands. Gently knead the leg, beginning with the fleshy part of the thigh and working down to the ankle.

2. Supporting the leg with one hand under the knee, stroke the leg from the ankle up the thigh and back down again.

3. Move your supporting hand down to the ankle. Gently smooth the palm of your other hand over the top of the foot to the toes.

4. Repeat steps 1 through 3 with the other leg.

5. Move your thumbs in a circular motion on the bottom of both feet.

After 2 months of age, you can begin massaging the baby's back.

❏ *Back and buttocks*

1. Lay the baby on his stomach with his feet toward you, making sure that he can breathe easily. Use long stroking motions to distribute some oil on his back.

2. Use the fingertips of both hands near the spine and slowly move them outward to the sides, following the ribs. Start at the shoulders and move all the way down the back to the buttocks.

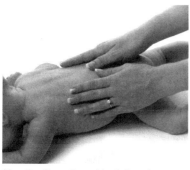

Use the fingertips of both hands near the spine and slowly move them outward to the sides, following the ribs.

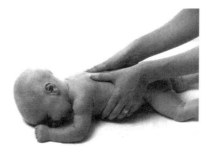

Cup your hands around his sides and use your thumbs to perform light massage from his shoulders to his buttocks.

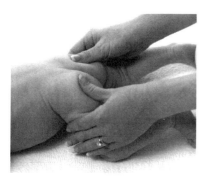

Gently knead the buttocks using a circular motion.

Repeat the long stroking motions, massaging from the shoulders to the toes and including the arms.

Back and Buttocks Massage

3. Cup your hands around his sides and use your thumbs to perform the same massage as in step 2.

4. Gently knead the buttocks using a circular motion.

5. Repeat the long stroking motions from step 1, massaging from the shoulders to the toes and including the arms.

6. As the massage ends, open your fingers and use a progressively lighter touch with each downward stroke.

For more detailed techniques, see *Infant Massage: A Handbook for Loving Parents* by Vimala Schneider McClure. Or, contact the International Association of Infant Massage at 800–248–5432. This group offers training programs for parents and can inform you about training in your area.

THE CHILDCARE DECISION

Sooner or later, you will have to face the situation of leaving your baby in someone else's care. You will feel most comfortable if, the first few times, you can leave him with a trusted relative or friend who is already familiar with him and his routines.

If you will be needing childcare on a regular basis, your best bet is to get references from other satisfied parents. You will need to decide whether you prefer care in your own home, in another home, or in a childcare center. Each type of care has its own advantages and disadvantages. For example, if having individual care or not exposing your baby to other children is your top priority, you should find a care provider who can come to your home. However, if leaving your baby with someone who is certified or has a license is most important, a licensed daycare center or a licensed family childcare home would be your best choice. Financial considerations may also influence your decision.

Most importantly, you need to meet with any potential childcare providers and observe their interaction with your baby. Try to find out their approaches to baby care, and make your views clear. Anyone you select should be willing to comply with your wishes, especially in areas such as holding your baby while he is being fed or not letting him cry alone in his crib. If you have any doubts about a certain person or facility, or you just "don't feel right" about it, do not leave your child there. Sometimes your gut feelings can provide the best indicators when making this important decision.

When you do leave your baby, be sure to provide explicit instructions for his care, along with plenty of breastmilk or formula, a familiar toy or blanket, extra diapers and clothes, and the phone numbers where you can be reached immediately.

CONCLUSION

Having a newborn is an exciting experience. Your new child will fill your life with discovery, amazement, and joy. Take the opportunity to marvel at each milestone and new adventure. Never again will this little person be changing and learning at such a rapid rate. Enjoy each moment, and invest the energy necessary to make sure that you are providing the best environment for his maximum emotional, mental, and physical development. Every daily interaction and each happy experience you share will help to establish a lifelong family bond.

Chapter Eleven

Infant Feeding
or Keeping Abreast

Both breastfeeding and bottlefeeding can produce babies that are physically and emotionally healthy, but there are differences. Breastfeeding is recognized as nutritionally superior by the American Academy of Pediatrics. This chapter presents the many advantages of breastfeeding and provides factual information on milk production and nursing techniques. It also discusses possible problems and their solutions.

A section on bottlefeeding offers helpful hints and suggestions for parents who choose this method of feeding. Mothers who return to work may combine the two methods.

BREASTFEEDING

Nursing is a natural continuation of the birth process because it completes the maternity cycle. Just as you nourished your baby prior to birth with nutrients from within your body, you continue to supply your baby with the food that is best suited to his needs—your breastmilk.

In addition to providing nutrients, breastfeeding also helps you foster a special relationship—a close physical and emotional bond with your baby. This relationship is unique in that your baby is totally dependent on you for his nourishment. This giving of yourself is an expression of your love for him, and it can result in many enjoyable and rewarding hours for both of you. Some of your fondest memories will be of the times spent nursing your baby.

Your success at breastfeeding will depend greatly on your desire to nurse, as well as on the encouragement you receive from those around you. Because of the importance of your husband's support, the decision to breastfeed should be a mutual one. His knowledge and understanding can provide you with a source of strength on those "trying" days when you might be tempted to give up. In addition, support from your caregiver, relatives, and friends is most helpful. Knowing a mother who successfully breastfed a child or who is a member of La Leche League can be extremely beneficial when you have questions. (For a complete discussion about this organization for nursing mothers, see "La Leche League" on page 266.)

Professional support can provide you with a higher level of expertise. Two types of counselors are available to answer your questions and to assist you if

More Than a Meal

Nursing is a symbiotic relationship between mother and baby. Both participants derive benefits, physically and emotionally, from the act of breastfeeding.

you have problems. A *certified lactation consultant* has completed a pre-scribed course and passed an exam to receive her certification. She is a spe-cialist in private practice and will charge a fee for her services, unless she is employed by your pediatrician or hospital. (For more information about lac-tation consultants, see "Certified Lactation Consultants" on page 267.)

Many women have been helped by counselors who volunteer their time and knowledge to promote breastfeeding and assist nursing mothers. A vol-unteer *breastfeeding counselor* has accumulated her knowledge through per-sonal experience, reading, and attending classes. She does not charge a fee. Counselors can provide phone consultations as well as instruction in group settings. They may be part of an organization such as La Leche League.

Several other important factors can help you have a successful breastfeed-ing experience. Understanding how breastmilk is produced and supplied to the baby, along with how to properly position your baby, will help to prevent most of the problems of nursing. Good personal care is another key element in successful nursing—nutritious food and adequate rest are mandatory. Plan for extra help around the house, especially if you have other children.

In 1997, the American Academy of Pediatrics updated its policy on breast-feeding to recommend that women breastfeed exclusively until the baby is 6 months old, when solids are introduced, and continue past the child's first birthday, for as long as is mutually desired. This expanded length for optimum nursing is in response to the increased knowledge about the health, nutrition-al, immunologic, developmental, psychological, social, economic, and envi-ronmental benefits of breastfeeding.

BENEFITS OF BREASTFEEDING

Researchers have documented the many advantages that breastfeeding offers to both mother and baby. First, and most important, breastmilk is the ideal food for an infant. Each species of mammal produces milk especially suited to the needs of its young. Human milk is biochemically suited to brain devel-opment, while animal milk promotes muscular development. Cow's milk was meant for baby cows. Most formulas are made from cow's milk. Formula companies often claim that their products are "most like mother's milk," but no formula can equal it. Many components of breastmilk—enzymes, living cells, hormones, and even vitamins—have been discovered over the years, but still other valuable constituents probably remain undetected.

Although cow's milk has a higher protein content, human milk has protein that is superior in quality and geared to the specific needs of the human infant. While a baby completely utilizes the protein in breastmilk, he excretes about half of the protein in cow's milk. Breastmilk promotes the growth of friendly bacteria in the baby's intestines. Additionally, the intestinal tract of a breast-fed baby is acidic, which is not conducive to the growth of harmful bacteria. The intestines of a formula-fed infant are alkaline, an environment in which many harmful bacteria thrive.

The amounts of fat in breastmilk and formula are similar, but breastmilk fat is more readily absorbed. To imitate mother's milk, formula companies replace the butterfat in cow's milk with mono- and polyunsaturated vegetable oils. However, this substitution also reduces the amount of cholesterol, which is necessary for several vital functions. Cholesterol aids in the absorption of nutrients and the development of the covering that surrounds and protects an infant's nerves. Breastmilk contains six times the amount of cholesterol that is present in formula. Some researchers believe that these high levels of cholesterol in infancy may protect babies from high levels later in life.[1]

Although low in content, the iron in human milk is in a form that is absorbed much more readily than the iron that is added to formula or given as a supplement. Formula-fed infants are at greater risk for iron deficiency anemia because only 4 percent of the iron in cow's milk is absorbed, as compared to 49 percent in mother's milk. Cow's milk can also cause minute bleeding in the intestines, which can further increase anemia. Full-term breastfed infants should not be supplemented with iron because it interferes with the iron binding ability of a special protein, lactoferrin. This protein binds the iron in the infant's intestinal tract and prevents harmful bacteria from multiplying, since the bacteria need iron to grow.

Human milk contains very small amounts of fat-soluble vitamin D, the "sunshine" vitamin that helps calcium to be metabolized and prevents rickets. A water-soluble vitamin D has also been isolated in breastmilk. Rickets is rarely observed in breastfed children if the mother is well nourished. A study in 1989 found that babies totally breastfed for the first 6 months showed no evidence of vitamin D deficiency.[2] A few minutes of sunshine a day on the baby's cheeks should ensure plenty of vitamin D. If the family lives in an area that does not receive much sunlight, it may be advisable for either the nursing mother or the child to take supplements of this vitamin.

During your baby's first weeks of life, your milk will undergo changes that will make it particularly suited for your baby's individual needs each day. It will begin as colostrum, a sticky yellowish fluid that contains immunity factors and has a high protein content. Your colostrum will also help rid your baby's body of mucus at birth and will cleanse his intestinal tract. The colostrum will gradually change to a thin white or bluish white liquid containing the exact combination of water, fat, protein, sugar, minerals, and vitamins that your baby needs, while continuing to provide immunities.

Breastmilk is raw and fresh. Formula is processed and must be stored and then reheated, all of which destroy important nutrients. Breastmilk is unprocessed and is fed to a baby when it is at its maximum nutritional value.

Breastmilk Has Unique Qualities

Breastmilk contains some amazing properties that cannot be duplicated or added to formula. These properties are perfectly devised to keep babies healthy and to protect them from disease. Because infants are born with immature immune systems, they are not equipped to fight off infection-causing bacteria and viruses. Breastmilk, however, provides the missing protective factors to combat foreign organisms. It is the *only* way your baby can receive this crucial protection.

During the first days of breastfeeding, a nursing baby receives protection through the high level of antibodies present in his mother's colostrum. Any immunities that the mother acquired over her lifetime are passed to her infant. Later, if the mother becomes ill, she builds up new antibodies, which are then also passed on to the baby. This is why breastfed babies rarely get colds, or may have just a mild case, even if everyone else in the family is sneezing and sniffling. In addition, breastfed infants have higher protective antibody responses to vaccinations than formula-fed infants. This protection is so great that some doctors have referred to breastmilk as "nature's vaccine."[3]

Breastmilk . . .

❑ Is the perfect food for human infants.

❑ Produces healthier babies.

❑ Is economical.

❑ Is always available and at the correct temperature.

❑ Promotes brain development and higher IQs.

❑ Protects against allergies.

❑ Offers emotional and physical benefits to the mother.

❑ Is easy to digest.

❑ Promotes good facial development.

❑ Produces bowel movements that do not stink!

Breastfeeding and Exercise

In a recent study, it was discovered that the level of immune proteins in breastmilk falls immediately after the mother exercises. The higher level is fully restored an hour later. To make sure your baby receives maximum immunity protection, nurse him *before* you exercise. [4]

Another protective factor comes from the mother's milk glands, which produce an immunity-inducing protein called secretory immunoglobulin A (IgA). This substance gives the baby protection against foreign molecules that might produce allergic reactions in him. It also gives him antibodies against the organisms that cause infant diarrhea and respiratory illness. Secretory IgA does not work by killing organisms, but by binding with them and preventing them from attaching themselves to the lining of the baby's intestines or respiratory tract, where they could multiply and cause disease. [5]

Even further protection results from living cells called leukocytes that are contained in breastmilk. These white cells attack foreign bacteria and destroy harmful disease-causing organisms. These cells are at their highest level right after birth and continue to be produced in sufficient quantities for up to 5 months. While these cells can survive freezing, they cannot survive heat. This is why stored breastmilk should never be heated to high temperatures or microwaved prior to use. Mother's milk also contains an antibacterial substance called lysozyme, which dissolves bacterial cell walls to destroy them. While this enzyme can be manufactured, it cannot be added to formula, since the sterilization process destroys it.

Another benefit of colostrum is that it provides a laxative effect to help rid the infant's intestinal tract of meconium. Meconium, the dark stool present in the bowel at birth, contains high levels of bilirubin. If the meconium is not excreted soon after birth, the bilirubin is reabsorbed into the bloodstream and can contribute to higher levels of jaundice in the newborn.

Breastmilk also helps protect babies against allergies. The intestines of a newborn are permeable and allow large molecules to pass through to the bloodstream. Allergies are the result of reactions to foreign molecules found in formula or foods. Colostrum contains epidermal growth factor, which coats the intestines and prevents the passage of large proteins into the bloodstream. Since breastmilk is not a foreign protein, an infant will not become allergic to it. Occasionally, if the mother drinks cow's milk, her infant may exhibit a reaction to the cow's milk proteins. Removing the cow's milk and all other dairy products from the mother's diet usually eliminates the fussiness in the baby. The longer an allergy-prone infant is breastfed, the better his chances are of reducing or eliminating the effects of allergies.

Breastmilk Is Better for Preterm Babies

Breastmilk is particularly important for the preterm infant's sensitive digestive system. Preterm babies have temporary deficiencies of certain enzymes and frequently suffer malabsorption problems. Breastmilk is perfectly suited to their special needs. Necrotizing enterocolitis, a severe and sometimes fatal bowel condition of preterm infants, is rarely found in babies that are fed breastmilk.

Because of the preterm baby's need to gain weight rapidly, his caloric intake must be higher than that of a term baby. Research has found that the milk from the mothers of preterm babies is higher in protein and fat than the breastmilk produced for full-term infants to meet this higher caloric demand.

A recent study comparing preterm infants fed breastmilk with preterm infants fed formula through a feeding tube showed that, 8 years later, the breastfed group had significantly higher IQs, even after adjusting for maternal education and social class. [6]

If your birth is preterm and your baby is too weak to suck, it is extremely important that you pump your breasts to give your baby the colostrum and mature milk that your body is producing for him. For the best results, use an electric breast pump to build and maintain your milk supply. This will take extra effort on your part, but it is well worth the benefits to your baby. Many hospitals rent electric pumps for this purpose.

While the baby is receiving milk via a feeding tube, it is recommended that he be allowed to suck to improve weight gain and to improve stomach emptying. Since a pacifier may impede his transition to the breast, authorities encourage mothers to nurse the baby while he is receiving the tube feeding.

Studies have shown that, contrary to popular medical belief, nursing from the breast is less stressful and easier for the preterm infant than sucking from a bottle.[7] Once the baby is able to suck, request that he be breastfed. Until you are able to feed the baby, cup feeding can be substituted for bottlefeeding. This takes lots of time and patience, but it is worth the effort.

Breastmilk Results In Better Health

Breastmilk contains antibodies that help prevent infection. Breastfed babies get fewer and milder colds than do bottlefed babies, and they have less eczema, ear infections, and diaper rash. In addition, a breastfed baby is less likely to be affected by allergies, either as a baby or later in life. No baby has ever been found to be allergic to his mother's milk. Occasionally, certain foods that you have eaten may cause a digestive upset, but eliminating those foods from your diet will usually solve the problem.

If you have a family history of allergies, it is especially important that you breastfeed your baby and delay introducing him to solid foods. Breastfeeding is the best way to prevent severe allergies in your child. You should continue giving your baby nothing but breastmilk for at least 6 months. As your baby gets older, his susceptibility to allergic reactions will diminish.

One of the most common causes of allergy in babies is cow's milk. Many parents switch their babies from one formula to another, hoping to find one— usually a soybean-based formula—that is agreeable. In the meantime, both baby and parents suffer.

On rare occasions, a baby is so allergic that he cannot tolerate any formula. In this case, breastmilk is crucial to the infant's survival. If his mother has not been nursing him, she must find another source of human milk until she can relactate and build up her own milk supply. Relactation is possible even for women who have not lactated for several months or who never nursed their babies. Indeed, some women have successfully nursed adopted babies, since the baby's sucking is what stimulates milk production.

Breastmilk Results In Better Digestion

A breastfed newborn's digestion is better than that of a bottlefed infant because breastmilk fosters the growth of "friendly" bacteria in the intestines. The presence of these bacteria results in fewer bowel upsets and less diarrhea. A baby's system utilizes breastmilk more completely than it does formula. Babies fed entirely on breastmilk rarely become constipated, whereas formula-fed babies occasionally do become constipated, resulting in painfully hard bowel movements.

Breastfed infants also receive a variety of flavors depending on the mother's diet and exercise. This may work to your advantage when you introduce solids to your baby, since he may try new foods more readily. Babies seem to like the taste of the milk, and may want to nurse more often, if their mothers have eaten garlic. Conversely, infants sometimes refuse to nurse after their mothers have exercised strenuously, possibly because exercise causes an increase in lactic acid, which makes milk taste sour. In this case, you will need to pump your breasts or feed your baby before you exercise. You may want to reduce the intensity of your exercise program.

Breastfeeding Produces Better Teeth

Breastfeeding promotes good facial development in babies. Babies suck differently when nursing from the breast than when sucking on a rubber nipple. Nursing results in superior facial muscle and jaw development. Bottlefeeding is considered to be a major cause of malocclusions and other facial and dental problems in children.[8]

Breastfeeding has also been associated with generally healthier teeth. In a study conducted at Oregon State University, children who were breastfed for 3 months or longer had 45 percent to 59 percent fewer cavities than their bottlefed counterparts in the same communities.[9]

Breastmilk Benefits the Skin

Breastfeeding encourages the close physical contact that is necessary for proper emotional development. Your new baby needs plenty of love and cuddling, and this is easily accomplished by nursing. A mother cannot "prop a breast" the way she can prop a bottle.

When you hold your baby, you will be struck by how soft his skin is. This softness will be enhanced by breastmilk. Some doctors even claim that they can tell the difference between bottlefed babies and breastfed babies by the feel of their skin.

Breastmilk Has Long-Term Benefits

Smarter Students

The journal *Pediatrics* recently published the results of a study that tracked 1,000 New Zealander children through age 18. This study confirmed what many experts had long suspected—children who were breastfed as infants, especially for a prolonged period, scored significantly higher on standardized achievement tests, including the SATs, many years later.[10]

Evidence exists that some of the benefits of breastfeeding remain with the infant throughout his lifetime. Breastfed babies have markedly lower incidences of ear infections, upper and lower respiratory tract infections, and gastrointestinal diseases, including diarrhea. Formula-fed infants have a higher risk of developing pneumonia, influenza, botulism, urinary tract infections, bacterial infections, and meningitis. They are also more likely to require hospitalization. Allergies occur at greater rates and are more severe in formula-fed infants.

Studies have shown that breastfed babies scored higher on mental development tests. Breastmilk contains very long chain fatty acids, which are necessary for proper brain growth. These fatty acids are not present in formula.[11]

A British study showed that ulcerative colitis in adults was 100 percent more common in patients who were not breastfed past 2 weeks of age than in those who were.[12]

In 1991, a New Zealand study linked formula feeding, the prone sleeping position, and maternal smoking to an increased risk of SIDS.[13] Another recent investigation linked formula feeding with the development of insulin-dependent diabetes in children.[14] Lymphomas are observed six times more often in children who were not breastfed for at least 6 months.[15]

Breastfeeding Is Better in Emergency Situations

During a major disaster such as a hurricane or earthquake, electricity and water are often cut off, and breastfeeding may be crucial to your baby's survival. In 1992, Hurricane Andrew devastated Florida and Louisiana, and Hurricane Iniki ravaged Hawaii. In some areas, power was not restored for several months, and the water supplies remained contaminated for weeks. Babies who were not breastfed were at serious risk during that time. In 1993, a young couple and their baby were stranded in a Nevada blizzard for 8 days. The parents survived by eating snow. Because the baby was breastfed, he remained healthy throughout the ordeal and survived in good condition. In situations such as these, nursing mothers can relax in the confidence that their babies will continue to receive the same plentiful and uncontaminated food supply.

Breastmilk Is Safer Than Formula

Formula may not always be safe. In 1978 and 1979, two soybean-based formulas, Neo-mull-soy and Cho-free, were found to contain insufficient amounts of an essential nutrient, chloride. At 8 and 9 years of age, children who had received these formulas as babies showed cognitive delays, language disorders, visual motor difficulties, fine motor difficulties, and attention deficit disorders.[16]

In 1992, it was reported that formula-fed infants were exposed to overdoses of vitamin D, which is toxic at high levels. Seven of the ten samples that were tested contained over 200 percent of the amount of vitamin D that was listed on the label.[17] Formula-fed infants may also be exposed to high levels of iodine (up to ten times the amount that is found in breastmilk), which may affect neonatal thyroid function.[18]

The FDA maintains a list of nutrients that are required components of all formulas. This list is updated infrequently, even though a new method may be discovered to synthesize a particular nutrient that has been missing from formulas. In 1996, the FDA discussed adding docosahexaenoic acid (DHA), an omega-3 fatty acid, to its required list. DHA is considered to be a major component of breastmilk and is a building block of brain tissue, yet it has not been required in formulas. In 1996, the director of the FDA's Office of Special Nutritionals, Elizabeth Yetley, stated that the FDA's list of required nutrients "is old and out of date."[19]

Contamination is another danger associated with formulas. As recently as 1993, a batch of Soy-a-lac formula was recalled because of salmonella contamination.

The method of preparation can also influence the safety of formula. In poverty-stricken areas, stretching formula to save money or providing low-cost substitutes such as tea or soft drinks results in the infant not receiving sufficient nutrients. A language barrier or the mother's inability to read may cause the infant to receive either too much or too little of the nutrients. Improper storage of prepared formula may result in bacterial contamination and illness. In areas where the water used for boiling contains lead, the infant is at increased risk for lead intoxication.

Additionally, using water from a contaminated water supply could have serious consequences. Unfortunately, it is not just in underdeveloped countries that this problem is encountered. Very recently, a number of American

*Price Fixing
of Formulas*

In 1996, a class action suit was settled against Bristol-Myers Squibb and Abbott Laboratories, the makers of Similac, Enfamil, Isomil, Prosobee, Nutramigen, Pregestimel, Alimentum, and Advance. Suits were filed in seventeen states alleging that these companies were guilty of fixing the prices of formulas from 1980 to 1992. While the companies did not admit to wrongdoing, they paid to settle the cases as a cost-saving measure, rather than going to court.

cities have found dangerous bacteria present in their water supplies. Each time, the residents were told not to drink the water until the source of the problem was pinpointed and eliminated. The real danger in these situations is to the babies who are given formula made with contaminated water *before* the contamination is discovered. No water supply can ever be assumed to be as safe as mother's milk!

Formula companies have changed their marketing strategies over the past few years. They now state that "breast is best" and provide breastfeeding discharge packs, publications, and videos to new mothers. While extolling the virtues of breastfeeding, these materials often imply that you will need a formula to supplement or to take over when you discontinue. In reality, if you continue to breastfeed your child throughout his first year of life, you will never need a formula. Every formula company says that its product is closest to mother's milk. Researchers have found that over 90 percent of mothers purchase the brand of formula that was provided in the discharge pack from the hospital.

None of the formula manufacturers benefit economically when you choose to breastfeed. The only economic advantages are to *you*, because you do not have to spend any money to feed your baby. Unfortunately, no company is willing to advertise the many benefits of breastmilk the way formula companies advertise formula.

Breastfeeding Has Benefits for Mothers

Advantages also exist for you, the nursing mother. Because breastmilk is available immediately, you can ease your baby's hunger without first having to warm a bottle. Breastfeeding is cheaper and easier than bottlefeeding because there is nothing to buy, measure, pour, heat, or sterilize. Your baby's sucking is beneficial to you because it stimulates your uterus to contract and to return to its prepregnant size sooner. In addition, since you burn more calories while nursing, it will be easier for you to lose weight without dieting and to regain your shape sooner. The extra fat that was deposited during pregnancy will be utilized during the early months of lactation.

Some evidence shows that breastfeeding decreases your chances of developing certain cancers. Studies have shown that a woman's risk of getting breast cancer is proportionately reduced by the length of time she breastfeeds. This means that the longer you nurse, the better protection you have.[20] A decrease in cervical[21] and ovarian[22] cancer has also been linked to breastfeeding.

Traveling is easier with a breastfed baby because you will not have to pack any supplies or warm any bottles. Nursing mothers have found that taking their babies along is easily accomplished by just grabbing an extra diaper or two. Outings are more relaxed because you do not have to rush home for feedings or worry if the formula is becoming sour without refrigeration. If you wear a blouse or sweater that you can pull up from the waist, you will be able to discreetly nurse your baby almost anywhere. Practice nursing in front of a mirror to become comfortable.

The emotional advantages of breastfeeding include more intimate contact between you and your baby, and the feeling of satisfaction and sense of fulfillment that you experience while nursing. In addition, the hormone prolactin, which causes the secretion of milk, helps you to feel motherly. It also has a soothing and tranquilizing effect, and thus causes you to feel calm and relaxed each time your baby nurses. Breastfeeding may also help you to cope

If you wear the right top, you will be able to discreetly nurse your baby anywhere.

in stressful situations. A recent study found that the release of stress hormones was suppressed in lactating women.[23]

Because you must sit or lie down to nurse, you are forced to get the rest that you need postpartum.

Nursing delays the return of the menstrual period because prolactin suppresses ovulation. Breastfeeding, therefore, is an aid to spacing children. However, you should use another method of contraception along with breastfeeding if you do not want another child right away because nursing is not 100-percent effective at birth control. The amount of breastfeeding necessary to suppress ovulation varies from woman to woman. In addition, you might ovulate prior to menstruating again and thus become pregnant without ever having a period. If your baby receives supplemental formula, begins eating solid foods, or regularly sleeps through the night, his less frequent nursings may cause a decrease in your production of prolactin.

For the Father: Breastfeeding Has Benefits for You

Your encouragement is crucial to your wife's success at breastfeeding. If you understand the benefits of nursing, you will be able to respond to comments and suggestions from friends and relatives that might discourage her or sabotage her efforts to nurse. Breastfeeding will help your child to achieve his full potential mentally, physically, and emotionally. Support and encourage your wife in providing these benefits to him.

You will discover that advantages also exist for you, the father of a breast-fed baby. For example, those middle-of-the-night feedings will not disrupt your sleep. Your wife will probably awaken as soon as the baby does, often before he even cries. (The two of them will seem to be on the same wavelength. You may often wonder which one of them wakes up first.) These nighttime feedings are easiest if the baby is simply tucked into bed with the two of you, allowing your wife to drift back to sleep while he nurses. In the early weeks, you can help out by getting up, changing the baby, and bringing him to his mother. Chances are, the closeness and body warmth will encourage him to fall asleep more quickly also. *Caution:* Do not bring your baby into bed with you if you sleep in a waterbed. He could suffocate in the soft mattress or against the frame if he rolled over.

Another benefit that you will certainly notice is that breastfed babies smell good. They do not have that sour milk smell that formula-fed babies often have, even when they spit up. Their stools do not have an offensive odor, so you will find that changing diapers is not as bad as you expected.

You will also appreciate the economic advantages of breastfeeding. Bottles, formula, and baby food cost money; breastmilk does not. The price of formula rose 150 percent from 1979 to 1990. Some couples have calculated that they saved enough in 6 months of breastfeeding to purchase a major appliance. You will also save money by having fewer doctor bills, since breastfed babies are healthier.

You should not feel left out or unimportant because you are unable to feed your baby. Feeding is just one part of his care. There are many other ways in which you can show your love—by bathing him, holding and cuddling him, rocking him, singing to him, taking him for walks in his stroller, and even changing his diapers. And you can have the satisfaction of knowing that, when it comes to milk, he is getting the "real thing."

An Added Bonus

Women who breastfeed have improved bone remineralization, which results in fewer hip fractures in the postmenopausal years.

MILK PRODUCTION

Within the breasts are grapelike clusters called alveoli in which milk is produced under the influence of the hormone prolactin. (See Figure 11.1.) The milk travels from these alveoli through lactiferous ducts until it reaches the fifteen to twenty lactiferous sinuses, in which it is stored. These sinuses are located under the areola, the darkened area around the nipple. The raised bumps on the areola that become prominent during pregnancy are called the Montgomery glands. They secrete a fluid that lubricates and prevents bacterial growth on the nipple and areola.

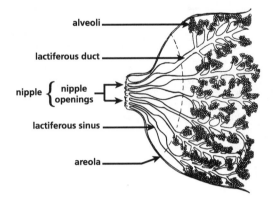

Figure 11.1.
Cross section of lactating breast.

Each nipple contains fifteen to twenty tiny openings—one from each sinus—through which the milk flows. Stimulation of the nipple by sucking, or even touching, causes the nipple to become more erect, which makes it easier for the infant to grasp. Sucking or touching also causes oxytocin to be released into the bloodstream. The oxytocin causes the alveoli to contract, which pushes the milk into the ducts and sinuses to make it available for your baby. This process is known as the milk ejection reflex or let-down reflex, and it occurs shortly after your baby begins each nursing. Most women experience a sort of tingling in their breasts during a let-down, along with a surge of milk from each breast, sometimes strong enough to cause a spray to shoot out as far as 12 inches. Occasionally, just hearing your baby cry or even thinking about him can cause a let-down. This let-down reflex can be inhibited by emotional upset, fatigue, or tension. Mothers having difficulty can condition the let-down by developing a nursing routine and using relaxation techniques.

Supply and Demand

Your milk supply is determined by the amount of milk your baby requires. The more he nurses, the more milk you will produce. This is why mothers are able to nurse twins. To establish an adequate supply, you should let the baby nurse whenever he is hungry and avoid the use of pacifiers and supplements (water, formula, or solid food), which would decrease the time the infant nurses at the breast. Encourage your baby to nurse every 2 to 3 hours (eight to twelve times a day). Wait until your baby is skilled at nursing and your milk supply is well established before introducing a pacifier or an occasional supplemental feeding. Otherwise, you might disturb this perfect demand-supply relationship that nature has devised and thus diminish your milk supply.

You will find that allowing your baby to set his own schedule will benefit both of you—the baby will be more content, and you will avoid both breast engorgement and an inadequate milk supply. As your baby grows, his body will require more milk. When he experiences growth spurts, he will want to spend more time at the breast to increase your milk supply. Do not misinterpret these increased feedings as a signal that your milk has "dried up." The initial fullness that is experienced, as a result of an increase in blood flow and tissue fluid, usually subsides by 6 weeks. If you allow your baby to nurse on demand, after 1 to 2 days of these more frequent feedings, your milk supply will increase and he will return to his normal schedule. The most common times for these growth spurts are between 10 and 14 days, between 4 and 6 weeks, at 3 months, and at around 6 months.

The majority of mothers can develop an adequate milk supply for nursing. Nursing is not possible in cases of complete mastectomy or breast surgery in which the milk ducts were severed. Certain other medical conditions can also affect the mother's ability to produce sufficient milk. (For a complete discussion of this problem, see "Inadequate Milk Supply" on page 260.) Women who have had breast augmentation may want to talk to a certified lactation consultant if problems arise. The size of the breasts has no effect on milk production. Size is determined by the amount of fatty tissue. Inability to produce milk is more often the result of cultural conditioning, such as negative myths and discouraging social influences.

Even if you become ill, such as with a cold or flu, you should continue to nurse. Your baby will receive the antibodies that you are producing to fight the illness and will probably not get sick. If he does become ill, he will have a very mild case. If you need to be hospitalized, use an electric pump to maintain your supply or arrange to have the baby brought to you for feedings.

You will feel better if you maintain a nutritious diet while nursing. Although it was previously believed that an extra 500 calories were needed while breastfeeding, recent studies indicate that this estimate is too high. The same principles of good nutrition apply to you as to the rest of the family. You do not need to follow any special or complex diets, although you may be thirstier than before. You should drink sufficient liquids to quench your thirst, but you do not need to drink milk to make milk. If you do not like milk, drink water and fruit juices, and eat foods such as cheese and yogurt to get your calcium. To avoid missing a meal, fix yourself a snack and a drink while your baby is napping. Then, when he wakes up wanting to nurse, grab your snack, and the two of you can relax and enjoy mealtime together. Having one hand free makes it easy!

Be careful to avoid exhaustion, especially during the first few weeks, by getting plenty of rest and relaxation. Do only those household chores that are absolutely essential—fixing simple meals, and doing laundry and light housekeeping. A spotless house is not necessary. Take care only of what bothers you the most, such as the dirty dishes and rumpled beds. Remember that your house will still be standing years from now, whereas your baby will be an infant for only a very short time.

Ideally, during the early weeks, you will have help from your husband, mother, mother-in-law, or a paid employee so that you can devote your time to your new baby. If you do not have help, you will need to use your time wisely. When your baby goes to sleep in the afternoon, you, too, should use that time for napping, rather than running around cleaning house. Your milk supply and your disposition will benefit.

HELPFUL HINTS FOR BREASTFEEDING

Women have been breastfeeding successfully for centuries. You can use the experiences of others to help make breastfeeding go more smoothly for you. This section offers some suggestions to make your experience easier.

During Pregnancy

One of your most important preparations is to choose your pediatrician carefully. Meet with him well before your due date to discuss your feelings and his ideas about breastfeeding. Ask him what percentage of his newborn patients are breastfed, how he treats jaundice, and if he refers women with breastfeeding problems to a certified lactation consultant. The early months with your baby will be much easier if you and your pediatrician agree on the use of supplements, the introduction of solid foods, and weaning. If you see eye to eye concerning rooming-in and "nothing but the breast" while in the hospital, have him write it on your record.

The use of nipple preparation to prevent sore nipples has varied over the years. It is now known that sore nipples are the result of improper positioning of the baby on the breast, not of inadequate nipple preparation. What you *can* do during pregnancy is to check to make sure that your nipples are not inverted. (For instructions, see "Flat or Inverted Nipples" on page 262.) If they are inverted, contact a breastfeeding counselor or certified lactation consultant for assistance. Otherwise, you can massage your breasts, or apply a lubricant or skin cream to your nipples, but it is not necessary. Avoid nipple stimulation if you have a history of preterm labor. Do not use soap or alcohol on them, as these tend to dry out the nipples. Washing with plain water will keep them clean. "Toughening" the nipples with a towel is no longer recommended.

Read about breastfeeding. Buy a book and take it to the hospital or birth center with you. Several good books are described in the "Recommended Reading List" on page 307.

Begin attending La Leche League meetings early in your pregnancy. You will get excellent advice on both breastfeeding and mothering. The advice on "getting started" will be invaluable once your baby comes. See a certified lactation consultant for classes or a personal visit. These consultants are available through most hospitals or on an independent basis. They are specially trained to detect breastfeeding problems and to help new mothers find solutions to breastfeeding difficulties. If you establish this support system of breastfeeding experts *before* you deliver, it will be much easier to get help if breastfeeding problems or questions come up later.

In the Hospital or Birth Center

Nurse your baby as soon as you can after delivery. The earlier you begin breastfeeding, the easier it will be for you and your baby. If the baby is born after an unmedicated labor, he will probably be eager to breastfeed, and the sooner he begins, the better he will nurse. His sucking reflex will be the

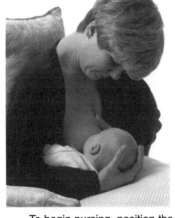

To begin nursing, position the baby with his tummy against you and cup your breast with your fingers in a *C* position . . .

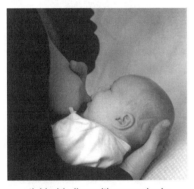

. . . tickle his lips with your nipple . . .

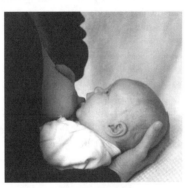

. . . wait until he opens his mouth wide, his tongue down . . .

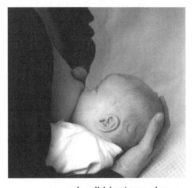

. . . and pull him toward you.

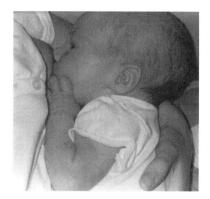

The tip of the baby's nose should touch your breast, and his lips should flare outward.

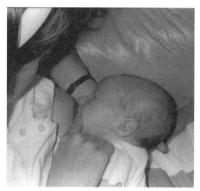

To remove the baby from your breast, place your finger in the corner of his mouth to break the suction.

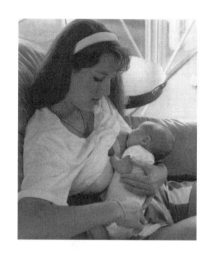

Cradle position.

strongest in the first hours after delivery. The longer you delay, the more difficult it will become. If the light in the birthing room is very bright, shield your baby's eyes or ask that it be dimmed.

Nursing will get off to its best start if you room-in with the baby day and night. You can nurse your baby when he is hungry and become familiar with his awake and sleep pattern. If you do send the baby to the nursery for any reason, place a note on the crib that states, "No bottles or pacifiers, please." Nursing on demand uses a baby's natural cues that he is ready to nurse and stimulates the milk to come in.

Some babies are very sleepy the first 1 to 2 days. Watch for your baby's quiet alert times and encourage him to nurse every 2 hours when he is awake. During the day, if he sleeps over 3 hours, you may want to try to wake him up so that his longer deep sleep will occur at night. Nursings are timed from the start of the feeding. Your baby should nurse eight to twelve times in a 24-hour period. Between the second and third day, these sleepy babies often become more alert and may want to nurse very frequently. Allow him to nurse, since his sucking will stimulate your mature milk to come in. Occasionally, a mother will give a bottle at these times because her "milk is not in and the baby is hungry," but this is counterproductive. Remember, breastfeeding is supply and demand. His demand builds your supply.

Proper positioning of your baby is very important. To nurse your baby in the cradle position, place his head in the bend of your arm, using a pillow under your arm and the baby to help raise his mouth up to your nipple. You can tuck his lower arm under your arm. With the baby facing you, tummy to tummy, cup your breast with your fingers in a *C* position, making sure that your fingers do not cover the areola. Tickle the baby's lips with your nipple, wait until he opens his mouth wide with his tongue down and extended over the bottom gum, and then pull him toward you. The nipple should be centered in the baby's mouth, with his jaw positioned behind the nipple and on the areola. The tip of his nose should touch the breast, and his lips should flare outward. If you are concerned that he cannot breathe, draw his bottom in closer or slightly lift the breast with your hand. Avoid pressing down on the breast as this may cause his jaw to slide down closer to the tip of the nipple. The baby should nurse in bursts of sucking, swallowing, and pausing. The sucking

The proper tongue position for latching-on is the mouth opened wide with the tongue down and extended over the bottom gum.

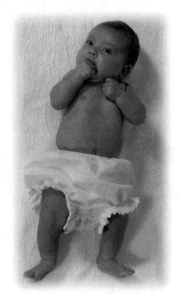

Sucking on the fist means this baby is ready to breastfeed.

Breastfeeding and Labor Medication

Narcotics given during labor may affect the infant's ability to initiate breastfeeding. An interesting study produced an amazing video of unmedicated infants who were placed on their mothers' abdomens immediately after birth. These newborns "crawled" up to the breast and latched on correctly, unaided. Infants from medicated births did not exhibit this behavior.

should not be painful for you. If it is, gently place your finger into the corner of the baby's mouth to release the suction, then try again. Do not allow the baby to slowly draw the nipple into his mouth because he will simply chew on the tip of the nipple and cause soreness. Also, make sure that your baby faces you and does not need to turn his head to the side to feed.

To nurse using the clutch position or football hold, place your baby's body next to your side and support his head with your hand. Use pillows as necessary. This position is very comfortable for large-breasted women and for mothers who delivered by cesarean section. In addition, large-breasted women may want to fold a diaper or hand towel, and place it under the breast for support. Some mothers prefer side-lying, especially for nighttime feedings.

Look for cues that your baby is ready to nurse. As he wakes up, he will stretch and squirm. Do not wait for him to begin crying. Look for him to make sucking motions or to move his hand to his mouth. If you wait until he screams, you will have to settle him down before nursing him.

Avoid supplements with the bottle. The extra liquid would fill him up and decrease his interest in nursing. Occasionally, you may be advised to let the baby spend the night in the nursery and be given a bottle by the nurse to allow you a night of rest. You may be told that it will not matter because "your milk is not in yet." While this may sound like a good idea, offering a bottle can cause nipple confusion. Since babies suck differently on the breast than on a rubber nipple, he might become confused and refuse the breast. Also, your baby does receive your rich colostrum; and the more he nurses, the sooner your mature milk will come in. Pacifiers can also cause nipple confusion. If the baby wants to suck, he should nurse at the breast to stimulate your milk production.

Do not use soap, oil, lotion, or a drying agent such as alcohol on your nipples. You will not need to wash them before each feeding, since they will secrete a substance that will keep them clean. If you are requested to wash your nipples while in the hospital, you can use water.

Do not try to prevent nipple soreness by restricting the length of the nursings. Nipple soreness is caused by improper positioning of the baby's mouth on the breast. Let the baby nurse for 10 to 15 minutes on the first breast, then switch him to the other breast and let him nurse until he is finished, about 5 to 20 minutes more. If he continues to act hungry, allow him to nurse on the first breast again.

Alternate the breast that you offer your baby first at each feeding because his initial sucking will be the strongest. By alternating the starting breast, you will ensure that an adequate supply of milk is built up in both breasts. To remind yourself which breast to offer first the next time, attach a safety pin to your bra on that side.

Do not use nipple shields for sore breasts. They inhibit adequate stimulation of the breasts and thus interfere with milk production. Their use creates more problems than it solves.

Do not be discouraged if you and your baby have trouble getting started with breastfeeding. He will be learning how to coordinate sucking and swallowing, and will create the stimulus for increasing your milk supply. If your hospital has a certified lactation consultant on staff, ask her to observe a feeding so you can be sure you are using proper technique. Remember, breastfeeding is new for both of you. Have patience. Before long, you both will be pros.

At Home

Give yourself about 6 weeks to establish a good nursing relationship. These first weeks may seem hectic and difficult, but any newborn, breastfed or not, is demanding. Just imagine having to wash bottles and prepare formula besides! After about 6 weeks, your life will calm down a bit as you and your baby adjust to each other.

Continue attending La Leche League meetings or seeking the counsel of a certified lactation consultant. Encouragement and support from other nursing mothers or professionals can be a lifesaver for you, particularly when problems arise.

Feed your baby whenever he is hungry. Because breastmilk is more easily digested than formula, breastfed babies need to eat more often, sometimes every 2 hours. Also, when many babies experience a growth spurt—usually at around 10 to 14 days, 4 to 6 weeks, 3 months, and 6 months—they want to nurse all day. By giving your baby extra nursings, you ensure that your milk supply will respond to his increased need. When the supply has built up sufficiently, the baby will cut back to his regular number of nursings.

Even though your breasts will be somewhat engorged at first, your milk supply will even out after a few weeks and your breasts will return to a more normal size. Do not confuse this with "losing your milk." You will still have plenty of milk for your baby.

Some babies have greater sucking needs than others. You can easily soothe your baby by putting him to the breast. Even if his need is not so much hunger as to be held close and to be comforted by the breast, it is still important. You will not be spoiling him by nursing him, but will simply be meeting his needs. It will be crucial to his security that you meet his needs as soon as possible. As New York Medical College professor Dr. Herbert Ratner says, "The quickest way to make your child independent is to take care of his needs when he is dependent."[24]

In the early weeks, your baby may have five or more bowel movements a day, sometimes as often as after every nursing. After 6 weeks of age, he may have a bowel movement as infrequently as once every 5 days. He may even switch from one routine to the other. You will soon know what is "normal" for your baby and will be able to recognize variations. The stools of a totally breastfed baby are yellow in color, and mushy or loose. These loose stools do not indicate diarrhea unless they are also green in color, contain mucus, or have a strong unpleasant odor.

You can be sure that you are producing enough milk if your baby has six or more wet diapers a day, along with two bowel movements per day, and is receiving only breastmilk. He will not need formula supplements or water. He will get plenty of water in your milk (breastmilk is 87.5 percent water), along with important nutrients, so do not fill him up on just plain water. In fact, researchers have found that giving a baby too much water could actually be dangerous. Oral water intoxication can occur when so much water has been ingested that the sodium in the blood becomes diluted. When this happens, the body cannot function properly. An altered mental state, abnormally low body temperature, bloating, or even seizures could result. Babies less than 1 month old are especially susceptible. While an infant *may* require more fluid in hot weather, encouraging him to nurse more frequently will ensure an adequate intake.

A Hungry Baby

The following are cues that your baby is ready to nurse:

❏ Sucking on his hands or fingers.

❏ Being in a quiet alert state.

❏ Making sucking motions with his mouth.

❏ Exhibiting the rooting reflex.

❏ Starting to fuss.

Watch your baby to learn what particular cues he tends to display.

Babies are individuals and gain weight at different rates. If your baby gains weight slower than "average," do not be alarmed. He is fine as long as he is happy and alert, and is feeding an average of eight to twelve times a day. Make sure your baby empties one breast before switching to the other to complete the feeding. Two kinds of milk are produced—the thinner *foremilk* and the more fatty *hindmilk*. Allowing him to empty one side will provide the proper balance of both kinds of milk and will encourage weight gain. Occasionally, a baby will nurse from only one breast at a feeding, but may nurse more frequently. If his weight gain is less than 4 ounces a week, however, you need to talk to a certified lactation consultant.

If your baby gains weight more rapidly than the average, he is probably fine also. You will not need to take any drastic action. An average weight is the median of all weights, from low to high. Even if your baby appears "fat," if his only food is breastmilk, you will not need to worry. He will be receiving the perfect food, containing no empty calories. This fat will not remain with him throughout life. Your breastfed baby will not need a reducing diet. Continue nursing him as usual, and he will slim down as soon as he begins actively moving around.

Many women appreciate the support of a good nursing bra. Choose one in a cotton fabric and avoid underwires because they can cause plugged ducts. (For other hints, see "How to Select a Nursing Bra" on page 118.) You should begin wearing a nursing bra in the hospital. During the early weeks, you may be most comfortable wearing one 24 hours a day—even to sleep in.

If you have a problem with leaking, place nursing pads or folded cotton handkerchiefs inside your bra. Do not use plastic pads or liners because they tend to keep the nipples wet. After each feeding, leave your flaps down for a few minutes to allow your nipples to thoroughly dry.

You will find that a comfortable chair, preferably a rocker, is mandatory. At times, you may want to breastfeed lying down. You can lie on your side with your baby next to you and snooze while he does.

Breastfeeding is convenient, since it leaves one hand free to do other things. You can keep a book, magazine, or paper and pen by your chair and catch up on your reading or correspondence. How about your thank-you notes for all the baby and shower gifts you received? If you are a list maker, this provides a perfect opportunity. You can make grocery lists, "things to do" lists, or Christmas lists. (It is never too early to start.)

If you have other children, nursing is a perfect time for reading to them, talking with them, or just being close. However, you should not feel that you always have to accomplish something while nursing. You might prefer to just enjoy this quiet time with your baby by cuddling, talking to him, or singing to him.

If you have an older child, nursing is the perfect time for reading a story, talking, or just being close.

Avoiding Harmful Substances

Check with your caregiver or certified lactation consultant before you take any medication or drug, even an over-the-counter drug. Some of them do show up in breastmilk and may affect your baby. Many medications can be safely used while nursing. If you are prescribed a drug that is contraindicated with nursing, your pediatrician or lactation consultant may be able to suggest an alternative. Do not take stimulant laxatives. These can upset your baby's system.

The National Institutes of Health recommend that you refrain from drinking alcohol during lactation because its effects on nursing babies are not known. Any alcohol that you consume will be readily transmitted to your baby in much the same concentration as is in your blood. While an infrequent social drink may have a mildly sedative effect on your newborn, it will probably not be harmful. The level of alcohol in milk is usually highest within the first 2 hours after drinking and gradually diminishes over the next hours. If you consume several drinks in an evening, it may be wise to avoid nursing until the next morning. Also, if you are intoxicated, you are in no condition to safely care for your baby. In addition, heavy alcohol consumption inhibits the flow of milk.

If you smoke over a pack of cigarettes a day, your baby may experience nausea, vomiting, abdominal cramps, and diarrhea. The level of vitamin C in your milk will also be reduced as your own stores are diminished.[25] Women who smoke produce less milk, and the milk they produce has a lower fat content.[26] Secondhand smoke is even more dangerous for babies. Children raised in smoking households experience more upper respiratory infections, pneumonia, bronchitis, and SIDS during their first year of life.[27] If anyone in your home smokes, insist that he or she do it outside and not in the presence of the baby.

Illegal recreational drugs are very dangerous. They impair a mother's ability to adequately care for her baby, and they pass into her breastmilk. Cocaine used by a nursing mother remains in her breastmilk for up to 36 hours and can be ingested by her infant. Children have become seriously ill and have even died as a result of cocaine use by a breastfeeding mother.[28]

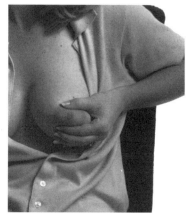

Hand-expressing milk.

Pumping and Storing Breastmilk

You will want to learn how to use a breast pump or how to hand-express your milk for future use. This milk can then be given to your baby when you are not available to nurse him. To hand-express milk, gently squeeze the outer edge of the areola using your thumb and forefinger. Some women find this works very well, while others have a difficult time and get only a drop or two. You may be more successful if you try it while your baby is nursing on your other breast.

Using a breast pump is often more effective than hand expression, but it, too, requires practice and patience. Placing a warm moist towel on the breasts for 10 minutes and then massaging them for 3 to 4 minutes just prior to using the pump can help stimulate the flow of milk. Many types of pumps are available, from hand pumps to electric ones. Follow the directions for whichever pump you use. For any pump, moisten your breast before applying the breast shield to improve the suction. Begin slowly, or on the lowest setting, to avoid discomfort. Pumping in a quiet, relaxed setting usually helps to get your milk flowing.

If you use a single pump, pump for 5 to 7 minutes on each breast, followed by an additional 3 to 5 minutes on each breast, for a total of 15 to 20 minutes. If you use a double pump, the total time should be 10 to 15 minutes. Electric and battery-operated pumps are usually the most efficient. See a breastfeeding counselor or certified lactation consultant if you want to buy or rent a breast pump. She can provide you with a good quality pump that will meet your needs.

Using a breast pump.

A Hint for the New Mother

❏ Store fresh breastmilk in plastic to maintain its protective properties.

Always make sure that your hands and the container you use for collecting the milk are clean. A good option for storage is specially designed milk storage bags. These durable bags are self-sealing and presterilized. Another option is bottle liners, although they are less durable and require the use of twist ties or clips for closing. You can double them to avoid tearing. Plastic is preferable to glass for milk storage because the leukocytes (white cells) in breastmilk adhere to glass. Milk stored in glass would therefore lose protective properties. If the milk is to be frozen, glass and plastic are equally acceptable because freezing destroys the leukocytes anyway.

Amazingly, breastmilk has properties that protect it from bacterial contamination. It can, therefore, be left out at room temperature for up to 10 hours.[29] Or, it can be refrigerated immediately and kept for up to 5 days. If you freeze the milk, it can be kept for 2 weeks in a freezer compartment located inside a refrigerator; 3 months, if stored in a separate freezer unit of a refrigerator; or 6 months, if in a separate deep freeze with a temperature of 0°F.[30] Place the container in the back of the freezer, away from the door.

It is most convenient to store milk in 2- to 4-ounce portions. Small quantities thaw and warm quickly, and there will be less waste if the baby does not take it all. Also, because babies utilize breastmilk so completely, less breastmilk is needed at a feeding than if the baby were taking formula.

To defrost frozen milk, simply run it under cold water until it gets mushy. Then use warmer water to take the chill off. Do not thaw in the microwave. Microwaving not only produces hot spots that can burn the baby, it also destroys the antibodies. Once milk is thawed, it cannot be refrozen, but it can be safely returned to the refrigerator for up to 9 hours.

Some mothers are concerned about the appearance of their milk when they see it in a container. It may separate into milk and cream because it is not homogenized the way cow's milk is. If this happens, shake the milk gently to mix before a feeding. Also, it is normal for human milk to be either bluish, yellowish, or even brownish in color. Frozen milk may turn yellow, but this does not mean it is spoiled unless it smells sour.

You will probably find that you will not want to go out very often without your baby. You will need him almost as much as he will need you. Breastfed babies are very portable and can be taken anywhere. However, you might want to keep some frozen milk on hand in case of an emergency or a situation in which you need to be away from your baby during a feeding.

Setting Priorities

Turn a deaf ear to criticism concerning breastfeeding or your method of caring for your baby. Your baby's happiness and comfort will be of the utmost importance—not your neighbor's (or your mother-in-law's) opinion. Remember, this baby will be your child to raise in the manner that you feel is most comfortable. Read and become knowledgeable, then decide what works best for you.

Do not forget to keep your priorities straight. Baby's happiness and your rest will be tops right now!

BREASTFEEDING PROBLEMS

Sometimes problems arise in connection with nursing, but you will be able to easily remedy them if you are properly prepared.

Nipple Soreness

Sore nipples are usually the result of improper positioning of the baby on your breast. It is crucial that he take the entire nipple into his mouth, along with a good portion of the areola—at least 1 inch of it—so that he does not "chew" on the end of your nipple. (See Figure 11.2.) In most cases, sore, cracked, or bleeding nipples can be remedied by adjusting the way the baby is positioned and latches onto the breast. A little tenderness is normal when you begin breastfeeding. Sore, cracked nipples are not. If you experience this, get help right away from a breastfeeding counselor or certified lactation consultant.

Frequent nursing can help reduce sore nipples. By nursing often, you will keep your baby from becoming so hungry that he latches on too strongly. Also, if you snuggle your baby up close to your breast, you will avoid unnecessary tugging.

Try not to let your breasts become engorged. The fullness may make it difficult for your baby to get hold of the breast, causing him to bite down on the nipple. If the breasts seem engorged, hand-express some of the milk before your baby nurses.

Even if your nipples become sore or cracked, continue nursing. Any blood swallowed by your baby will not hurt him. After feeding, express some of your milk and apply it to the nipples. Warm water compresses may also be soothing. Do not use soap or drying agents on your breasts because they wash away the natural protection. Expose your breasts to air and sunshine, or use a blow dryer on the warm setting, to help the nipples heal. Placing ice chips in a washcloth on your nipples prior to feeding may numb them.

Remember that nipple soreness is a temporary condition. With good care and perseverance, you can help your nipples heal in a very short time. However, if the pain becomes worse or lasts beyond the first week, it may be the result of other causes. Make sure your baby is well propped and remains at the level of the breast throughout the entire feeding. The weight of his head may cause your arm to drop and slide his jaw closer to the nipple during the feeding. Use a variety of nursing positions that will allow his jaws to apply pressure to different areas of the areola. Do not allow wet nursing pads to remain on your nipples for long periods. Never use plastic liners. If a pad is stuck, wet it with warm water to loosen it before removing.

Persistent sore nipples or nipples that become sore after weeks of comfortable nursing may be caused by thrush, a harmless yeast infection that the baby may have acquired as he traveled down the birth canal. This is then transmitted to the mother's nipples during nursing. Thrush may appear as white patches on your nipples and in the baby's mouth, or as a diaper rash. It is most important that both mother and baby be treated to eliminate this cause of nipple soreness.

Your sore nipples may be baby related. If the baby's tongue is not extended over the bottom jaw, he will be unable to latch on effectively. A baby who is tongue-tied (has a short frenulum, the attachment under the tongue) may be unable to latch on effectively. Some doctors will clip a short frenulum if it interferes with nursing. Babies may become confused by sucking on a rubber nipple and may have difficulty switching back and forth between the breast and rubber nipple. If you are unable to identify and remedy the cause of painful nipples, do not hesitate to use the services of a certified lactation consultant.

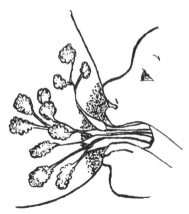

Figure 11.2.
The proper positioning of the baby's mouth on the breast.

To avoid nipple soreness, make sure the baby's mouth is positioned correctly.

Inadequate Milk Supply

An inadequate milk supply can result from a rigid or infrequent feeding schedule, the use of supplements, or stress. The early introduction of supplements can result in a vicious cycle—the more supplements you give, the less milk you produce, the more supplements you need to give, and the further your milk supply diminishes.

The signs in a baby of an inadequate milk supply include low weight gain, few wet diapers, dark concentrated urine when a diaper is wet, and unhappiness. If your baby develops these symptoms, call your pediatrician immediately. If the baby is severely dehydrated, he may require hospitalization, although most mild cases can be remedied at home. Use the services of a certified lactation consultant. She is trained to assess the nursing couple to determine the problem, provide a solution, and monitor progress.

If the problem is the result of any of the above reasons (rigid or infrequent feeding schedule, the use of supplements, or stress), you will probably be instructed to nurse frequently, every 1 1/2 to 2 hours during the day and every 3 hours at night. Make sure that you offer the baby both breasts at each feeding and nurse long enough for him to receive the high-calorie hindmilk. You may be instructed to use a breast pump to further stimulate milk production. If supplements are required, this milk can then be offered with a flexible cup or finger feeding. To finger feed, place your finger in the baby's mouth to stimulate him to suck, then drip the milk into his mouth with a syringe or dropper. Your lactation consultant can give you more detailed instructions on how to perform this technique.

Infrequently, the problem is physical and requires professional help. A woman may be unable to produce sufficient milk if her thyroid is underactive, if she is severely anemic, or if she has untreated diabetes. These conditions can all be treated. Rarely, a woman's breasts may have developed improperly and may not contain the necessary glandular tissue for nursing. With this situation, there is usually no change in the breasts during pregnancy or with continued nursing. In addition, if a piece of the placenta was retained after the birth, the woman's body may think she is still pregnant and not produce enough hormones for lactation. Excessive or long-term bleeding should be reported to your caregiver.

If you are taking certain medications and are experiencing an inadequate milk supply, you may want to check with a lactation consultant. These medications include prescription drugs and over-the-counter preparations for allergies, asthma, depression, hypertension, migraines, insomnia, autoimmune diseases, and heart problems. Other factors that may decrease the mother's milk supply are smoking, alcohol consumption, large amounts of caffeine, combined (estrogen and progestin) oral contraceptives, and high doses of vitamins.

You may think that your baby is not getting enough milk if he wants to nurse every 2 hours. This desire to nurse frequently is normal in a baby in the early weeks and during growth spurts, and is not a cause for alarm as long as he is not showing any of the symptoms mentioned above. Your baby may just need to suck a lot.

Normal Breast Fullness Versus Engorgement

Most new mothers experience a normal increase in the size and fullness of their breasts around the second to the sixth day after birth. This occurs as the milk "comes in" and is also the result of the extra blood and lymph fluids that assist in the production of milk. If the breasts become overfull and hardened, if pain or fever accompany the increase, or if the infant is unable to latch onto the severely swollen breast, the condition is known as engorgement. Engorgement is usually due to infrequent or insufficient feedings. It occurs most often in first-time mothers, but varies considerably among individuals. Engorgement is temporary and can be remedied by frequent nursing. The milk supply and excess swelling will readjust within a short time.

If you become engorged, you can relieve the discomfort by taking a hot shower or placing hot cloths on your breasts to encourage the milk to let down. If your baby has difficulty grasping the nipple, he may become frustrated and cry. Hand-express a little milk or use a pump before nursing to make the nipple soft and pliable. After the feeding, apply cool compresses to the breasts to reduce circulation and relieve pain.

Folklore has provided a technique for relieving engorgement that has been found to produce excellent results. Cover your breasts with cold cabbage leaves, leaving the nipples exposed, and use a bra to hold the cabbage in place. Apply the leaves for 20 minutes every 2 or 3 hours until the engorgement has improved. Cold cabbage leaves can also be used to help mothers who weaned abruptly, or who chose not to breastfeed and thus became engorged. In these cases, you should wear the leaves continuously and change them every 2 hours.

"Oops! Looks like it's time to nurse."

Milk Leaking

Milk leaking or spraying is usually a temporary condition. If you experience it, you can stop it by pushing the heel of your hand against the nipple. Wear nursing pads to protect your blouse against wet spots.

Mastitis and Plugged Ducts

Mastitis refers to any inflammation of the breast. A plugged duct is one type of mastitis. If you notice soreness and a lump in one area of your breast, you may have a plugged duct. This is caused by incomplete emptying of the duct by the baby, by missed feedings, or by wearing a tight bra. Avoid bras with underwires. You can clear a plugged duct within 24 hours by resting, drinking plenty of fluids, and nursing the baby frequently on the affected breast. Massage the breast with gentle pressure from the chest wall toward the nipple to help stimulate the flow of milk. Remove any dried milk secretions from your nipple. Also, apply warm compresses to the breast to promote milk flow.

Alter your baby's position on the nipple while he is nursing to help him drain all the ducts. Make sure to offer him the affected breast first, when his sucking is the strongest.

Breast Infection

If a tender area, lump, or redness in the breast is accompanied by a fever and flu-like symptoms, you may have a breast infection. In fact, all flu symptoms in a nursing mother should be considered a breast infection until proven otherwise.

If you have a breast infection, continue to nurse your baby frequently to empty all your ducts. *Do not stop nursing.* Stopping would be an emotional and physical shock to both you and the baby. It could actually make the problem worse because the ducts would become overfilled.

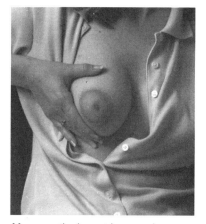

Massage the breast by pressing gently from the chest wall towards the nipple.

Drink plenty of fluids and get a lot of rest. Take your baby and go to bed. Apply heat to the infected area in the form of a heating pad or hot water bottle. Your caregiver may prescribe antibiotics that are safe to take while nursing.

Breast Abscess

Occasionally, a breast infection progresses to a breast abscess, a sore area filled with pus. Along with antibiotics, you may need to have the abscess incised and drained. This minor surgery is normally done in the doctor's office and heals quickly. Until it is healed, hand-express the milk from the affected breast and discard it; nurse your baby on the other breast. Once the healing is complete, you can resume nursing on both sides.

Flat or Inverted Nipples

To determine if your nipples are inverted, place your thumb and index finger around the base of the nipple and press together. If the nipple shrinks inward, the nipple is inverted. Flat or inverted nipples frequently improve as the pregnancy progresses. If the inversion continues past your seventh month of pregnancy, see a breastfeeding counselor or certified lactation consultant.

You will still be able to breastfeed your baby because babies nurse by applying pressure on the areola, not the nipple. Also, the sucking will naturally draw out the nipple. Flat nipples can be made more erect by stimulation or by the application of ice prior to a feeding.

If your nipples are severely inverted, you might want to wear a special breast shell during your last trimester of pregnancy to encourage the nipple to protrude. Or, you can use a breast pump or a special syringe called Evert-It to draw out the nipple prior to a feeding. All of these products are available from breastfeeding counselors and lactation consultants.

BABY-RELATED BREASTFEEDING DIFFICULTIES

Your baby's unique personality or his condition at birth may affect your nursing relationship. Remember that every baby is an individual and that no baby "goes by the book." Meet his individual needs and hopefully these difficulties will quickly be overcome. If the problems continue, call a breastfeeding counselor or visit a certified lactation consultant.

A Sleepy Baby

If you were medicated shortly before birth or received general anesthesia for a cesarean, your baby may be sleepy and somewhat sluggish about nursing. To stimulate him, change his diaper, move him around, or gently rub his back. Uncover him and expose him to the air. Alternately sit him up and lay him down, supporting his head and back. Pat his feet, and talk and play with him. Wipe his face with a cool washcloth. Feed him as often as possible to prevent weight loss. Offer him the breast every 2 hours.

Many babies have short quiet alert periods followed by deep sleep in the first days after birth. Take advantage of the awake times to nurse, instead of allowing visitors to play with the new baby. Often, by the time you get the baby back, he has fallen into his deep sleep again. Also, watch for cues that he wants to nurse, such as sucking movements or bringing his hand up to his mouth. Try nursing him immediately when you see those signals.

A Baby Who Refuses the Breast

If your baby has been given pacifiers or bottles, you may notice that when he latches onto the breast, he pushes the nipple out with his tongue, releases the breast, shakes his head, and screams. He has become nipple confused and is attempting to suck from the breast in the same manner that he did on the rubber nipple. You may have to retrain his sucking with your finger to encourage his tongue to "milk" the nipple, rather than push against it. Do not give him any more rubber nipples. It is best to delay the introduction of rubber nipples until at least 3 to 4 weeks of age to prevent nipple confusion.

If his nose is stuffy, he may latch on but pull away from the breast to breathe. Since infants are nose breathers, you may need to suction his nose with a bulb syringe so that he can nurse without difficulty.

When the let-down is delayed, the baby may not like to wait for his meal and may become frustrated. This may occur if the mother is under a lot of stress, smokes, or drinks excessive amounts of alcohol or caffeine. Some of these causes can be eliminated. If you feel tense, try playing soft music, using warm compresses on the breasts, massaging the breasts, and visualizing the milk flowing to your baby.

A Fussy Baby

Occasionally, your diet may include foods that upset your baby. First, try cutting out all dairy products. The protein in cow's milk passes through to the baby, and your baby may be sensitive to it. Spicy or gassy foods cause fussiness in some babies. Does your diet contain large amounts of caffeine? If you consume it in the evening, you may find that your baby is wide awake when you are ready for him to go to sleep. Do you exercise vigorously? The buildup of lactic acid after strenuous exercise can cause your milk to taste sour. Are you menstruating? Some babies become fussy or reject the breast at the beginning of the mother's period. Also, if you use hair spray, deodorant, or any other perfumes or sprays, keep them off your breasts. They may mask your normal scent and cause your baby to become fussy or reject the breast.

A Vigorous Nurser

If your baby nurses vigorously, he may gulp too much milk and air. If this occurs in response to a strong let-down, hand-express some milk before nursing to allow the let-down to subside. Also, taking him off your breast several times and burping him will reduce spitting up and gas discomfort.

If your baby is overly hungry, he may bite down hard on your breast and cause a sore nipple. Avoid making him wait too long before feeding him. Watch for cues that he is hungry.

An Ineffective Nurser

A baby may be a weak nurser due to preterm birth, a birth defect, cesarean delivery, or a medicated delivery. If your baby is a weak nurser, feed him more frequently and longer. Nurse him for as long as he wants. Help him to get started at each nursing by hand-expressing some milk into his mouth. You may need to pump your breasts to maintain an adequate supply.

A Hint for the New Mother

❏ Avoid giving your baby rubber nipples, including pacifiers, to prevent nipple confusion.

BREASTFEEDING FOLLOWING A CESAREAN DELIVERY

The special closeness that breastfeeding provides will be particularly important if you deliver by cesarean section. Since you will not have experienced the physical sensations of birth, nursing will afford you the intimate contact and comfort that are essential to both mother and baby. Your breasts will fill up with milk just as if you had delivered vaginally. Because you will need extra rest, you will appreciate being able to just take your baby to bed with you and leisurely feed him, instead of having to get up to wash bottles or prepare formula.

You should plan to nurse as soon after delivery as possible, just as you would after a vaginal delivery. If you have epidural anesthesia, you can hold and nurse your baby right in the recovery room. If you have general anesthesia, however, you will have to wait until you are alert before getting started.

Your abdominal incision will necessitate finding alternate nursing positions. Experiment until you find one that is easy and comfortable. Many cesarean mothers prefer the side-lying position. To assume this position, use pillows to support your back, your abdomen, and possibly your upper leg. Place your baby on his side, facing you, and cradle him in your arm. Pull him in close to you until your nipple touches his lip. Wait for him to open his mouth, then make sure that his jaws are well past the nipple. To burp him, roll onto your back and roll the baby onto your chest, face down. Then roll onto your other side to nurse him from the other breast.

Some women prefer to nurse in a sitting position. If you do, bend your knees somewhat and support your feet to lessen the strain on your abdomen. Place your baby on a pillow in your lap and cradle him in your arm. The clutch position or football hold is another position that relieves pressure on the abdomen. While sitting, hold your baby on a pillow at your side as if he were a football. Use your hand to support his head at your breast.

Continue taking your pain medication as needed. Most analgesics do

"What do you mean I can't nurse after a cesarean? I have all the right equipment!"

Side-lying position.

Football hold.

If you are a cesarean mother who prefers the cradle position, use a pillow in your lap to support the baby up at your breast.

not affect the baby. However, check with your doctor to be sure.

Do not become discouraged if you and your baby seem to get off to a slow start. Remember that this will be the beginning of many months of a happy, rewarding nursing relationship.

BREASTFEEDING BY WORKING MOTHERS

If you plan to return to work after your baby is born, you can still enjoy a happy and successful nursing experience. Your baby will benefit from whatever time you spend breastfeeding, as he continues to receive your breastmilk and its protective properties. Your baby will be healthier, resulting in fewer sick days.

If possible, arrange to visit and nurse your baby on your lunch hour, or have your baby brought to you. If this is not possible, leave either breastmilk or formula with his sitter to be given to him while you are at work. Many women prefer their infants to continue having only breastmilk and arrange to pump their breasts once or twice each day while they are at work. Many excellent breast pumps are available from your breastfeeding counselor or certified lactation consultant. Continue nursing your baby on request while you are at home. If you do not pump while you are at work, your milk supply will even out to meet the reduced demand.

If at all possible, delay returning to work outside the home until your baby is a year old. The first year is very important in a child's development and a very precious time for mothers. Unless you have severe financial problems, the time you spend with your baby will be more beneficial to your family than the income you will receive from working, especially after you deduct taxes, baby-sitting fees, the cost of formula and extra clothes, and the other expenses related to work. You may find that the money left over is not as significant as you thought it would be.

If you must work, choose your baby sitter carefully. A trusted relative or friend is your best choice. Otherwise, you will need to thoroughly check references before leaving your child with a stranger. Ideally, you will find someone who will care for your baby as you would. A person who keeps only one or two children can provide a more homelike atmosphere and plenty of cuddling. In addition, exposure to fewer children will reduce your baby's chances of catching colds or other illnesses, which would further increase your doctor bills, as well as create concern and cause you to miss work. (For a further discussion of childcare, see "The Childcare Decision" on page 239.)

BREASTFEEDING IN SPECIAL OR UNUSUAL SITUATIONS

Many mothers have successfully breastfed in special or unusual situations. If you have twins, triplets, or a preterm baby, you can receive valuable support from a certified lactation consultant or La Leche League International. You can also get information on continuing to nurse if you need to be hospitalized for an illness such as tuberculosis, hepatitis, epilepsy, or cancer. Help is also available if your baby has Down syndrome, a cleft palate, or a mental or physical handicap, or if he must be hospitalized. For information or support, contact a certified lactation consultant or La Leche League International. You will

Pumping Away From Baby

Many working mothers regularly spend their breaks and lunch hours with a breast pump. The following tips should help you get started:

❑ Wear clothing that makes it easy to pump.

❑ Find a quiet, private area with a comfortable chair.

❑ Listen to soft, relaxing music.

❑ Look at a picture of your baby.

❑ Place a baby blanket, with the scent of baby powder or lotion, over your shoulders or on your lap.

❑ Place a warm cloth on your breasts.

❑ Massage your breasts.

❑ Relax your shoulders and visualize your baby or the milk flowing.

❑ Drink a beverage while you are expressing.

Daily pumping will soon be a natural part of your routine.

receive specific guidelines, as well as help in contacting other mothers who have nursed in circumstances similar to yours.

CONTRAINDICATIONS TO BREASTFEEDING

A few situations exist in which breastfeeding is contraindicated. If you have had a double mastectomy or breast reduction surgery in which your nipples were surgically removed and reattached, you will not be able to breastfeed. Additionally, if you were ever exposed to the AIDS virus, you should not breastfeed. Rare cases have been reported of infants acquiring the virus through their mothers' breastmilk. A woman with untreated active tuberculosis should also refrain from breastfeeding.

A mother who uses cocaine or any other illegal recreational drugs should not breastfeed because these substances pass readily through the milk and can cause serious or fatal reactions in the baby. Several other substances may require temporary cessation of nursing. These include radioactive isotopes, antimetabolites, cancer chemotherapy drugs, and a small number of other medications.

If your baby is diagnosed with galactosemia, he is missing a liver enzyme and is unable to metabolize lactose. Since breastmilk is high in lactose, breastfeeding is contraindicated in this case. Continuation would cause mental retardation. The baby must be placed on a special formula such as Nutramigen. Some states check for this disease as part of the infant screening test.

LA LECHE LEAGUE

La Leche League is an organization of women who have successfully breast-fed their children and who enjoy helping others do the same. The organization had its beginnings at a family picnic in Franklin Park, Illinois, in 1956. Two nursing mothers attending the picnic recognized the need of new mothers to receive factual advice on breastfeeding. Previous generations had had mothers and grandmothers within their households who could supply this assistance. Our changing family structure, however, had left mothers without good role models, resulting in a lack of information.

Today, La Leche League is an international organization with over 3,000 groups in forty-eight countries. Each chapter meets monthly and covers a series of four topics concerning nursing. If you are considering breastfeeding, you should begin attending La Leche League meetings at least 4 months before your due date to complete the series. There is no charge to attend the meetings, although you may be encouraged to join La Leche League. After your baby is born, you can take him with you to the meetings. To find the chapter nearest you, check your local telephone directory or contact La Leche League International at 9616 Minneapolis Avenue, Franklin Park, Illinois 60131; telephone 800–LA–LECHE (800–525–3243).

Keep the telephone number of your La Leche League leader handy and feel free to call her at any time if a problem arises. Her knowledge and experience can help ease you through any rough spot. The advice of these breastfeeding counselors is free. They volunteer their time and knowledge to assist mothers with breastfeeding.

CERTIFIED LACTATION CONSULTANTS

Certified lactation consultants are paid professionals who have completed a prescribed course of study and passed an examination. They are qualified to do breastfeeding assessments on mothers and babies, and to assist with all types of breastfeeding problems. Their services include providing at-home or office consultations, conducting prenatal and working mothers' classes, and offering breastfeeding supplies. The first lactation consultants were La Leche League volunteers who felt that the field of breastfeeding counseling would be legitimized by certifying competence in minimal standards of knowledge and skills. The first test was administered in 1985, and since that time, this specialty has gained wide acceptance in the medical community.

Many hospitals employ certified lactation consultants to assist new mothers with breastfeeding. The consultations are often covered by health insurance if they are ordered by a pediatrician. Ask your pediatrician, local hospital, or childbirth instructor to recommend a certified lactation consultant or contact the International Lactation Consultant Association (ILCA) Headquarters at 200 North Michigan Avenue, Suite 300, Chicago, Illinois 60601; telephone 312–541–1710.

BOTTLE FEEDING

When you feed your baby, you will be providing him with more than nourishment. You will also be giving him love, warmth, intimate human contact, and a feeling of security. Close physical contact, especially skin-to-skin, as well as cuddling are extremely important in the psychological and physical development of a baby.

Neither propping a bottle nor sitting your baby in an infant seat and holding his bottle provide these necessary elements. Even when your baby can hold his own bottle, he should not be left alone, as this can be dangerous and can also lead to dental problems. He will still need to be held and cuddled when he is fed.

Make each feeding time special by cradling your baby close to you in the bend of your arm (the nursing position) and not rushing the feeding. Talking and singing to your baby make feeding time sociable and pleasant for both of you. Alternate arms at each feeding. Babies who are always held on the same side develop different strengths in their eyes. The eye that is closest to your breast will not receive adequate stimulation and will become weak from nonuse.

Types of Formula

The type of formula that you use will probably depend upon your pediatrician's preference. Formula is made from cow's milk or soybeans, and modified to resemble mother's milk as much as possible. Some babies do not tolerate certain formulas. They may become constipated or suffer digestive upsets. If your baby is allergic to cow's milk–based formulas, your pediatrician may try a soybean-based one. The signs of allergy include rash (eczema), diarrhea, chronic cold symptoms, colic, and asthma. Occasionally, a baby is so allergic that he can tolerate only breastmilk.

Formula comes in several forms. The single serving ready-to-feed bottle is

Bottle Mouth Syndrome

Doctors heartily discourage putting a baby to bed with a bottle. If unattended, the baby could choke. If you do choose to give him a bottle in bed, give him plain water. Formula and juice contain sugar that can remain on the baby's teeth while he sleeps and can lead to bottle mouth syndrome, which is evidenced by extensive cavities. Better yet, hold and rock your baby as he enjoys his night feeding and then put him to bed without a bottle. This not only prevents tooth problems, but gives him that extra love and cuddling that every child needs.

the easiest to use, but is also the most expensive. Liquid formula concentrate, which you need to mix with water, should be refrigerated once the can is opened and then it should be used within 24 hours. The powdered type does not need refrigeration until it is mixed with water, but once it is mixed, it also needs to be used within 24 hours. Make sure that you follow the directions on the can for preparation. Adding extra water to stretch the formula or not adding enough water is dangerous to your baby's health and development. Formula should be given at room temperature because overheating destroys important vitamins. Never microwave a bottle of formula. While the bottle may feel cool, the formula will continue to heat. Microwaving can also produce hot spots, which can burn your baby. Overheating might even cause the bottle to explode.

Basics of Bottle Feeding

Many doctors now say that bottles and nipples do not need to be sterilized if they are washed in a dishwasher. They should be sterilized before their first use, however. After each use, nipples should be washed in hot soapy water and rinsed well, making sure the nipple holes are open. You will need to have about eight nipples and bottles. Plastic nurser bags are convenient because they are sterile and disposable.

Nipples come in many shapes and varieties. Be sure that your baby will accept a certain kind of nipple before you stock up on it. Make sure that the hole in the nipple is the correct size. When you hold the bottle upside down and shake it, the formula should drip easily, one drop at a time. If your baby takes a long time (over 30 minutes) to finish a bottle, or if he becomes fussy or tired before finishing, the hole may be too small. If he takes in a lot of air or finishes the bottle very quickly, the hole is probably too large.

When you feed your baby, cradle him in your arms in a semi-upright position. Hold the bottle at a 45-degree angle so that the milk always fills the nipple. Otherwise, the baby will take in a lot of air. Burp your baby halfway through and at the end of each feeding. If he cried hard before being fed, or if he gulped his milk, he may need extra burping. Place a diaper over your shoulder to prevent stains on your clothes. If you do get a stain, you can soak it out in a solution of baking soda and water, or vinegar and water.

Do not place an unfinished bottle of formula in the refrigerator for later use. The baby's saliva will already be working on the formula and may promote the growth of bacteria. Do not save formula for reuse if it has been out of refrigeration for several hours. With "ready to feed" bottles, you will not have to worry about formula spoiling. Contaminated or spoiled milk can cause vomiting and diarrhea, which in turn can lead to dehydration, a serious problem in infants because of their size.

Canned liquid formula should be stored at temperatures below 72°F. If it was stored in a hot warehouse during the summer, it may have curdled. Do not use canned formula that smells "funny" or that has separated into layers with an oily yellow substance on top that cannot be dispersed by shaking. Also, check the expiration date, especially if you bought the container when the store was having a sale.

Feed your baby every 2 to 4 hours, or whenever he seems hungry. Begin with about 3 ounces of formula in the bottle. If he falls asleep during a feeding, he has probably had enough. After feeding and burping him, place him on his right side or in a sitting position to help his digestion.

Bottle Feeding Tips

The following tips should help make bottle feeding a healthy and rewarding experience:

❏ Alternate the side you hold the baby on so that both of his eyes will be equally stimulated.

❏ Remember to check the expiration date on every can of formula.

❏ Always hold your baby while he is feeding.

❏ Do not heat bottles in the microwave.

❏ After an hour, throw out any formula that was left in the bottle to prevent contamination.

Your pediatrician may have other tips to add to this list.

INTRODUCING OTHER FOODS

Breastmilk or formula is a complete food for your baby until around 6 months of age. At that time, the iron supply that he was born with may begin to diminish. Many babies also start teething at this time, indicating that nature intended for them to begin chewing. This is usually the time to introduce solid foods. Let your baby be your guide. Some babies are eager to eat at this time and will reach for food. Others are still not ready and will refuse it. Proceed very slowly. If your baby does not want food, do not force him to eat. Continue to offer it occasionally, and when he is ready, he will take it. Do not concern yourself with how much he eats. He will just be learning to eat and will still need some time before he is ready for three "square meals" a day. Mashed banana is a good food to offer first. Breastmilk or formula, however, should remain his primary source of nutrition throughout the first year. The American Academy of Pediatrics recommends that babies receive only breastmilk for the first 6 months of life and then continue to receive breastmilk as the primary source of nutrition throughout the second half of the first year while starting to eat solid foods. Mothers are encouraged to continue breastfeeding for as long as is mutually desired. If you do not breastfeed for the entire first year, you should substitute formula.

Experts say that introducing solids before 6 months of age offers no advantages. The enzymes that are necessary to completely digest cereal and other foods are not present in full quantity until a baby is 3 to 6 months old. Also, before 3 to 4 months, a baby does not have the ability to move food from the front of his mouth to the back. Most of the food that you would feed your baby at this time would therefore be wasted. You would spend a lot of time catching the food his tongue thrust back out. Furthermore, because a baby's gastrointestinal tract is not yet mature, the early introduction of solids can cause improper absorption and food allergies. It might also lead to obesity in later life, since many mothers encourage their babies to finish the jar or to clean the plate to prevent wasting food.

Solid foods also do not make a baby sleep through the night. Sleeping all night is a function of neurological maturity and is independent of feeding. Babies usually begin to sleep through the night at 2 to 3 months of age.

When you do begin giving solid foods to your baby, introduce one food at a time. Allow 1 week between new foods. If your baby has an adverse reaction such as a rash or stomach upset, you will know which food is responsible.

Certain foods are highly allergenic and should be delayed to prevent reactions. For example, do not give your baby cow's milk until he is 1 year of age because approximately 20 percent of children are allergic to cow's milk. Dairy products such as yogurt, cottage cheese, and natural cheeses can be started at 9 to 10 months. Orange juice, citrus fruits, and eggs should not be introduced until 1 year of age.

Some foods are dangerous for babies for other reasons. Once you give your child cow's milk, give him whole milk until he is 2 or 3 years old. The high protein and salt contents of skim milk and 2-percent milk put too much stress on a young child's kidneys. In addition, skim milk does not contain enough calories to meet a toddler's energy and growth needs, and it is deficient in iron, vitamin C, and the essential fatty acids. Honey is another food that should not be given to babies, because of the risk of infant botulism, which can be fatal. Wait until your child is 12 months old before giving him honey.

Caution . . .

Do not give unpasteurized apple juice or cider to infants or young children. These may contain harmful bacteria.

Older siblings often want to help. This big brother is helping to feed his sister.

You can avoid using expensive, overprocessed commercial baby foods by taking the nutritious (and nonsalted) foods from your table, and mashing or blending them for your baby. You can even freeze portions of these mashed foods to give to your baby when the rest of your family is enjoying a "combination" dish, such as a casserole, that includes foods not yet introduced into the baby's diet. Freeze these leftover single foods in ice cube trays. When they are frozen, pack the individual cubes in plastic bags and store them in your freezer. To use them, simply defrost to room temperature and serve. Even baby cereals are unnecessary if you regularly serve your family cooked cereals that are low in salt and sugar, such as oatmeal and Cream of Wheat. Make the cereal with water instead of milk, and serve it to the baby with no added sweetener.

Many women find that running the baby's foods through the blender is unnecessary. You can avoid the expense and trouble of puréeing foods by waiting until your baby is truly ready for finger foods. At about 8 to 10 months of age, your baby will be able to handle the foods from your table and will enjoy the independence of feeding himself. Offer him small pieces of softened vegetable, such as baked white or sweet potato, or tiny pieces of chicken, fish, or beef. Foods that you can easily mash between your fingers are good choices. Finger-size pieces of dried or toasted whole wheat bread are convenient and easy for the baby to chew. Also, packaged cereals that are low in salt and sugar, such as Cheerios, make good finger foods. In this way, you will eliminate the headache of spoon feeding, and mealtimes will be more pleasurable.

Some foods should not be offered until your child is 3 years old because of the possibility of choking. These include nuts, grapes, popcorn, spoonfuls of peanut butter, and carrot and celery sticks.

Commercial baby food manufacturers have been tremendously successful at marketing their products by convincing mothers that puréed food is a necessary step before table food. They have even invented different levels of prepared foods from "smooth" to "chunky" to prolong the length of time that parents "need" to purchase these foods. Advertising experts have influenced our culture so strongly that mothers feel negligent if they do not use these expensive products. The baby food manufacturers even promote the purchase of small jars of special "baby" fruit juices when the same juices are available much more economically in larger bottles.

What other mammal purées food for its young? Most mammals breastfeed their infants until they are able to feed themselves adult-type food. By breastfeeding and delaying the introduction of solids until the baby is ready, human infants can also avoid commercial or even homemade puréed foods. To know when your child is ready, watch for him to grab for your glass or reach for your food.

If you do decide to purchase prepared baby foods, look for varieties that have no added salt, sugar, starches, or other fillers. Many brands now offer products that contain only the puréed food and no additives. These provide more nutrition, so read the labels carefully. Do not feed your baby right from the jar, since his saliva contains enzymes and bacteria that will start to break down the food and thus prevent you from saving the leftover for later use. In addition, be aware of products containing chicken. High levels of fluoride have been found in some commercial baby food containing chicken. Fluoride is stored in bone, and it may be released during the deboning process. Too much fluoride can result in fluorosis, which causes light spots on the permanent teeth.[31] If you use commercial baby food, offer chicken products sparingly. Better yet, grind your own chicken or wait until your child can handle small pieces of chicken.

Children's Snacks

With so many quality foods available, it should be easy to avoid giving your child packaged cookies and soft drinks as snacks. When mothers simply do not purchase junk foods, children readily accept and come to prefer the more nutritious foods. Offer your child cheese, whole wheat crackers, fresh fruit and vegetables, raisins and other dried fruit, and popcorn. However, do not offer nuts, seeds, or popcorn if your child is under 3.

You can turn your favorite cookie recipes into health cookies by substituting whole wheat flour for a portion of the white flour and adding wheat germ, brewer's yeast, and powdered milk. If your child is over 12 months old, you can also substitute honey for the refined sugar. The cookies should turn out fine as long as your total dry ingredients equal the total dry ingredients in the recipe. If the batter is too thick, just add an extra egg. Many cookie recipes call for raisins, nuts, peanut butter, or oatmeal, which make them doubly nutritious.

Soft drinks are devoid of any food element except sugar. They are full of acids, preservatives, emulsifiers, stabilizers, artificial flavorings, and dyes. While researchers have tested these additives individually for safety, little is known about their combined effect on the human body. Soft drinks cause tooth decay and take away the appetite for more nutritious foods. They act as stimulants by causing the blood sugar to soar temporarily. However, this boost is rapidly followed by a drop in blood sugar and energy. Give your child milk, water, or unsweetened fruit juice when he is thirsty.

Packaged gelatin desserts are about 85-percent sugar. Instead, use unflavored gelatin and prepare it with fresh fruit juice.

WEANING

Many women find that their views on weaning change after they begin nursing. Often, an expectant mother will plan to nurse for 3 months, 6 months, or some other set amount of time. However, once she begins the nursing relationship with her baby, she finds it so rewarding that she is not anxious for it to end. She knows, too, that breastfeeding is more than just a method of physical nourishment. It is an emotional bond. An abrupt severing of that bond could be traumatic for both mother and baby.

Most nursing mothers find that weaning is easiest for both partners if it is done gradually. Authorities, too, are realizing that weaning is individual and should be determined by each baby's needs. Just as babies begin sitting up, rolling over, walking, and talking at different ages, their needs to continue nursing vary. Therefore, weaning ideally should be a baby-led process. You will know when your baby is ready, and it will probably be so gradual that you will hardly even realize it. As he becomes more interested in other activities and in the world around him, and as he becomes better at feeding himself from the table and drinking from a cup, his need to nurse will diminish. Of course, when he is hurt or ill, he will want to resort to his "baby" ways, and you will be glad that you are able to comfort him through nursing. (In fact,

Hints for the New Father

❏ Be knowledgeable about breastfeeding. Attend a class with your mate.

❏ Defend your mate against negative comments.

❏ Massage your mate's shoulders to help her relax at the start of a feeding.

❏ Assist your mate with positioning the baby at the breast.

❏ Observe your mate and the baby for proper mouth positioning on the breast.

❏ Look for signals that the baby is ready to nurse—for example, sucking motions and putting his fist in his mouth.

❏ Burp the baby.

❏ Bring the baby to your mate in the middle of the night.

❏ Encourage eight to twelve feedings in a 24-hour period.

❏ Do not encourage supplements or pacifiers during the first weeks.

❏ Wait until the baby is a month old before feeding him a bottle.

❏ Support your mate's decision to breastfeed if it becomes difficult.

❏ Know that your baby is getting the best possible start.

❏ Let your mate know that you are proud of her.

❏ Decide on a major purchase with all the money your mate will save by breastfeeding for a year.

nursing can be a real "lifesaver" when your toddler is so sick that he does not want to eat or drink, but does want to nurse. Nursing can prevent dehydration.) Gradually, however, you will find that he will be asking to nurse less frequently. Your best way to assist him will be to stop offering him the breast, while at the same time not denying it when he needs it.

Remember that you will be helping your child to become an independent human being at his own rate. Your months of involvement in the nursing relationship will make you sensitive to his exact needs. Do not let comments from others deny him this right. Our society supports babies remaining attached to the bottle until age 2 or 3. It is so much better to be attached to a person than to a thing. If you feel that prolonged nursing is best for you and your baby, do not allow public opinion to affect your decision. The American Academy of Pediatrics supports continuing to breastfeed as long as is mutually desired. The nutritional and psychological benefits from nursing will continue, and you will be helping to create a happy, healthy, well-adjusted human being.

CONCLUSION

Feeding your baby is a natural continuation of your role of protecting and nourishing him before he was born. Your breastmilk is the food nature intended your baby to have. It is a living tissue whose nutritional and immunological properties can never be duplicated. Receiving these benefits is your baby's birthright.

Breastmilk is the "gold standard" to which all formulas are compared. Why give your baby artificial baby milk when you can provide him with the "real thing"? Formula manufacturers would have you believe that their product is almost as good as yours. But these companies are not in the mother's milk business—they are in the business of making money. Your milk is far superior to all the substitutes, and it is free!

By breastfeeding, you can relax in the knowledge that you are providing your baby with the best possible start in life. Educate yourself about breastfeeding beforehand, attend La Leche League meetings, talk with mothers who have nursed successfully, and line up a certified lactation consultant, and you and your baby will share many happy hours of a rewarding breastfeeding experience.

The New Parent
or Happy Daze

Your first days as a new parent will include a wide range of feelings and emotions—from relief and excitement that your baby is finally here, to fear and apprehension about the tremendous responsibility you have undertaken. Most of all will be your feelings of love for this unique little person you helped to create. Yet, at the same time, you may have unexplained feelings of sadness and a sense of being overwhelmed. Sometimes, all you may feel is total exhaustion! All of these are normal reactions to new parenthood. This chapter discusses the physical and emotional changes that are experienced by most new parents and offers suggestions for making this period of adjustment a little easier.

PHYSICAL CHANGES

During your first 6 weeks postpartum, your body will return to its prepregnant state. You will eliminate the extra fluid that you retained during pregnancy by frequent urination and perspiration.

Your uterus will gradually return to its prepregnant size and position in a process called involution. You may notice periodic contractions as it becomes smaller. If you nurse your baby, you will feel the uterus contract each time you put your baby to your breast for the first few days. Because of this, involution of the uterus occurs faster in breastfeeding mothers. If this is your second or subsequent child, you may find these "after pains" to be painful. A mild pain reliever such as ibuprofen or acetaminophen may provide some relief.

You will have a vaginal discharge for 3 to 4 weeks as the lining of your uterus returns to normal. The discharge will begin as bright red, will then become light pink, will gradually turn brownish, and will finally be clear. If it becomes bright red again after it has become clear, you have overexerted yourself. Slow down, go to bed for a couple of days, and get plenty of rest. If the bleeding is excessive, call your caregiver. You may have a postpartum hemorrhage. Do not use tampons during the postpartum period.

Continue the comfort measures that you used in the hospital for your stitches or hemorrhoids. For pain relief, place cool witch hazel compresses (refrigerate homemade ones or use commercial brands) directly onto your pad before applying it to the perineum. If you did not receive a portable sitz bath

When to Call Your Caregiver

The following symptoms are warning signs and may indicate a serious problem in the postpartum period. Do not hesitate to call and report any of these signs. Minor breast-related problems can be handled by a certified lactation consultant.

❏ Temperature over 100°F and chills.

❏ Heavy bleeding. Bleeding should gradually decrease, not increase.

❏ Passing a large clot or many clots.

❏ Unpleasant odor from the vaginal discharge.

❏ Increased pain or swelling in the vaginal and perineal area.

❏ Abdominal pain or tenderness (other than the normal uterine cramping).

❏ Hot, sore breasts with a lump or area of redness.

❏ Cracked and bleeding nipples.

❏ A lump or pain in the calves or severe swelling in the legs.

❏ Pain in the mid to lower back.

❏ Burning, frequency, difficulty, or urgency with urinating.

❏ Severe depression, sadness, or withdrawal.

Immediate treatment may prevent these conditions from becoming serious.

in the hospital, you can sit in a clean tub of warm water or use a portable showerhead to run water over the perineal area. You will find that squeezing your buttocks together before you sit down or stand up helps to reduce the strain on the episiotomy stitches. Some women prefer sitting slightly to the side of their buttock.

Many women are concerned about having their first bowel movement after the delivery, especially if they have stitches or hemorrhoids. Your bowel movements should resume within 4 to 5 days. Eat a diet with sufficient green leafy vegetables and whole grain products, and drink plenty of fluids. Prune juice or prunes may also help. Your caregiver may recommend a stool softener, if necessary. Hemorrhoids will gradually shrink over time.

During the next few days, your breasts will change from their size at the end of pregnancy to possibly several sizes larger. Your body sends additional blood and fluids to aid in the production of milk. If you do not breastfeed, your breasts will still undergo these changes. Medication is no longer given to suppress the production of milk. Non-nursing mothers may want to wear a tight sports bra and apply ice to reduce the swelling. Cabbage leaves may also provide relief. (For instructions, see "Normal Breast Fullness Versus Engorgement" on page 260.)

Weight loss will be gradual, sometimes taking months. Remember that it took you 9 months to put the weight on, so you cannot expect to lose all the pounds overnight. Nursing will help, since your body will use 500 to 800 calories each day in the production of milk. Continue to eat well and take your prenatal vitamins. Do not go on a strict reducing diet if you are breastfeeding. When you first come home, your abdomen will be flabby and you may still look 4 or 5 months pregnant. If you begin the exercise program described on page 285 while you are still in the hospital, you will have a head start on reconditioning the muscles that were stretched during pregnancy.

You may experience both emotional highs and lows during the first weeks after birth. It is not surprising that many women have the "baby blues," since many sudden changes occur. While most women expect to be consistently happy and loving toward their new babies, they may be surprised to also experience the "blues," characterized by episodes of crying, moodiness, sleeping difficulty, irritability, anxiety, lack of sexual desire, and ambivalence about the decision to have a baby and the change in their lifestyle. And when they do have these negative thoughts and feelings, they feel guilty about it.

Physically, your body will undergo abrupt shifts in hormonal levels, a 30-percent decrease in blood volume, possibly painful uterine contractions, and/or a sore bottom. Pregnancy grows on you month by month, but motherhood is thrust on you very suddenly. One moment your baby is still a part of you, and the next he is a separate, unique human being. To further compound the shock, the spotlight shifts from you to the baby. You are no longer the center of attention, pampered and coddled by family, friends, and even strangers. In the early days, this loss of the spotlight may make you feel isolated and unimportant.

Your husband may also be affected by these changes. No longer will he be the primary focus of your attention. He may feel resentment and jealousy toward the baby if he is not allowed to be an active partner in the newcomer's care and nurturing. In addition, the sudden awareness of the enormous responsibility that he has just assumed may overwhelm him and even frighten him for a time.

More than any other factor, exhaustion is the primary reason women experience the blues. Therefore, you should consider it a priority to get as much rest as possible during your first 2 weeks at home. Since it will be several weeks before you can fit into your prepregnant clothes again, stay in your nightgown and be comfortable. You will also appear to be recovering and will be treated as such. If you get dressed as soon as you arrive home, you will appear fully recovered and will find yourself pushed into hostess and housekeeper roles before you are ready. This will result in fatigue and irritability, and your recovery will be slower. If possible, nap whenever your baby does. In fact, the two of you should spend the first days at home in bed together. Do not feel guilty about this. Your body needs the extra rest at this time.

If you take care of yourself and follow the suggestions in this chapter, you can minimize and possibly avoid the down feelings that women have come to expect following childbirth. If, however, you become severely depressed and lose interest in taking care of yourself and the baby, you need to seek professional help. (For a discussion of severe depression following childbirth, see "Postpartum Depression.")

ADJUSTMENT TO PARENTHOOD

Imagine this scene: You are home with your new baby. You have just bathed, fed, and cuddled him, and he is now sleeping peacefully in a clean and tidy house. You are relaxing with your feet up and reading a good book, exchanging occasional fond glances with your loving, content mate. This is a wonderful picture, but is it realistic? And if you do have moments like this, how long do they last? No matter what romanticized ideas you may have developed about being a parent, you will have times (and many of them) when your reality will just not match these ideals. You cannot program yourself to have boundless energy, be

---

Postpartum Depression

While many women experience a mild case of "the blues," some women suffer a more debilitating condition known as postpartum depression. These women develop prolonged feelings of sadness, anxiety, insomnia, extreme fatigue, and possibly even thoughts of suicide or of causing harm to the infant.

The most widely accepted theory relates postpartum depression to the drastic hormonal changes that accompany birth. In addition, the constant demands of a newborn can leave a woman completely fatigued and overwhelmed. A woman who has high expectations and tries to accomplish too much may set herself up for depression. The inability to be the "perfect parent" may affect her self-esteem and increase her feelings of failure. If the birth did not go according to her plans, this may add to her feelings of failure. Heredity or previous history may also play a role. A history of mental illness or a difficult postpartum adjustment either by the woman or by another family member may increase her risk. A woman who abruptly stops breastfeeding may experience a drop in hormone levels, which can increase feelings of depression. Breastfeeding releases hormones that help new mothers feel calm and relaxed. It has also been shown to prevent the release of stress hormones in new mothers.

Identifying postpartum depression is the first step. Understanding and compassion from family members, adequate rest, good nutrition, and assistance with daily activities is a must. Counseling and support groups may also benefit some women. Occasionally, drug therapy with antidepressants can be used. Some physicians have found that injections of progesterone after delivery may reduce the symptoms in women whose depression is caused by severe hormone withdrawal. Others have used vitamin B_6 with some success.[1] A British study has reported improvement in postpartum depression with the use of the estrogen patch.[2]

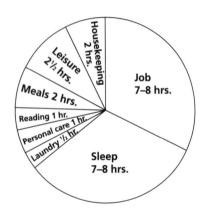

Figure 12.1.
A sample "Before Baby" time
management chart.

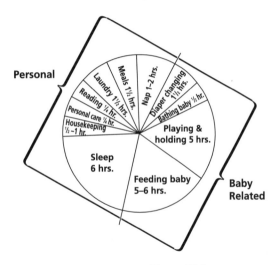

Figure 12.2.
A sample "After Baby" time
management chart.

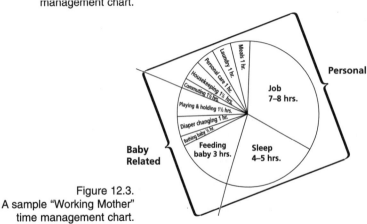

Figure 12.3.
A sample "Working Mother"
time management chart.

relaxed and confident, be consistently loving, and meet all of your baby's (and spouse's) needs. You cannot be a perfect parent. Parents are human beings! The "perfect parent" image we often try to project to those around us—our parents, relatives, and friends—is plainly unrealistic. And if you take time to discuss this openly with them, you will find that they, too, have had some frenzied and anxious moments as new parents.

The adjustments that you will make after having your baby are similar in many ways to the adjustments that you had to make following marriage. New roles will be defined; new household tasks will be assigned. To help you prepare more realistically for the days that lie ahead, you and your husband should sit down together and do the following exercise while you are still pregnant.

Each of you take a piece of paper and draw two circles on it. Each circle will represent a 24-hour period. Label the first circle "Before Baby," and the second circle "After Baby." Divide the "Before Baby" circle into sections representing the different activities that currently make up your day, such as working, preparing and eating meals, housekeeping, paying bills and banking, being a companion, making love, gardening, relaxing, enjoying a hobby, sleeping, bathing, and so on. (See Figure 12.1.) Size each section in this pie chart to reflect the percentage of time that you spend on the activity. For example, if you work 8 hours a day, make the work section one-third of the chart. In the "After Baby" chart, note the activities that you must, or hope to, continue, as well as the new baby-related activities such as feeding, bathing, soothing, diaper changing, and doing the laundry. (See Figure 12.2.) Sizewise, make these sections indicate the amount of time per day that you expect to devote to each of these activities.

When you are both finished, compare your pie charts with one another. Is one partner indicating more changes than the other? Are the "After Baby" charts realistic? Do the childcare activities and time estimates that each of you indicated match each other's expectations? How will the "After Baby" chart change if the mother returns to outside employment? (See Figure 12.3.) Discuss any differences in your expectations now. This way, after the baby is born, you will not argue over who should do what and when. Save your charts. You will have fun looking at them again after your baby is born.

You should see clearly after doing this exercise, if you did not before, that the time you devote to your different roles will change considerably once you add the role of parent to your life.

CONFUSING EMOTIONS

When you and your partner become new parents, you will share many positive feelings—feelings of personal gratification, challenge, and achievement; a deepened love; and a renewed appreciation of each other. You will enjoy discovering new dimensions in each other as parents and may even find the relationships with your own parents becoming closer.

The negative feelings that accompany new parenthood may come as a surprise to you, however, as may the feelings of guilt that often follow. When you have done simply everything to soothe a fussy baby and he is still crying, when you have gotten up for the third time during the night to feed him, or when the anticipated 2-hour nap lasts for only 30 minutes, you may find yourself getting upset or even hostile toward this baby who is so "ungrateful" for all that you have done for him. You are not alone! Parents are human and have feelings of anger and guilt from time to time, whether they admit it or not. The feelings are not the problem, however. Rather, the concern is over how you handle the feelings and cope with the situation at hand. Often, just talking with other new mothers who are experiencing the same feelings and difficulties will help you put the situation in perspective and arrive at a creative solution.

Sometimes, the baby is not the reason that these emotions surface in a mother. Instead, "cabin fever," loss of freedom, lack of intellectual stimulation, or lowered self-confidence is the cause. If you feel upset in any way after your baby is born, try to find the reason you feel as you do. You will then be able to work toward a solution. Be sure to share your feelings with your mate. Problems seem less important when they are shared and solved together.

TAKE TIME TO ADJUST

Do not have exceedingly high expectations for yourself, your spouse, or your baby in the first months after birth. Both you and your spouse will be adjusting to tremendous changes in your lives in the forms of an altered family structure, new demands on your time, and changes in your relationship.

The early months will be the most demanding—on your time alone and on your time as a couple. Communication will be essential. Be assured that as you grow as parents and as the baby matures, your lifestyle can and will adjust to what you want it to be.

Simplify Your Housework

Try to get household assistance for your first 1 to 2 weeks at home to help ease you through the adjustment period. A relative with whom you feel truly comfortable is a joy. She can prepare the meals, wash the dishes, do the laundry and cleaning, and care for your older children. This will allow you to better care for yourself and your baby.

Make sure your helper understands her role. These first weeks will be essential to help you bond with your baby and to become confident in baby care. She can provide you with her expertise as she watches you care for your new infant. But, if she becomes the "baby nurse," you will not become proficient in baby-related skills and you will overtire yourself with hostess duties. Once your assistant goes home, you may feel inadequate to care for your new baby. It is extremely important for the breastfeeding mother to have a supportive atmosphere for success. If your helper has not breastfed, have her read Chapter 11 prior to the baby's arrival so that she will become familiar with ways to help you. Family members who offer to feed the baby so that you can rest may sabotage your breastfeeding efforts. If you are concerned that your visitors will bring more stress than assistance, you can ask them to come over for just short visits. You may find it most beneficial if these well-intentioned friends and relatives simply provide nutritious meals and help with some light housekeeping chores.

Occasionally, couples find that it is better for out-of-town visitors to wait a few weeks before coming. Your partner can take off a week or two as you settle into your new roles as parents. You may appreciate this opportunity to be alone as you help each other learn new responsibilities. Then, after you begin to feel better physically and are more comfortable with baby care, you may be ready to handle visitors.

Organize your priorities together, as a couple, and agree to do only those things that both of you feel are important and necessary. The new baby, who will need almost constant physical care, will be most demanding on your time during the first few weeks. In addition, your body will undergo tremendous physical changes, which will affect your energy level. Many people find that to-do lists are helpful. You could include things that you *must* do, things that you can do if time permits (things that are nice, but not essential), and things that can wait until the baby is older. You could also make a list of substitutes that could save you work. Besides listing all the jobs and their importance, you should also note who will do each job. You may find that temporarily paying for some of the jobs to be done is well worth the money. Consider hiring a housecleaning service or lawn care company, or paying a teenager to do those jobs or to help with the other children, the meals, or the laundry.

Although your baby may want to nurse nearly every 2 to 3 hours around the clock during the first weeks, you will find more and more time elapsing between feedings as he grows older. You will be able to catch up on your housework later. Donna Ewy, a noted childbirth educator and author, suggests that the best gift you can give your baby is *you* for the first 6 weeks of his life.

Stretch Your Limited Time

You need to become aware of the things in your current lifestyle that are important to you individually and as a couple. Try to find ways to maintain some of these activities after the baby arrives, since it will be impossible to continue them all. A simple exercise will help you clarify what these important things are.

You and your husband should sit down together and, on separate sheets of paper, complete the phrases, "Three things that I like to do alone are . . ." and "Three things that I like to do with my mate are . . ." Then, answer the question, "How will the baby change these activities?" When you both have finished writing your answers, trade lists with each other. You may find items missing from your partner's list that you thought were important, as well as things on his list that you did not realize were important. Decide together which activities are most important, which ones you can give up for a time, and how to maintain the important activities. For example, if you enjoy going to the movies but do not want to leave the baby, go to an early show or rent a video. (Nursing babies do very well in theaters.) Entertain friends at home for dinner, rather than going out with them to a restaurant. Order take-out food from your favorite restaurant and set the table with flowers, candles, and your best china. Take turns watching the baby for a few hours so that each of you can do something alone. Find chunks of time to spend alone together that may be different from the time blocks you currently share. Take advantage of the baby's naptimes for conversation and shared activity, rather than using them to rush to the supermarket or do yard work.

You can accomplish many things while you nurse your baby—make a list, read a book, listen to music, eat a snack, or lie down and rest. Learn to utilize nursing time in whatever ways you find most satisfying. Do not feel guilty, however, if you just want to relax and enjoy these quiet moments.

Use Your Resources

Parenthood is one of life's most thrilling adventures, and yet, you may be entering it feeling an array of fears, anxieties, and doubts. Be assured that you both will bring many strengths to your new roles as parents.

Spend time talking about the special qualities that each of you will be bringing to parenthood. Take turns discussing your own strengths and then those of your partner. You will probably find that your positive attributes complement each other's to make you well-rounded parents. Qualities like a good sense of humor, self-confidence, flexibility, organizational ability, compassion, and an affectionate nature will go a long way to get you over the rough spots during the early weeks and all the years of parenthood. Build on these strengths to become the kind of parents you want to be.

Analyzing what you liked and disliked about the parenting you received as a child can also be helpful. Try to remember the things your parents did that you would like to copy. Also, try to recall the weaknesses in your parents' methods. In this way, you can avoid becoming trapped in the same negative patterns that you disliked as a child.

You may also want to talk about your concerns and perceived weaknesses. Many young couples feel unprepared for the immense job of parenting. You have many resources available to help you in this task. Included are your pediatrician, friends, relatives, books, and classes. Talk with others about your new roles as parents. Share your feelings with friends. Compare notes with other parents, and spend time with them and their babies. A new parents' group or class may be available in your area and can provide wonderful opportunities for sharing concerns and helpful hints, and for acting as a support group for you. If not, you can start one. Place a notice in your church bulletin or in your community newsletter. Hang a flyer in the grocery store or the neighborhood park. Set a day and time, and encourage new mothers to meet at the designated location and to bring a bag lunch, their baby, their concerns, and advice. You may be surprised at the response you receive. New mothers, especially, benefit from time out with their babies in an atmosphere of acceptance and common experience.

A new mothers' group is ideal for sharing concerns and helpful hints, and for getting much-needed support.

Make the Most of Those Special Times

Make the most of all the precious, close, happy times you share with each other and your baby. Feelings are very catching, and the baby who is surrounded by loving feelings in the early years is able to give them back later. Most of all, however, *remember your sense of humor*!

HELPING YOUR OTHER CHILDREN ADJUST

If you have other children, you should prepare them for the new arrival and also plan ways to help them get accustomed to having a new baby in the house. Their adjustment, in fact, will probably be greater than yours, since you did most of your adjusting with your first child.

During Pregnancy

The time to start preparing your other children for the new baby depends on their ages. Toddlers have no conception of time, so talking about a new baby before your seventh or eighth month will only make the wait more difficult. You can tell a preschooler of 3 or 4 when he begins showing an interest in your growing abdomen. He may also ask questions if he hears you discussing the topic. However, preschoolers, too, have limited time conception, so the wait can seem endless if you start talking about the baby too soon. Older children can be told immediately and be involved in the preparations for the baby from the beginning.

Two big-brothers-to-be learn about pregnancy and birth in a sibling preparation class.

If your children are going to attend the birth, they will need further preparation. Many facilities offer sibling preparation classes. This may be either a short class providing basic information and a tour of the facility, or more detailed instruction. (For a discussion of this, see "Children at Birth" on page 140.)

Most children love to look at their baby pictures and hear the story of their own birth. By sharing these with your other children, you can assure them that the same excitement and anticipation surrounded their arrivals as well. You can also use these stories to paint a realistic picture of what the new baby will be like. Many young children expect a ready-made playmate and are greatly disappointed when they find a baby who does little more than eat, sleep, wet, and cry. If you have friends who have young babies, take your preschooler to visit so that he can get an idea of what babies are really like.

If you still have a toddler sleeping in the crib that you plan to use for the baby, move him to his "grown-up" bed at least 2 months before your due date. Dismantle the crib and put it out of sight until the baby is born. This way, your toddler will not feel that the baby has stolen his bed. In the same vein, do not take away stuffed animals and baby toys from your older child and give them to the baby. Let him do this when he is ready. He is going to feel that the baby has taken over as it is. Do not add to his distress by asking him to give up some of his possessions.

During Your Hospital Stay

If possible, have someone whom your child likes stay with him at your home when you go to the hospital. If this is not possible, have him stay overnight with the person who will care for him before your due date so that he does not become frightened when you go to the hospital or birth center.

Call home at set times each day to talk to him. Do not be upset if he refuses to come to the telephone. He might feel angry that you left him. He might enjoy it if you hide several small toys or treats around the house before you leave, then give him directions to find one each time you call.

Take advantage of sibling visiting hours at your hospital. You can ease your child's anxiety about your absence and give him a chance to meet his new brother or sister. Celebrate the baby's birth day with a cake and a *0* candle, and maybe even gifts to the siblings from the baby.

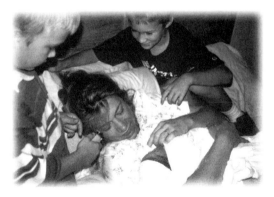

Greeting little brother.

At Home

When you arrive home from the hospital or birth center, let your husband carry the baby into the house so that your arms are free to hold and cuddle your other child. You may be amazed at how *big* he suddenly appears to you. If you like, bring him some gifts. Visit and play with him. Wait until he asks to see the baby, then satisfy his curiosity by letting him touch, hold, and talk to (and about) this new family member.

Jealousy is a fact of life and cannot be completely prevented. It is usually stronger in children under 5 because they are more dependent on their parents and have few outside interests. Older children adapt more easily because less of their time and interest is centered on the home. You can lessen feelings of jealousy in your preschooler by spending time alone with him each day. Make the baby's morning naptime your preschooler's special play time, during which he can do whatever he wants. Children also enjoy doing special things with Dad—a trip to the park or lunch at a restaurant can be a special treat for a child of any age.

Another way to decrease a preschooler's feelings of jealousy is to give him a doll to play with so that he has a "baby" to take care of while you take care of yours. Also, keep little wrapped gifts on hand to give him when friends bring presents for his new brother or sister. Letting him help you take care of the baby, even in little ways, will make him feel like an important member of the family.

Keep a close eye on 3- and 4-year-olds. They are wonderful "helpers," but sometimes they attempt tasks that could endanger the baby. The preschooler may try to pick up and carry the baby, or even attempt to get the newborn from the crib. Putting the infant in a playpen is often helpful just to protect him from a sibling's "help." The older child may try to share his food with the baby or try to change his diaper. Also, keep baby supplies out of his reach so that powders and creams are not available. Place a baby monitor near the infant and keep the receiver on or near you. That way, you can be aware of any unwanted "assistance."

If your child shows anger or other negative feelings toward you or the baby, encourage him to talk about them. Tell him that you understand these feelings and, in fact, even feel them yourself sometimes. Assure him that you love him, but tell him firmly that you cannot allow him to strike out at the baby. Give him a substitute—for example, a punching bag, or a hammer and pegboard—that he can use to vent his anger safely.

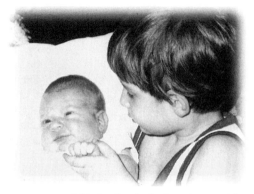

A big brother lovingly welcomes his new sister into the family.

Expect some regressive behavior on the part of your toddler or preschooler. If he is not already potty trained by the time the baby is born, wait at least 4 to 6 months or until you are sure that he is ready. Wet or soiled pants, and requests for the breast or a bottle are common. If you look at the situation from his point of view, it makes sense. He reasons that if the baby gets so much attention doing these things, he will, too. Let your child try to nurse or drink from a bottle if he wishes. Most children do not remember how to nurse if it has been a while. After a few attempts, he will realize that it is not much fun and will head off to do something else. Rarely, a toddler who was recently weaned may return to breastfeeding for a time. If you are uncomfortable with allowing your child to nurse, express some milk into a cup for him to taste. This may satisfy his curiosity.

Use the baby's feeding times as moments to share with your older child. Read a book, share a snack, or play a quiet game. If your child uses feeding times to act up, prepare a basket of special toys and treats that he can have only at those times. In this way, he will feel as important to you as the baby.

Support the side of your child that wants to grow up. Give him a chance to be proud of his maturity, and make comments that foster his self-esteem: "You do that so well." "You are such a help to Mommy." Remind him that there are disadvantages to being a baby—babies cannot play ball, go to birthday parties, or eat ice cream, for example. Have lots of patience and be prepared for the adjustment to take some time.

PETS AND THE NEW BABY

Sharing a pacifier moment.

Just as siblings need to be prepared for the new baby's arrival, so do pets. To many couples, their pet is their "first baby," and they are concerned about how the pet will adapt to the new baby and even about whether the pet will endanger him. Most pets adapt very well and grow to accept and love the new addition. Some pets, though, show signs that they need more attention or even become aggressive. It is very important to remember that close supervision of all pets is required. Because a dog is a pack animal, he sees the people in his home as the members of his pack. His view of his place in the pack and of this "new" pack member will affect his response to the baby. If he believes this new addition threatens his position, he may not adapt as well.

Your pet's personality will also help to determine how he reacts to the baby. Is he good with other children? How does he react when a baby cries? Is he tolerant of being handled, or does he snap if certain areas of his body are touched or possibly grabbed? Does he become aggressive if his food bowl is touched or if you try to take something from his mouth? Is he easily excited or nippy? Is he protective of his territory, or does he welcome strangers into his home? If your dog shows aggressive behavior, it is important to invest in specialized training to alter this behavior. Teach your dog the commands *sit*, *stay*, *down*, *no*, and *come*.

Begin to prepare your pet for the baby during the last weeks of pregnancy. A dog uses his senses of smell and sound to learn about his environment. Allow him to investigate the nursery and sniff the new scents. Cradle a blanket that has been sprinkled with powder, lotion, or even diaper cream. Speak to him in a pleasant, soothing tone of voice, pet him, and offer him a treat so he has a positive association with these smells. Never play tug of war with a baby blanket or baby toy. Reinforce calm interest, and discourage jumping or aggressive behavior. Play a tape of a baby crying to see how he reacts. If you have friends or family members with babies or young children, ask them to visit, especially if your dog has not been around many children.

If your pet has not had a physical recently or is not on monthly heartworm/parasite medication, it may be a good idea to take him to the veterinarian to have a complete physical, including a stool examination for parasites. Make sure he is current on all vaccinations. This would also provide an opportunity to discuss the subject of the new baby with a veterinarian who knows your pet.

While you are still in the hospital, have your husband wrap the baby in a blanket, then take the blanket home so the dog can become familiar with the smell of the baby. When you arrive home, you may want to have your husband carry the baby and place him directly in the crib. You can then greet your pet, who will be excited to see you after your absence. A little later, you can gradually introduce the pet and the baby. He can look at the baby first in the crib, then in your arms. Allow him to be curious and observe you feeding, changing, and holding the baby. Do not act overly frightened or react angrily if your pet approaches or licks the baby. This would reinforce that the baby is something negative. If your pet becomes upset when the baby cries, reassure and stroke him just as you would if he were frightened by thunder or other loud noises.

If your pet is territorial, it may be best to bring him outside (a neutral location) for his first view of the baby. Then you can all enter the house together. If he becomes overly excited with lots of company, do not have extra people present for the first meeting.

Occasionally, a pet will react to this new addition by having accidents, chewing, refusing to eat, or other signs that he is feeling abandoned. Make sure his routine is not altered drastically and that he is given the attention he is used to having. Continue taking him for his daily walk. Take time to play with him, and offer him lots of pats and kind words. Do not hit your dog for bad deeds. Reward positive behavior, rather than accentuating the negatives. A dog who becomes aggressive is instinctively protecting his territory from an invader. This can have very serious consequences. If the behavior is not altered, you may have to find another home for the dog.

To avoid a possible tragedy, do not leave your pet alone with the baby until you are absolutely sure you can trust the dog. When your baby starts to crawl, you need to be equally alert, as a dog can be an attractive plaything. Even the best animal may not take kindly to being grabbed or pinched. Teach your child to stroke and pet the dog; never allow hair pulling or ear tugging.

Cats are more independent than dogs and need to be handled a little differently. In general, follow the suggestions for introducing a dog to a new baby. Knowing your cat's personality and how he responds to people and new situations is your best guide to how he will act with the baby. An older cat who is used to lots of attention may act jealous or misbehave. Extra attention, especially when the baby is awake, should solve the problem.

Contrary to popular myth, cats cannot suck the air out of a baby's mouth. Occasionally, a cat may cuddle up with or sleep on top of an infant and may accidentally smother the baby. Because they can easily jump onto dressers or into cribs, cats should not be allowed into the baby's room unless you are

A Hint for the New Mother

❏ Do not get a new puppy when your baby is first born thinking that you will have plenty of time to train him.

there. Securely fasten netting over the crib to discourage jumping. Clip your cat's nails to prevent accidental scratches. If you have a mature male cat, he may spray to mark his territory. You may want to have him neutered prior to the arrival of the new baby. Neutering may also diminish aggressive behavior.

Most pets learn to love the new addition to the family, with the pet and child becoming close companions. Avoid problems by preparing your pet, identifying possible problems and remedying them before they become worse. Some couples plan to get a puppy during their first weeks at home with a new baby, thinking that they will have lots of time to spend training the puppy. But most parents are already overwhelmed by the lack of sleep and the responsibility of the new baby. It would be best to delay getting a puppy until the baby is older and sleeping better, and you are able to give a new puppy the attention he deserves.

FOR THE NEW FATHER: CHANGES IN YOUR LIFE

Bonding with Daddy.

While Mom adjusts to the major physical and emotional changes that the birth of a baby brings, you will also experience a major alteration in your life. You may find that this new addition requires your mate's undivided attention. In addition, visitors will also concentrate on the new baby and mother. At times, you may experience feelings of jealousy toward the infant if you feel neglected and left out. To avoid these feelings, become an active participant in the baby's care. Offer to change diapers, give baths, and take the baby for walks. Do not hesitate to perform these tasks because you fear you may not do them exactly as your mate does. The important thing is that you are bonding with your baby and developing a lasting relationship. You may even be more skilled than your mate at performing certain baby-related jobs. You can do anything Mom can do—with the exception of breastfeeding.

If you are concerned that a family member will take over and not allow you the opportunity to interact with your newborn, encourage her to delay her visit until you go back to work. This way, your mate will have help for a longer period of time, and you can enjoy the first weeks with your new baby.

Remember the positive attributes of your parents and try to duplicate them. If you have any negative childhood memories, try to avoid the things your parents did to cause them and develop your own style of fathering. Learn from your parents' mistakes and remember that no parent is perfect. Build on your strengths and those of your mate to develop a parenting style on which you can both agree.

You may find that your sexual feelings have changed since the birth of the baby. Some men find it difficult to view a woman who has become "a mother" as sexy right away. This Madonna complex may cause you to believe that sexual feelings are inappropriate. Others express ambivalence toward sex after viewing the birth of their baby. It may take some time before they can view the vagina as sexual, rather than as the opening that brought the new baby into the world. Your mate's body will also have changed and may still retain some of the effects of pregnancy, including added weight and breasts that secrete milk. While many men find the larger breasts attractive, some are uncomfortable with touching or kissing breasts that may respond by squirting milk. They may feel that the breasts are no longer for their enjoyment, but only to nourish the baby. There may also be great concern over initiating intercourse if the woman had an episiotomy or a laceration.

Your partner may also be reluctant to resume intimacy if she is exhausted, worried that the baby will wake up, or concerned about pain. Take it slowly, and start by being romantic. Take her out on a date. Offer a full body massage. Gradually, you will find that she is more receptive to your touch and may be ready for sexual intercourse. If you are concerned about pain, first check the area for sensitivity by performing perineal massage and ask for feedback. Massage vitamin E oil into the scar tissue. During sex, use a good water-soluble lubricant and provide adequate foreplay. If the woman assumes the superior position, she can control the depth of penetration. This is especially important for women who had cesarean sections, since having the man on top may be too uncomfortable on the incision. While resuming sex may not be automatic and exactly as before, patience and understanding can make this aspect of your relationship just as fulfilling.

You may be pleasantly surprised by the enormity of your love for the new baby, even finding excuses to reduce outside interests so you can spend time with the baby. Many men reorganize their priorities and become more mature in the process. The huge responsibility of having a baby will offer you an opportunity to bond and to develop a lasting relationship with your child. While parenting is not easy, it offers tremendous satisfaction and benefits to those parents who invest their time and energy in their children.

POSTPARTUM EXERCISES

You should begin exercising as soon as possible after childbirth, even within 24 hours. In fact, if your perineum is not numb from anesthesia, begin doing Kegels within the first 2 hours.

The muscle work involved in immediate postpartum exercise is not strenuous or harmful. It will help restore tone to your pelvic floor and abdominal muscles, as well as encourage good circulation in your legs. Your caregiver may give you a list of exercises to begin after delivery. If not, show him the following exercises and get his approval, as well as any modifications that he feels may be necessary in your particular case. Start gradually, and add exercises and repetitions as your strength and comfort permit. Do not overdo!

Unless otherwise noted, do each exercise twice a day, beginning with 2 to 3 repetitions and gradually working up to the number of repetitions listed. Consistency is much more important than the length of the session.

If you have a cesarean delivery, get your doctor's permission before starting a vigorous exercise program. For a suggested exercise program, see "Exercise After a Cesarean" on page 197.

First Day

Do the following exercises while still in the birthing room or as soon as you can in your regular room.

Super Kegel Exercise

Benefits: Tones the pelvic floor muscles. Improves circulation. Promotes healing of the perineum.

Directions: While lying down, sitting, or standing, contract the muscles of the pelvic floor and hold for 20 seconds. Continue to breathe normally.

Frequency: 1 rep every 2 hours, for a total of 10 reps a day. Do the first rep in the birthing room and 1 rep after every urination.

Abdominal Tightening

Benefits: Decreases abdominal flabbiness and helps restore muscle tone to the abdominal wall.

Directions: While sitting or standing, pull in the abdominal muscles and hold tightly for 5 seconds. Continue to breathe normally. Gradually increase the holding time to 10 seconds.

Frequency: As often as possible.

Ankle Rotating

Benefits: Aids blood circulation and prevents blood clots.

Directions: In bed, lie down or sit with your legs stretched out in front of you. Rotate your foot at the ankle three times in one direction, then three times in the other direction. Repeat with the other foot.

Frequency: 5 to 10 reps with each ankle per exercise session.

Foot Flexing and Stretching

Benefits: Aids blood circulation and prevents blood clots.

Directions: In bed, lie down or sit with your legs stretched out in front of you. Flex your foot, slowly bringing your toes toward your body. You will feel stretching in the calf muscle. Then release your foot, slowly pointing your toes away from you. Repeat with the other foot.

Frequency: 5 to 10 reps with each foot per exercise session.

Second Day

Continue the super Kegel exercise and abdominal tightening from the first day and add the following two exercises.

Pelvic Tilt

Benefit: Tones the abdominal muscles.

Directions: Lie on your back with your knees bent and your feet flat on the floor. Arch your back and press your buttocks against the floor. Then release your buttocks and press the small of your back against the floor, contracting your abdominal muscles. Continue to breathe normally.

Frequency: 5 to 10 reps per exercise session.

Prone Resting Position

Benefit: Helps the uterus return to its normal position.

Directions: Lie on your stomach with a folded blanket or pillow under your abdomen and upper thighs, and another one under your ankles. Turn your face to one side, eyes opened or closed, and rest for as long as you wish.

Prone resting position.

Frequency: As often as possible.

Third Day

On the third day, check for separation of the recti muscles before you do any further abdominal exercising. The recti muscles are a band of muscles that runs vertically through the center of the abdomen. The band is divided into two halves, which are joined by connective tissue. Many pregnant women experience separation of the recti muscles, especially if they did not use good body mechanics while lifting.

Checking for separation of the recti muscles.

To check for separation, lie on your back with your legs bent and your feet flat on the floor. Press the fingers of one hand in a horizontal line into the area below your navel, then slowly raise your head and shoulders about 8 inches off the floor. You should feel the bands of muscles on both sides of your abdomen pull toward the center and move your fingers out of the way. If three or more fingers slide into a gap between the muscle bands, you have separated recti muscles.

To correct the problem, do head lifting (see below) to close the gap before continuing with your regular exercises. The gap should close to the normal 1/2 inch within 7 to 10 days. Until the gap is closed, do not rotate or bend your trunk from side to side, or twist your hips. These movements could pull your recti muscles further apart.

If your recti muscles are fine, continue doing the super Kegel exercise, abdominal tightening, pelvic tilt, and prone resting position from the first 2 days.

Head Lifting

Benefit: Restores the recti muscles to their proper position.

Directions: Lie on your back with your knees bent and your feet flat on the floor. Cross your arms over your abdomen and take a deep breath. Slowly exhale and raise your head off the floor, pulling your abdominal muscles together with your hands. Inhale and slowly lower your head.

Head lifting to correct separated recti muscles.

Frequency: 10 reps per set, 5 sets per day.

Second Week

Continue the super Kegel exercise from the first week. Replace the remainder of the exercises with the following exercises, which are more advanced versions of the earlier ones.

Modified Sit-Up

Benefit: Tones the abdominal muscles.

Directions: Lie on your back with your knees bent and your feet flat on the floor. Inhale, then exhale, raising your head and shoulders off the floor and reaching both your hands toward your knees. Inhale, lying back down.

Variation: As you exhale and raise your head and shoul-

Modified sit-up.

Variation of modified sit-up.

ders off the floor, reach both your hands to the outside of your right knee. Inhale and lie back down, then exhale, raise your head and shoulders, and reach both hands to the outside of your left knee. Inhale and lie back down.

Caution: If the recti muscles are still separated, support them as you do this advanced version of the head lifting exercise. Do not do the variation of this exercise until the recti muscles are restored.

Frequency: 5 to 10 reps per exercise session.

Pelvic Rock

Benefit: Tones the abdominal muscles.

Directions: Kneel on the floor on your hands and knees. Align your head with your spine, tuck in your bottom, pull up your abdominal muscles, and press up your spine at the lower back. Hold this position for a few seconds, then return to the starting position. Repeat the exercise with a constant rhythm and a rocking motion.

Frequency: 5 to 10 reps per set, 3 sets per day.

Knee-Chest Position

Benefit: Helps the uterus return to its proper position.

Knee-chest position.

Directions: Get down on your knees, spacing them about 12 to 18 inches apart. Bend forward at the hips, lowering your chest to the floor and placing the side of your face on top of your folded hands, your elbows pointing out to the sides. If desired, position a pillow under your face and chest. Contract and relax your abdominal muscles as many times as you wish, then rest for at least 5 minutes.

Frequency: 2 sets per day.

Third Week

Continue the super Kegel exercise, pelvic rock, and knee-chest position from the first 2 weeks and add the following five exercises. In addition, to strengthen your cardiovascular system and tone your body in general, begin walking briskly around your neighborhood every day.

Side Kicks

Benefit: Helps restore the waistline.

Side kicks.

Directions: Lie on the floor on your right side with your arms over your head and your head resting on your right arm. Keeping your right leg slightly bent, raise your left arm and leg toward the ceiling and touch your hand to your knee. Return your arm and leg to the starting position, stretching the arm over your head and elongating your waist and rib cage. Repeat 5 to 10 times on that side. Relax. Turn to your left side and repeat with the other arm and leg.

Frequency: 5 to 10 reps with each arm and leg per exercise session.

Modified Sit-Up II

Benefit: Tones the abdominal muscles.

Directions: Lie on your back with your knees bent, your feet flat on the floor, and your hands clasped behind your head. Inhale, then exhale, raising your head and shoulders off the floor and reaching your elbows toward your knees; do not touch the knees. Inhale, lying back down.

Frequency: 5 to 10 reps per exercise session.

Modified sit-up II.

Modified Sit-Up III

Benefit: Tones the abdominal muscles.

Directions: Lie on your back with your knees bent, your feet flat on the floor, and your hands clasped behind your head. Inhale, then exhale, raising your head and shoulders off the floor and reaching both your elbows to the outside of your right knee; do not touch the knee. Inhale and lie back down, then exhale, raise your head and shoulders, and reach both elbows to the outside of your left knee. Inhale and lie back down.

Frequency: 5 to 10 reps per exercise session.

Modified sit-up III.

Single Leg Raises

Benefits: Tones the leg and abdominal muscles. Improves the blood circulation.

Directions: Lie on your back with your knees bent, your feet flat on the floor, and your hands clasped behind your head. Draw your right knee toward your chest, then inhale, point your toes, and continue raising the leg toward the ceiling until the knee is straight. Exhale, flex the foot, and slowly lower the straightened leg to the floor. Return the leg to the starting position and repeat the movement with the left leg.

Frequency: 5 to 10 reps with each leg per exercise session.

Single leg raises: Draw your knee toward your chest . . .

. . . raise your leg with the toes pointed . . .

. . . then flex your foot and slowly lower your leg.

Single leg sliding.

Single Leg Sliding

Benefits: Tones the leg and abdominal muscles. Improves the blood circulation.

Directions: Lie on your back with your knees bent, your feet flat on the floor, and your hands clasped behind your head. Inhaling through your nose, draw your right knee toward your chest, flexing your foot. Then exhaling through your mouth, slowly return the foot to the floor and slide the leg downward, pressing the small of your back to the floor and contracting your abdominal muscles. Return the leg to the starting position and repeat the movement with the left leg.

Frequency: 5 to 10 reps with each leg per exercise session.

Fourth Through Sixth Weeks

Continue doing the super Kegel exercise, side kicks, single leg raises, and single leg sliding from the first 3 weeks and add the following two exercises. In addition, increase the length of time you spend walking around your neighborhood.

Hip rolls.

Hip Rolls

Benefit: Helps restore the waistline.

Directions: Lie on your back with your arms stretched out sideways like a *T.* Draw your knees toward your chest, then roll your hips to the right, lowering your knees and legs to the floor on your right side; keep your back and arms flat on the floor. Return your hips and knees to the center position, then roll your hips to the left, and lower your knees and legs to the floor on your left. Return to the center position.

Frequency: 5 to 10 reps to both sides per exercise session.

Modified sit-up IV.

Modified Sit-Up IV

Benefit: Strengthens the abdominal muscles.

Directions: Lie on your back with your knees bent, your feet flat on the floor, and your arms folded across your chest. Inhale, then exhale, raising your head and shoulders to a 30-degree angle. Inhale, lying back down.

Frequency: 5 to 10 reps per exercise session.

After the 6-Week Checkup

Continue practicing all the exercises from the fourth through sixth weeks—side kicks, single leg raises, single leg sliding, hip rolls, and modified sit-up IV—for at least the next 2 months. In addition, continue walking briskly around your neighborhood and add an aerobic exercise such as jogging, swimming, or bicycle riding. Continue doing your super Kegels, which are an exercise that you should do for the rest of your life.

POSTPARTUM SEX

The time following the birth of your baby will be exciting, complicated, and busy. Your body will go through rapid changes, adjusting from the pregnant to the nonpregnant state. As new parents, you and your husband will have an altered relationship. Being pregnant and in love is quite different from being parents and in love. After being free and spontaneous as lovers, you will now also be parents, with new roles, new responsibilities, and a whole new life.

The love relationship between you and your husband will continue to grow in many ways, and part of that love relationship will be the enjoyment of sex. You may be confused by what you are told or even by your own feelings as individuals and as a couple. A number of factors will influence your decision about when to resume sexual intercourse.

Medical Advice

Some caregivers advise their patients to delay having sex again until after the 6-week postpartum checkup. Others suggest waiting until the vaginal discharge has stopped. Waiting ensures that both the stitches and the placental site within the uterus have healed. With a cesarean birth, the abdominal scar must also heal. Until these areas have healed completely, bacteria could be introduced and cause an infection.

Fatigue

The first few weeks and months with the new baby will be the busiest. Your time will not really be your own. You might not get a decent night's sleep for a while, and the days will be exhausting. Although your husband's routine will be somewhat changed, your lifestyle will be changed much more dramatically. It will be difficult to be a good parent around the clock—but sexy, too? It just will not seem possible for a while!

Hormones

Your body's hormones are actively involved in all the changes connected with birth and breastfeeding. It may take them some time to get back into balance. These hormonal changes may affect your feelings and sexual responsiveness. You may want very much to make love, or you may feel turned off by sex for a time. If you are turned off, do not berate yourself—the desire will return. The following four-step method[3] can be used to help reawaken your sexual desire:

1. *Nonsexual touch.* Daily hugging and cuddling, showering together, and nonsexual massage can help both partners to rediscover the pleasure of touch and to increase their anticipation.

2. *Sexual touch.* Using massage on each other in a sexual way while continuing to avoid all genital contact will further increase desire and enhance awareness of each other's sexuality.

3. *Genital stimulation.* Gentle massage of the vagina, using a sterile water-soluble lubricating jelly, will help to determine the woman's sensitivity and whether she is ready for intercourse. She can reciprocate by massaging her partner's genital area manually or orally.

Hints for the New Father

❑ After the birth of your baby, stay overnight in the hospital with your mate.

❑ Encourage your mate to begin doing super Kegels.

❑ Change the baby and bring him to his mother for feeding in the middle of the night.

❑ Cuddle the newborn on your bare chest.

❑ Take time off from work to be with your mate and baby.

❑ Assist your mate with the household chores.

❑ Encourage your mate to nap.

❑ Spend time with your other children.

❑ Ask your mate out for a date.

❑ Discuss the birth control options with your mate.

❑ Express your affection for your mate and make her feel special by bringing home flowers, a gift, or dinner, or just saying, "I love you."

❑ Give your mate a massage.

❑ Allow yourself time to adjust to your new role as a parent.

❑ Enjoy being a dad.

4. *Sexual intercourse.* Using repeated *partial* penetration and withdrawal will ease the stretching of the vagina by the penis.

Practice these steps with a relaxed attitude.

Pain

Some new mothers find intercourse painful or uncomfortable, especially if they resume it too soon after giving birth. Some men are hesitant because of concern for their mates. Patience and gentleness are important. Your perineum and vagina must heal. If your episiotomy is overcorrected, making your vaginal opening smaller than it was before, or if you have vaginal adhesions, you should try gentle dilation, first using the fingers and then vaginal dilators from your caregiver. If your vaginal area is still tender, you may find that the most comfortable position is lying side by side, which takes the pressure off the episiotomy site. A warm bath before lovemaking may also help.

Decreased vaginal lubrication due to hormonal changes might also make intercourse painful. This situation may last longer for the breastfeeding mother. Applying a water-soluble jelly to the penis and vagina remedies this problem. Do not use a non-water-soluble lubricant, such as petroleum jelly, because it keeps air out and allows bacteria to grow.

Breastfeeding

Some breastfeeding mothers enjoy sex immensely; others do not for a while. Fathers have feelings about breastfeeding also. Some find it very attractive, while others find it is somewhat inhibiting to their sexual feelings.

Breasts are an important part of human sexuality—first, as the means of nourishment for babies, and second, as a source of sexual stimulation and pleasure. If you have been thinking of breasts as being intended solely for sexual pleasure, both of you will need some time to get used to the idea of breasts filled with milk. Some nursing mothers do not enjoy breast stimulation, and many couples find new areas of the body for sexual foreplay. At the same time, you need to be assured that your baby will not contract an infection if your love play includes your breasts.

One thing that may catch you unaware is a leaking of milk during love play or orgasm, resulting in both of you getting soaked. This happens because oxytocin is released during breast stimulation and orgasm, and oxytocin is the hormone that triggers milk let-down. This release of milk is normal and natural. It may help to make love after nursing, when the breasts are relatively empty (and the baby is more likely to be asleep). You could also try wearing a nursing bra and pads to prevent leaking at a stimulating moment. Towels to keep the bedding dry are also a logical preparation.

If you bottlefeed your baby, you may still have an uncomfortable amount of milk within your breasts for a few weeks after delivery. Since sexual activity involving the breasts encourages milk production, you should avoid the breasts during sexual foreplay to discourage milk production.

New Responsibilities

The baby, no matter how adorable he is, may almost seem to function as a "chaperone," which can be very inhibiting at times. The spontaneity in your love life may take a dive: "Is the baby going to wake up?" "Do we have enough time between feedings?" Sexy feelings hardly get a chance if you are always listening for a cry.

Your new responsibilities may fatigue both of you, especially during the early weeks of adjustment. But the tension and fatigue may build even further if you do not take some time out for yourselves. Change, feed, and cuddle the baby, then put him to bed, shut the door, and take time to talk to each other, relax, caress, and make love.

Fear of Becoming Pregnant

No matter how thrilled you both will be with the new baby, the thought of having another one right away may be alarming. The two of you will need to address family planning before the postpartum checkup and then discuss it with your caregiver. Exclusive and frequent breastfeeding may inhibit ovulation and the onset of your period, but it is not 100-percent effective at preventing pregnancy.

Combined oral contraceptives that contain both estrogen and progestin are not compatible with breastfeeding, since the estrogen reduces milk production and alters the composition of the milk. This results in babies who gain weight slowly and require supplementing with formula. To ensure an adequate milk supply and success with breastfeeding, wait 6 months before starting combined pills. Progestin-only birth control pills, Norplant, and Depo-Provera are compatible with breastfeeding, since they do not contain estrogen. There is a concern among some professionals, however, that even though the quantities are small, these synthetic hormones do pass into the breastmilk. The long-term effects of early exposure to contraceptive hormones are not known.[4] The potential effects on the baby may be reduced if these hormonal methods are delayed until the baby is 6 months old.

Due to changes in the vagina and uterus following childbirth, your old diaphragm may not fit correctly. It may also be dried out and contain tiny holes. You can be refitted at your 6-week checkup. The sponge method of contraception is no longer available in the United States. Menstrual periods must resume with regularity before the rhythm method can be used. A condom and foam or jelly may be best for the first few weeks. The condom will decrease the possibility of introducing infection, and the foam or jelly will lubricate the vagina. Remember that all methods are only as reliable as those who use them. For a summary of the birth control methods currently available in the United States, see Table 12.1 on page 294.

In 1996, the FDA endorsed two methods that could be used for emergency contraception in cases of unprotected sex or in cases where the primary method failed (for example, condom breakage). One method involves the woman using a high-dose birth control pill. The first dose must be taken within 72 hours after unprotected intercourse, with the second dose taken 12 hours later. (For the dosages, see "Morning After Doses" on page 300.) This method is considered a one-time method and 75-percent effective. When using this method, it is important that the woman also begin using a reliable form of birth control. Another, more effective method is the insertion of a copper-T intrauterine device (IUD) within 7 days after unprotected intercourse. Following the insertion, the IUD can be left in place for up to 10 years. Emergency contraception is not well known in this country. Studies have shown no long-term or serious side effects.[5] For more information or if your

Table 12.1. Methods of Contraception Used in the United States [6,7,8]

Method	What Is It?	How Does It Work?	How Reliable or Effective Is It?
BARRIER			
Condom	A sheath, made of either latex rubber or lamb intestinal membrane ("skin"), designed to fit snugly over the erect penis. May be prelubricated. May have a reservoir to hold the sperm.	Prevents sperm from getting inside the vagina during intercourse.	64%–97%; effectiveness is greatest when used with another method, such as a spermicide.
Female condom	A lubricated polyurethane sheath with flexible rings on each end.	Prevents sperm from getting inside the uterus during intercourse.	88%–97% when used alone; effectiveness is greater when combined with a condom.
Diaphragm	A shallow rubber cup with a firm, but pliant rim. Should always be used with a spermicidal jelly or cream.	Fits inside the vagina and forms a barrier between the cervix and the sperm. The jelly or cream kills the sperm.	70%–98%.
Cervical cap	A large, soft rubber thimble with a firm, but pliant rim. Should always be used with a spermicidal jelly or cream.	Fits inside the vagina, snugly against the cervix, and forms a barrier between the uterus and the sperm. The jelly or cream kills the sperm.	78%–94%.
SPERMICIDE			
Foam, jelly, cream, film	A cream or jelly, available in tubes, a foam, available in cans or individual applicators, or a dissolvable film.	Acts as a physical barrier between the sperm and the uterus, and contains a chemical that kills sperm.	60%–98%; effectiveness is greatest when used with another method, such as a condom.

How Is It Used?	What Are the Advantages?	What Are the Disadvantages?	What Are the Side Effects or Complications?
Placed on the erect penis prior to contact with the vagina. After ejaculation, the penis should be removed from the vagina immediately.	Effective; safe; available without a prescription; latex provides protection against AIDS and other sexually transmitted diseases (STDs).	Often found objectionable. Interrupts intercourse. Can be messy. Can break. Should be used only with a water-based lubricant such as K-Y jelly; is weakened by petroleum-based products such as Vaseline petroleum jelly. Lambskin does not protect against AIDS or other STDs.	Allergic reaction to latex.
Inserted in the vagina before intercourse, with one ring in and the other left out. Must be removed afterwards very carefully.	Available without a prescription; protects somewhat against AIDS and other STDs.	Awkward to insert. Slips during use. Not aesthetically appealing to some couples.	Vaginal irritation. Penile irritation.
Coated with spermicide and inserted in the vagina before intercourse. Can be inserted up to 6 hours beforehand. Must stay in at least 6 hours afterwards.	Effective; safe; may reduce the risk of cervical cancer; may protect somewhat against STDs.	Must be fitted by a health-care professional. Can be difficult to insert. Can be inconvenient or messy. Requires reapplication of spermicide for repeated intercourse. Weight gain or loss of over 10 pounds may affect the fit.	Vaginal irritation. Very rarely, toxic shock syndrome if allowed to remain in for a prolonged period of time.
Inserted in the vagina before intercourse. Can be inserted many hours beforehand. Must remain in for at least 8 hours afterwards, but not for more than 48 hours.	Convenient, reapplication of spermicide is not necessary for repeated intercourse; may protect somewhat against STDs.	Cannot always be fitted properly. May be difficult to insert. Should be used only by women with normal Pap tests.	Uterine or cervical infection. Possible increased risk of toxic shock syndrome. Genital burning, irritation.
Inserted in the vagina before intercourse. Can be used up to 30 minutes beforehand. Must be reapplied with repeated intercourse. Must remain undisturbed (no douching) for at least 8 hours afterwards.	Effective; safe; good lubrication; available without a prescription; products containing nonoxynol-9 may protect somewhat against AIDS.	Must be inserted just before intercourse. Can be inconvenient or messy.	Vaginal irritation. Penile irritation.

Method	What Is It?	How Does It Work?	How Reliable or Effective Is It?
HORMONAL			
Combined pill, progestin-only pill	Pills containing synthetic hormones similar to the ones made in the ovaries. The combined pill contains two hormones, estrogen and progestin; the progestin-only pill contains one hormone.	Prevents the egg's release from the ovary, plus thickens the cervical mucus and changes the lining of the uterus, making it difficult for a fertilized egg to begin growing.	97%–99% if used consistently; much less if used carelessly.
Norplant	Hormone implant consisting of six small silicone rubber capsules or two slightly larger rods.	Continuously releases a small amount of progestin into the body to inhibit ovulation and to thicken the cervical mucus.	99%.
Depo-Provera	An intramuscular injection of the hormone progestin.	Inhibits ovulation.	99%.
INTRAUTERINE DEVICES (IUDs)			
Progestasert, Copper-T	A small plastic *T*-shaped device with a thin string that is inserted into the uterus by your caregiver.	Causes a reaction within the uterus that impedes fertilization or that keeps a fertilized egg from becoming attached to the uterine wall.	95%–99%.

How Is It Used?	What Are the Advantages?	What Are the Disadvantages?	What Are the Side Effects or Complications?
Taken orally. One combined pill is taken every day for 3 weeks, with 1 week off. One progestin-only pill is taken every day, with no time off.	Convenient; extremely effective; does not interfere with sex; may reduce menstrual cramps.	Requires a prescription. A medical exam is recommended. Cannot be taken by all women. Does not protect against AIDS or other STDs.	Nausea, weight gain, headache, irregular periods, missed periods, spotting, darkened facial skin, depression. Rarely, blood clots in the legs, lungs, or brain; heart attack (with the combined pill).
Implanted under the skin of the upper arm by your caregiver in a simple office procedure.	Long-lasting (up to 5 years); convenient; effective; does not interfere with sex; contraceptive effects are easily reversed.	Implant procedure requires special training. Removal may be difficult. Does not protect against AIDS or other STDs; expensive initially, but cost effective in the long run. Protection may not last 5 years in overweight women.	Irregular periods, spotting, depression, headache, nervousness, weight gain, acne, hair loss, infection of the implant site, scarring at the site after removal.
Injected every 3 months by the office nurse.	Convenient; effective.	The level of progestin is high immediately following the injection. Must be re-injected every 3 months. Does not protect against AIDS or other STDs; takes 6 months or more to regain fertility.	Irregular periods, headache, weight gain, increased risk of osteoporosis, delayed fertility when the injections are discontinued.
Inserted in the uterus by your caregiver. The type that releases progesterone must be replaced yearly; the type that releases copper can remain in for up to 10 years. The string must be checked by the woman after each menstrual period to make sure the device is still in place.	Effective; allows spontaneity; usually not felt by either partner during sex.	A mutually monogamous relationship is desirable because of the risk of STDs. Should not be used by women with a history of pelvic inflammatory disease. Can be expelled by the uterus. Does not protect against AIDS or other STDs. The yearly removal and reinsertion of the Progestasert IUD makes this an expensive method. Copper-T used more commonly.	Cramps, bleeding, spotting. Uterine infection or inflammation, resulting in scarring of the reproductive organs or sterility. Pain, bleeding, fever, discharge. Rarely, uterine perforation during insertion.

Method	What Is It?	How Does It Work?	How Reliable or Effective Is It?
STERILIZATION			
Tubal ligation	A surgical procedure in which a section of each fallopian tube is cut out and the ends are tied off.	Prevents the sperm from reaching the egg and the egg from reaching the uterus.	Almost 100%.
Vasectomy	A surgical procedure in which a section of the vas deferens is cut out and the ends are tied off.	Prevents the sperm from being released during ejaculation.	99%.
NATURAL FAMILY PLANNING			
Periodic abstinence	The avoidance of intercourse each month on the days on which a woman would most likely become pregnant.	The release of the egg is predicted through methods such as maintaining a chart of the basal body temperature, checking the vaginal secretions, and keeping a calendar of the menstrual periods.	90%–97% or less, depending on the method and the consistency of use; effectiveness is greatest when all these natural family planning techniques are combined.
EMERGENCY CONTRACEPTION			
Morning After Pill	A high-dose birth control pill taken after unprotected intercourse.	Prevents the fertilized egg from implanting by altering the lining of the uterus.	75%.

How Is It Used?	What Are the Advantages?	What Are the Disadvantages?	What Are the Side Effects or Complications?
Performed by a surgeon either postpartum or on an outpatient basis.	Effective; low rate of complications; improved sexual relations due to removal of the fear of pregnancy; no loss of sexual desire or ability.	Involves surgery. Is not usually reversible. Does not protect against AIDS or other STDs.	Pain for several days. Rarely, the wrong structure is tied off or the tube grows back together.
Performed by a urologist in his office.	Effective; low rate of complications; improved sexual relations due to removal of the fear of pregnancy; no loss of sexual desire or ability; less invasive than tubal ligation.	Involves surgery. Is not usually reversible. Does not protect against AIDS or other STDs.	Pain and possible swelling for several days. Rarely, the wrong structure is tied off or the tube grows back together. Should have sperm count taken prior to having unprotected intercourse.
Careful records are maintained on several factors (such as the basal body temperature, vaginal secretions, and onset of menstrual bleeding), then studied to predict ovulation.	Safe; can be effective; no religious objection; teaches women about their menstrual cycles.	Difficult to use if the menstrual cycle is irregular. Requires abstinence for a significant part of each cycle. Does not protect against AIDS or other STDs.	None.
Taken orally. The first dose must be taken within 72 hours after unprotected intercourse, with the second dose taken 12 hours later.	Convenient; no long-term or serious side effects.	Must be prescribed by your caregiver.	If vomiting occurs within 2 hours of taking a dose, the dose must be retaken. The following danger signs should be reported immediately—severe abdominal pain; chest pain, cough, shortness of breath; severe headache, dizziness, weakness, numbness; vision loss or blurring, difficulty speaking; severe pain in leg (calf or thigh); jaundice; severe depression.

Method	What Is It?	How Does It Work?	How Reliable or Effective Is It?
Copper-T IUD	A small plastic *T*-shaped device with a thin string that is inserted into the uterus by your caregiver. For emergency contraception, it must be inserted within 7 days of intercourse.	Causes a reaction within the uterus that impedes fertilization or that keeps a fertilized egg from becoming attached to the uterine wall.	99%.

caregiver is not familiar with the methods, you can call the Emergency Contraceptive Hotline at 800–584–9911. This is operated 24 hours a day by the Washington-based Reproductive Health Technologies Project and Bridging the Gap Foundation. For summaries of these methods, see Table 12.1.

Feelings

Warmth and affection mean a lot to new parents, especially during the early adjustment period. A cuddle and hug may mean more to you than making love for a while. For many couples, the baby arrives before they have a chance to become content with their sexual life. The movies do not tell you that a satisfying and exciting sex life can take years to develop.

Many a man feels pushed aside when a baby arrives needing so much attention. Instead of feeling that he has gained a child, he may feel that he has lost a lover. If your husband feels this way, you will need to reassure him and to tell him that your seemingly endless involvement with the baby does not mean that your love for him has diminished. You will receive a lot of touching and body contact while caring for your baby all day, but your husband, at work, will not and will need this when he gets home. Encourage him to help with the baby, and do not forget to give him an extra hug and kiss now and then.

You may find it quite a change to be home alone with a baby, especially if you have always worked outside the home. You will need to be reassured that your new role as a mother is important, even though you will not be earning

---

Morning After Doses

The FDA has issued these instructions for using six brands of birth control pills as emergency contraception.[9] Take the following number of pills up to 72 hours after unprotected sex, then again 12 hours later.

❑ *For Wyeth-Ayerst Laboratories' brands,* take two white tablets of Ovral, four light orange tablets of Nordette, four white tablets of Lo/Ovral, or four yellow tablets of Triphasil.

❑ *For Berlex Laboratories' brands,* take four light orange tablets of Levlen or four yellow tablets of Tri-Levlen.

It is vital to take the proper color pill because birth control pills come in different levels of hormones. In addition, some brands contain placebo pills that women take for 1 week each month.

How Is It Used?	What Are the Advantages?	What Are the Disadvantages?	What Are the Side Effects or Complications?
Must be inserted by your caregiver.	Has a high level of effectiveness.	Expensive. Should not be used by women with a history of pelvic inflammatory disease. Can be expelled by the uterus.	Cramps, bleeding, spotting. Uterine infection or inflammation, resulting in scarring of the reproductive organs or sterility. Pain, bleeding, fever, discharge. Rarely, uterine perforation during insertion.

money for it. You will require love and confidence boosting, and will need your husband to tell you that you are still desirable. If he takes no special notice of you until you flop into bed exhausted, your frustration and resentment may build.

It would be sad if you chose to forgo warmth and affection from your husband out of concern that they would lead to sex. Try not to put so much emphasis on having sexual intercourse and wondering if "tonight is the night." Loving each other does not have to be sexual intercourse or nothing at all. Cuddling in each other's arms, touching, kissing, giving or receiving a massage, and enjoying each other are very important ways of feeling close.

The main thing that you and your husband should try to do is to keep in touch with each other's feelings. The concerns that you will have as new parents will not really be isolated problems, but rather typical of what you will find throughout your life as a couple. If you can talk about your feelings and needs now, you will find that your understanding of each other will enhance your sexual relationship for the rest of your life together. Couples who are honest and patient with each other do not have trouble finding solutions to sexual problems. Talk about your feelings, keep your senses of humor, and look together for solutions. After all, you will be friends and lovers long after your child has grown up and left home.

Warmth and affection are vital for new parents.

CONCLUSION

Having a baby will be one of the most exciting adventures of your life. This single act, more than any other, will change your lifestyle. The journey begins during pregnancy as you learn new things about your body and unborn child. Your awareness of your baby and his sensations will begin to develop the mother-child bond and your communication with him. The act of labor and giving birth will help to cement this relationship. The commitment you make to this tiny individual will last throughout his lifetime. Make wise and informed choices right from the start of the pregnancy and continue that philosophy into his childhood. Parenthood is the most important and the most challenging job that you will ever do, and it can be the most rewarding.

Appendix A
Labor Record

For the labor partner: Use this form to keep track of your partner's progress during labor. You do not need to record every contraction, just enough to keep you aware of any changes in frequency and duration of the contractions. As the contractions become stronger and closer together, your partner will need encouragement and support.

Keep this as a personal record of the baby's birth. Use the "Comments" column to record your partner's feelings, as well as any significant events. You can also keep track of the medications that your partner is given and when, the interventions that are used and when they are started, when your partner urinates (she should do this every 1 to 2 hours), when the membranes rupture, and so on. Note effacement, dilation, and station whenever they are checked.

Personal Labor Record

Time Contraction Began	Length of Contraction	Effacement, Dilation, Station	Comments

Time Contraction Began	Length of Contraction	Effacement, Dilation, Station	Comments

Appendix B
Recommended Reading List

Pregnancy to Parenthood provides basic information on many topics related to pregnancy, birth, and the newborn. For more information on these topics, see the following books. If you cannot find a certain book in the public library or local bookstore, you may be able to order it directly from the ICEA Bookcenter, P.O. Box 20048, Minneapolis, Minnesota 55420-0048.

Breastfeeding

Eiger, Marvin S., and Sally W. Olds, *The Complete Book of Breastfeeding*, Workman Publishing, 1987. A complete examination of the subject, with much practical information.

La Leche League International, *The Womanly Art of Breastfeeding*, 5th edition, Penguin Books, 1991. A valuable, complete, and practical guide. A must for every woman planning to nurse her baby.

Pryor, Gale, *Nursing Mother, Working Mother*, Harvard Common Press, 1997. Covers all aspects of the breastfeeding–working mother experience. Offers clear, practical solutions.

Pryor, Karen, *Nursing Your Baby*, Pocket Books, 1991. Valuable and interesting information on the physiology of the breasts and on the nursing process.

Woessner, Candace, Judith Lauwers, and Barbara Bernard, *Breastfeeding Today: A Mother's Companion*, Avery Publishing Group, 1996. A comprehensive, up-to-date guide designed for today's woman.

Cesarean Birth

Cohen, Nancy Wainer, *Open Season: A Survival Guide for Natural Childbirth and VBAC in the 90s*, Greenwood Publishing Group, 1991. Provides the information and confidence necessary for achieving a vaginal delivery.

Flamm, Bruce L., *Birth After Cesarean: The Medical Facts*, Simon & Schuster Trade, 1992. A complete guide to vaginal birth after cesarean section, with crucial information to assist in avoiding an unnecessary cesarean.

Young, Diony, and Charles Mahan, *Unnecessary Cesareans: Ways to Avoid Them*, 2nd edition, International Childbirth Education Association, 1989. Explains what to do during your pregnancy, labor, and delivery to decrease the chance of having a cesarean and how to have a positive experience if a cesarean is necessary.

For Children

Carroll, Teresa, *Mommy Breastfeeds Our Baby*, n.p., 1990. A booklet teaching children that breastfeeding is a natural and special way to feed a baby.

Malecki, Maryann, *Mom and Dad and I Are Having a Baby!* Pennypress, 1982. A picture book to prepare children of all ages to be present at birth.

Mayle, Peter, *Where Did I Come From*, Carol Publishing Group, 1973. A clear presentation of the physiology of conception, pregnancy, and birth, presented with humor. Intended for 8- to 12-year-olds.

Neri, Renee B., *Our Family Grows*, Avery Publishing Group, 1985. Delightful coloring and activity book to encourage the involvement of a young child in the planning and excitement surrounding a sibling's arrival.

Nilsson, Lennart, and Lena K. Swanberg, *How Was I Born?* Delacorte, 1994. Basic, clear presentation of pregnancy, from conception to childbirth. Beautifully illustrated.

Rogers, Fred, *The New Baby*, Putnam Publishing Group, 1996. Examines the feelings a child may have about a new baby. Includes photographs of family scenes.

Scott, Ann H., *On Mother's Lap*, Houghton Mifflin, 1992. A young Eskimo boy discovers that even though a new baby has joined the family, there is still room for him.

Sheffield, Margaret, and Sheila Bewley, *Where Do*

Babies Come From? Alfred A. Knopf, 1973. A good basic exploration of the physiology of intercourse, conception, pregnancy, and birth. Sensitively illustrated with colorful drawings.

Nutrition

Goldbeck, Nikki, *As You Eat, So Your Baby Grows*, Ceres Press, 1994. A brief guide to nutrition during pregnancy.

Lansky, Vicki, *Feed Me! I'm Yours*, Meadowbrook Press, 1994. Helpful information and recipes to make eating fun for your toddler.

Parenthood, Childcare, and Child Development

Bing, Elisabeth, and Libby Colman, *Laughter and Tears*, Henry Holt & Co., 1996. Tells mothers what to expect emotionally at various stages during the first year after giving birth.

Brazelton, T. Berry, *Working and Caring*, Addison-Wesley Publishing Co., 1987. Sensible, comforting advice for working parents on raising a family while both parents hold full-time jobs.

Brinkley, Ginny, and Sherry Sampson, *You and Your New Baby*, Pink Inc! 1991. A basic baby-care guide, presented in a simplified format.

Burck, Frances Wells, *Babysense: A Practical and Supportive Guide to Baby Care*, St. Martin's Press, 2nd edition, 1991. A unique guide that answers most of your "how-to" questions and explains both the mental and physical aspects of infant development.

Caplan, Frank, *The Second Twelve Months of Life*, Berkley Publishing Group, 1983. A month-by-month guide to development in the second year.

Caplan, Theresa, *Early Childhood Years*, Bantam, 1984. Discusses the development of the young child.

Caplan, Theresa, *The First Twelve Months of Life: Your Baby's Growth Month by Month*, Berkley Publishing Group, 1993. Month-by-month guide to infant development, with detailed charts and many good photographs.

Elgin, Suzette H., and Rebecca Haden, *The Gentle Art of Communicating With Kids*, John Wiley & Sons, 1996. A direct, down-to-earth book that illustrates how to talk with your child (toddler through teen years) positively, productively, and peacefully. Uses scenarios and dialogs to illustrate communication without confrontation.

Heinl, Tina, *Baby Massage*, Sigo Press, 1991. Explains the positive physical and emotional effects of massaging your baby. Includes step-by-step directions.

Lansky, Vicky, *Practical Parenting Tips*, Meadow-brook, 1992. Over 1,000 ideas to save you time, trouble, and money.

Leach, Penelope, *Your Baby and Child*, Alfred A. Knopf, 1989. A comprehensive and sensitive guide to childcare and development during the first five years. Beautifully illustrated.

McClure, Vimala Schneider, *Infant Massage*, Bantam, 1989. A clearly illustrated guide to massaging your baby, including songs to sing and games to play.

Olkin, Sylvia Klein, *Positive Parenting Fitness*, Avery Publishing Group, 1992. An illustrated handbook covering exercise for new mothers and fathers, postpartum problems, baby massage, baby movements, and acupressure.

Rakowitz, Elly, and Gloria S. Rubin, *Living With Your New Baby*, 2nd edition, Berkley Publishing Group, 1986. An excellent guide to understanding and coping with parenthood.

Samuels, Mike, and Nancy H. Samuels, *The Well Baby Book*, Summit Books, 1991. Preventive medicine for pregnancy through age 4.

Thevenin, Tine, *The Family Bed: An Age-Old Concept in Child Rearing*, Avery Publishing Group, 1987. Explores the pros and cons of siblings' sleeping with one another and with their parents.

Weiss, Joan S., *Your Second Child*, Summit Books, 1981. A detailed presentation of the impact of a second baby on the family. Discusses pregnancy, childbirth, and sibling rivalry.

White, Burton L., *The First Three Years of Life*, Simon & Schuster Trade, 1995. A detailed guide to the child's development in the early years.

Zand, Janet, Rachel Walton, and Bob Rountree, *A Parent's Guide to Medical Emergencies: First Aid for Your Child*, Avery Publishing Group, 1997. An easy-to-follow, illustrated guide to handling emergencies such as seizures and near-drowning.

Zand, Janet, Rachel Walton, and Bob Rountree, *Smart Medicine for a Healthier Child*, Avery Publishing Group, 1994. An A-to-Z guide to childhood illnesses and injuries, and their treatment using conventional methods, herbal and homeopathic remedies, diet, and nutritional supplements. Written by a medical doctor, a naturopath, and a registered nurse.

Pregnancy, Birth, and Childbirth Preparation

Balaskas, Janet, *Active Birth*, Harvard Common Press, 1992. Descriptions of all the stages of labor, demonstrating how a woman's choice of position during labor can reduce her discomfort. Includes an illustrated section on stretching exercises.

Baldwin, Rahima, *Special Delivery: The Complete Guide to Informed Birth*, Celestial Arts, 1986. Comprehensive guide for couples wanting to take greater responsibility for their birth experiences at home, in a birth center, or in a hospital.

Bing, Elisabeth, *Elisabeth Bing's Guide to Moving Through Pregnancy*, Farrar, Straus & Giroux, 1991. Photographs and helpful hints on exercise for physical comfort and well-being during pregnancy.

Bing, Elisabeth D., and Libby Colman, *Making Love During Pregnancy*, Farrar, Straus & Giroux, 1989. Facts about intercourse during pregnancy. Examines many myths about the subject and offers good, practical information. Extensive illustrations.

Bradley, Robert A., *Husband-Coached Childbirth*, HarperCollins Publishers, 1981. Information for husbands on helping their wives from pregnancy through birth. The Bradley method.

Brinkley, Ginny, and Sherry Sampson, *Young and Pregnant*, Pink Inc! 1989. A pregnancy manual written specifically for teens. Encourages the teen to take responsibility for her own well-being and that of her baby, and to consider her future.

Flanagan, Geraldine L., *Beginning Life*, D.K. Publishing, 1996. The story of life from conception to birth told through beautiful photographs.

Gaskin, Ina M., *Spiritual Midwifery*, 3rd edition, Book Publishing Co., 1990. Advice on the spiritual and physical aspects of birth. Includes accounts of births at The Farm in Tennessee.

Harper, Barbara, *Gentle Birth Choices*, Inner Traditions, 1994. Gentle birth explored in hospitals, in free-standing birth centers, and at home. Includes advice on water birth.

Hathaway, Marjie, and Jay Hathaway, *Children at Birth*, Academy Publications, 1978. A positive report on children's presence during the birth of their siblings. Includes over 125 photographs.

Jiménez, Sherry L. M., *The Pregnant Woman's Comfort Guide*, Avery Publishing Group, 1992. A handbook providing expectant mothers with natural, safe, and effective treatments for more than seventy of the most common discomforts of pregnancy and postpartum.

Kitzinger, Sheila, *The Experience of Childbirth*, Viking Penguin, 1990. Discusses the emotional aspects of pregnancy, with the emphasis on relaxation.

Klaus, Marshall, John Kennell, and Phyllis Klaus, *Bonding: Building the Foundations of Secure Attachment and Independence*, Addison-Wesley Publishing Co., 1995. Explains how to build the foundations of secure attachment and independence between mother and child.

Korte, Diana, and Roberta Scaer, *A Good Birth, a Safe Birth*, Harvard Common Press, 1992. Provides the tools needed to experience the best possible birth. Includes documented studies.

Leboyer, Frederick, *Birth Without Violence*, Inner Traditions International Ltd., 1995. Poetic and powerful, with beautiful photographs showing techniques for easing the trauma of birth for the baby.

Lieberman, Adrienne B., *Easing Labor Pain*, Harvard Common Press, 1992. A practical guide that explains what happens during labor and birth. Includes first-person accounts of birth.

Nilsson, Lennart, *A Child Is Born*, Delacorte, 1990. Brilliant photographs that capture the mystery of life within the womb from conception to birth, along with up-to-date advice on childbearing methods.

Noble, Elizabeth, *Essential Exercises for the Childbearing Year*, 4th edition, New Life Images, 1995. A very good presentation of valuable exercises for mothers before and after birth. Offers particularly good information for the mother recovering from a cesarean delivery.

Noble, Elizabeth, *Having Twins*, Houghton Mifflin, 1991. Tips on prenatal care and parenting, as well as fascinating facts on multiple birth.

Odent, Michel, *Birth Reborn*, Birth Works, 1994. Descriptions of the labor positions and delivery methods used in Odent's famous clinic in Pithiviers, France.

Olkin, Slyvia Klein, *Positive Pregnancy Fitness*, Avery Publishing Group, 1987. An illustrated handbook on relaxation, stress management, nutrition, and exercises to prepare for childbirth.

Panuthos, Claudia, *Transformation Through Birth*, Greenwood, 1984. Explores the relationship between a woman's psychological well-being and her ability to experience a healthy and rewarding birth.

Perez, Paulina, *The Nurturing Touch at Birth*, Cutting Edge Press, 1997. Covers all the techniques and "tricks of the trade" that are needed when caring for a laboring woman.

Peterson, Gayle, *Birthing Normally*, Shadow & Light, 1991. Holistic approach providing ways to maximize the chance of giving birth naturally, without intervention.

Samuels, Mike, and Nancy H. Samuels, *The Well Pregnancy Book*, Summit Books, 1986. A comprehensive guide covering the emotional and physical aspects of pregnancy, birth, and breastfeeding.

Simkin, Penny, *The Birth Partner: Everything You Need to Know to Help a Woman Through Childbirth*, Harvard Common Press, 1989. A guide to providing effective support during labor. Emphasizes the importance of making informed choices.

Tupler, Julie, *Maternal Fitness*, Simon & Schuster Trade, 1996. A clearly illustrated exercise program for pregnancy. Focuses on exercises for the muscle groups used during labor, as well as on exercises to relieve pregnancy discomforts.

Verny, Thomas, with John Kelly, *The Secret Life of the Unborn Child*, Dell Trade Paperbacks, 1982. Startling information on the physical and emotional influences on the unborn baby.

Unexpected Outcomes and Pregnancy Loss

Friedman, Rochelle, and Bonnie Gradstein, *Surviving Pregnancy Loss*, Little, Brown and Company, 1982. Discusses many types of losses. Includes an appendix of grief counselors, adoption services, and support organizations.

Ilse, Sherokee, *Empty Arms*, Wintergreen, 1990. A small, concise book that answers most of the questions that parents may have when confronted with a stillbirth or the death of a newborn.

Kohn, Ingrid, and Perry-Lynn Moffitt, *A Silent Sorrow: Pregnancy Loss Guidance and Support for You and Your Family*, Dell Publishing, 1993. A comprehensive book dealing with all forms of pregnancy loss. Includes separate sections on mothers' and fathers' perspectives.

Panuthos, Claudia, and Catherine Romeo, *Ended Beginnings: Healing Childbearing Losses*, Greenwood, 1984. How to use inner resources to help heal losses from miscarriage, stillbirth, abortion, or a traumatic birth experience.

Rich, Laurie A., *When Pregnancy Isn't Perfect*, NAL-Dutton, 1993. A mother's experience with a high-risk pregnancy. Describes the emotional and psychological aspects, as well as the medical aspects.

Miscellaneous

Boston Women's Health Book Collective Staff, *The New Our Bodies, Ourselves*, Simon & Schuster Trade, 1992. Complete information on all aspects of a woman's biological and psychological health.

Kippley, John F., and Sheila K. Kippley, *The Art of Natural Family Planning*, 4th edition, Couple to Couple, 1996. Complete information on temperature, mucus, and cervix changes as related to fertility.

Kitzinger, Sheila, *Woman's Experience of Sex*, Viking Penguin, 1985. A detailed explanation of women's feelings about their bodies. Includes many drawings and photographs.

Notes

Preface

1. "Labor Support Linked to Fewer Cesareans," *Childbirth Forum*, Fall 1991, p. 6.

Chapter 1
The Optimum Birth Experience

1. Silvia Feldman, *Choices in Childbirth* (New York: Grosset and Dunlap, 1978), p. 160.
2. "New Crop of Midwives Shatter Stereotype," *The Florida Times-Union*, 22 October 1996.
3. Gail Sforza Brewer, *Pregnancy After 30 Workbook* (Emmaus, Pennsylvania: Rodale Press, 1978), p. 43.
4. "Maternal Position During Labor and Birth," *ICEA Review* 2 (Summer 1978), pp. 2–3.
5. David Banta and Stephen Thacker, "Electronic Fetal Monitoring: Is It a Benefit?" *Birth and the Family Journal*, Winter 1979, p. 247.
6. Diony Young and Charles Mahan, *Unnecessary Cesareans: Ways to Avoid Them* (Minneapolis: International Childbirth Education Association, 1989), p. 6.
7. Brewer, p. 61.
8. Brewer, p. 61.
9. "Maternal Position During Labor and Birth," pp. 2–3.
10. Young and Mahan, p. 30.
11. Doris Haire, "The Pregnant Patient's Bill of Rights" and "The Pregnant Patient's Responsibilities," papers, International Childbirth Education Association, Minneapolis.

Chapter 2
Pregnancy

1. Arthur Colman and Libby Colman, *Pregnancy: The Psychological Experience* (New York: Seabury Press, 1978), pp. 9–11.
2. Jean Campen, "Medical Update: Group Beta Strep: A New Way of Treating an Old Foe," *Childbirth Instructor Magazine*, First Quarter 1996, p. 9.
3. Campen, p. 9.
4. "Baby Poisoned by Food Spurs Couple's Crusade," *New York Post*, 18 August 1997.
5. "Companies Wrestle With Threats to Workers' Reproductive Health," *The Wall Street Journal*, 5 February 1987, p. 23.
6. "News," *Birth* 24 (December 1997), p. 266.
7. "New Marker for Preterm Labor," *Childbirth Instructor Magazine*, First Quarter 1996, p. 7.
8. Henci Goer, "Antenatal Corticosteroids: Wonder Drug for Preterm Infants," *Childbirth Forum*, Spring 1996, p. 5.
9. Sundberg, J. Bang, S. Smidt-Jensen, V. Brooks, C. Lundsteen, J. Parner, K. Keiding, and J. Philip, "Randomized Study of Risk of Fetal Loss Related to Early Amniocentesis Versus Chorionic Villus Sampling," *Lancet* 350 (1997), pp. 697–703.
10. Silvia Feldman, *Choices in Childbirth* (New York: Grosset and Dunlap, 1978), pp. 63–64.
11. Jean Caldwell, "CVS: An Early Test for Genetic Problems," *American Baby*, February 1985, p. 21.
12. "Limb-Reduction Defects and Chorion Villus

Sampling," *The Lancet*, 4 May 1991, pp. 1091–1092.

13. *AFP Plus: An Office Guide for Prenatal Care Providers* (N.p.: Integrated Genetics Laboratories, Inc., 1991).

14. Bernard G. Ewigman, et al., "Effect of Prenatal Ultrasound Screening on Perinatal Outcome," *The New England Journal of Medicine* 329 (16 September 1993), p. 821.

15. Carolyn L. Gegor, "Obstetric Ultrasound: Who Should Perform Sonograms?" *Birth* 19 (June 1992), p. 98.

Chapter 3
Nutrition

1. Gail Sforza Brewer, *What Every Pregnant Woman Should Know: The Truth About Diet and Drugs During Pregnancy* (New York: Penguin Press, 1985), p. 22.

2. Penny Simkin, Janet Whalley, and Ann Keppler, *Pregnancy, Childbirth and the Newborn* (New York: Meadowbrook Press, 1991), p. 73.

3. *What Every Pregnant Woman Should Know*, p. 25.

4. Madeline Shearer, "Malnutrition in Middle Class Pregnant Women," *Birth and the Family Journal* 7 (Spring 1980), p. 30.

5. Bonnie Worthington, *Nutrition in Pregnancy and Lactation* (St. Louis: C. V. Mosby Co., 1977), p. 9.

6. "Health and Fitness," *The Orlando Sentinel*, 30 April 1996, p. E-4.

7. "Folic Acid May Help Prevent Heart Disease and Stroke," *Miracles: A Quarterly Newsletter for Loyal Donors to the March of Dimes* 4 (1996).

8. "Coalition Urges Folic Acid Addition to Food," *Childbirth Instructor Magazine*, First Quarter 1996, p. 7.

9. "Vitamin A May Increase Risk of Birth Defects," *The Orlando Sentinel*, 7 October 1995, p. A-1.

10. R. Louise Floyd, et al., "Smoking During Pregnancy: Prevalence, Effects, and Intervention Strategies," *Birth* 18 (March 1991), p. 48.

11. "Recent Advances in Research," fact sheet, Florida SIDS Information Exchange, March 1979, p. 2.

12. "Lesser Known Facts," fact sheet, American Cancer Society, 1980, p. 1.

13. "Smoking Can Raise SIDS Risk," *The Orlando Sentinel*, 8 March 1995.

14. "Moms Who Smoke Increase Babies' Risk of Ear Infections," *Growing Child Research Review*, May 1995.

15. Ellen H. Yoshiuchi, "Fetal Alcohol Syndrome," *Childbirth Instructor Magazine*, Spring 1992, p. 27.

16. "Study: Drinking Multiplies Risks of Infant Leukemia," *The Orlando Sentinel*, 3 January 1996, p. A-3.

17. Samantha Jannke, "When the Mother-to-Be Drinks," *Childbirth Instructor Magazine*, Winter 1994, p. 30.

18. A. Jakubovic, T. Hattori, and P. McGee, "Radioactivity in Suckling Rats After Giving C-14-Tetrahydrocannabinol to the Mother," *European Journal of Pharmacy* 22 (1973), pp. 221–223.

19. Cynthia W. Cooke and Susan Dworkin, *The Ms. Guide to a Woman's Health* (New York: Doubleday, 1979), p. 184.

20. "Cocaine Follow-up," *Childbirth Instructor Magazine*, Winter 1994, p. 8.

21. L. Fenster, et al., "Caffeine Consumption During Pregnancy and Fetal Growth," *American Journal of Public Health* 81 (1991), p. 458.

22. "Study Links Miscarriages to Caffeine Consumption," *Childbirth Instructor Magazine*, Winter 1994, p. 8.

23. Nikki Goldbeck, *As You Eat, So Your Baby Grows* (New York: Ceres Press, 1978), p. 13.

24. Cherry Wunderlich, "Unborn Males: Children at Risk With Saccharin," *ICEA News* 18 (1979), p. 1.

25. Silvia Feldman, *Choices in Childbirth* (New York: Grosset and Dunlap, 1978), p. 35.

26. "Decongestant Danger," *Midwifery Today* 26 (Summer 1993), p. 48.

27. *Physicians' Desk Reference*, 41st edition (Oradell, New Jersey: Medical Economics Co., 1987), p. 1641.

Chapter 4
Exercise

1. Robin Bell and Maureen O'Neill, "Exercise and Pregnancy: A Review," *Birth* 21 (June 1994), p. 85.

2. Bell and O'Neill, p. 85.

3. "Pregnancy Outcomes Among Active and Sedentary Women," *Baby Care Forum*, Summer 1996, p. 5.

Chapter 5
Tools for Labor

1. Mike Samuels and Nancy H. Samuels, *The Well Pregnancy Book* (New York: Summit Books, 1986), pp. 147–148.

2. Adapted from Gayle Peterson, *Birthing Normally*, 2nd edition (Berkeley, California: Mindbody Press, 1984), pp. 57–72.

3. Barbara Harper, "Waterbirth: An Increasingly Attractive Gentle Birth Choice," *International Journal of Childbirth Education* 9 (February-March 1994), p. 17.

4. Roberto Caldeyro-Barcia, "The Influence of

Maternal Bearing-Down Effort During Second Stage on Fetal Well-Being," *Birth and the Family Journal* 6 (Spring 1979), pp. 17–21.

5. Morris Notelovitz, "Commentary," *ICEA Review* 2 (Summer 1978), p. 6.

6. M. Hugo, "A Look at Maternal Position During Labor," *Journal of Nurse Midwifery* 22 (Fall 1977), pp. 26–27, as cited in "Maternal Position During Labor and Birth," *ICEA Review* 2 (Summer 1978), p. 2.

7. Katherine Camacho Carr, "Obstetric Practices Which Protect Against Neonatal Morbidity: Focus on Maternal Position in Labor and Birth," *Birth and the Family Journal* 7 (Winter 1980), p. 251.

Chapter 6
Labor and Birth

1. Marshall Klaus, John Kennell, and Phyllis Klaus, *Bonding: Building the Foundations of Secure Attachment and Independence* (New York: Addison-Wesley Publishing Co., 1995), p. 38.

2. Catherine C. Roberts and Leslie M. Ludka, "Food for Thought: The Debate Over Eating and Drinking in Labor," *Childbirth Instructor Magazine*, Spring 1994, pp. 25–29.

3. Roberts and Ludka, p. 27.

4. Marshall Klaus and John Kennell, *Maternal-Infant Bonding* (St. Louis: C. V. Mosby Co., 1976), p. 2.

5. Klaus, Kennell, and Klaus, pp. 68–73.

6. Klaus, Kennell, and Klaus, p. 64.

7. Avis J. Ericson, *Medications Used During Labor and Birth: A Resource for Childbirth Educators* (Milwaukee: International Childbirth Education Association, 1978), p. iii ("Foreword" by Murray Enkin).

8. Diony Young, "Editorial: Early Discharge: Whose Decision, Whose Responsibility?" *Birth* 23 (June 1996), p. 62.

Chapter 7
Medications and Anesthesia

1. Diana Korte and Roberta Scaer, *A Good Birth, a Safe Birth* (New York: Bantam Books, 1984), p. 223.

2. Avis J. Ericson, *Medications Used During Labor and Birth: A Resource for Childbirth Educators* (Milwaukee: International Childbirth Education Association, 1978), p. 5.

3. Ericson, p. 4.

4. James A. Thorp and Ginger Breedlove, "Epidural Analgesia in Labor: An Evaluation of Risks and Benefits," *Birth* 23 (June 1996), pp. 69–73.

5. Thorp and Breedlove, p. 74.

6. Henci Goer, "Epidural: Myth Vs. Reality," *Childbirth Instructor Magazine*, Special Issue 1997, p. 22.

7. Tim Chard and Martin Richards, *Benefits and Hazards of the New Obstetrics* (Suffolk, England: Lavenham Press, 1977), p. 112.

8. C. MacArthur, M. Lewis, E. G. Knox, and J. S. Crawford, "Epidural Anesthesia on Long-Term Backache After Childbirth," *British Medical Journal* 301 (7 July 1990), pp. 9–12, as cited in Penny Simkin, "Weighing the Pros and Cons of the Epidural," *Childbirth Forum*, Fall 1991, p. 4.

9. Diony Young and Charles Mahan, *Unnecessary Cesareans: Ways to Avoid Them* (Minneapolis: International Childbirth Education Association, 1989), p. 9.

10. K. Dickerson, "Pharmacological Control of Pain During Labour," in I. Chalmers, M. Enkin, and M. Keirse, editors, *Effective Care in Pregnancy and Childbirth* (New York: Oxford University Press, 1989), as cited in Penny Simkin, "Weighing the Pros and Cons of the Epidural," *Childbirth Forum*, Fall 1991, p. 4.

11. Marshall Klaus, John Kennell, and Phyllis Klaus, *Bonding: Building the Foundations of Secure Attachment and Independence* (New York: Addison-Wesley Publishing Co., 1995), p. 32.

12. Thorp and Breedlove, p. 81.

Chapter 8
Variations and Interventions

1. Nancy Wainer Cohen and Lois J. Estner, *Silent Knife: Cesarean Prevention and Vaginal Birth After Cesarean* (South Hadley, Massachusetts: Bergin & Garvey, 1983), p. 310.

2. Henci Goer, "The Occiput Posterior Baby," *Childbirth Instructor Magazine*, Summer 1994, pp. 36–40.

3. Kathy Charbonneau, "Healthy Lifestyles: Intravenous Infusion: The Chemical Impact," *International Journal of Childbirth Education* 9 (February-March 1994).

4. Margot Edwards and Penny Simkin, *Obstetric Tests and Technology: A Consumer's Guide* (Minneapolis: International Childbirth Education Association, n.d.), p. 7.

5. Edwards and Simkin, p. 7.

6. Lynn Borgatta, "Recent Reports: Electronic Fetal Monitoring," *Childbirth Instructor Magazine*, Autumn 1993, p. 39.

7. "One Mother Dies for 8 Newborns Saved With

Electronic Monitoring," *Obstetrics and Gynecology News* 12 (15 December 1978), p. 1.

8. "News," *Birth* 23 (March 1996), pp. 49–50.

9. Leah L. Albers, "Clinical Issues in Electronic Fetal Monitoring," *Birth* 21 (June 1994), p. 109.

10. Bonnie Ennis Cox, "Prenatal Procedures: What's New, What's Being Used," *Childbirth Instructor Magazine* 1 (Spring 1991), p. 30.

11. Sally C. Clarke and Selma Taffel, "Changes in Cesarean Delivery in the United States, 1988 and 1993," *Birth* 22 (June 1995).

12. E. A. Friedman and M. R. Sachtleben, "Amniotomy and the Course of Labor," *Obstetrics and Gynecology* 22 (1963), p. 767, as cited in *ICEA Review* 3 (Summer 1979).

13. "Amniotomy," *ICEA Review* 3 (Summer 1979), p. 2.

14. Jean Marie Campen, "Routine Episiotomy," *Childbirth Instructor Magazine* 1 (Winter 1991), p. 29.

15. Campen, p. 31.

16. Nancy Berezin, *The Gentle Birth Book* (New York: Simon & Schuster, 1980), p. 21.

17. Barbara Harper, "Waterbirth: An Increasingly Attractive Gentle Birth Choice," *International Journal of Childbirth Education* 9 (February-March 1994).

18. Adrienne Lieberman, *Easing Labor Pain* (Boston: The Harvard Common Press, 1992), p. 113.

19. Lieberman, p. 49.

20. Lieberman, p. 49.

Chapter 9
Cesarean Birth

1. George Nolan, *Family Centered Cesarean Maternity Care Policy* (Ann Arbor: University of Michigan Hospital, n.d.), p. 1.

2. Diony Young and Charles Mahan, *Unnecessary Cesareans: Ways to Avoid Them* (Minneapolis: International Childbirth Education Association, 1989), p. 3.

3. Bruce Flamm, "Cesarean Delivery 1970–1995: Where Have We Been and Where Are We Going?" *International Journal of Childbirth Education* 9 (November 1994), p. 7.

4. Sally C. Clarke and Selma Taffel, "Changes in Cesarean Delivery in the United States, 1988 and 1993," *Birth* 22 (June 1995), p. 66.

5. Young and Mahan, p. 5.

6. Jean Campen, "Statistics Corner," *International Journal of Childbirth Education* 6 (August 1991), p. 15.

7. Young and Mahan, p. 6.

8. Young and Mahan, p. 6.

9. Clarke and Taffel, p. 66.

10. Young and Mahan, p. 8.

11. Young and Mahan, p. 8.

12. Young and Mahan, p. 9.

13. Diana Korte and Roberta Scaer, *A Good Birth, a Safe Birth* (New York: Bantam Books, 1984), p. 148.

14. M. J. Maiselle, et al., "Elective Delivery of the Term Fetus: An Obstetrical Hazard," *Journal of the American Medical Association* 238 (7 November 1977), p. 2036.

15. Sidney M. Wolfe, "Unnecessary Cesarean Section: Halting a National Epidemic," *Health Letter* 8 (June 1992), p. 2.

16. Young and Mahan, p. 24.

17. Nicette Jukelevics, "Vaginal Birth After Cesarean (VBAC) Sheet," *International Journal of Childbirth Education* 9 (November 1994), p. 41.

18. Jukelevics, p. 41.

19. Susan G. Doering, "Unnecessary Cesareans: Doctor's Choice, Parent's Dilemma," *Compulsory Hospitalization or Freedom of Choice in Childbirth?* 1 (1976), pp. 145–152.

Chapter 10
The Newborn

1. "News," *Birth* 23 (March 1996), p. 49.

2. Barbara Kay Turner, *Baby Names for the 90s* (New York: Berkley Books, 1991), p. 4.

3. Marshall Klaus, John Kennell, and Phyllis Klaus, *Bonding: Building the Foundations of Secure Attachment and Independence* (New York: Addison-Wesley Publishing Co., 1995), p. 53.

4. Frank A. Oski, "Hyperbilirubinemia in the Term Infant: An Unjaundiced Approach," *Contemporary Pediatrics*, April 1992, p. 152.

5. Oski, p. 150.

6. La Leche League International, *Newborn Jaundice* (Franklin Park, Illinois: La Leche League International, 1989), p. 2.

7. David Grimes, "Routine Circumcision Reconsidered," *American Journal of Nursing*, January 1980, p. 108.

8. Belinda Lassen, "Newborn Circumcision," *International Journal of Childbirth Education* 6 (February 1991), pp. 9–10.

9. Janice Cox, "Information Alert," *International Journal of Childbirth Education* 3 (August 1988), p. 45.

10. *New England Journal of Medicine*, 24 April 1997,

as cited in "Lidocaine-Prilocaine for Circumcision Pain," *Childbirth Instructor Magazine*, Third Quarter 1997, p.6.

11. Noreen Humphrey, "Care of the Circumcised and Uncircumcised Penis," *Baby Care Forum* (Fall 1992), p. 3.

12. Steven P. Shelov and Robert E. Hannemann, *Caring for Your Baby and Young Child* (New York: Bantam Books, 1994), p. 46.

13. Jean Campen, "Statistics Corner," *International Journal of Childbirth Education* 7 (1992), p. 6.

14. Campen, p. 6.

15. "Official Credits Education Campaign for Decline in Sudden Infant Deaths," *The Orlando Sentinel*, 25 June 1996, p. A-1.

16. Campen, p. 7.

17. Ashley Montagu, *Touching: The Human Significance of the Skin*, 2nd edition (New York: Harper and Row, 1978), pp. 39–41.

18. "Small Study Casts Doubt on the Reliability of Ear Thermometers," *Growing Child: Research Review*, 1994, No. 3, p. 1, as cited in *American Family Physician* 48, p. 1525.

19. "Should Immunization Against Varicella [Chickenpox] Be Restricted to the Immunocompromised?" *Physician's Weekly* 12 (10 July 1995).

20. American Heart Association, *Basic Life Support, Heartsaver Guide* (Tulsa: CPR Publishers, Inc., 1993), pp. 40–49.

21. "Auto Air Bags Can Kill Kids, Study Says," *The Orlando Sentinel*, 18 September 1996, p. A-3.

22. "Infant Eye Cues," *Childbirth Instructor Magazine*, First Quarter 1996, p. 32.

Chapter 11
Infant Feeding

1. "Breastfeeding and Cholesterol," *Childbirth Instructor Magazine*, Winter 1994, p. 8.

2. La Leche League International, *The Womanly Art of Breastfeeding*, 5th edition (New York: Penguin Books, 1991), p. 347.

3. *The Womanly Art of Breastfeeding*, p. 349.

4. "Health and Fitness," *The Orlando Sentinel*, 13 January 1998, p. E-4.

5. Karen Pryor, *Nursing Your Baby* (New York: Pocket Books, 1991), p. 64.

6. Ruth A. Lawrence, "Can We Expect Greater Intelligence From Human Milk Feedings?" *Birth* 19 (June 1992), p. 105.

7. Nancy Mohrbacher and Julie Stock, *The Breastfeeding Answer Book* (Franklin Park, Illinois: La Leche League International, 1991), pp. 306–307.

8. Pryor, pp. 83–84.

9. Pryor, p. 83.

10. "Breastmilk: Wide-Ranging Benefits," *The Florida Times-Union*, 13 January 1998, p. C-1.

11. Marsha Walker, "Why Aren't More Mothers Breastfeeding?" *Childbirth Instructor Magazine* 2 (Winter 1992), p. 20.

12. Pryor, p. 84.

13. Walker, p. 20.

14. Walker, p. 20.

15. Walker, p. 20.

16. T. A. Kaleita, M. Kinsbourne, and J. H. Menkes, "A Neurobehavioral Syndrome After Failure to Thrive on Chloride-Deficient Formula," *Developmental Medicine and Child Neurology* 33 (1991), as cited in Marsha Walker, "Summary of the Hazards of Infant Formula," handout, International Lactation Consultant Association, 1992, p. 3.

17. M. F. Holick, Q. Shao, W. W. Lieu, et al., "The Vitamin D Content of Fortified Milk and Infant Formula," *New England Journal of Medicine* 326 (1992), as cited in Marsha Walker, "Summary of the Hazards of Infant Formula," handout, International Lactation Consultant Association, 1992, p. 3.

18. D. Fisher, "Upper Limit of Iodine in Infant Formulas," *Journal of Nutrition* 119 (1989), as cited in Marsha Walker, "Summary of the Hazards of Infant Formula," handout, International Lactation Consultant Association, 1992, p. 3.

19. "News," *Birth* 23 (September 1996), p. 177.

20. Pryor, p. 57.

21. Kaye E. Brock, Geoffrey Berry, et al., "Sexual, Reproductive and Contraceptive Risk Factors for Carcinoma–*In Situ* of the Uterine Cervix in Sydney," *The Medical Journal of Australia* 150 (6 February 1989), p. 127.

22. Marta L. Gwinn, Nancy C. Lee, et al., "Pregnancy, Breast Feeding, and Oral Contraceptives and the Risk of Epithelial Ovarian Cancer," *Journal of Clinical Epidemiology* 43 (1990), p. 566.

23. "News," *Birth* 23 (June 1996), p. 113.

24. Pryor, pp. 12–13.

25. Candace Woessner, Judith Lauwers, and Barbara Bernard, *Breastfeeding Today: A Mother's Companion* (Garden City Park, New York: Avery Publishing Group, 1994), pp. 39–40.

26. "Cigarette Smoking and Breastfeeding," *Childbirth Instructor Magazine*, Autumn 1993, p. 10.

27. *The Womanly Art of Breastfeeding*, p. 234.

28. "News," *Birth* 16 (March 1988), p. 43.

29. *The Womanly Art of Breastfeeding*, p. 167.

30. Mohrbacher and Stock, p. 100.

31. Judy Heilman, et al., "Fluoride Concentrations of Infant Foods," *Journal of the American Dental Association* 128 (July 1997), p. 857.

Chapter 12
The New Parent

1. Brenda Cicchinelli, "A Cry for Help: Postpartum Depression," *International Journal of Childbirth Education* 10 (February-March 1995), pp. 42–43.

2. "In Brief," *Childbirth Instructor Magazine*, Third Quarter 1996, p. 7.

3. Viola Polomeno, "Sexual Intercourse After the Birth of a Baby," *International Journal of Childbirth Education* 11 (December 1996), pp. 13–15.

4. Judith Lauwers and Candace Woessner, *Counseling the Nursing Mother* (Garden City Park, New York: Avery Publishing Group, 1990), pp. 21–22, 53.

5. "News," *Birth* 23 (September 1996), p. 177.

6. F. Gary Cunningham, Paul C. MacDonald, and Norman G. Gant, *Williams Obstetrics*, 18th edition (Norwalk, Connecticut: Appleton & Lange, 1989), pp. 922–941.

7. Robert A. Hatcher, et al., *Contraceptive Technology 1990–1992*, 15th edition (New York: Irvington Publishers, Inc., 1990), pp. 423–427.

8. Sherry L. M. Jiménez, "'Safe Sex' After Baby," *American Baby Magazine*, December 1996, pp. 51–58.

9. "'Morning After' Doses Outlined," *The Florida Times-Union*, 25 February 1997, p. A-11.

Glossary

Italicized words are defined elsewhere in the glossary.

abdomen. The area between the ribs and the *pubic bones*.

abortion. Any termination of pregnancy, either spontaneously (*miscarriage*) or intentionally, before the *fetus* is able to survive outside the *uterus*.

abruptio placentae. Premature separation of the *placenta* from the *uterus*.

acquired immune deficiency syndrome (AIDS). A viral disease that attacks the body's natural defenses.

active labor. The second phase of the *first stage of labor*; the phase during which the *cervix* dilates from 4 to 8 *centimeters*.

active management of labor. The use of *amniotomy* and augmentation to ensure a *labor* under 12 hours.

acupressure. The use of fingertip pressure on specific body points for the relief of such problems as pain, nausea, and fatigue.

acupuncture. The insertion of fine needles into specific points on the body for pain relief or relief from other problems.

adrenal glands. Two small glands, located on the upper part of the kidneys, that secrete *hormones*.

AFP. See *alpha-fetoprotein*.

afterbirth. The *placenta* and *membranes*, which pass out of the *uterus* during the *third stage of labor*.

afterpains. Contractions of the *uterus* following birth.

AIDS. See *acquired immune deficiency syndrome*.

albumin. A simple protein.

alpha-fetoprotein (AFP). A protein produced by the baby.

alpha-fetoprotein (AFP) screening. A blood test to screen for open neural tube defects (spina bifida) and Down syndrome.

alveoli. Grapelike clusters of sacs. In the breasts, they produce milk; in the lungs, they absorb oxygen.

amino acids. The building blocks of protein molecules.

amnihook. An instrument that is used to perform an *amniotomy*.

amniocentesis. The removal of a small amount of *amniotic fluid*, usually to determine fetal age and genetic composition.

amnioinfusion. The technique of infusing saline through an *intrauterine pressure catheter* to provide additional fluid within the *uterus*.

amnion. The innermost *membrane* of the *amniotic sac*.

amniotic fluid. The liquid contained in the *amniotic sac*.

amniotic sac. The two layers of *membranes* (the *amnion* and the *chorion*) containing the *fetus* and the *amniotic fluid*; also called the bag of waters.

amniotomy. The artificial rupture of the *amniotic sac*.

analgesic. A drug that relieves or reduces pain without causing unconsciousness.

anesthetic. An agent that produces loss of sensation, with or without loss of consciousness.

angel kisses. See *stork bites*.

anoxia. Deficiency of oxygen.

antibody. A substance produced by the body in response to an *antigen* that recognizes and attacks the *antigen* to resist illness.

antigen. A foreign substance, such as dust, food, or bacteria, that stimulates *antibody* production.

anus. The outlet of the rectum, located directly behind the *vagina*.

Apgar score. Evaluation of the infant's condition at 1 and 5 minutes after birth.

areola. The pigmented area surrounding the nipple of the breast. Pronounced *a RE o la*.

Babinski toe reflex. A reflex, elicited by stroking the sole of the foot, in which the toes fan outward.

baby blues. A temporary period of sadness that sometimes occurs after giving birth.

barbiturate. A depressant drug that induces sleep.

beta strep. See *group B streptococcus*.

bilirubin. A product of the breakdown of red blood cells, an excess of which can cause *jaundice*.

biophysical profile. An *ultrasound* test to check for fetal well-being.

birth canal. The passageway from the *uterus* through which the baby is born; the *vagina*.

blastocyst. A stage in the development of the *embryo*.

blood pH. Blood alkalinity or acidity.

bloody show. A blood-tinged vaginal discharge seen at the beginning of or during *labor*.

bonding. The process of a mother and father becoming attached to their new baby.

Braxton-Hicks contractions. The intermittent and usually painless contractions of the *uterus* noticed during pregnancy.

breastfeeding counselor. A volunteer who promotes breastfeeding through telephone consultations and in group settings.

breech. A *presentation* of the baby in which the buttocks or feet (footling breech) present first.

caput succedaneum. Swelling of the scalp. Pronounced *KA put suk se DA ne um*.

cardinal movements. The rotations of the baby through the *pelvis*.

catheterization. The method used to empty the bladder by inserting a small pliable tube through the *urethra*.

caudal anesthesia. The injection of an *anesthetic* into the caudal space, which is at the base of the spine. Causes a loss of sensation from the hips to the toes; not commonly used.

centimeter. A unit of measure used to describe progress in the dilation of the *cervix* during *labor*.

cephalhematoma. A collection of blood under the scalp.

cephalic. Pertaining to the head.

cephalopelvic disproportion (CPD). A condition in which the baby's head cannot fit through the pelvic opening; usually an indication for a *cesarean birth*.

certified lactation consultant. A person who completed a prescribed course and is authorized to assist mothers with breastfeeding problems.

certified nurse-midwife (CNM). A registered nurse who has completed an accredited midwifery program and is licensed by the state to manage low-risk pregnancies and deliveries.

cervix. The narrow necklike end of the *uterus* that leads into the *vagina*, and that must thin out and open during *labor* to allow the baby to pass into the *birth canal*.

cesarean birth. *Delivery* of the baby by means of incisions in the abdominal and uterine walls; also called *cesarean section, c-section,* or section.

cesarean section. See *cesarean birth*.

chlamydia. A sexually transmitted disease.

chorion. The outermost *membrane* of the *amniotic sac*.

chorionic villi. Fingerlike projections covering the developing *embryo* and containing cells that have the same genetic composition as the *embryo*.

chorionic villus sampling (CVS). A procedure in which a sample of the *chorionic villi* is removed to determine genetic composition.

cilia. Hairlike projections that propel the egg through the *fallopian tube* toward the *uterus*.

circumcision. Surgical removal of the *foreskin* of the *penis*.

CNM. See *certified nurse-midwife*.

coccyx. The small bone at the end of the spinal column; the tailbone. Pronounced *KOK siks*.

colostrum. A sticky yellowish fluid secreted by the breasts in small quantities during late pregnancy and for several days following birth before the mature milk comes in.

complete. When the *cervix* is sufficiently dilated and effaced for the baby to pass through; usually 10 *centimeters* and 100-percent effaced.

conception. *Fertilization;* the union of a *sperm* and an egg, resulting in a new life.

congenital. Existing at or before birth; hereditary.

contraceptive. Any device used to prevent pregnancy.

contraction. A tightening and shortening of the uterine muscles during *labor* that causes *effacement* and *dilation* of the *cervix*, and contributes to the descent of the baby.

cord blood. Blood from the *umbilical cord*.

cord blood banking. The process of collecting and freezing blood from the *umbilical cord* after birth.

CPD. See *cephalopelvic disproportion*.

cradle cap. A crusting on the scalp of an infant.

crowning. When the *presenting part* of the baby (usually the crown of the head) is visible at the vaginal opening and no longer slipping back out of sight between *contractions*.

cryobank. A blood bank that freezes and stores blood.

c-section. See *cesarean birth*.

CVS. See *chorionic villus sampling*.

delivery. Birth; the baby's passage from the *uterus* into the external world through the *birth canal* or via *cesarean section*.

dilation. The gradual opening of the *cervix*, accomplished through uterine *contractions*, to permit passage of the baby out of the *uterus*. *Dilation* is *complete* at 10 *centimeters*. Also called dilatation.

diuretic. A medication that removes water from the body; also called *water pills*.

doptone. A hand-held device used to listen to the *fetal heart rate*.

doula. A trained *labor* companion.

dry birth. A birth without *amniotic fluid*. It is a misconception that if the *membranes* rupture, all the *amniotic fluid* is lost.

due date. The estimated date of birth; also called the estimated date of confinement (EDC).

dystocia. An abnormal or prolonged *labor*.

early labor. The first phase of the *first stage of labor*; the phase during which the *cervix* dilates from 0 to 4 *centimeters*.

eclampsia. A serious form of *pregnancy-induced hypertension* accompanied by convulsions and coma that can occur before, during, or after *delivery*.

edema. The presence of excessive amounts of fluid in the body tissues.

effacement. Thinning and shortening of the *cervix*, occurring before or during *dilation*, and expressed in terms of a percentage from 0 to 100.

effleurage. A very light fingertip massage of the *abdomen*, buttocks, or thighs that aids relaxation during *labor*.

electronic fetal monitor. See *fetal monitor*.

embolism. The presence of an air bubble or blood clot in a blood vessel.

embryo. The baby during the first 8 weeks of life in the *uterus*.

endorphins. Natural painkillers that are produced by the body.

enema. A solution that is inserted into the rectum and colon to empty the lower intestine.

engagement. The process in which the baby's *presenting part* becomes secured in the upper opening (inlet) of the woman's pelvic cavity in preparation for passage through the pelvic bones; may be felt as *lightening* by the woman.

engorgement. Excessive fullness, usually referring to the breasts.

epidermal growth factor. A property of breastmilk that promotes the growth of cells and strengthens the intestinal walls to act as a barrier against foreign substances.

epidural anesthesia. The injection of an *anesthetic* into the epidural space, which surrounds the spinal fluid.

Causes a loss of sensation from the *abdomen* to the toes.

episiotomy. An incision made into the *perineum* prior to *delivery* to enlarge the vaginal outlet.

erythema toxicum. A normal newborn rash.

estriol. An *estrogen*-type *hormone* that is made by the *placenta*.

estriol excretion study. A test to measure the *estriol* level in blood or urine that is used to determine placental functioning.

estrogen. A female *hormone* produced in the *ovaries* and *placenta*.

expulsion. The actual movement of the baby through and out of the *birth canal*, accomplished via the *contractions* of the *uterus* and the pushing efforts of the woman.

external version. The process of manually turning a baby from a *breech* or *transverse lie* to a head-down *presentation*.

fallopian tubes. Two small tubes extending from the *uterus* toward the left and right *ovaries*.

false labor. See *prelabor*.

fertilization. The meeting of a *sperm* and an egg, normally occurring in the *fallopian tube*.

fetal distress. A condition in which the oxygen supply of the *fetus* is threatened, detected by a change in the *fetal heart rate* or the presence of *meconium*-stained *amniotic fluid*.

fetal heart rate (FHR). The *fetus's* heartbeat, normally 120 to 160 beats per minute.

fetal monitor. An electronic machine used to detect and record the *fetal heart rate* in relation to the *contractions* of the *uterus*; also called an *electronic fetal monitor*.

fetal movement evaluation. A method of determining fetal well-being by keeping track of the baby's movements; also called the fetal kick count.

fetal scalp sampling. A test during *labor* in which a sample of blood is obtained from the *fetus's* scalp to determine the *blood pH*.

fetoscope. An instrument used for listening to the *fetal heart rate* and placental sounds.

fetus. The baby from the eighth week of pregnancy until birth.

FHR. See *fetal heart rate*.

finger. A unit of measure used to describe the progress of *dilation*. One finger equals 2 *centimeters*.

first stage of labor. The period of *labor* during which the *cervix* dilates to 10 *centimeters*. Includes *early labor*, *active labor*, and *transition*.

fluorosis. A cosmetic defect that occurs when more

than an optimal amount of fluoride is ingested. The result is light spots on the permanent teeth.

folic acid. An important B vitamin believed to help prevent certain birth defects.

fontanels. The soft spots on the top of the baby's head that enable the *molding* necessary during birth.

forceps. An obstetrical instrument resembling a pair of tongs that is occasionally used to aid in *delivery*.

foreskin. The fold of skin covering the head of the *penis*.

fourth stage of labor. The first hours after birth; the recovery period.

frenulum. The membrane that connects the tongue to the bottom of the mouth.

fundus. The top, or upper portion, of the *uterus*.

GBS. See *group B streptococcus*.

general anesthesia. The inhalation of gas or an *intravenous* injection that is used to produce a loss of consciousness.

genitals. The external reproductive organs.

gentle birth. See *Leboyer delivery*.

gestation. The condition or period of carrying a baby in the *uterus*; approximately 40 weeks long.

gestational age. The age of the *fetus* as determined from the first day of the last menstrual period.

gestational diabetes. Diabetes that occurs during pregnancy; usually temporary.

glucose tolerance test (GTT). A blood test to screen for diabetes.

gonorrhea. A sexually transmitted disease.

gravida. Literally, a pregnant woman; used with a numeral to designate the number of times a woman has been pregnant—that is, a woman pregnant for the first time is a gravida I, a woman pregnant for the second time is a gravida II, and so on.

group B streptococcus (GBS). A bacterium that causes illness in newborns and pregnant women; also called *beta strep* or group B strep.

GTT. See *glucose tolerance test*.

heartburn. A burning sensation in the esophagus caused by the seepage of gastric juices from the stomach.

hemolytic disease of the newborn. A severe illness characterized by massive destruction of red blood cells, usually from Rh incompatibility.

hemorrhoids. *Varicose veins* of the *anus*, usually temporary when they begin during pregnancy.

hepatitis B. A viral infection transmitted sexually or by contact with body fluids.

herpes simplex virus II (HSVII). A contagious venereal virus that, if active, can have disastrous effects on the *fetus* during vaginal *delivery*. It is an indication for a *cesarean section*.

higher-risk pregnancy. A pregnancy in which the mother and/or baby is thought to be at risk for developing complications.

HIV. See *human immunodeficiency virus*.

hormone. A chemical substance produced by a gland or organ.

HSVII. See *herpes simplex virus II*.

human immunodeficiency virus (HIV). The virus that causes *AIDS*.

hyperglycemia. High blood sugar.

hypertension. High blood pressure.

hyperventilation. Rapid breathing that causes excessive depletion of carbon dioxide in the blood, characterized by dizziness and tingling of the extremities.

hypoglycemia. Low blood sugar.

hypotension. Blood pressure that is lower than normal.

immunity. Resistance to a particular disease.

implantation. The attachment of the fertilized egg to the wall of the *uterus*.

in utero. Within the *uterus*.

incompetent cervix. A *cervix* that begins dilating too early, usually in the second *trimester*.

incontinence. The inability to control the flow of urine.

induction. The artificial initiation of *labor* through the use of medication or mechanical techniques.

infant screening test. A blood test done on the infant within the first week of life to screen for several metabolic diseases.

intradermal. Under the skin.

intrathecal. Into the spine. Used to refer to *spinal anesthesia*.

intrauterine. Within the *uterus*.

intrauterine pressure catheter (IUPC). A catheter that is inserted into the *uterus* to measure the exact pressure exerted by the *contraction*.

intravenous (IV). In the vein.

intravenous (IV) fluid. A sterile fluid that is fed into the body through a vein for the purpose of nutrition, hydration, or medication.

intubation. The insertion of a breathing tube into the windpipe for the administration of *general anesthesia*.

involution. The process by which the *uterus* returns to its nonpregnant size and position, usually taking approximately 4 to 6 weeks.

IUPC. See *intrauterine pressure catheter*.

IV. See *intravenous*.

jaundice. Yellow discoloration of the skin, the whites of the eyes, and the mucous membranes because of a high level of *bilirubin*.

Kegel exercises. A set of exercises devised by Dr. Arnold Kegel to strengthen the *pelvic floor* muscles. Pronounced *KEE gull*.

labia. The lips, or external folds, surrounding the *vagina* and *urethra*. Pronounced *LAY bee a*.

labor. Uterine *contractions* that are productive, causing *effacement* and *dilation* of the *cervix*, and descent and *expulsion* of the baby.

lactation. The production and secretion of milk by the breasts.

lactation consultant. See *certified lactation consultant*.

lactiferous ducts. Milk ducts.

lactiferous sinuses. Small milk reservoirs located under the *areola*.

Lamaze. A method of childbirth, developed by Dr. Fernand Lamaze, that involves emotional and physical preparation; also called *psychoprophylaxis*. Pronounced *le MAHZ*.

lanugo. The fine downy hair on the body of the *fetus* after the fourth month.

Leboyer delivery. A quiet, peaceful *delivery* experience, designed by Dr. Frederick Leboyer, to reduce birth trauma in infants; also called *gentle birth*.

let-down reflex. The involuntary ejection of milk that occurs during breastfeeding; also called the *milk ejection reflex*.

leukocytes. White blood cells that attack bacteria.

lightening. The shifting of the baby and *uterus* down into the pelvic cavity, noticed by the mother as a change in abdominal contours.

linea nigra. The dark vertical line appearing on the *abdomen* during pregnancy. Pronounced *LIN e ah NI gra*.

listeria. A bacterium that can contaminate food and, if ingested, can cause *miscarriages* and stillbirths in pregnant women.

lithotomy. A *delivery position* in which the woman lies on her back with her feet in stirrups.

local anesthetic. An *anesthetic* designed to numb a specific area; used in childbirth to numb the *perineum* for the repair of the *episiotomy*.

lochia. The discharge, consisting of blood, mucus, and tissue, that is expelled from the *uterus* after the birth of the baby.

lysozyme. An antibacterial substance found in breastmilk that dissolves bacterial cell walls.

macrosomia. Abnormal size of body. Used to describe a baby of excessive size.

mask of pregnancy. A brownish pigmentation of the forehead, cheeks, and nose during pregnancy.

mastitis. Inflammation of the breast.

meconium. The dark green or black tarry substance that is present in the baby's large intestine and forms his first stools after birth.

membranes. The two layers of tissue—the *amnion* and the *chorion*—that form the *amniotic sac*.

milia. Tiny white bumps that may appear on a newborn's face.

milk ejection reflex. The involuntary ejection of milk that occurs during breastfeeding; also called the *letdown reflex*.

miscarriage. Spontaneous *abortion*.

molding. An elongation of the baby's head as it adjusts to the size and shape of the *birth canal*.

Mongolian spots. A temporary purplish brown discoloration that is found on the backs of some dark- or olive-skinned babies.

Montgomery glands. Small prominences on the *areola* that enlarge during pregnancy and *lactation*.

morbidity. Illness.

morning sickness. The nausea or vomiting that is experienced by many women during the first *trimester* of pregnancy.

Moro reflex. A reflex that causes an infant to thrust his arms out when he is startled.

mortality. Death.

morula. The mass of cells resulting from the early cell division of the *ovum*. Pronounced *MOR u la*.

mucous plug. The heavy mucus that blocks the cervical canal during pregnancy.

multigravida. A woman who is experiencing her second or subsequent pregnancy.

multipara. A woman who has given birth to more than one child; also called a multip. Pronounced *mul TIP ar ah*.

multiple pregnancy. A pregnancy in which the woman is carrying more than one baby.

natal. Pertaining to birth or the day of birth.

navel. The site where the *umbilical cord* was attached to the baby in utero; also called the belly button or umbilicus.

necrotizing enterocolitis. A severe and sometimes fatal bowel condition of *preterm* infants.

neonatal period. The first 4 weeks of life.

nonstress test. A noninvasive test for fetal well-being.

obstetrics. The branch of medicine covering the care of women during pregnancy, childbirth, and *postpartum*.

occiput. The back part of the baby's head. Pronounced *OK sip ut*.

ovaries. The two female glands of reproduction.

ovulation. The monthly release of a ripe *ovum* from an *ovary*.

ovum. The female egg cell; the plural is "ova."

oxytocin. The *hormone* that stimulates uterine *contractions* and the *let-down reflex*.

oxytocin challenge test. A test that is used to determine how the baby will handle *labor*. The woman is connected to a *fetal monitor*, and *contractions* are induced with *oxytocin*.

para. Literally, a woman who has given birth; used with a numeral to designate the number of children a woman has had—that is, a woman who has had one child is a para I, a woman who has had two children is a para II, and so on.

paracervical anesthetic. An *anesthetic* that is injected into the *cervix*; not commonly used.

paraphimosis. The inability to return the *foreskin* to its original position.

patient controlled analgesia (PCA). A device that allows the patient to control the administration of narcotics through an *IV*.

PCA. See *patient controlled analgesia*.

pelvic floor. The hammocklike ligaments and muscles supporting the reproductive organs.

pelvimetry. A method of determining pelvic measurement by X-ray.

pelvis. The bony ring that joins the spine and legs. In the female, its central opening encases the walls of the *birth canal*.

penis. The male sex organ.

perineal. Pertaining to the *perineum*.

perineal massage. Massage of the *perineal* tissues.

perineum. The area between the *vagina* and the *anus*. Pronounced *per i NE um*.

phenylketonuria (PKU) test. A procedure in which a small drop of the newborn's blood is examined for a specific *amino acid* deficiency.

phimosis. The inability of the *foreskin* to be pulled back.

phototherapy. The use of ultraviolet light to treat newborn *jaundice*.

physiological. Pertaining to the normal functioning of the body.

pica. An unusual craving for and ingestion of nonfood items. Pronounced *PI ca*.

PIH. See *pregnancy-induced hypertension*.

pitocin. An oxytocic *hormone* used to induce or stimulate uterine *contractions*.

PKU test. See *phenylketonuria test*.

placenta. The temporary organ of pregnancy that exchanges oxygen, nutrients, and wastes between the mother and the *fetus*; part of the *afterbirth*.

placenta previa. A *placenta* that is implanted in the lower uterine segment, possibly covering the cervical opening partially or completely.

plantar toe reflex. A reflex in infants that causes the toes to curl when the base of the toes is pressed on the underside of the foot.

position. The way the *presenting part* of the *fetus* is situated in the *pelvis* of the mother.

posterior. The *position* in which the back part of the baby's head is against the woman's spine.

postpartum. The time following birth.

postpartum depression. A prolonged period of melancholy that some women experience after childbirth.

post-term. A prenancy at 42 or more weeks *gestation*.

potentiate. To intensify the action of a medication or substance.

precipitate delivery. A sudden and unexpected birth, usually following a very short *labor*.

precipitate labor. A *labor* completed within 3 hours.

preeclampsia. A severe form of *pregnancy-induced hypertension* that, if left untreated, may lead to *eclampsia*.

pregnancy-induced hypertension (PIH). A metabolic disorder of pregnancy. The symptoms include *hypertension*, *edema*, and *albumin* in the urine. Formerly called *toxemia*.

prelabor. Contractions of the *uterus* that are strong enough to be interpreted as true *labor*, but that have no dilating effect on the *cervix*; also called *false labor*.

premature. Referring to an infant weighing less than 2,500 grams (5 pounds 8 ounces) at birth or a *delivery* before 37 weeks *gestation*; also called *preterm*.

prenatal. The period of pregnancy from *conception* to birth; also called antepartum.

prep. The shaving or trimming of the pubic hair in preparation for the *delivery*.

presentation. The way the baby is positioned for birth.

presenting part. The part of the baby that is closest to the *cervix*.

preterm. Prior to 37 weeks *gestation*.

primigravida. A woman who is pregnant for the first time.

primipara. A woman who has given birth to one child; also called a primip. Pronounced *pry MIP ah rah*.

progesterone. The *hormone* responsible for the building up of the lining of the *uterus* and for maintaining that lining during pregnancy.

prolactin. The *hormone* that stimulates *lactation* and maternal feelings.

prostaglandins. A substance released at the end of pregnancy to *ripen* the *cervix* and cause *contractions*.

psychoprophylaxis. Mind prevention; also see *Lamaze*.

pubic bones. The front bones that join the two hip bones to form the pelvic girdle. The pubic bones are connected by the *symphysis pubis* and ligaments, which soften during pregnancy.

pudendal block. The loss of sensation in the *vagina* and *perineum* produced by the injection of an *anesthetic* into the pudendal nerves.

pulse oximeter. A device placed on the finger to measure the oxygen level in the blood.

quickening. The first movements of the *fetus* felt by the woman, usually between 16 and 18 weeks.

relaxin. The *hormone* that relaxes the pelvic ligaments and other joints during pregnancy.

Rh factor. A blood factor found in the red blood cells that is present in 85 percent of the population. When it is absent, the person is Rh negative.

Rh-immune globulin. A medication given to an Rh-negative woman within 72 hours of the birth of an Rh-positive baby, or after an *abortion* or *amniocentesis*, to prevent her body from producing *antibodies* that could endanger subsequent babies; one brand is RhoGAM.

ripen. Soften; used in reference to the *cervix*, which becomes soft when it is ready for the onset of *labor*.

rooming-in. The situation in which the mother and baby stay in the same hospital room for extended periods, rather than just for feedings.

rooting reflex. The instinctive movement of the baby's head and mouth toward a touch on the cheek or mouth.

round ligaments. The two ligaments that are the main support of the uterus.

rubella. German measles.

sacrum. The triangular bone situated below the last spinal vertebra and above the *coccyx*.

saddle block. The injection of an *anesthetic* into the lower spinal canal causing a loss of sensation from the pubic area to the toes; not commonly used.

scopolamine. A medication used for its amnesic effects; also called scope; rarely used.

second stage of labor. The period of *labor* from *complete* dilation through the birth of the baby.

secretory immunoglobulin A (IgA). An *immunity*-inducing substance in breastmilk.

sibling. A brother or sister.

sickle cell anemia. An anemia caused by a trait inherited from both parents; more common in black people of African descent.

SIDS. See *sudden infant death syndrome*.

sonogram. See *ultrasound*.

sperm. The male reproductive cell produced in the *testes*.

sphincter. A ringlike muscle that closes a natural opening, such as the *anus* or *urethra*.

spinal anesthesia. The injection of an *anesthetic* into the spinal fluid causing a loss of sensation; *intrathecal*.

station. The location of the baby's *presenting part* in relation to the woman's pelvic bones.

stem cells. Immature blood cells.

stork bites. A reddened area on a newborn's skin caused by capillaries close to the skin; also called *angel kisses*.

stretch marks. See *striae gravidarium*.

striae gravidarium. The pinkish or purplish lines seen on the *abdomen* and breasts during pregnancy; also called *stretch marks*. Pronounced *STRI ee gra vee DAR ee um*.

stripping the membranes. The procedure in which the *amniotic sac* is pulled away from the *cervix* to induce *labor*.

sudden infant death syndrome (SIDS). The unexplained death of a baby under 1 year of age.

super Kegel. An improved version of the *Kegel exercise*.

symphysis pubis. The cartilage that connects the *pubic bones* and softens during pregnancy.

Tay-Sachs disease. A genetic disorder of fat metabolism; more common in people of Jewish descent.

TENS. See *transcutaneous electrical nerve stimulation*.

term. The completed cycle of pregnancy; full term is 40 weeks.

testes. The two organs, located in the scrotum, that produce *sperm*.

tetanic contraction. A uterine *contraction* that is extremely long and strong; usually associated with induced *labor*.

thalassemia. A hereditary disease that is manifested by anemia; more common in people of Mediterranean descent.

third stage of labor. The period of *labor* from the birth of the baby through the *delivery* of the *placenta*.

tocolytic. A type of medication used to stop uterine *contractions*.

tonic neck reflex. A reflex in infants in which they assume a fencing position when lying on their backs.

toxemia. The common name for *pregnancy-induced hypertension*.

toxoplasmosis. A disease, contracted from eating rare meat or handling cat feces, that can cause birth defects.

tranquilizer. A medication that relieves anxiety.

transcutaneous electrical nerve stimulation (TENS).

A small battery-operated device used for pain relief.

transition. The last phase of the *first stage of labor*; the phase during which the *cervix* dilates from 8 to 10 *centimeters*.

transverse lie. A *presentation* in which the baby lies sideways in the uterus.

trimester. A period of three months.

twilight sleep. A combination of an *analgesic* and *scopolamine*; rarely used.

tympanic thermometer. A thermometer that records the temperature via the ear.

ultrasound. High frequency sound waves used for diagnostic purposes; also called a *sonogram*.

umbilical cord. The cordlike structure containing two arteries and one vein that connects the baby and the *placenta*.

urethra. The tube that carries the urine from the bladder to the outside of the body.

uterus. The muscular pear-shaped organ of *gestation*; also called the *womb*.

vacuum extractor. A suction device used to assist in the *delivery* of the head.

vagina. The curved, very elastic canal, measuring 4 to 6 inches long, between the *uterus* and the *vulva*.

Valsalva maneuver. Long breath holding and forceful pushing.

varicose veins. Unnaturally distended veins, commonly found during pregnancy in the legs, *vulva*, and *anus*.

vernix caseosa. White, cheeselike protective coating covering the baby's skin in utero. Pronounced *VER niks kay se O sah.*

vertex. The crown, or top, of the head.

viability. The ability to survive outside the *uterus*.

vibroacoustic stimulation test (VST). A *nonstress test* that utilizes a small transducer to make a buzzing sound.

visualization. A technique of picturing an image in the mind.

VST. See *vibroacoustic stimulation test*.

vulva. The external female reproductive organs, consisting of the clitoris and the *labia*.

walking epidural. An *epidural* using narcotics but not affecting motor sensations, thus allowing the woman to walk.

water intoxication. A serious complication that occurs if large amounts of electrolyte-free *intravenous fluids* are infused or too much water is ingested.

water pills. See *diuretic*.

Wharton's jelly. The jellylike material surrounding the vessels of the *umbilical cord*.

womb. See *uterus*.

Bibliography

The following books, articles, and other materials were used as reference sources in the preparation of *Pregnancy to Parenthood*. For a list of books for further information on pregnancy, birth, or childcare, see the "Recommended Reading List" on page 309.

Books

American Heart Association. *Basic Life Support, Heart-saver Guide.* Tulsa: CPR Publishers, Inc., 1993.

Berezin, Nancy. *The Gentle Birth Book.* New York: Simon & Schuster, 1980.

Bing, Elisabeth D., and Libby Colman. *Making Love During Pregnancy.* New York: Farrar, Straus & Giroux, 1989.

Brewer, Gail Sforza. *Pregnancy After 30 Workbook.* Emmaus, Pennsylvania: Rodale Press, 1978.

Brewer, Gail Sforza. *What Every Pregnant Woman Should Know: The Truth About Diet and Drugs During Pregnancy.* New York: Penguin Press, 1985.

Chard, Tim, and Martin Richards. *Benefits and Hazards of the New Obstetrics.* Suffolk, England: Lavenham Press, 1977.

Cohen, Nancy Wainer, and Lois J. Estner. *Silent Knife: Cesarean Prevention and Vaginal Birth After Cesarean.* South Hadley, Massachusetts: Bergin & Garvey, 1983.

Colman, Arthur, and Libby Colman. *Pregnancy: The Psychological Experience.* New York: Seabury Press, 1978.

Cooke, Cynthia W., and Susan Dworkin. *The Ms. Guide to a Woman's Health.* New York: Doubleday, 1979.

Cunningham, F. Gary, Paul C. MacDonald, and Norman G. Gant. *Williams Obstetrics*, 18th edition. Norwalk, Connecticut: Appleton & Lange, 1989.

Dick-Read, Grantly. *Childbirth Without Fear.* New York: Harper and Row, 1959.

Ericson, Avis J. *Medications Used During Labor and Birth: A Resource for Childbirth Educators.* Milwaukee: International Childbirth Education Association, 1978.

Edwards, Margot, and Penny Simkin. *Obstetric Tests and Technology: A Consumer's Guide.* Minneapolis: International Childbirth Education Association, n.d.

Feldman, Silvia. *Choices in Childbirth.* New York: Grosset and Dunlap, 1978.

Flamm, Bruce L. *Birth After Cesarean: The Medical Facts.* New York: Simon & Schuster Trade, 1992.

Goldbeck, Nikki. *As You Eat, So Your Baby Grows.* New York: Ceres Press, 1978.

Hatcher, Robert A., et al. *Contraceptive Technology 1990–1992*, 15th edition. New York: Irvington Publishers, Inc., 1990.

Ilse, Sherokee. *Empty Arms.* Minneapolis: Wintergreen Press, 1990.

Jordan, Kate, and Carole Osborne-Sheets. *Bodywork for the Childbearing Year*, 10th edition. La Jolla, California: American Massage Therapy Association, 1995.

Karmel, Marjorie. *Thank You, Dr. Lamaze.* New York: Dolphin Books, 1965.

Klaus, Marshall, and John Kennell. *Maternal-Infant Bonding.* St. Louis: C. V. Mosby Co., 1976.

Klaus, Marshall, John Kennell, and Phyllis Klaus. *Bonding: Building the Foundations of Secure Attachment and Independence.* New York: Addison-Wesley Publishing Co., 1995.

Korte, Diana, and Roberta Scaer. *A Good Birth, a Safe Birth.* New York: Bantam Books, 1984.

Krause, Marie V. *Food, Nutrition and Diet Therapy*, 4th edition. Philadelphia: W. B. Saunders Co., 1966.

La Leche League International. *Newborn Jaundice.* Franklin Park, Illinois: La Leche League International, 1989.

La Leche League International. *The Womanly Art of*

Breastfeeding, 5th edition. New York: Penguin Books, 1991.

Lauwers, Judith, and Candace Woessner. *Counseling the Nursing Mother*. Garden City Park, New York: Avery Publishing Group, 1990.

Leboyer, Frederick. *Birth Without Violence*. Rochester, Vermont: Inner Traditions International Ltd., 1995.

Lieberman, Adrienne. *Easing Labor Pain*. Boston: Harvard Common Press, 1992.

Mohrbacher, Nancy, and Julie Stock. *The Breastfeeding Answer Book*. Franklin Park, Illinois: La Leche League International, 1991.

Montagu, Ashley. *Touching: The Human Significance of the Skin*, 2nd edition. New York: Harper and Row, 1978.

Nilsson, Lennart. *A Child Is Born*. New York: Delacorte, 1990.

Nolan, George. *Family Centered Cesarean Maternity Care Policy*. Ann Arbor: University of Michigan Hospital, n.d.

Oxorn, Harry. *Oxorn-Foote Human Labor and Birth*, 5th edition. Norwalk, Connecticut: Appleton-Century-Crofts, 1986.

Palmer, Gabrielle. *The Politics of Breastfeeding*. London: Pandora Press, 1988.

Peterson, Gayle. *Birthing Normally*, 2nd edition. Berkeley, California: Mindbody Press, 1984.

Physicians' Desk Reference, 41st edition. Oradell, New Jersey: Medical Economics Co., 1987.

Pryor, Karen. *Nursing Your Baby*. New York: Pocket Books, 1991.

Riordan, Jan, and Kathleen Auerback. *Breastfeeding and Human Lactation*. Boston: Jones and Bartlett Publishers, 1993.

Samuels, Mike, and Nancy H. Samuels. *The Well Pregnancy Book*. New York: Summit Books, 1986.

Shelov, Steven P., and Robert E. Hannemann. *Caring for Your Baby and Young Child*. New York: Bantam Books, 1994.

Simkin, Penny. *The Birth Partner: Everything You Need to Know to Help a Woman Through Childbirth*. Boston: Harvard Common Press, 1989.

Simkin, Penny, Janet Whalley, and Ann Keppler. *Pregnancy, Childbirth and the Newborn*. New York: Meadowbrook Press, 1991.

Turner, Barbara Kay. *Baby Names for the 90s*. New York: Berkley Books, 1991.

Verny, Thomas, with John Kelly. *The Secret Life of the Unborn Child*. New York: Dell Publishing Co., 1981.

Woessner, Candace, Judith Lauwers, and Barbara Bernard. *Breastfeeding Today: A Mother's Companion*. Garden City Park, New York: Avery Publishing Group, 1994.

Worthington, Bonnie. *Nutrition in Pregnancy and Lactation*. St. Louis: C. V. Mosby Co., 1977.

Young, Diony, and Charles Mahan. *Unnecessary Cesareans: Ways to Avoid Them*. Minneapolis: International Childbirth Education Association, 1989.

Articles and Other Materials

AFP Plus: An Office Guide for Prenatal Care Providers (pamphlet). N.p.: Integrated Genetics Laboratories, Inc., 1991.

Albers, Leah L. "Clinical Issues in Electronic Fetal Monitoring." *Birth* 21 (June 1994).

American Family Physician 48.

"Amniotomy." *ICEA Review* 3 (Summer 1979).

"Auto Air Bags Can Kill Kids, Study Says." *The Orlando Sentinel*, 18 September 1996.

"Baby Poisoned by Food Spurs Couple's Crusade." *New York Post*, 18 August 1997.

Banta, David, and Stephen Thacker. "Electronic Fetal Monitoring: Is It a Benefit?" *Birth and the Family Journal*, Winter 1979.

Bell, Robin, and Maureen O'Neill. "Exercise and Pregnancy: A Review." *Birth* 21 (June 1994).

Borgatta, Lynn. "Recent Reports: Electronic Fetal Monitoring." *Childbirth Instructor Magazine*, Autumn 1993.

"Breastfeeding and Cholesterol." *Childbirth Instructor Magazine*, Winter 1994.

"Breastmilk: Wide-Ranging Benefits." *The Florida Times-Union*, 13 January 1998.

Brock, Kaye E., Geoffrey Berry, et al. "Sexual, Reproductive and Contraceptive Risk Factors for Carcinoma–In Situ of the Uterine Cervix in Sydney." *The Medical Journal of Australia* 150 (6 February 1989).

Caldeyro-Barcia, Roberto. "The Influence of Maternal Bearing-Down Effort During Second Stage on Fetal Well-Being." *Birth and the Family Journal* 6 (Spring 1979).

Caldwell, Jean. "CVS: An Early Test for Genetic Problems." *American Baby*, February 1985.

Campen, Jean. "Medical Update: Group Beta Strep: A New Way of Treating an Old Foe." *Childbirth Instructor Magazine*, First Quarter 1996.

Campen, Jean. "Statistics Corner." *International Journal of Childbirth Education* 6 (August 1991).

Campen, Jean. "Statistics Corner." *International Journal of Childbirth Education* 7 (1992).

Campen, Jean Marie. "Routine Episiotomy." *Childbirth Instructor Magazine* 1 (Winter 1991).

Carr, Katherine Camacho. "Obstetric Practices Which Protect Against Neonatal Morbidity: Focus on Maternal Position in Labor and Birth." *Birth and the Family Journal* 7 (Winter 1980).

Charbonneau, Kathy. "Healthy Lifestyles: Intravenous Infusion: The Chemical Impact." *International Journal of Childbirth Education* 9 (February-March 1994).

Cicchinelli, Brenda. "A Cry for Help: Postpartum Depression." *International Journal of Childbirth Education* 10 (February-March 1995).

"Cigarette Smoking and Breastfeeding." *Childbirth Instructor Magazine*, Autumn 1993.

Clarke, Sally C., and Selma Taffel. "Changes in Cesarean Delivery in the United States, 1988 and 1993." *Birth* 22 (June 1995).

"Coalition Urges Folic Acid Addition to Food." *Childbirth Instructor Magazine*, First Quarter 1996.

"Cocaine Follow-up." *Childbirth Instructor Magazine*, Winter 1994.

"Companies Wrestle With Threats to Workers' Reproductive Health." *The Wall Street Journal*, 5 February 1987.

Cox, Bonnie Ennis. "Prenatal Procedures: What's New, What's Being Used." *Childbirth Instructor Magazine* 1 (Spring 1991).

Cox, Janice. "Information Alert." *International Journal of Childbirth Education* 3 (August 1988).

"Decongestant Danger." *Midwifery Today* 26 (Summer 1993).

Doering, Susan G. "Unnecessary Cesareans: Doctor's Choice, Parent's Dilemma." *Compulsory Hospitalization or Freedom of Choice in Childbirth?* 1 (1976).

Ewigman, Bernard G., et al. "Effect of Prenatal Ultrasound Screening on Perinatal Outcome." *The New England Journal of Medicine* 329 (16 September 1993).

Fenster, L., et al. "Caffeine Consumption During Pregnancy and Fetal Growth." *American Journal of Public Health* 81 (1991).

Flamm, Bruce. "Cesarean Delivery 1970–1995: Where Have We Been and Where Are We Going?" *International Journal of Childbirth Education* 9 (November 1994).

Floyd, R. Louise, et al. "Smoking During Pregnancy: Prevalence, Effects, and Intervention Strategies." *Birth* 18 (March 1991).

"Folic Acid May Help Prevent Heart Disease and Stroke." *Miracles: A Quarterly Newsletter for Loyal Donors to the March of Dimes* 4 (1996).

Gegor, Carolyn L. "Obstetric Ultrasound: Who Should Perform Sonograms?" *Birth* 19 (June 1992).

Goer, Henci. "Antenatal Corticosteroids: Wonder Drug for Preterm Infants." *Childbirth Forum*, Spring 1996.

Goer, Henci. "Epidural: Myth Vs. Reality." *Childbirth Instructor Magazine*, Special Issue 1997.

Goer, Henci. "The Occiput Posterior Baby." *Childbirth Instructor Magazine*, Summer 1994.

Grimes, David. "Routine Circumcision Reconsidered." *American Journal of Nursing*, January 1980.

Gwinn, Marta L., Nancy C. Lee, et al. "Pregnancy, Breast Feeding, and Oral Contraceptives and the Risk of Epithelial Ovarian Cancer." *Journal of Clinical Epidemiology* 43 (1990).

Haire, Doris. "The Pregnant Patient's Bill of Rights" (paper). International Childbirth Education Association, Minneapolis.

Haire, Doris. "The Pregnant Patient's Responsibilities" (paper). International Childbirth Education Association, Minneapolis.

Harper, Barbara. "Waterbirth: An Increasingly Attractive Gentle Birth Choice." *International Journal of Childbirth Education* 9 (February-March 1994).

"Health and Fitness." *The Orlando Sentinel*, 30 April 1996.

"Health and Fitness." *The Orlando Sentinel*, 13 January 1998.

Heilman, Judy, et al. "Fluoride Concentrations of Infant Foods." *Journal of the American Dental Association* 128 (July 1997).

Humphrey, Noreen. "Care of the Circumcised and Uncircumcised Penis." *Baby Care Forum* (Fall 1992).

ICEA Review 3 (Summer 1979).

"In Brief." *Childbirth Instructor Magazine*, Third Quarter 1996.

"Infant Eye Cues." *Childbirth Instructor Magazine*, First Quarter 1996.

Jakubovic, A., T. Hattori, and P. McGee. "Radioactivity in Suckling Rats After Giving C-14-Tetrahydrocannabinol to the Mother." *European Journal of Pharmacy* 22 (1973).

Jannke, Samantha. "When the Mother-to-Be Drinks." *Childbirth Instructor Magazine*, Winter 1994.

Jiménez, Sherry L. M. "'Safe Sex' After Baby." *American Baby Magazine*, December 1996.

Jukelevics, Nicette. "Vaginal Birth After Cesarean (VBAC) Sheet." *International Journal of Childbirth Education* 9 (November 1994).

"Labor Support Linked to Fewer Cesareans." *Childbirth Forum*, Fall 1991.

Lassen, Belinda. "Newborn Circumcision." *International Journal of Childbirth Education* 6 (February 1991).

Lawrence, Ruth A. "Can We Expect Greater Intelligence From Human Milk Feedings?" *Birth* 19 (June 1992).

"Lesser Known Facts" (fact sheet). American Cancer Society, 1980.

"Lidocaine-Prilocaine for Circumcision Pain." *Childbirth Instructor Magazine*, Third Quarter, 1997.

"Limb-Reduction Defects and Chorion Villus Sampling." *The Lancet*, 4 May 1991.

Maiselle, M. J., et al. "Elective Delivery of the Term Fetus: An Obstetrical Hazard." *Journal of the American Medical Association* 238 (7 November 1977).

"Maternal Position During Labor and Birth." *ICEA Review* 2 (Summer 1978).

"Moms Who Smoke Increase Babies' Risk of Ear Infections." *Growing Child Research Review*, May 1995.

"'Morning After' Doses Outlined." *The Florida Times-Union*, 25 February 1997.

"New Crop of Midwives Shatter Stereotype." *The Florida Times-Union*, 22 October 1996.

"New Marker for Preterm Labor." *Childbirth Instructor Magazine,* First Quarter 1996.

"News." *Birth* 16 (March 1988).

"News." *Birth* 23 (March 1996).

"News." *Birth* 23 (June 1996).

"News." *Birth* 23 (September 1996).

"News." *Birth* 24 (December 1997).

Notelovitz, Morris. "Commentary." *ICEA Review* 2 (Summer 1978).

"Official Credits Education Campaign for Decline in Sudden Infant Deaths." *The Orlando Sentinel*, 25 June 1996.

"One Mother Dies for 8 Newborns Saved With Electronic Monitoring." *Obstetrics and Gynecology News* 12 (15 December 1978).

Oski, Frank A. "Hyperbilirubinemia in the Term Infant: An Unjaundiced Approach." *Contemporary Pediatrics*, April 1992.

Polomeno, Viola. "Sexual Intercourse After the Birth of a Baby." *International Journal of Childbirth Education* 11 (December 1996).

"Pregnancy Outcomes Among Active and Sedentary Women." *Baby Care Forum*, Summer 1996.

"Recent Advances in Research" (fact sheet). Florida SIDS Information Exchange, March 1979.

Roberts, Catherine C., and Leslie M. Ludka. "Food for Thought: The Debate Over Eating and Drinking in Labor." *Childbirth Instructor Magazine*, Spring 1994.

Shearer, Madeline. "Malnutrition in Middle Class Pregnant Women." *Birth and the Family Journal* 7 (Spring 1980).

"Should Immunization Against Varicella [Chickenpox] Be Restricted to the Immunocompromised?" *Physician's Weekly* 12 (10 July 1995).

Simkin, Penny. "Weighing the Pros and Cons of the Epidural." *Childbirth Forum*, Fall 1991.

"Smoking Can Raise SIDS Risk." *The Orlando Sentinel*, 8 March 1995.

"Study: Drinking Multiplies Risks of Infant Leukemia." *The Orlando Sentinel*, 3 January 1996.

"Study Links Miscarriages to Caffeine Consumption." *Childbirth Instructor Magazine*, Winter 1994.

Sundberg, J. Bang, S. Smidt-Jensen, V. Brooks, C. Lundsteen, J. Parner, K. Keiding, and J. Philip. "Randomized Study of Risk of Fetal Loss Related to Early Amniocentesis Versus Chorionic Villus Sampling." *Lancet* 350 (1997).

Thorp, James A., and Ginger Breedlove. "Epidural Analgesia in Labor: An Evaluation of Risks and Benefits." *Birth* 23 (June 1996).

"Vitamin A May Increase Risk of Birth Defects." *The Orlando Sentinel*, 7 October 1995.

Walker, Marsha. "Summary of the Hazards of Infant Formula" (handout). International Lactation Consultant Association, 1992.

Walker, Marsha. "Why Aren't More Mothers Breastfeeding?" *Childbirth Instructor* 2 (Winter 1992).

Wolfe, Sidney M. "Unnecessary Cesarean Section: Halting a National Epidemic." *Health Letter* 8 (June 1992).

Wunderlich, Cherry. "Unborn Males: Children at Risk With Saccharin." *ICEA News* 18 (1979).

Yoshiuchi, Ellen H. "Fetal Alcohol Syndrome." *Childbirth Instructor Magazine*, Spring 1992.

Young, Diony. "Editorial: Early Discharge: Whose Decision, Whose Responsibility?" *Birth* 23 (June 1996).

About the Authors

Linda Goldberg, RN, CCE, is a graduate of the Helene Fuld School of Nursing at West Jersey Hospital. She has taught childbirth classes since 1977 and served as Director of Instructor Training and Certification for the Childbirth Education Association (CEA) of Jacksonville, Florida. She also served as Vice President and President of the CEA of Jacksonville, as well as President of its Board of Directors, before moving to Winter Springs, Florida, in 1984. Since 1985, Linda has taught childbirth education for Special Beginnings, an out-of-hospital birth center in Orlando. She also teaches private classes and is continuing her work with mothers and babies as a staff RN at a local hospital. She is a coauthor of the childbirth manual *Your Child's First Journey*.

Linda Goldberg

Linda and her husband, Bill, have three children—Jeff, Becky, and Jonathan—all born after unmedicated labors and all breastfed. Jeff and Becky were delivered in a hospital by a supportive physician, and Jonathan was born in an out-of-hospital birth center attended by a certified nurse-midwife.

Ginny Brinkley, BS, MBA, completed her undergraduate studies at Mary Washington College of the University of Virginia and her graduate studies at the University of North Florida. One of the original members of the Childbirth Education Association of Jacksonville, she served that organization as both Childbirth Education Coordinator and Executive Director. In addition, she was a member of its Board of Directors for over 10 years. In 1989, Ginny cofounded Pink Inc! Publishing, producer of pregnancy and parenting materials for pregnant teens, and pregnancy prevention materials for adolescent males and females. Other books she has written include *Young & Pregnant, You & Your New Baby, Baby and Me, "You're WHAT?"* and *What's Right for Me?* and she is a coauthor of *Your Child's First Journey*.

Ginny Brinkley

Ginny's family consists of her husband, Bill; two biological sons, Scott and Brett Hewitt (both prepared births and both breastfed)¦ three stepchildren, Bill Jr., Bob, and Samantha; and four grandchildren, Brad, Bobbie Janene, Kelli, and Hunter.

Janice Kukar, BA, ACCE, is a graduate of Michigan State University with a degree in home economics education and human development. An adult educator for 10 years before adopting a baby, Janice served the Childbirth Education Association of Jacksonville as Instructor, Volunteer Coordinator, and Associate Director. Her recent activities include leadership positions on Parent-Teacher Association boards at the local and county levels, as well as appointments to the Human Sexuality Task Force for the Duval County School Board and the Health Education Curriculum Committee. She is a coauthor of *Your Child's First Journey*.

Janice Kukar

Jan and her husband, David, have two sons—Bobby, adopted at 4 months, and Tommy, delivered using the Lamaze method and breastfed. Her advocacy of prepared childbirth was reinforced by her recent participation in the unmedicated birth of her first grandchild, Page Marie, who is a happy breastfed baby.

Index

Abdominal tightening, 197, 286
Abruptio placentae, 186
Accelerated-decelerated breathing, 98
Accident prevention, 116, 224, 226–232
Accutane, 24, 62
Acetaminophen, 156, 219, 221, 273
Acquired immune deficiency syndrome, 32, 266, 295, 297
Active labor, 129, 142–143
Active management of labor, 173
Acupressure, 59, 102–104
Acupuncture, 105
Adjustment to parenthood, 275–280
Admission to birth facility, routine procedures for, 124–125
AFP screening. *See* Alpha-fetoprotein screening.
Afterbirth. *See* Placenta.
Afterpains, 138, 144, 156, 273
AIDS. *See* Acquired immune deficiency syndrome.
Air embolism, 29
Albumin, 47
Alcohol, 3, 60, 257, 260
Allergies, baby
    breastmilk and, 244, 245
    to cow's milk, 244, 245, 269
    to formula, 245, 267
    to solid foods, 245, 269
Alpha-fetoprotein screening, 38–39

Ambivalent feelings, 24, 274–275, 277, 279
American Academy of Pediatrics, 211, 216, 241, 242, 269
American Academy of Pediatrics' Committee on Drugs, 9, 149
American College of Obstetricians and Gynecologists, 40, 66, 174, 185, 190
Amino acids, 48
Amniocentesis, 37–38, 190
Amnioinfusion, 169, 185–186
Amniotic fluid, 16, 18, 37–38, 46, 48, 123, 185
Amniotic sac, 16, 46, 123
Amniotomy, 171, 173
Analgesics, 150, 152–153, 189
    combined spinal/epidural, 158–159
    epidural, 150–151
    patient controlled, 195–196
    postpartum, 156–157
    saddle block, 158
    spinal, 158
Anesthesia, 6, 8, 147–150, 154–157
    epidural, 150–151, 154–155, 158, 189, 191
    general, 156–157, 184, 191, 192, 194
    local infiltration, 154–155
    pudendal block, 154–155
    regional, 6, 8, 150–151,

154–155, 158–159, 184, 191, 192, 194
    saddle block, 154–155, 158, 191
    spinal, 154–155, 158, 191
Anesthesiologist, 151, 185, 191, 192
Ankle rotating, 197, 286
Anoxia, 135, 178
Anterior position, 163
Antibiotic ointment, 6, 136, 204
Antibodies, 48, 141, 186, 243, 244, 245, 251
Antibody screening, 31
Antiemetics, 152–153
Anxiety, 24, 26, 28, 121, 181, 274
Apgar, Virginia, 203
Apgar score, 202–203
Areola, 23, 250, 253, 259, 262
Arm circles, 70
Arteries, umbilical, 21
Artificial respiration, 176–177, 224–226
Artificial rupture of the membranes, 171, 173, 188
Artificial sweeteners, 62
Aspartame, 62
Aspirin, 62, 218
Atarax, 152–153
Atropine, 191
Augmentation of labor, 172–173
Automobile safety, 42–43, 119, 231–232

Babinski toe reflex, 209
Baby, at birth
    adjustment to extrauterine life,
        202–203
    Apgar scoring, 202–203
    appearance, 194, 201–202
    blood tests, 204–205, 209
    circulatory changes, 202
    delivery room care, 202–204
    temperature, maintaining, 137,
        203–204
    vernix caseosa, 18, 202
    weight, 201
    See also Baby, newborn, charac-
        teristics of.
Baby, common concerns regarding
    baby-proofing, 116, 226–232
    bathing, 209, 214, 217, 234
    bowel movements, 213, 218,
        233, 245, 249, 255, 267
    breastfeeding problems. *See*
        Breastfeeding problems.
    burping, 263, 268
    circumcision, 7, 210–212
    colic, 215
    constipation, 213, 245, 267
    cord care, 209
    cradle cap, 213
    crying, 137, 214–215
    diaper rash, 212, 233
    diarrhea, 213, 218, 229, 245,
        255, 267, 268
    feeding. *See* Bottle feeding;
        Breastfeeding.
    food. *See* Baby food; Solid
        food.
    growth spurts, 250, 255
    jaundice, 153, 172, 209–210,
        244
    massage, 236–239
    playing, 234–236
    rashes, 212–213, 219
    skin care, 212–213, 246
    sleeping, 215–217
    spitting up, 213–214
    spoiling, 217
    traveling, 231–232, 234
    vomiting, 214, 218, 268

weaning, 271–272
weight gain, 201, 256
Baby, items needed for
    clothes, 229, 232, 233–234
    diapers, 233
    equipment, 227, 228, 230,
        232–234
    toys, 216, 235–236
Baby, medical concerns regarding
    choking, 221–224, 270
    coughing, 219
    eye problems, 219, 267
    fever, 218
    immunizations, 219–221
    poisoning, 219, 231
    preterm, 164, 189, 244–245
    temperature taking, 218
    See also Baby, common con-
        cerns regarding.
Baby, newborn, characteristics of
    breasts, 207
    breathing, 202, 207
    eyes, 202, 204, 206
    fingernails, 207
    fontanels, 205–206
    genitals, 202, 207
    hair, 206
    hearing, 206
    heart rate, 207
    hiccups, 207
    lanugo, 18, 19, 207
    meconium, 18, 123, 137, 185,
        210, 213, 233, 244
    milia, 206
    molding, 173, 194, 201, 206
    Mongolian spots, 207
    reflexes, 207–209
    senses, 178, 206
    skin, 207
    soft spots, 205–206
    stork bites, 207
    tear ducts, 206
    umbilical cord stump, 207, 209
    vision, 136, 206
Baby blues, 274–275
Baby bottles, sterilizing, 268
Baby equipment, 227, 228, 230,
    232–234

Baby food
    commercial, 270–271
    making your own, 270
Baby-proofing, 116, 226–232
Back blows, 221–222
Back care, 59, 66–68, 69–70, 71,
    72, 78
Back labor, 101–102, 104, 165–167
Backache, 59, 68, 70, 71, 78, 120
Bathing baby, 217
    as comfort measure, 214
    equipment needed for, 234
    umbilical cord stump and, 209
Bikini incision, 193
Bili-lights, 210
Bilirubin, 209–210, 244
Birth, 5–6, 132–133, 135, 144–145,
    175–180
Birth center. *See* Birth facility.
Birth control
    breastfeeding and, 249, 293
    after childbirth, 293
    emergency, 293–300
    methods of, 294–301
Birth facility
    admission to, 124–125
    delivery procedures at, 134
    discharge from, 139, 141, 204
    pre-registering at, 114–115
    stay in, 139, 141, 195–196
    tour of, 114
    when to go to, 124
Birth options, 3–7, 134, 140
Birth Partner, The, 114
Birth plan, 2–7, 180
Birth Visualization, 93–95
Birth without interventions, 180
Birthing ball, 100
Birthing room, 5, 134
Bladder
    cesarean delivery and, 192, 195
    during labor, 129
    postpartum, 138, 141
    during pregnancy, 23
    vacuum extractor and, 175
Blastocyst, 15
Bleeding
    postpartum, 6, 138, 177, 194

during pregnancy, 30, 34
Blood
    fetal, 21
    Rh factor, 30, 31, 32, 141,
        186–187
    type, 30, 32
    volume, 25, 46
Blood pressure, 31, 34, 35, 159
    effect of medication on, 149,
        151, 153, 155, 157, 159, 189
Blood tests
    newborn, 204–205, 209
    prenatal, 30, 31
Bloody show. *See* Mucous plug.
Body Awareness/Tension
        Recognition exercise, 86–88
Body changes during pregnancy,
    22–24, 25–26, 27, 29
Body mechanics, 66–68, 197
Bonding, 6, 7, 8, 136–138, 139,
    144–145, 194
    delayed, 136, 137
    effects of medications on, 137,
        148
    maintaining baby's temperature
        during, 6, 137
Bottle feeding, 246, 247–248,
    267–268
Bottle mouth syndrome, 267
Bowel movement
    baby, 213, 218, 233, 245, 249,
        255, 267
    postpartum, 141, 274
Brain development, 16, 17, 19, 45,
    47, 235
Braxton-Hicks contractions, 25, 26,
    35, 112, 121
Breast abscess, 262
Breast fullness, 260–261
Breast infection, 261–262
Breast pump, 245, 257, 265
Breastfeeding
    advantages of, 6, 177, 241,
        242–249
    AIDS and, 266
    alcohol consumption and, 257,
        260
    birth control and, 249, 293

cancer and, 248
after a cesarean, 8, 196, 264–265
contractions during, 248, 273
contraindications to, 266
facial development and, 246
father's role in, 241, 249
getting started at, 136, 196,
    252–254
growth spurts and, 250, 255
hormones and, 137, 177, 249,
    250
jaundice and, 210
let-down reflex and, 250, 263
maternal fluid intake and, 251,
    262
medications and, 155, 157,
    256–257, 260, 262, 264–265
menstrual cycle and, 249
nipple care, 252, 254, 259
nutrition and, 251
nutritional supplements and,
    248, 250, 254, 260
pediatrician and, 251–252
preparation for, 251–252, 262
preterm baby and, 244–245
problems. *See* Breastfeeding
    problems.
in public, 248
sexual relations and, 292
smoking and, 257, 260
in special situations, 265–266
succeeding at, 241–242, 249
traveling and, 248
twins, 250
weaning, 271–272
working and, 265
Breastfeeding counselor, 242
Breastfeeding problems
    baby-related, 262–263
    breast abscess, 262
    breast fullness, 260–261
    breast infection, 261–262
    engorgement, 250, 255, 259,
        260–261
    flat nipples, 262
    inadequate milk supply, 260
    inverted nipples, 252, 262
    mastitis, 261

milk leaking, 256, 261, 292
nipple soreness, 252, 254, 259
plugged ducts, 256, 261
Breastmilk
    advantages of, 242–246,
        247–248
    allergies and, 244, 245
    antibodies in, 243, 244, 245,
        251, 258
    caloric content of, 244, 248, 256
    colostrum, 6, 25, 136–137, 243,
        244
    composition of, 242
    digestion and, 244, 245–246
    hand expression of, 257, 261
    iron content of, 48, 243
    production of, 250–251, 260
    storage of, 258
Breasts
    baby, 207
    postpartum, 274, 292
    during pregnancy, 23, 25
Breathing, newborns, 202, 207
Breathing techniques
    basics of, 96
    for labor, 95–99
    for pushing, 106–107
Breech presentation, 161–162, 165,
    186
    exercise to rotate baby, 162
Brewer, Gail Sforza, 48
Brewer's yeast, 52
Bupivacaine, 150, 154–155
Burping, 263, 268

Caffeine, 61–62
Calcium, 49–50, 54–58
Calf stretch, 76–77
Caloric content
    of breastmilk, 244
    of honey versus sugar, 52–53
    of selected foods, 54–58
Caloric requirement
    during breastfeeding, 251
    during pregnancy, 47, 48, 51
    of preterm infants, 244
Calories
    burned by breastfeeding, 248

empty. *See* Junk food.

Cancer, 248

Caput succedaneum, 173, 175, 201–202

Car safety. *See* Automobile safety.

Carbohydrates, 48

Cardinal movements of labor, 164

Cardiopulmonary resuscitation, 176–177, 221, 224–226

Caregiver
choosing a, 1–2
when to call your, 32, 34, 123, 274
See also Pediatrician.

Carpal tunnel syndrome, 51

Catheter, suction, 138

Catheter, urinary, 138, 192, 195

Centers for Disease Control, 33, 170, 220

Cephalhematoma, 173, 175, 206

Cephalic presentation, 161

Cephalopelvic disproportion, 185

Certified lactation consultant, 242, 252, 255, 265–266, 267

Certified nurse-midwife, 2, 134

Cervical cap, 294–295

Cervix
dilation and effacement of, 121, 127, 128, 129, 130, 131, 132, 142, 144
during third trimester, 26

Cesarean baby, 194–195

Cesarean birth
anesthesia for, 8, 148, 154–157, 184, 191, 192
avoiding, 188–189
breastfeeding after, 8, 196, 264–265
complications of, 199
exercise after, 197–198, 285
family-centered, 8, 184–185
father-attended, 8, 184, 192, 193
incisions used for, 192, 193–194, 196, 198
indications for, 161, 162, 185–187
medications for, 156–157
options for, 7–8

planned and unplanned, 189–190
postpartum, 195–197
preoperative procedures for, 8, 190–191
rates of, 169–170, 187
recovery from, 194, 196–197
rooming-in following, 8, 185, 196
sexual relations following, 196
surgical procedure for, 191–193

Chest thrusts, 222

Chickenpox vaccine, 220–221

Childbirth options, 3–8

Childcare providers, 239–240, 265

Children's snacks, 271

Chlamydia, 32

Choices in Childbirth, 1

Choking, 221–224, 270

Cholesterol, 242–243

Chorion, 16

Chorionic villus sampling, 38

Chromosomes, 13

Cigarettes, 59–60

Circulatory system, baby, 202

Circumcision, 7, 210–212

Classes
childbirth, 3, 28
early pregnancy, 28

Clothing
baby, 229, 232, 233–234
maternity, 68–69

Cocaine, 60–61, 266

Colic, 215

Colostrum, 6, 25, 136–137, 243, 244

Comfort measures for labor, 101–105, 129, 131, 135, 167

Compazine, 152–153

Complications, tests to detect, 37–41

Conception, 13–15

Conditioning exercises, 65, 69–73

Condoms, 294–295

Constipation
in baby, 213, 245, 267
postpartum, 141, 274
pregnancy, 23, 27, 48, 59

Consumer Product Safety Commission, 226

Contraception. *See* Birth control.

Contractions
afterpains, 138, 144, 156
Braxton-Hicks, 25, 26, 112, 121
breastfeeding and, 248, 273
induced, 172
labor, 122, 123, 127, 128, 129, 130, 131, 132
nipples and, 30
prelabor versus true labor, 121
prostaglandins and, 30
sexual orgasm and, 30
timing of, 122

Convulsions, 219

Copper-T intrauterine device, 300–301

Cord. *See* Umbilical cord.

Cough reflex, 208

Coughing, 219

Counterpressure, 101, 166–167

CPD. *See* Cephalopelvic disproportion.

CPR. *See* Cardiopulmonary resuscitation.

Cradle cap, 213

Cramps, 34, 76, 130

Crowning, 110, 133

Crying in newborns, 137, 214–215

CVS. *See* Chorionic villus sampling.

Darvocet, 156–157

Dehydration
in baby, 218
during labor, 4, 167

Delivery
of baby, 132–133, 134, 135, 144–145, 175–180
of placenta, 135, 144–145

Delivery options, 5–6

Delivery room, 5, 134

Delivery room prodecures, 5–6, 202–204

Demerol, 149, 152–153, 154–155, 156–157

Depo-Provera, 296–297

Depression
postpartum, 196–197, 199,
274–275
during pregnancy, 27–28, 121
Diabetes, gestational, 34–35
Diabetic mother, early delivery of,
186
Diagnostic tests, 37–41
Diaper rash, 212, 233
Diapers, 233
Diaphragm
after a cesarean delivery, 195
during pregnancy, 27
during pushing, 106, 107
Diaphragm (contraceptive device),
293, 294–295
Diarrhea
in allergic baby, 267
in baby, 213, 218, 255
bad formula and, 268
breastmilk and, 245
swimming pools and, 229
Dick-Read, Grantly, 81
Diet
after ceserean birth, 195, 196
during labor, 128
during multiple pregnancy, 36,
48
No-Risk Pregnancy Diet, 3, 48,
49
during pregnancy, 3, 23, 45,
51–53, 61–62
Digestion
after a cesean, 196
during labor, 128
during pregnancy, 23, 27
Digestion in baby
breastmilk and, 245–246
formula and, 267
introduction of solids and, 269
Dilation, 121, 126, 127, 128, 129,
130, 132, 142, 144
Discharge, vaginal. *See* Vaginal
discharge.
Discharge from hospital, 7, 139,
195, 204
early 141
Diuretics, 46–47

Dizziness, 34
Doctor. *See* Caregiver; Pediatrician.
Doptone, 18, 39, 124
Double hip squeeze, 102, 166
Douching, 123
Doula, 82, 114, 188
Dreams, 26
Drugs. *See* Medications.
Drugs, recreational, 59–62
Dry birth, 123
Due date, 15, 22, 39
Duramorph, 156–157

Early labor, 128–129
Eclampsia, 35
Edema, 25, 46–47, 48
Effacement, 121, 126, 127, 128,
132, 142, 144
Effleurage, 101
Electronic fetal monitor, 4, 39, 41,
124, 168–171, 173, 188–189
Embryo, 16–17
Emergency childbirth, 119,
175–177
Emotional changes during pregnan-
cy, 24, 26, 27–28
Emotional support during labor, 3,
82, 125, 129, 130–131, 135,
143, 145, 148
Endorphins, 66, 104, 105, 125, 147
Enema, 3, 124, 190
Energy before onset of labor, 121
Engagement, 127
Engorgement, 250, 255, 259,
260–261
Epidural anesthesia, 149, 150–151,
158, 189, 191, 194, 195
Episiotomy, 5, 75, 108, 109, 110,
135, 138, 141, 154, 156, 174,
273–274
avoiding an, 73, 75, 108, 135,
174
Equal sugar substitute, 62
Equipment, baby. *See* Baby equip-
ment.
Ergotrate, 152–153
Erythema toxicum, 207
Erythroblastosis fetalis, 186–187

Estriol excretion study, 40
Estrogen, 13, 22–23, 46, 48 122
Exercise
conditioning, 65, 69–73
Kegel, 73–75, 110, 123, 132,
138, 174, 285–286, 287, 288,
290
postpartum, 197–198, 285–290
postpartum, cesarean, 197–198,
285
for relief of discomfort, 76, 77,
166
to rotate baby, 162, 166
sustained, 65, 69, 290
Expulsion. *See* Delivery.
External fetal monitor, 168–169
External version, 163
Eye ointment, 6, 136, 204
Eyes, baby, 202, 204, 206, 219, 267

Facial development and breastfeed-
ing, 246
Failure to thrive, 136
Fallopian tube, 13–14, 15
False labor. *See* Braxton-Hicks
contractions; Prelabor.
Family-centered maternity care,
3–7, 8, 138, 184–185, 188
Father
bonding and, 136–138
cesarean birth and, 184–185,
191, 192, 193, 194
postpartum and, 241, 249,
284–285
role in breastfeeding, 241, 249
See also Labor partner.
Fatigue
postpartum, 275, 291
during pregnancy, 24, 27
Fats, 48, 242
FDA. *See* U.S. Food and Drug
Administration.
Fears, 24, 26, 28, 81–82
Fear-tension-pain cycle, 81–82
Feeding baby. *See* Bottle feeding;
Breastfeeding.
Feldman, Silvia, 1
Fentanyl, 154–155, 156–157

Fertilization, 13–15
Fetal
    development, 15–19
    distress, 36, 168, 169–170, 172, 173, 185, 186, 199
    emotions, 19–21
    maturity, 39, 171, 189–190
    position, 163–164
    presentation, 161–163, 186
    See also Fetus.
Fetal alcohol syndrome, 60
Fetal fibronectin, 36
Fetal heart monitor, 4, 39, 41, 124, 168–171, 173, 188–189
Fetal movement evaluation, 41
Fetal scalp sampling, 169
Fetus, 17–19. *See also* Fetal.
Fever
    in baby, 218
    during pregnancy, 33, 34
Fiber, 23, 48, 59
Fingernails, baby, 207
First aid, 176–177, 221–226
First stage of labor, 127–131
Flamm, Bruce, 199
Flat nipples, 262
Focal point, 96
Folic acid, 26, 50
Fontanels, 205–206
Food additives, 62
Foods, solid, for baby, 269–271
Foot flexing and stretching, 197, 286
Foot massage, 80
Footprint, 204
Forceps delivery, 162, 175, 187
Foreskin, 210, 211, 212
Formula, 267–268
    allergies to, 245, 267
    nutritional deficiencies of, 242, 243, 247–248
Front-pack baby carrier, 232, 234
Fundal pressure, 192
Fundus, 141
    massage of, 138

Gag reflex, 208
Galactosemia, 266

Gender of baby, 17, 18
General anesthesia, 156–157, 184, 191, 192, 194
Genitals, baby, 202, 207
Gentle birth, 177–180
Gentle pushing, 106
Gestational diabetes, 34–35
Global Maternal Child Health Association, 180
Glucose tolerance test, 31
Gonorrhea, 32, 204
Grasp reflex, 208–209
Growth spurts, 250, 255
GTT. *See* Glucose tolerance test.

Hair, baby, 206
Hand expression of milk, 257, 259, 261, 263
Head injury, 219
Head lifting, 287
Hearing, baby, 206
Heart rate, baby, 207
    late decelerations of, 169
Heartburn, 23, 27
Heimlich maneuver, 223
Hemoglobin, 50
Hemorrhage
    abruptio placentae and, 186
    postpartum, 273
    as risk of cesarean, 188
Hemorrhoids, 27, 141, 273–274
Hepatitis B vaccination, 219
Herpes simplex virus II, 76, 187
Herpesvirus, 32
Hiccups
    in newborns, 207
    as sign of transition, 130
High blood pressure, 35, 159
Higher-risk pregnancy, 34–37, 169
Hip rolls, 290
Honey, 52–53, 269
Honeymoon stitch, 174, 292
Hormones
    breastfeeding and, 137, 177, 249, 250
    postpartum, 274, 291–292
    See also Endorphins; Estrogen;

Oxytocin; Progesterone; Prolactin; Relaxin.
Hospital. *See* Birth facility.
Hospital bag
    for baby, 118
    for woman, 118
HSVII. *See* Herpes simplex virus II.
Hyperventilation, 95, 98
    as sign of transition, 130
Hypnotics, 152–153
    as sign of transition, 130
Hypotension, supine, 67, 108, 172, 189
Hypovolemia, 47

Ibuprofen, 156–157
Identification bracelets, 204
IgA. *See* Secretory immunoglobulin A.
Immunizations, 219–221
Implantation, 15, 23
Incisions
    cesarean, 192, 193–194, 196
    episiotomy, 135, 141, 174, 274
Indigestion, 23, 27
Induction of labor
    by amniotomy, 4, 171
    using Pitocin, 5, 152–153, 172
    after premature rupture of the membranes, 171
    prostaglandins and, 172
    by stripping the membranes, 171
Infant massage. *See* Massage, infant.
Infant screening test, 204–205, 266
Informed consent, 9
Internal fetal monitor, 168–169
International Childbirth Education Association, 9, 114
Interventions, 167–171
    early, 188
Intrauterine device
    for birth control, 296–297
    for emergency contraception, 300–301
Intrauterine growth retardation, 46
Intrauterine pressure catheter, 169

Intravenous fluids, 4, 125, 165, 167–168, 191, 192, 195
Inverted nipples, 252, 262
Involution, 273
Iron, 47, 50, 54–58, 243
Ischial spines, 127
Isoflurane, 156–157
Isometric tailor press, 72
IUD. *See* Intrauterine device.
IUPC. *See* Intrauterine pressure catheter.
IVs. *See* Intravenous fluids.

Jaundice, 153, 172, 209–210, 244
Jogging, 66, 290
Journal of the American Medical Association, 61–62
Junk food, 45, 47, 53, 271
Juvenile Products Manufacturers Association, 226

Karmel, Marjorie, 81
Kegel, Arnold, 73
Kegel exercises, 73–75
    to avoid episiotomy, 174
    postpartum, 138, 285–286, 287, 288, 290
Kennel, John, 136, 139
Klaus, Marshall, 136, 139
Knee reaching, 198
Knee-chest position, 186, 288
Kneeling on hands and knees, 109, 166
Kneeling position, 100, 109, 166

La Leche League, 241, 255, 265–266
Labor
    active management of, 173
    augmentation of, 172–173
    back, 101–102, 104, 165–167
    cardinal movements of, 164
    effects of medications on, 4, 130–131, 147–148, 150–159
    false, 121
    first stage, 127–131, 142–143
    first stage, active phase, 129, 142–143

first stage, early phase, 128–129, 142–143
first stage, transition phase, 130–131, 142–143
fourth stage, 135–138, 144–145
induction of. *See* Induction of labor.
labor partner's role during. *See* Labor partner, role during labor.
onset of, 122
second stage, 132–133, 135, 144–145
signs of true, 122–123
third stage, 135, 144–145
variations, 164–167
warm-up signs of, 120–121
Labor massage, 101
Labor partner
    choosing a, 114
    role in emergency childbirth, 176–177
    role during labor, 129, 130–131, 135, 142–145, 171, 172
    role as a support person, 125
Laboring in water, 4, 104, 125, 179
Lactation. *See* Breastfeeding.
Lamaze
    benefits of, 81–82, 95, 99
    techniques, 81–112
    theory, 81–82
Lamaze, Fernand, 81
Lamaze bag, 117
Lanugo, 18, 19, 207
Largon, 152–153
Lateral Sims' position, 108–109
Leboyer, Frederick, 135, 177–178
Leboyer delivery, 6, 177–179
Lecithin, 19, 190
Let-down reflex, 250, 263, 292
Lidocaine, 150, 154–155, 211
Lifting during pregnancy, 68
Lightening, 26, 120
Linea negra, 25
Listeria, 32–33
Lithotomy position, 5, 109
Liver function
    in baby, 149, 209

during pregnancy, 47
Local anesthesia, 154–155, 174, 211
Lochia, 138. *See also* Vaginal discharge.
Log rolling, 197
L/S ratio, 190
Lunar month, 15, 17–19
Lunging position, 70, 99–100, 109, 166

Mahan, Charles, 2
Making Love During Pregnancy, 28
Malnutrition during pregnancy, 45, 47
Marijuana, 60–61
Mask of pregnancy, 26
Massage, infant, 236–239
    arms and hands, 237
    back and buttocks, 238–239
    chest and abdomen, 237
    legs and feet, 238
Massage, labor, 101
Massage, perineal, 75–76, 174
Massage, pregnancy, 77–80
    back and shoulder, 78
    foot, 80
    hand and arm, 79–80
Mastitis, 261
Masturbation, 29, 30, 210
Maternity support, 68–69
Meconium, 18, 123, 137, 185, 210, 213, 233, 244
Medications
    benefits of, 148–149, 150, 152, 154, 156, 158
    breastfeeding and, 155, 157, 256–257, 260, 262, 264–265
    cesarean birth and, 8, 148, 154–157, 184, 191, 192
    effects on baby when directly administered, 136, 152–153, 204
    effects on bonding, 137, 148
    effects on fetus when given to woman, 59–62, 137, 149, 151, 153, 155, 157, 158
    during labor, 4, 130–131,

147–148, 150–159
postpartum, 152–153, 156–157
during pregnancy, 24, 51, 62
refusing, 148, 149–150
Melanocyte stimulating hormone, 26
Membranes
artificial rupture of, 4, 171
function of, 16
spontaneous rupture of, 4, 123, 129, 130
stripping of, 171
Methergine, 152–153
Midwife. 114. *See also* Caregiver.
Milia, 206
Milk leaking, 256, 261, 292
Milk production, 250–251
Milk supply, inadequate, 260
Modified paced breathing, 97, 111
Modified sit-up, 287–288
Modified sit-up II, 289
Modified sit-up III, 290
Modified sit-up IV, 290
Modified Valsalva maneuver, 106–107
Molding, 173, 194, 201, 206
Mongolian spots, 207
Monitrice, 82
Montagu, Ashley, 217
Montgomery glands, 23, 250
Moodiness, 24, 27, 28, 274–275
Morning after doses, 300
Morning after pill, 293–300
Morning sickness, 23, 45, 51
Moro reflex, 209
Morphine, 154–155, 156–157, 194
Morula, 15
MSH. *See* Melanocyte stimulating hormone.
Mucous plug, 121, 123, 132
Multiple pregnancy, 36, 48

Naming your baby, 205
Narcan, 152–153
Narcotic antagonists, 152–153
National Association of Childbearing Centers, 139, 141

National Cancer Institute, 60
National Institutes of Health, 3, 37, 40, 257
Natural family planning, 298–299
Nausea, 23, 130. *See also* Morning sickness.
Neck circles, 76
Necrotizing enterocolitis, 244
Nembutal, 152–153
Nesting urge, 121
Neuromuscular control, 83
Newborn. *See* Baby, at birth; Baby, common concerns regarding; Baby, medical concerns regarding; Baby, newborn, characteristics of.
NIH. *See* National Institutes of Health.
Nipple confusion, 259, 263
Nipple shields, 254
Nipples
care of, 252, 254, 259
flat, 262
inverted, 252, 262
plugged ducts, 256, 261
preparing for nursing, 251–252, 262
sore, 252, 254, 259
stimulation of, 30, 165
Nisentil, 152–153
Nitrous oxide, 156–157
Nolan, George, 184
Nonfood items during pregnancy, 59–63
Nonstress test, 41
No-Risk Pregnancy Diet, 3, 48, 49
Norplant, 296–297
Nubain, 152–153
Nursing bras, 68, 118, 256
Nutrasweet, 62
Nutrition
hints, 51–53
during lactation, 251
No-Risk Pregnancy Diet, 3, 48, 49
during pregnancy, 3, 23, 46–51, 59–63

Obesity, 47

Obstetrician. *See* Caregiver.
OCT. *See* Oxytocin challenge test.
Odent, Michael, 179
Oral contraceptives, 293, 296–297, 298–299, 300
Oral sex, 29
Orgasm, 30, 292
Ovaries, 13
Ovulation, 13–14, 249
Ovum, 15–16
Oxytocics, 152–153
Oxytocin, 6, 30, 41, 137, 152–153, 165, 172, 177, 250, 292
Oxytocin challenge test, 41

Pain
exercise during pregnancy and, 66
during labor, 81–82
during labor, techniques to reduce. *See* Breathing techniques.
medications for. *See* Medications.
postpartum, 195–196
postpartum sex and, 292
during pushing, 132
during recovery, 138, 194
as a warning sign during pregnancy, 30, 34,
Pant-blow, 98, 111
Parenthood, adjustment to, 275–280
Patient controlled analgesia, 195–196
Patterned paced breathing, 98, 111
Pavlov, Ivan, 81
PCA. *See* Patient controlled analgesia.
Peanut butter, 53
Pediatrician
choosing a, 115–116, 251–252
when to call your, 218–219
Pelvic floor
during delivery, 110, 132
exercises. *See* Kegel exercises.
muscles, 73
Pelvic rock, 71, 166, 288
Pelvic tilt, 198, 286

Pelvis, 25, 67, 109, 127

Penis, 14. *See also* Circumcision.

Perineal care, 118, 141

Perineal massage, 75–76, 174

Perineum, 75, 110, 132–133, 135, 141, 174, 273–274

Petrikovsky, Boris, 33

Pets, 282–283

Pfannenstiel incision, 193

Phenergan, 152–153

Phenylketonuria, 205

Phototherapy, 210

Physician. *See* Caregiver; Pediatrician.

Pica, 62–63

Pitocin, 114, 152–153
    to aid contractions following birth, 192
    to augment labor, 5, 173
    to induce labor, 5, 171–172
    prolonged labor and, 165
    as a risk for cesarean section, 188
    rupture of the membranes and, 123

PKU. *See* Phenylketonuria.

Placenta
    delivery of, 6, 113, 135, 144–145, 177, 192
    development of, 21
    function of, 21, 46

Placenta abruptio, 186

Placenta previa, 186

Plantar toe reflex, 209

Playing with baby, 234–236

Plugged ducts, 256, 261

Poison Control Center, 219, 231

Poisoning, 219, 231

Polio vaccine, 219–220

Position, fetal, 163–164
    back labor and, 165, 166
    forceps and, 175
    prolonged labor and, 165
    vacuum extractor and, 175

Positions, pushing. *See* Pushing positions.

Positions for labor, 4, 99–100
    kneeling, 100

side-lying, 100

sitting, 100

upright position, 99–100

Posterior position, 109, 163, 165, 166
    rotating a, 166, 175

Postpartum
    care following cesarean, 139, 194, 195–197
    care following vaginal delivery, 138, 139, 141
    exercises, 197–198, 285–290
    help at home during, 196, 277–278
    medications and, 152–153, 156–157
    physical changes during, 273–275
    sex, 196, 284–285, 291–301

Postpartum depression, 197, 275

Post-term pregnancy, 160

Posture, 66–68

Practice for labor, 110–112

Precipitate delivery, 164–165, 175–177

Precipitate labor, 164–165

Preeclampsia, 35, 186

Pregnancy
    alcohol and, 3, 60
    caffeine and, 61–62
    discomforts of, 23, 24, 25, 26, 27, 76–77
    first trimester of, 15, 22–24, 28, 51
    food additives and, 62
    higher-risk, 34–37, 169
    length of, 15, 22
    medications and, 24, 51, 62
    nutrition during, 3, 45–51
    options during, 3
    recreational drugs and, 59–62
    second trimester of, 16, 25–26, 29, 51
    sex during, 28–30
    signs of, 22–23
    smoking and, 3, 21, 59–60
    third trimester of, 16, 26–28, 29, 51

weight gain during, 47, 48

Pregnancy massage. *See* Massage, pregnancy.

Pregnancy-induced hypertension, 25, 31, 35, 47, 50, 159–160, 186

"Pregnant Patient's Bill of Rights, The," 9–10

"Pregnant Patient's Responsibilities, The," 9, 11

Prelabor, 121. *See also* Braxton-Hicks contractions.

Premature baby. *See* Preterm baby.

Premature rupture of the membranes, 171

Premature urge to push, 131
    blowing for, 98–99
    as sign of transition, 130

Prenatal care, 30–34

Prenatal testing
    alpha-fetoprotein screening, 38–39
    amniocentesis, 37–38, 190
    chorionic villus sampling, 38
    estriol excretion study, 40
    fetal movement evaluation, 41
    nonstress test, 41
    oxytocin challenge test, 41
    ultrasound, 3, 39–40, 190
    X-ray pelvimetry, 40, 162

Prep, 125, 190
    complete, 4, 190
    mini, 125
    partial, 8, 190

Presentation, 161–163, 186

Pressure point massage, 59, 102–104

Preterm baby, 164, 189, 244–245

Preterm labor, 36, 159, 164

Procaine, 150, 154–155

Progesterone, 14, 23

Prolactin, 137, 248, 249, 250

Prolapsed cord, 162, 186

Prolonged labor, 162, 165

PROM. *See* Premature rupture of the membranes.

Prostaglandins, 30, 122

Protein, 45, 47, 48, 51, 52, 53, 54–58, 196

Psychoprophylaxis, 81, 102

Pubic hair, shaving. *See* Prep.

Pubococcygeus muscle group, 73

Pudendal block, 154–155

Push, urge to, 105, 132

Pushing, 132–133
  breathing patterns for, 106–107
  positions for. *See* Pushing positions.

Pushing positions
  kneeling on hands and knees, 109
  kneeling position, 109
  lateral Sims' position, 108–109
  lithotomy position, 5, 109
  lunging position, 109
  semireclined position, 5, 107
  side-lying position, 108–109
  squatting position, 5, 107–108, 166

Quickening, 18, 25

Quiet alert state, 136

Rash, in baby, 212–213, 219

Ratner, Herbert, 255

Recovery. *See* Postpartum.

Recovery room, 138, 194

Recti muscles, 198, 287

Reflexes in baby, 207–209

Regional anesthesia, 6, 8, 150–151, 154–155, 158–159, 184, 191, 192, 194

Relaxation
  active, 83
  basics, 83–84
  benefits of, 81–83
  during birth, 132, 191
  Birth Visualization, 93–95
  Body Awareness/Tension Recognition exercise, 86–88
  checking for, 84–85
  during labor, 81–95
  passive, 83
  A Special Place visualization, 92–93

  techniques, 86–95
  Total Body Relaxation exercise, 88–90
  Touch Relaxation exercise, 90–92
  visualization, 92–95

Relaxin, 23

Relaxing breath, 96

Reproduction. *See* Fertilization.

Reproductive organs, 13–15

Respiratory distress syndrome, 189

Rest, postpartum, importance of, 196, 275

Restoril, 152–153

Retin A, 24

Reyes Syndrome, 218

Rh incompatibility, 32, 141, 186–187

RhoGam, 31, 32, 141, 186–187

Rib cage stretch, 69, 76

Rooming-in, 78, 138–139, 196

Rooting reflex, 208

Ropivacaine, 154–155

Rotating a breech baby, 162–163

Rotating a posterior baby, 166, 175

Rotation and extraction, 175

Rupture of the membranes
  artificial, 4, 171
  spontaneous, 4, 123, 129, 130

Saccharin, 62

Saddle block anesthesia, 154–155, 158, 191

Salt, 46, 47

Sanger, Max, 183

Sanitary pads, 118, 195

Seconal, 152–153

Second stage of labor, 132–133, 135, 144–145

Secondhand smoke, 257

Secretory immunoglobulin A, 244

Sedatives, 152–153, 191

Self-inducing labor, 159

Semen, 14, 30

Semireclined position, 5, 107

Senses, baby, 178, 206

Sexual relations
  postpartum, 196, 284–285, 291–301
  during pregnancy, 24, 27, 28–30
  after rupture of the membranes, 123

Shaken baby syndrome, 215

Shortness of breath, 27

Shoulder dystocia, 187

Shoulder presentation, 161, 186

Shoulder rotation, 70, 76

Sibling visitation, 7, 139, 281

Siblings, 116, 134, 140, 280–282

Side kicks, 288–289

Side-lying position, 5, 67, 84, 100, 108–109, 166

SIDS. *See* Sudden infant death syndrome.

Silver nitrate, 6, 136, 204, 206

Simkin, Penny, 73, 75, 114

Sims' position, 84

Single leg raises, 289

Single leg sliding, 290

Sitz bath, 141, 273

Skin
  baby, 207, 212–213, 246
  during pregnancy, 23–24

Skin-to-skin contact, 134, 137, 267

Sleep
  baby, 215–217
  postpartum, 276, 291
  during pregnancy, 24, 142

Slow paced breathing, 97, 111

Smoking, 3, 59–60, 230, 257, 260

Sodium pentathol, 156–157

Soft drinks, 49, 61–62, 271

Soft spots, 205–206

Solid food, 269–271

Sonogram, 39–40, 190

Special Place visualization, 92–93

Sperm, 14–15

Spermicides, 294–295

Sphingomyelin, 190

Spinal anesthesia, 150, 154–155, 158, 191

Spitting up, 213–214

Spoiling your baby, 217

Squatting position, 5, 107–108, 166

Stadol, 152–153

Stages of labor
first stage, 127–131, 142–143
fourth stage, 135–138, 144–145
second stage, 132–133, 135, 144–145
third stage, 135, 144–145

Station of presenting part, 127

Stem cells, 115

Stepping reflex, 209

Sterilization, 298–299

Stillbirth, 181

Stirrups, 5, 109, 134, 174

Stork bites, 207

Stress test, 41

Stretch marks, 25

Stripping the membranes, 171

Sucking
on breast versus on bottle, 246
needs, 255
as sign of hunger, 254

Sucking reflex, 208

Sudden infant death syndrome, 60, 216–217

Sufentanil, 154–155

Sugar, 48

Super Kegel Exercise, 285–286. *See also* Kegel exercises.

Supine hypotension, 67, 108, 172, 189

Support person, 3, 5. *See also* Doula; Labor partner; Monitrice.

Sustained exercise, 65, 69

Swaddling, 215

Swallowing reflex, 208

Swelling, 25, 34, 46–47

Synthetic hormones, 152–153

Syntocinon, 152–153

Syphilis, 32

Syrup of ipecac, 231

Tailor press, 71

Tailor sitting, 67

Tailor stretch, 72

Tear ducts, baby, 206

Temperature, baby
maintaining, 137, 203–204

taking, 218

TENS. *See* Transcutaneous electrical nerve stimulation.

Testes, 14, 18, 207

Thermometers, 218

Third stage of labor, 135, 144–145

Thrush, 259

Time management, 276, 278–279

Tonic neck reflex, 209

Topical anesthetic, 211

Total Body Relaxation exercise, 88–90

Touch Relaxation exercise, 90–92

Toxemia. *See* Pregnancy-induced hypertension.

Toxoplasmosis, 32

Toys, 216, 235–236

Tranquilizers, 152–153, 191

Transcutaneous electrical nerve stimulation, 104–105

Transition, 130–131, 142–143

Transverse lie, 161, 186

Traveling
with baby, 231–232, 234
breastfeeding and, 248
during pregnancy, 43

Trimesters of pregnancy
first trimester, 15–16, 22–24, 28, 51
second trimester, 16, 25–26, 29, 51
third trimester, 16, 26–28, 29, 51, 115

Tubal ligation, 298

Twins, 36, 48, 250

Tylenol With Codeine, 156–157

Ultrasound, 3, 39–40, 190

Umbilical cord, 21–22
around baby's neck, 176
blood from, 6, 115, 135
compression of, 185
cutting of, 6, 135, 177, 178
prolapse of, 186

Umbilical cord stump, 207, 209

Underwater birth, 179–180

Upright position, 99–100

Urethra, 14

Urination
by baby, 218, 255, 260
by fetus, 18, 208
during labor, 129
postpartum, 138, 141, 195, 273
during pregnancy, 23, 27, 120

Urine tests, 31, 40

U.S. Food and Drug Administration, 36, 40, 62, 172, 247

Uterus
breastfeeding and, 136, 177, 248
cesarean birth and, 192
contractions of. *See* Contractions.
postpartum, 135, 136, 138, 177, 273
during pregnancy, 18, 22–23, 25, 26–27
rupture of, 153, 172, 198, 199

Vaccinations, 219–221, 243

Vacuum extractor, 175, 201

Vagina, 14–15
episiotomy and, 174
Kegel exercises and, 73
during pregnancy, 23, 25, 27
postpartum sex and, 292

Vaginal birth after cesarean, 185, 198–199

Vaginal discharge
baby, 207
during pregnancy, 23, 27, 121
postpartum, 138, 195, 273
as a warning sign, 32, 34

Vaginal secretions. *See* Vaginal discharge.

Vaginal sponge, 293

Valsalva maneuver, 106–107

Varicose veins, 27, 68

Vasectomy, 298

VBAC. *See* Vaginal birth after cesarean.

Veneral disease, 32

Vernix caseosa, 18, 202

Vertex presentation, 161

Vibroacoustic stimulation test, 41

Villi, 16, 21, 38

Vision
    baby, 136, 206
    during pregnancy, 27
Vistaril, 152–153
Visualization, 92–95
Vitamin A, 50
Vitamin B complex, 23, 50, 52
Vitamin B$_1$, 52
Vitamin B$_6$, 23, 51
Vitamin D, 243
Vitamin K injection, 204
Vitamins, 48, 50, 51, 52
Vomiting
    baby, as a warning sign, 214,
        218

bad formula and, 268
during pregnancy, 23, 51
as a sign of transition, 130
VST. *See* Vibroacoustic stimulation
    test.

Walking
    during labor, 128, 165, 166, 173,
        188
    during pregnancy, 66, 68, 69
Warm-up signs of labor, 120–121
Warning signs during pregnancy,
    34
Water intoxication, 229, 255
Weaning, 271–272

Weight
    baby, 201, 256
    postpartum, 248, 274
    during pregnancy, 45, 47, 48,
        121
Wharton's jelly, 21
Wheat germ, 52
Working
    breastfeeding and, 265
    during pregnancy, 41–42
World Health Organization, 187

X-ray pelvimetry, 40, 162

Yolk sac, 16

FOR A COPY OF AVERY'S CATALOG CALL 1-800-548-5757

0-89529-481-8 • $12.95

0-89529-723-X • $6.95

0-89529-373-0 • $14.95

0-89529-490-7 • $10.95

0-89529-772-8 • $4.95

0-89529-545-8 • $19.95

OTHER BOOKS OF INTEREST FROM AVERY

0-89529-489-3 • $8.95

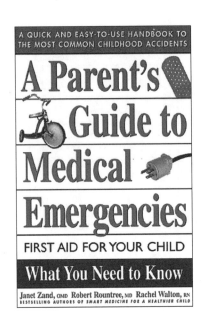

0-89529-736-1 • $11.95

0-89529-597-0 • $11.95

0-89529-694-2 • $5.95

0-89529-693-4 • $5.95

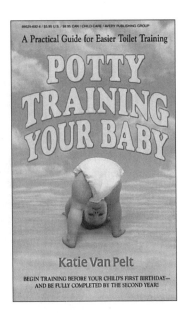

0-89529-692-6 • $5.95